1976

W9-AEE-683

The History of Civilization
Edited by C. K. OGDEN, M.A.

Art in Greece

Art in Greece

By

A. DE RIDDER

AND

W. DEONNA

NEW YORK
BARNES & NOBLE, INC.

First published in Great Britain 1927
by Kegan Paul, Trench, Trubner & Co. Ltd

Published in the United States of America 1968
by Barnes & Noble, Inc., New York, N.Y.

TRANSLATED BY
V. C. C. COLLUM
*(The transliteration and spelling of Greek names and words in
this translation follow the Rules adopted by the Hellenic Society)*

Printed in Great Britain

CONTENTS

PART ONE

THE AIM OF GREEK ART. ART AND THE CITY

PART TWO

AGENTS FOR THE PRACTICAL APPLICATION OF ARTISTIC AIMS. GROUPS OF ARTISTS AND ARTISTIC PERSONALITIES

PART THREE

REALIZATION. TECHNICAL PROBLEMS

CONTENTS

CONTENTS

PART FOUR

CONTENTS

CONCLUSION

THE PLACE OF GREEK ART IN THE HISTORY OF CIVILIZATION

LIST OF FIGURES AND PLATES

FIGURES

xi

FOREWORD

PURE ART

LEISURE AND PLAY

Art does not date from the Greeks, but, under the Greeks, art in diverse forms grew and blossomed amazingly so that one may say of this privileged people that they were the creators of pure *art. Thus it is here, perhaps, that we should try to distinguish, by linking up this magnificent achievement with the data of the preceding period,[1] what is the rôle of art in the evolution of humanity.*

It is of capital importance for the understanding of life and history to observe that the activities of living beings, of all living creatures, presents itself under two opposite aspects: Work *and* Play.

Life, in whatever degree, is for ever at work—whether it be the life individual or the life collective or the infinitely varied and increasingly complex combinations of both. Life travails that it may maintain itself—that is to say, in order to repair itself (since there is wear and tear) and in order to protect itself (since every living thing is menaced to greater or lesser extent by its physical environment and by other living beings). Life labours, too, that it may expand if—as we have postulated in preceding volumes—it is essentially a tendency, an endeavour, a nisus. It grows by effort and it grows by union.

[1] *See* De Morgan, " Prehistoric Man," *pp.* 174 *ff. on " Dress and Ornament," and pp.* 185 *ff. on " The Arts of Prehistoric Peoples " ;* Moret, " From Tribe to Empire" ; *and* Delaporte, " Chaldæo-Assyrian Civilization," *the Foreword, and the chapters on Babylonian and Assyrian Art ;* Glotz, " The Ægean Civilization," *the Foreword, and the chapters on " Games" and " Art." Magdalenian art, as we know, was blotted out completely, to humanity's " great loss." Ægean art, rich and varied, more realistic than the arts of the East, less concerned, too, with practical preoccupations and more individualistic, exercised a considerable influence, for long unsuspected, on the art of those Greeks who caused the downfall of Ægean civilization. But Greek art has superior qualities : " All that went before it was in reality merely the incubation period that led to this æsthetic zenith "* (De Morgan, " Les Premières Civilisations," *p.* 499).

Work has a practical object in view—utility. But progress in life, won by work, brings about escape from pressing need, creates the possibility of leisure and liberates energy for play. To work is to maintain life. To play is to enjoy it.[1]

All organization, all progress in life tends more and more to enfranchise it from immediate want, to procure it leisure— not merely a passive leisure of relaxation, of repose and slumber, but an active leisure for enjoyment.

In leisure, from the moment that there is energy available (the invalid has leisure but he does not play) this energy tends to employ itself for the pleasure of so being employed, for the relief of thus expending itself.[2] *The surplus energy permits of active play. And just as there are primordial needs which are the expression of elementary life—the need for luxury which is the expression of the increase and perfecting of life—so is there a need for play which results from the very enfranchisement from need and which is the luxury of life* par excellence.

It must be noted, moreover, that this theoretical opposition of work and play is not realized absolutely except in the case of immediate and pressing need. Work and play, interest and disinterested enjoyment may be blended in an infinitude of different ways and in infinitely variable quantities.[3]

All this, however, is quite general in character. Our aim was once again to link history with life. These principles stated, we must pass on to the particular consideration of man and of human society.

One might well say, without being paradoxical, that the history of human society is the history of leisure, of the progress of leisure, of its distribution among different social classes, and of its utilization.

Of its distribution.—Political institutions, like economic organization, tend toward the general good of society, to the lightening of the difficulties and hardships of the life of the group ; but those who hold power for the general good tend to use it for their own good and to relieve themselves of labour.

---

[1] *Work, labour,* travail, *from* tripalium, *a three-staked instrument of torture. To* travail—*to toil, to struggle, to fashion—make a continuous effort. Leisure, from* licere, *to be allowed to . . ., to have freedom.*

[2] *Cf. the* χάθαρσιs *of Aristotle.*

[3] *See* K. Groos, " Les jeux des animaux," *pp.* 301, 308 ; *and* Grosse, " Les débuts de l'Art."

*Whereas, those, on whom labour presses heavily, clamour for
their share of the good things of life and make efforts—efforts
which even culminate in revolutions—to win what is at bottom
the right to leisure.*

Of its utilization.—*The modalities of play are virtually as
many as the powers of the individual ; and, as a fact, there is the
play of the physical organs, the play of the different senses, and
the play of the various higher faculties : everything which has
seemed to protect and maintain life has afterwards served in its
expansion. And the aspects of play are extremely varied
according to the stages of historic evolution, and to the period
of the life of the individual.*

*In the first place we must establish a distinction between
play and games—which one sees arise among animals, but which
only come to full development in human societies.*

*Play is the spontaneous employment of the living being of
superabundant energy. Games are practical exercises intended
to organize the employment of leisure. And it is under the form
of games—and then of arts—that play may be brought under
the influence of society, perhaps even institutionalised although
responding to a need originally entirely individual : further on
we shall emphasize this important point à propos art.*

*If play, as it has been said, is a transitional form between
practical activity and activity that is purely contemplative or
æsthetic, between life and art,*[1] *games equally bear the imprint
of this twofold character. Children and adolescents who bring
their physical nature into play, at the same time that they " give
it vent " have also the satisfaction of proving their energy and
of exercising their powers whether on their own bodies, on the
outside world, on things or on other beings. Physical games,
and also most kinds of games which have been invented or
instituted for young people or adults, produce—actually tend to
produce—some practical advantage along with the pleasure of
playing. Physical games are a simulation of work which
enables real work to be done more easily ; they assure victories
without the practical necessity to vanquish, yet not without
facilitating ulterior victories. To conquer difficulties for
pleasure and at the same time for profit is the aim of games and
of competitions of every kind. A thousand examples could be*

[1] *See* K. Groos, *work quoted,* p. 303; *also* Ebbinghaus, " Précis de
Psychologie," p. 283.

B

*cited to illustrate the proposition that a useless expenditure of
energy is often crowned with utility.*

*Many games—such as the gymnastic games of the Greeks—
many periodic and regulated festivals, entail the appearance of
a special element whose rôle, in play, is neither active nor direct—
the public. One cannot say that this rôle is purely contemplative
because divers interests—religious and civic in the case of the
Greek games—may be mixed with the pleasure of being a spectator. But there is the pleasure, to lesser or greater degree, of
the spectacle—a pleasure that is properly œsthetic.*

*This term—œsthetic pleasure—employed by some for all
pleasure in play, we would rather reserve for contemplative
enjoyment ; it even seems to us that it is preferable to restrict
its use to that contemplative enjoyment linked with the arts. Is
it not better, in fact, to distinguish the emotion born of the games
of the circus, of the combats of gladiators and of bull fights, from
those created by an artistic spectacle ? The reality of flowing
blood—in a cruel game—and the illusion of pain in the drama
produce pleasures of the same kind but of different quality.*

*Let us then distinguish the arts clearly, and, among the arts,
let us further distinguish those which are major and those which
are minor, or in other words the occasional or decorative arts
from those that are arts by intention.*

*The proper object of art is to give œsthetic pleasure to the
senses and the higher faculties, through the medium of techniques
—which are the arts—by various elements borrowed from the
real and variously combined spatially or in time,[1] or in both space
and time at once. That which brings about this kind of pleasure
is the beautiful; the aim of art is to manufacture it ; it regulates
the permanent sources of enjoyment in the highest order of play.*

*Art has two sides : it utilizes the surplus energy of those
whose senses are most highly developed, whose faculties are the
richest, and who, if one can so put it, are bursting with vigour
and who take pleasure in creative acts ; it utilizes this surplus
for the contemplative enjoyment of those who have the same
aptitudes and needs to a lesser degree and who are quite unable,
without the first, to satisfy their being's hunger. There is the
artist, and the work of art; and there is the amateur of art, and*

---

[1] *Th. Ribot distinguishes the Static Arts from the Active Arts.*

æsthetic *contemplation. The differences between the two should be clearly expressed in terminology.*

But art, in the beginning, was never completely dissociated from the useful : it was superimposed on it. Man began his career as artist by ornamenting objects that were necessary to him, by embellishing the décor of a life which escaped from rigorous need.

We believe that our distinguished collaborator, W. Deonna, who has given much thought to the nature of art and its beginnings, is both right and wrong when he leans to the identification of technical inventions, civilization in general, and art properly so-called, and when he confounds or classes together practical " arts " and æsthetic arts in a single " archæology " understood in an extraordinarily wide sense. The word art, originally combination—from which we get artisan and artist— ought to have given us artial *and* artistic. *In our view, one should not say—there is no point in saying : " A creator, fashioning raw material, whether of the most practical techniques or of the fine arts, man is an artist, the author of art. . . . The day when he freed himself from servitude to nature in order to react on materials is an important date in the history of humanity—the day when art was first invented."*[1] *Doubtless art applied itself at first, and continued to apply itself, to the products of human industry : there is none the less an intimate and radical difference, in human inventions, between those destined to increase the commodities of life and those which set* a-playing *some one or other, or more than one, of man's faculties.*

The preceding volumes have shown us that man, from the moment the conditions of his existence permitted him to do so, diffused around him the possibilities of enjoyment that he might continually draw from this ever ready source. Articles of use may possess a pleasing value : " In primitive times, when the hard necessity of the struggle for existence dominated everything, this special value is hardly to be discerned. But little by little, as success in this struggle for life came to him, and as man became possessed of leisure, he began to pay attention to it. He noticed that the means of combat, which at first had for him merely

[1] W. Deonna, " *L'Archéologie, son domaine, son but* " (" Bibl. de Phil. scientifique," 1922), *p.* 71; *Cf. pp.* 75-76.

the value of a means of nourishment or of a weapon, was also an agreeable thing independently of its usefulness."[1] Gradually all useful articles rose in his estimation in that they could be made the instruments of enjoyment.

Very likely he began with his body—following thus the example of lower animals which know the luxury and pride of adornment. The male animal seeks to make a conquest of the female by colour, sound and odour: in this force of desire there is a blossoming of life and an effort to achieve beauty.[2] In man, costume, weapons, utensils, furniture, dwelling—all are adorned, and each one becomes an " object of art."[3] The domain of the arts known as minor, decorative or applied—and which we define as occasional arts—is immense. Architecture—born of the tree and the cavern—which is considered a major art, no doubt because of the development it has received and the various elements embraced by it, nevertheless retains its character as a useful craft: " It might strictly be assimilated to an extension of clothing."[4]

When we seek the historical origin, the germinating point, so to speak, of the various ornaments and successive embellishments which human life has acquired, we may well come upon, indeed, we are bound to find, as a rule, practical intentions and social circumstances. Tattooing, the painting and cutting of the body, feather plumes and animal skins, no doubt correspond to tribal distinctions, to rank, religious belief, and magical ends. Still, there may have been in all this a more or less vague œsthetic element from the very beginning : " To the mythical and social motives for the decoration of the person is added the attraction exercised by strong colours easily to be seen, such as the

[1] Ebbinghaus, *work quoted*, p. 283.

[2] *See* Espinas, " Les Sociétés animales "; K. Groos, *work quoted;* Ribot, " Psychologie des sentiments," *II*, 10, " *le sentiment esthétique* " (*p.* 344, *Note* 2, *where he quotes some suggestive lines of Th. Gautier's :* " *The savage who tattoos himself, who smears himself with red and blue, and sticks a fishbone in his nose, is following some confused notion of beauty* "); *and* P. Lacombe, " Introduction à l'Histoire littéraire," *p.* 17.

[3] " *Round and about the arts of the furnisher and costumier there is unfolded the brilliant and ever-growing procession of the attendant arts of the gold- and silver-smith, the gem-setter and jeweller, the enameller and the coach-builder—for the embellishment of carriages, those miniature movable houses—of the armourer and the smith, the arts of the oven and the forge, and the textile arts* " (P. Lorquet, " l'Art et l'Histoire," *p.* 90). *See also the entire chapter on the* minor arts.

[4] Th. Ribot, *work quoted*, p. 345.

*contrast of black and white, of yellow, and above all of red
which is reminiscent of blood."[1] And the time comes when
symbolism fades while the æsthetic aim is more and more
pronounced.*

*There are senses to which æsthetic enjoyment is no stranger
but from which no organized art has evolved because they are too
closely bound up with the immediate necessities of life ; such are
taste, touch and sense of smell.[2] The nobler senses are those of
sight and hearing, because these two are linked to the higher
faculties. From these two proceed not merely the decorative[3]
but the principal arts. Detached—apparently at all events—
from utility, they make play with the world of images which
reflects external reality and with the inner world of feeling.
Reaching beyond the senses they make their appeal to the highest
faculties—to understanding, imagination, and sensibility—
and this is what lends to them their high dignity.*

*According as to whether they lean to imitation or expression
the higher arts form two groups : painting and sculpture on the
one hand, and the dance and music on the other. Literary art,
the richest and most complex of all, has an equal part in both
imitation and expression.[4]*

*The literature of expression—lyrical writing—is closely
related to those incontestably ancient, and for some people
primitive, arts, music and the dance. Music and dancing are
an extension of the spontaneous expression of overflowing feeling.
Emotional needs satisfy themselves in regulated manifestations
of sexual, warlike, or religious signification. Thus song and
dance not only have their actors but their audience, and this
audience associates itself with the feelings expressed, extracting
therefrom æsthetic pleasure. But it also extracts this pleasure*

---

[1] M. H. Cornejo, " Sociologie générale," *vol. II, p.* 261.

[2] *We lay claim, nevertheless, to a " culinary art " and we take great
pains to satisfy both the sense of smell and of touch. See* P. Lorquet,
" l'Art et l'Histoire," *pp.* 110-12.

[3] *Hearing, like sight, has its minor arts, pendants to the decorative
arts—" modulated calls, ditties and chanties, ' Cries of Paris,' and the
' Ranz des Vaches' melody of the shepherd." See* P. Lorquet, *work
quoted, p.* 96.

[4] *Cf. Wundt's distinction between the imitative and the musical arts,
and Cornejo's between the constructive and rhythmic arts. See* Cornejo,
work quoted, vol. II, p. 253.

from another source—from unison, from the rhythm created by these sounds and motions.[1]

Rhythm—which already exists in the cries and chanties which aim at accompanying, facilitating and lessening the burden of labour, such as threshing, spinning, weaving and sea ditties—constitutes a very important source of enjoyment. The arts of form and colour, in their various degrees, and above all architecture, evoke the same pleasure by means of symmetry and harmony. Here we have the most general element in art, common to its most diverse manifestations. But in the subjective —by some people called the rhythmic—arts, this element plays a larger and more apparent part than in others, because in them feeling is stronger and impresses on them more directly this law of life itself—unity in variety.[2]

The various arts are nowhere in their inner characters completely in opposition one to the other, from whatever angle they are regarded. The dance and music, which often evoke definite circumstances ; lyrical language, which associates itself with the events of individual and collective life—are not more strangers to the element of imitation[3] *than are painting and sculpture to the element of expression.*

But these last have for their object essentially the reproduction of the real. And there is a genuine literature of imitation— narrative, descriptive, dramatic—which provides us with an inexhaustible fount of enjoyment from the unfettered contemplation and the disinterested knowledge of all the things and creatures with which our life is bound up.

This art which reflects reality and life sometimes follows them as closely and as obediently as may be, and sometimes amends, recreates and touches them up. Both the imagination which reproduces and the imagination which creates, both realism and idealism in different fashion, bring about the same satisfaction, each one as disinterestedly as the other.

We will no more attempt to deny for the great arts than for the minor arts which are obviously linked to utility, that the activity

[1] *See* Cornejo, *ibid., pp.* 288, 293; Ribot, *work quoted, pp.* 336, 338. *On the origin of musical instruments, see* Cornejo, *p.* 294.

[2] *See* Ebbinghaus, " Précis de Psychologie," *p.* 288.

[3] *See* G. H. Luquet, " *Les débuts de l'art,*" *in the* " Revue du Mois," 1920, *and* " *Genèse de l'art figuré,*" *in the* " Journal de Psychologie," *October and November,* 1922; Deonna, " L'Archéologie," *vol. II. Cf.* V. Chapot, " *Les Methodes archéologiques,*" *in the* " Rev. de Synth. hist.," *February* 1914, *p.* 13.

of play has issued from practical activity ; and we recognize that it is of considerable moment that the genesis of each of them should be defined.

That, for instance, it is possible, nay probable, that totemism —which we must not exaggerate—and magic have played a large part in the beginnings of the pictorial arts : but that a time came when the image, over and above its utilitarian character, its efficacy in conjuring danger, procuring game, or expressing veneration, admiration or fear, took on, as an image, the value of a thing of beauty. *It was the same with literary art. It is linked with myth and legend, that is to say, with the beliefs, self-interest, loves and hatreds of the group. " The important gain made by ethnography and folk-lore in the domain of literature during these recent years consists in having brought out the fact that literary production known as ' popular ' is a useful activity . . . especially in its inception it is an organic element and not, as has been imagined, a superfluous æsthetic activity—a luxury ":[1] but it increasingly became so.—Thus were produced the higher arts—that is to say the techniques in which certain individuals exercised exceptional faculties for the sole pleasure of so exercising them, and so bringing to others the same exclusive pleasure.[2]*

**

What we are here concerned with is the nature of art and the part it has to play : it is therefore beside the point to lay stress on the specific differences between the arts, and it would be of little use to try to work out with exactitude the order of their succession. All the arts derive from the same source and share the same far-off origin because all of them are an expression of the diverse faculties of human nature and of the potency of life. Complex and synthetic at the beginning (as witness the dance, architecture, the epic), even if they were clearly differentiated they reacted the one on the other and combined in an infinite variety of ways. When, at last, speculation on art began, and when æsthetics developed out of didactic treatises, a number of different hypo-

---

[1] *See* A. Van Gennep, " La formation des Légendes," *pp.* 14, 16.

[2] " *In primitive times art was not a profession ; the creator, even while occupied in other ways, produced naturally, spontaneously, as a rose-tree yields roses ; it was a superabundance, an overflow. Gradually it became a profession, and, the victim of its own glory, it was obliged to produce whether it would or no . . . manufacturing works of art as others manufactured articles of trade ": there was a return to practical interestedness. See* Ribot, *work quoted,* p. 364.

*theses were put forward—which were mutually complementary
rather than exclusive in so far as they dealt more particularly
with the artist, the public, the work of art itself, or this or that
branch of art—which often tended to magnify art, and to hyposta-
tize it, and all these hypotheses expressed, at bottom, the widening
and deepening of life through play : play had become complicated,
diversified, refined, sublimated ; but art is quite simply and un-
equivocally a game.*

*The thesis that would explain this play by society seems to
us a false one, or at all events confused. Let us revert, à propos
the arts, to a question which arose in connection with games.*[1]

*There have been attempts to constitute an " œsthetic
sociology."*[2] *These are legitimate and may bear interesting
fruit in measure as they show all that society has contributed to
the development of art and all that art has borrowed from different
social institutions, or even in so far as they reveal all the social
element implicit in œsthetic feeling, which is the profound echo
that sociability awakens in the emotions of the individual.*[3]
*On the other hand, such attempts are altogether chimerical in so
far as they seek to demonstrate that society created art, that,
for example, society " secreted the epopee."*[4]

*Ribot, in his " Psychologie des sentiments," has illustrated
the importance of " œsthetic needs " in the development of social
life, without, however, making them social in their origin.
The examples he quotes confirm our suggested law of three phases.*[5]
*As he puts it, " Man is an œsthetic animal," and this is what he
sets out from : the art which is born of this property of the human
being goes through a strongly social phase before it becomes
sharply individualized. But even when we find the most obvious
and most profound imprint of its environment we must not forget
that art at its source is human and therefore individual. Art
springs from the individual and comes back to the individual.*[6]

---

[1] *See* p. xvii.

[2] *The rubric " Sociologie esthétique " appeared in vol. 5 of " l'Année
Sociologique."*

[3] *See* Guyau, " l'Art au point de vue Sociologique."

[4] " Année Sociologique," *vol. XI*, p. 784. *See vol. V, pp. 578-85,
Durkheim's review of* Yrjo Hirn's *book,* " The Origins of Art, a Psychological and Sociological Enquiry," *in which there is too much psychology
for Durkheim.*

[5] *See the Foreword to* " From Tribe to Empire."

[6] Ribot, *work quoted, pp.* 340 *ff. On the rôle of individualities see*
Chapot, *article quoted, in the* " Rev. de Synth. hist.," *February,* 1914,
p. 11.

Furthermore, this individualism in which it ends is not without its dangers, for if it be pushed to extremes the social link becomes relaxed and the desire for action weakened.

Normally, art, because it crowns life and action, contains elements that are useful to action, however pure and disinterested it may be. The pleasure it procures may also minister to knowledge and morality. The intellect may be enriched and rendered more lucid, the soul strengthened, the entire being brought into harmony by the virtue of order and rhythm as a result of art when the æsthetic enjoyment is no more than a memory, just as the lungs expand more freely and the muscles are invigorated after physical games. Literature and the fine arts do not exist for education; nevertheless, they do educate. The humanities, the liberal arts—these terms express their essential generousness. According to a happy formula, they give pleasure without lust (Ebbinghaus), but not necessarily without utility.

Pleasure without utility, " art for art's sake," is putting " life for art " in the place of " art for life." The life of pure pleasure—dilettantism—is altogether contrary to the deeper tendencies of man's being. He can arrive at making his entire existence a game if he saturates himself with literature and art. There are individuals who have completely lost sight of the good and the true so obsessed have they been by the desire for æsthetic pleasure, and there have been whole classes, and epochs, in which this happened. Linked with this constant seeking after the joys of art are the gallantries of love, witty talk, the fashionable life of society drawing-rooms, the amused onlooking of men, the detached contemplation of nature : this sheer play with men and things, devoid as it is of any vital enthusiasm or forceful passion, is vitiating and in the end may prove lethal.

The search for what is good and true responds to the tendency of a man's being : the search for pleasure ends in immobility. Whatever fundamental analogy there may be between art and science—for science, too, is a game; and from the animal stage upwards curiosity manifests a surplusage of life, the beginnings of enfranchisement—the more disinterested science is, the greater become its practical potentialities and its power over things, and the more it increases our consciousness of human ends. Science seeks Paradise above all. Art can create an artificial paradise and cause forgetfulness of life's aims : it is then a kind of Nirvana.

In fine, if art is a symbol of progress and an agency for the evolutionary development of humanity, the abuse of art is both a sign and a factor of decadence.

* *

We think that the foregoing considerations are well illustrated by this volume. It is not an archæological treatise. Its title is not " Greek Art " but " Art in Greece " ; and de Ridder clearly sets forth its aim in the introductory pages.

This aim—to show the part which art has played in the life of the Greeks, and the character it took on among them, in such fashion as to explain the influence exercised by Greek artists on the art of other peoples and later ages—is in harmony with his lifelong preoccupations. Greece attracted him from his earliest youth, held him, and finally haunted him. Excavations, the editing of catalogues, various undertakings, official functions, everything throughout his life was associated with this corner of the earth, with this elect people whom he desired to know well because he loved them and whom he loved the more in measure as he knew them better. Hence he was immediately tempted by the subject I suggested to him. Since everything in his life was linked with Greece, his whole life was to be focussed in this book.

He had sketched the plan of the book in November, 1913. Gifted with an extraordinary memory, he had got every detail clearly arranged in his head as the result of prolonged thought. The war delayed the writing of the manuscript. When I asked him to set to work, the book was ready—though not a line of it had been written. In response to my call he put down on paper, in his neat and elegant handwriting, three chapters, and this first draft was practically final. The other chapters are buried together with that well-stored and lucid brain in the grave that prematurely claimed them.[1]

I hoped that the precious pages of him who from 1913 to 1921 had concentrated his thought on this book, that this relic at least should not be lost, and I was successful in persuading Deonna to undertake the work, preserving these pages as an introduction and filling in, in his own way, de Ridder's framework.

Deonna's important labours—for he, too, is an "Athenian"

[1] *See* J. Chamonard's *notice in the Annuaire for 1922 of the Association of Former Students of the École Normale supérieure.*

and a curator of a museum—together with his particular know-
ledge of Greek archæology, his immense curiosity, his devoted
efforts to widen the field of archæology and to go back to the
earliest source of art and to link it up with the other manifestations
of human activity, rendered his collaboration in " l'Évolution
de L'Humanité " highly desirable.

In this book he has not only studied with a penetrating
ingeniousness every detail of technique but he has forcibly
brought out the relations of Greek art with social life in all its
different aspects. He has shown that if the gigantesque art of
the Oriental peoples corresponds to their monarchical organiza-
tion, Greek art, which is well-proportioned and anthropomorphic,
and in which the human personality plays so novel a part, is in
harmony with the constitution of the city. He has thrown a
vivid light on the religious origins of this art. Perhaps he may
sometimes seem to have exaggerated the part played by religion.
When he declares that art " was for long only a form of cult "
(p. 57), that Greek art is " the docile servant of official religion,"
and that " it keeps this character, which is older in origin than
any other, throughout its entire existence " (p. 54), that " religion
penetrates even the industrial arts destined to practical ends "
(p. 58), it must be remembered that he likewise lays stress on the
close liaison between technique and play and that in his eyes the
entire material life of the Greeks is influenced by æsthetic pre-
occupations.

Art exercises an influence on religion even when it is most
closely linked with it, and it moulds religion as much as it
ministers to and expresses it. And the time came when art
freed itself from religion, and, in a general way, " the dissocia-
tion of the beautiful and the useful" (pp. 117-8) came about.
Art blossomed for itself, and " individualism triumphs " (p. 112).
This is the return to the individual after the very pronounced
socialization phase of which we spoke a while back. If art
became a " social language," if it established " a communion
between men," it is none the less, we repeat, individual in its
origin.

At first sight one might be tempted to find a certain contra-
diction between Deonna and de Ridder. De Ridder, a close
historian but profoundly impressed by Greek beauty, is above all
concerned with achievement, perfection—with the Greek " miracle."
There was an epoch " privileged above all others " in which the

Greeks " translated their dreams and chimeras of beauty into living reality "; it is here that de Ridder would seek the " hall mark " of the Hellenic genius which was to be so deeply impressed on all subsequent art. He deliberately limits the concept of art and sees in it a " creation of beauty " destined to satisfy " one of the higher needs of humanity " (p. 8). Deonna declares that " beauty was not an end in itself in Greece," but a means to an end (p. 49) ; and for him no single form or stage of Greek art is negligible. Still, if we look close enough there is no more than a difference in the point of view and in the proportions in which they see the object which divides these two writers. De Ridder recognizes that the artist is hardly distinguishable from the artisan in the beginning ; while getting his enjoyment out of perfection, he indicates what has gone before and what follows after. Deonna, more preoccupied with the successive phases of evolution, with the historical problem, recognizes no less the " superior gift " of the Greeks, and brings out equally forcibly the essential character of their art—the feeling for life, the ideal of a nobly human life, of a balanced and harmonious life, and, finally, the taste for order and proportion. Both are in agreement in portraying Greek art as the " human " art par excellence, *the art " that generalizes " in the words of Henri Lechat.*[1] *In this, as in everything she created, the contribution of Greece is essentially reason.*[2]

Here we are brought up against a problem which confronted us in " Language " in connection with language—the problem of progress. Vendryes is inclined to think that we must not see in the evolution of languages " a steady and continuous advance

---

[1] " La Sculpture grecque," p. 143.

[2] " *This so noble art is abstract, rational, idealist ; it addresses itself more to the intelligence than to the heart ; and with this art we find ourselves in the domain of the pure idea of Plato. The fugitive and changing side of things is displeasing to it, and for it the only truth is eternal truth,"* p. 312.

See also J. Vendryes' " Language," p. 347 : " *The Greek tongue is a language whose very essence is godlike. . . . It is not a matter of the ideas this language has served to express or of its literature, which is an education in wisdom and beauty. . . . The outward form of the Greek language is in itself a delight to the soul. The harmony of its rhythm, the grace of its sounds, and the richness of its vocabulary even, are not the most precious of its qualities. In the grammatical field, Greek is distinguished above all other languages by the precision of its morphemes which renders the word-formation so lucid, and the graceful suppleness of its syntax which gives to every thought its full value, following its every movement and reflecting each fine shade in its transparent depths. Never has a more beautiful instrument been fashioned to express human thought.*"

towards a definite end." He refuses to take into account any relation between languages and degrees of civilization: " We have no right" he says, " to consider a rational and abstract language, because it happens to be our own [or that of the Greeks], as in any way superior to a mystical and concrete one. It is entirely a question of two different types of mentality, each of which may have its merits. There is nothing to prove that, in the eyes of an inhabitant of Sirius, the civilized person's mentality does not represent degeneration" (p. 358).[1] Without going to quite such lengths of scepticism, perhaps Deonna would be disposed to consider the successive forms of art as expressions, all equally interesting, of different historical states.[2]

Reason, however, and, in a general way, psychic development, play a part in human life that it is impossible to neglect. From this point of view it is legitimate to establish degrees in the evolution of humanity even in matters relating to its linguistic or æsthetic activity.

If we consider the form of a work of art, certain qualities heighten æsthetic enjoyment by lending to it rational dignity— and it is here that Greek art provided what is an eternal model, especially during the brief years of the Athenian splendour. If we consider the content of a work of art, there are differences in the exactitude, the depth, the amplitude of the reproduction of the real and in the tendencies this reproduction expresses which lend such works an unequal value. Hence diverse potentialities of variable number come into play in æsthetic enjoyment, and, by setting them in motion, the repercussion of the pleasure experienced may minister to life to a smaller or greater degree. Too much stress cannot be laid on this point, that art, in measure as the beings to whom it appeals are complete, must in itself be complete in order to give them more lively enjoyment. Every great work of art contains an intellectual and moral element which is a consequence and source of psychic progress. The coincidence of powerful geniuses with a high human ideal gives its value and singular efficaciousness to the art of the great

---

[1] *We have shown (in the Foreword to "Language") that even in Vendryes' book there is to be found an attenuated form of this thesis. See also the discussion at the Société française de Philosophie in the Bulletin for November to December, 1922, on "The Progress of Language."*

[2] *In "Archéologie," vol. III, "Les Rythmes artistiques," Deonna suggested " a law of cycles," discussed by V. Chapot in the already quoted article in the " Rev. de Synth. hist.," pp. 14-17.*

Hellenic epoch.   Art for art's sake (towards which the succeeding period leans)—over and above the momentary pleasure it evokes—may refine taste, but it does not greatly conduce to human progress, and from being amoral it may become immoral.

It would be utterly vain to search the history of art for any regular development. " Moderns " are not necessarily superior to " ancients." Peoples and periods have been more or less favourable fields for art, and the coming of genius obeys no laws. The chef-d'œuvres of Greece were for long unequal. Yet the artistic wealth of humanity was increased by each succeeding form and attempt. There was produced alike that sort of cumulative technique and the material which, in science, provides the needed progress. So long as there are none of those cataclysms in which tradition for the time is broken, those middle ages of set-back and fresh beginnings, even if the artist does not create great works, or works equal to those of the past, the mass of amateurs of art understand and savour aspects of beauty that are ever more and more varied, and the game of art is played with an extraordinary intensity. To browse on idealistic Greek art, or realistic Greek art ; to taste of the art of Greece and also all that Greece missed and which is to be found in Gothic, in the Romantic—the sentiment of the infinite, for instance—this is to enjoy incontestable superiority. In art, progress should not only be envisaged from the point of view of genius, in the creations of the artist, but also from that of the public, in its comprehension of the æsthetic.[1]

**
* **

In our reflection on art in general, on art in Greece, literary art is naturally implied. Surprise may therefore be felt that this volume is devoted almost exclusively to plastic art. Greece shone in literary arts and was at least as original here as in the other arts ; she manifested the same qualities, realized the same ideal, created simple and noble beauty, and inculcated order and proportion in her literary art, and in it she bore testimony to a fertility of invention and stored a wealth of observation and ideas—by which the plastic arts have benefited.

Louis Hourticq, in a study in which he shows that these very

---

[1] *On the question of progress see P. Lacombe, " Introduction à l'Histoire littéraire," book III. Increasing illumination will be thrown on all these questions in the volumes of this series which are to deal with art.*

*arts respond to needs, and yield pleasures of a different order
from those of literary art and do not follow a strictly parallel
line of advance, puts forward the opinion that their progress in
general was even more precocious : " Far from deriving from
the book, the work of the sculptor and the painter often preceded
the literature to which it is likened in the attempt to find therein
the desired explanation."*[1] *What is true of epochs in which
sculpture and painting are mature and rich in tradition and
models would not seem to apply to the early days. There, though
plastic realizations may have given precision to myth, myths
preceded its plastic realization.*[2]

*Myths are spontaneous and naïve attempts to interpret
nature and life. " Into the empty heaven " the fertile imagination of the poets of Greece " projected a multitude of divine
beings." Myth taught the minstrels to see into the soul of
their characters ; and the passions which drove Agamemnon,
Diomedes, and Achilles, were first studied in Zeus, Ares and
Poseidon."*[3] *The anthropomorphism of the earlier Greek poets
translated, with an efflorescence of physical life, a lively and sharp
consciousness of the ego, an exalted idea of the human personality,
a firm confidence in the* Νοῦς. *The Homeric epopee and the
poems of Hesiod " reveal that the representation of life was the
material most calculated to touch men and to kindle in them
the impression of beauty."*[4]

*Why, then, should literary art be consigned to the background ?
Just because, in Greece, literary art is linked so closely with life
and thought that every volume of the Greek series is bound to be
concerned with it and with writers and their works. If we
wanted to deal with Greek literature by itself we should be forced
to much vain repetition and we should be obliged to lay stress
on highly technical and special details—if we were not merely
to content ourselves with a dry and useless summary.*

*Moreover, we must here make this capital distinction :
literary history, as it is usually given, embraces two kinds of
works. The one belongs to literary art and ministers especially*

---

[1] " La méthode en Histoire de l'art," *in the* " Rev. de Synth. hist.,"
vol. XXVIII, February, 1914, *p.* 31.

[2] " *Antique statuary issued from Greek paganism, without a doubt ;
but, conversely, is not Greek paganism in part the creation of artists, as of
poets?*" *Of poets particularly, in our view. See* Hourticq, *ibid., p.* 40.

[3] *See* Ouvré, " Les formes littéraires de la Pensée grecque," pp. 17, 50.

[4] M. Croiset, " La Civilization hellénique," *vol. I, p.* 50.

to æsthetic pleasure. The other serves various practical ends and has no part in literary art except by virtue of supplementary qualities, so to speak, from which—as in the decorative arts— æsthetic pleasure may be derived.

Oratory, history, philosophy, and those kinds of prose emanating from action or speculation, will find their natural place in those volumes devoted to political life and thought. As for those genres that are really literary—epic (a mixed genre which contains everything in embryo, but more especially narrative and description), lyric, and dramatic—they issue from religion, which itself is associated with the entire life of young peoples : and the study of Greek religion evokes many of the masterpieces of literature.[1]

Perhaps it would not have been without interest to lay stress on these literary " genres " which Greece, in particular, has made and on the laws of beauty she formulated—the poetic and rhetorical—new vehicles of literary art by which her reason hoped to fortify creative spontaneity. But we shall find again the genres, the canons and the models of Greece in the Alexandrian period, again in Rome, and then again in the Renaissance and in the classical epoch.

For the rest we shall have to revert in a general way to the diverse forms of art, and we shall see all that humanity owes to Greece for having organized the nobler pleasures.

HENRI BERR.

[1] *See vol. XI of the French Series, " Le Génie grec dans la Religion."*

INTRODUCTION

I

THIS book is not a history of Greek art. There are many in print already, both in French and in other languages, and, even if fitted to undertake it, I could hardly treat a subject of such importance—for many reasons one of the most difficult there is—in a few hundred pages. It would barely be possible to give a dry summary gleaned from my predecessors, savants to whose labours I have gone for guidance, and I should not have been able to take into account those numberless detailed monographs which, keeping pace with new discoveries, ofttimes complete and revise the conclusions already arrived at. I shall refer with all the less scruple to those general histories of art[1] which each have their own merit and of which France has so generous a share, thanks to Collignon[2] and Perrot.[3] Thus it will be easy for the reader to check what I say and himself to add abundant examples to those which I select.

Neither do I claim to set forth a philosophy of Greek art. Not that the subject lacks interest: I know of none more interesting nor which more merits the undertaking; but not only is it a subject which few could handle, but equally the complete initiation that would be necessary, even before one could begin to study it, is far from being within the reach of everybody. Nothing, indeed, is less clear in most people's minds than their notion of æsthetics, and the principle of æsthetics is the corner-stone of the whole question. Thus the first thing necessary would be for the author and reader to understand one another on this essential point, and a whole series of abstruse and nice definitions would be required to introduce the subject, and however brief one essayed to be, however patiently the reader might follow these deductions step by step, the *hors d'œuvre* would be in danger of becoming

[1] **I-XXII.**   [2] **V, LXII-III.**   [3] **XXXVIII, LXXXIV, C, CXLIV.**

the main dish at the feast and the theme itself would fade away before those philosophic discussions that would be foreign, and in a sense, exterior to it. I may add that, at the risk of speaking and arguing about abstractions, nothing less would be required in order to check these ideas of æsthetics and even merely to verify our definitions, than a most minute and thorough knowledge of Greek art. Maybe there is as great a contradiction in demanding from a philosopher a practical knowledge of monuments as in asking from an archæologist lucid philosophic concepts, but supposing the two disciplines to exist side by side in a person of unusual powers in whom the two contraries should be reconciled, it would still be impossible to expect such an effort from the average person; and, however interesting this delicate problem might be, it would hardly seem to be one that could come within general knowledge, or even be within the grasp of, or be found intelligible by, everybody.

I would simply seek to discover what art was for the Greeks and what were the ideas they entertained about art. That they were amazing artists, no one, I think, doubts, but what most people want to know is how and why they were such wonderful artists, and that is a question that cannot be answered without first discovering what art meant to the Hellenes and what place it occupied in their lives and in the Greek city. If we can get an exact idea of this rôle, and if we can understand what the Greeks thought about it, perhaps we shall be better able to understand the essential character of their art and what it was that constituted its originality and beauty.

In order to support the demonstrations which I shall attempt in the course of this study, illustrated examples must be given. Reproductions of sufficient exactitude to enable the reader to follow the argument will be provided. We shall not restrict our illustrations to a single category of monuments, such as statuary, and we shall not limit our studies to marble statues; other and more humble examples may supply us with more direct testimony, as I shall hope to prove, and in a sense will be more characteristic. It must be clearly understood, however, that the monuments chosen are chosen simply as illustrations; they do not comprise the whole of Greek art, nor are they by any means the principal masterpieces. Their rôle is more modest, and in a sense more useful; for us they have to take the place of what no longer exists in antiquity and to make us understand the beauty of that ancient art whose reflection still glows in them as in humble disciples who have been near to their master and so rendered worthy that we should listen to and venerate them.

II

The first question we have to resolve is to define what we mean by Greek art, or, what amounts to the same thing, to distinguish among those monuments preserved to our own times those which really represent Greek art and without which we should have no knowledge of its character and main qualities. Indeed, it would be quite wrong to imagine that all the objects illustrated are in the same degree capable of revealing to us the secret of the race, and equally wrong to think that art has always been the same at all periods or that it has remained unchanged from the beginning until later times, unalterable as an entity or as a creation of the reason. Had it been so, Greek art, whether or no it has been superior to all others, would have differed from them by possessing a unique privilege which would have placed it apart as the most surprising of exceptions. Everywhere, indeed, among all peoples and in every civilization, just as races are transformed and modified as the result of wars and conquests or by the peaceful influx of foreign elements, so does their art change, like their history, and their pictorial and plastic creations evolve and differ to such an extent that at a few centuries' distance the link between these products of an identical soil and population escapes us. Barely 300 years separates a Jean Malouel or a Jacques Froment from a Fragonard; yet, between the two, what a difference there is, not only in talent or technique but in ideals and in the manner in which they conceive of art and life ! If we did not know it otherwise, should we ever have thought of attributing to the same people works not only so diverse but so opposite, and should we have approved anyone who might attempt with a great effort of sophistic ratiocination to join together, artificially, these paintings, explaining one by the other and seeing in them two links of the same chain or successive phases in a single evolutionary scheme ?

We could evoke in other exotic or antique civilizations examples similar to this which France has provided. For long Egypt has been thought of as the land of a uniform art, where everything was mechanical and regulated, where immutable canons determined representations that were always alike, where there was no individual sentiment, and where the liberty of the artist was unknown and proscribed, where all that was demanded of him was to conform to a narrow program and to work it out faithfully and literally down to the smallest details. Archæological discoveries since the beginning of the 19th century have testified and are still testifying year by year that this view was mistaken and was only justified by a single moment in Egyptian art, whereas gradual changes were transforming it incessantly, and that these modifications were due to individual and personal efforts or to influences coming from without to which it was neither insensible nor a stranger. In the same way the hieraticism of Byzantine art, as we are constantly discovering with greater clearness, was greatly exaggerated by critics; here, too, when it became possible to distinguish the periods, there was seen to be an evolution in which different manners, opposite conceptions and diverse techniques, either more refined or more imperfect, succeeded one another. So, too, at the beginnings of Hindu art, and of Chinese, and Japanese art, we perceive and each day we discern more clearly, foreign influences succeeding one another and in each particular case gradually modifying and transforming the old native stock, while a whole succession of incessant efforts, often unfortunate, goes on in order to develop a fresh originality; all of them external manifestations revealing to us so many living and extremely flourishing organisms receiving much from outside but assimilating this foreign food and leaving their own mark on what they borrow without losing their originality and as though they thus paid a forfeit to existence.

Greek art is neither more nor less immutable than these others, and, like them, it has passed through many and divers phases. From its origins up to the Byzantine period it has undergone continuous evolution and transformation. Just as political and historical Greece is as unlike itself as can be at intervals of a couple of centuries or even shorter periods, so is Greek civilization and art continually undergoing modification, sometimes for the better, when the change means progress, and sometimes for the worse, and then Hellas takes the downward path; but whether for good or ill, whether we grieve over it or rejoice, this change is always going on and is a fact that is not to be denied. Nothing could be more interesting than to follow this ceaseless movement and to note the successive differences; but neither could any study be more difficult because we do not know when to seize the psychological moment and because one has to be on one's guard, in seeking to establish it, not to attach too much importance to passing phases which are but accidental variations.

For, indeed, the diversity of those monuments which alone can serve to reconstitute Greek art is very great. Without going back over history, even cursorily—and we have already stated that such is not our purpose—we must, if only to set a limit to our subject, outline the principal phases. For details we must refer the reader to the more comprehensive histories already indicated.

An earlier volume of this series[1] treated of the art which has been denominated Mycenæan since Schliemann and Minoan since Evans, and to which Dussaud, with greater simplicity and justice, would give the title Ægean. Between this civilization and the Greece of the 5th or 4th centuries there lies not merely the lapse of a thousand years or more but complete change in ideas or conceptions of life. The rare merit of the Ægean artists is to have given an amazingly realistic and picturesque impression of life with very limited means and despite the handicap of conventions which they could not, or knew not how to, overcome. There was as yet little order in these compositions in which human beings and beasts were crowded together at random, and scarcely any sense of rhythm or harmony (at all events during the primitive and creative period of art), but a lively sense of nature and a minute and faithful observation of external life together with a true appreciation of effect. This instinct, this need, almost, for reality was not altogether unknown to the Greeks; the Ionians appear to have come into and transmitted the heritage, and even in the classic period such

[1] Glotz, *Ægean Civilization*.

humble artisans as Pistoxenus, the painter of vases, bear
witness that the lesson had not been lost; still it must be
frankly recognized that in the great period of Greek art, the
4th century, the qualities which distinguish it and which
we shall try to define further on are entirely and essentially
different even in principle.   A gulf separates the two worlds,
and such frail bridges as are thrown across it consist of transmitted motifs or relationships of details.   This is comprehensible if, as it would seem and as has almost been proved to
be the case, the Cretans were of a different race from the Greeks
and if two invading waves, coming perhaps from the North—
the Achæans and later the Dorians—flowed one after the other
over the old stock of Hellas.   According to this hypothesis
the newcomers did learn in the school of the more advanced
masters with whom the chances of migration had brought
them into contact, but the pupils modified what they had
learned, and when a fresh wave of peoples pushed back these
earlier invaders, there remained nothing, or at all events very
little, of the precious heritage they had received but had
assimilated with difficulty and which they were incapable of
passing on to their conquerors and successors.

Once the curtain had fallen on this opening scene, not
long after the commencement of the first millennium, at the
beginning of the Iron Age and on the threshold of the period
when the Olympiads begin, Greece historically was but a
disorganized collection of peoples whose political system was
unstable, revolutions being frequent, but among whom
wealthier and more active cities developed as the result of
trading and before long sent out colonies. These colonies
and the commercial relations which the Hellenes established
with the surrounding peoples placed them in contact with
foreign and more advanced civilizations from which they
were to learn precious lessons and to receive fruitful teaching.
The Ionians who were settled on the Asiatic coast and neighbouring islands preserved some of the Ægean traditions brought
to them by the backwash of the great tidal wave which swept
the eastern Mediterranean towards the end of the second millennium.   These precious fundamental ideas they were able to
develop, transforming them by contact with the neighbouring
Babylonian, Hittite, Assyrian, and Egyptian empires; sea-
going peoples, such as the Cypriots and especially the Phœni-

cians, played a part whose importance should not be exaggerated but is not to be denied, in this migration of the forms of art and in this succession of exchanges which was to lead to the invention of types and motifs. Nearly all the elements came from the East and from Egypt, not merely the fabulous beasts and some of the legends attached to them, but textiles, pottery, ivories, bronzes and even the precious metals which were the artists' material, and, up to a certain point, the decorative sense and even the great ideas of ornamentation. All these principles, without which Greek art would not be, the Greeks gradually transformed and modified; this inert and composite matter they animated with a new spirit which was their own, and they created out of borrowed material a whole new world which was both original and personal.

Three centuries at least, the 8th to the end of the 5th, are consecrated to this slow elaboration, to this apprenticeship of the Hellenes who assimilated foreign techniques and made of their borrowed acquisitions something of their own which was to bear the hall-mark of their race. Discoveries on the Acropolis dating from the dawn of the 5th century and at the time of the Persian wars permit us to sum up with considerable accuracy that of which these Athenians were capable whom an intelligent tyranny had brought to the forefront of the Greek world and who, from this time forward, seem to have a sense of art and to care for the things of art.

Excavation has not yielded to us the valuable ex voto objects in metal or precious substances which were naturally pillaged by foreign invaders, and which, too, were never very numerous in Greece, which was both poor and less ostentatious in its taste than the Oriental monarchies. On the other hand, the abundant discoveries of pottery[1] and the little masterpieces made by the more skilful artisans such as Euthymides and Euphronius permit us to divine without exactly revealing to us the relative point of perfection which was achieved from this time onward by great decorative painting.[2] It was not yet master of all its means nor freed from all shackles, but it was not far off, since the great works of Polygnotus and Micon, whose influence was so great on Greek art, came soon after the departure of Xerxes. Thenceforward, and after a long evolutionary period, whose several successive stages we

[1] **CXXIX** ff.   [2] **CXV** ff.

divine rather than know, we no longer have to do with
prentice hands who can be content with what is less than
perfection, and happy if they have rendered a form approximately and filled up surfaces at haphazard, but with artists
who strain every nerve to express things exactly as they see
them, and who, when they set themselves to clothe their
observation in a form that is perfect and precise, are conscious
of satisfying one of the higher needs of humanity, and who
possess a sense of and a love for beauty—in short, with artists
who, in their fashion, are already producing works of art.[1]

It is the same for their confrères the sculptors[2] and for
all the workers who model in relief or in the round. Here,
too, the masterpieces are no more. The great statues in
bronze, the famous group of the Tyrannicides carried off by
the Persians, even the replicas which Critius and Nesiotes
were to do soon after, have disappeared almost without leaving a trace, and now we have great difficulty in imagining
what they were like; yet there remain more humble witnesses
to the perfection to which such works of art attained. Excavation has revealed a fair number of terra-cotta[3] and bronze
statuettes which were sometimes votive, of plaques and even
fragments of big statues. These fragments, for the most
part in bad preservation, have given us at least an inkling
of the form and aspect of the more important monuments,
although it has been impossible—or we have not known how—
to preserve their patina. These reproductions made indus-
trially at a period when it was not easy to draw a line between
artisan and artist are sometimes little inferior in merit to the
large statues. Certain faults born of the inexperience of the
modeller and his scanty acquaintance with anatomy might
be less obvious in these small figurines in which detail disappears. Taking all this into consideration, and allowing
the imagination to fill in the gaps in the evidence, we can
get a fairly good idea of the relative degree of perfection to
which the sculptor's art attained at this period. The remains
of pediments and the large number of wooden and marble
statues found in clearing the Acropolis also help to this end.[4]
The greater part of these latter represent the Korai, orantes,
and priestesses which the cult of Athena grouped on the

---

[1] LVIII ff.   [2] LVIII ff.   [3] CV ff.
[4] LXXII, LXXVIII, LXXX, LXXXIX, XC, XCIV.

sacred hill. Despite the imperfections of their structure and despite the many conventions to be seen in their pose and costume, their youthful and smiling grace has conquered even the most obstinate, and the art, already sure, with which they are modelled, the simplicity and the breadth of their style, and the decorative quality of their high and joyous silhouette is apparent to everyone. It should be noted in passing, however, that it was not here that secondary votive gifts or polychrome painting helped to hide the faults of the modelling, and the company of skilled workmen to whom we owe them merely repeated with insignificant variations the originals designed by creative master-artists. We have proof of this in the fact that similar statues have been discovered in other great sanctuaries such as Delphi and Delos, without counting all those that have vanished; it was simply the exceptional finding together of such a large number of well-preserved examples on the Acropolis that gave the mistaken impression of an Attic speciality, for we must not forget that these are votive statues, manufactured by the dozen, and only very exceptionally original works or genuine creations. Their testimony is but the more eloquent in favour of Attic art at the beginning of the 5th century. These average productions show us clearly and decisively the average level of art at the time of the Persian wars. Many conventions still regulate it. The attitudes are stiff, the details and features ill-observed or rendered ill, the anatomy is defective, the draperies too symmetrical or else cling to the form in an incomprehensible manner, but all these defects will be practically invisible if we think of the progress realized since this century or even in a shorter space of time. And we can well conceive that it was about this period that Ageladas appeared, the sculptor to whom a false tradition has given Myron, Phidias, and Polyclitus as pupils—that is to say the three masters whose fame fills the entire 5th century. It mattered little to us here whether the legend of Ageladas is true or false; suffice it that, looking at things broadly, sculpture, in a general way, if not in possession of all the means of expression, was at least nearing emancipation and final liberty towards 480.[1]

Thus painting and sculpture, the plane image and the

[1] **LXXVIII**, p. 351.

plastic representation are about equally advanced, or if it is
preferred, are at about the same point of perfection. We are
the less surprised that the practice of polychrome decoration,
then more general, rendered the frontiers between these two
arts very indistinct and often difficult or almost impossible
to determine. It does not matter to us here, and anyhow the
question is futile, which of these arts is anterior to the other,
and which of them made the faster progress; if we cannot
say that they went hand in hand, at least we shall see later
that many a celebrated sculptor was a painter and many a
painter occasionally modelled.

Given this point of departure, with art, in its two forms,
nearing, towards the year 480 B.C., its maturity and full
development, the entire history of the 5th century will be
marked by ceaseless progress in art and by the masterpieces
which appear almost annually. Possibly as great promise
has been seen elsewhere, but if Greek art had stopped there,
and however rare may have been the qualities then revealed,
that art would not be to-day what it is. Its singular and
it would seem, unique good fortune lies in the fact that,
almost arriving at perfection, it always tended to get still
closer, and though it may not be given to human nature to
achieve it, it succeeded better than any other art in transforming its chimeras of beauty and its dreams into living
realities. There is here a continuous effort, a steadily maintained progress, a perseverance in creative energy which not
only is a great testimonial to the Greek race, but to humanity
itself. Such success is unique, but it is a great thing and
highly consoling that we can quote at least one such
example.

This is not the place in which to set down the history of
this incomparable period which is so little known. Suffice
it to call to mind that Myron, Phidias, and Polyclitus, to
quote only the very great names, then created their toreutic
masterpieces and carved their great chryselephantine statues.
Polygnotus and Micon, on the other hand, painted their
great frescoes, and at the end of the century, Zeuxis and
Parrhasius their miniatures. Finally, Athens, at the apogee
of her power under Pericles, covered herself with monuments
till she rivalled the great sanctuaries of Olympia, of Delphi
and Delos. If we reflect that this was also the period of the

great tragic writers we shall agree that never were there known so many great talents and masterpieces nor so great a concourse of poets and artists, when the influence of creative thought on plastic or pictorial invention must have been as great as that of the artists on the poets. We can understand that all, even the humblest of artisans and disciples, coming into contact with this great interplay of ideas and having before them works which both served them as examples and spurred them to emulation in that pre-eminently privileged period, were alive to these fertilizing influences and that their ruder productions reflected the glow in their own way.

The Peloponnesian wars which put a period to Athens' brief hegemony did not cause any sudden interruption to her artistic destinies. Leaving aside a later renaissance which was to be less fruitful, Praxiteles was to make the Attic workshops famous once again in the 4th century, and his masterpieces were to make known a new form of art. Only it was to be a new form in fact, since neither 4th century art in general nor Praxiteles' art in particular is the Attic art of the 5th century. The spirit of it is different, as, in some respects, is the technique and even the material, up to a point. The gulf between the two schools is not impassable but it is sufficiently wide and deep to make one feel that the atmosphere is different, and that one is almost in another world.

If we follow the evolution of art very closely perhaps we shall altogether miss or scarcely be aware of the metamorphosis. The change, indeed, is slow and gradual. With sculptors of the transition who still work in the 5th century manner it is certain traits and details alone which herald the coming revolution. It is ever thus in art. To cite an instance nearer home, it is maintained to-day that the shell, so dear to the century before last, had already appeared under Louis XIV., and if we go further than mere ornament, Watteau, in whom we can trace much of the 18th-century spirit, scarcely comes into Louis XV. and barely survives the Regency. Yet it is undeniable that the difference between his art and that of a Poussin or a Lesueur, even a Lebrun or a Mignard, leaps to the eye and that the contrast is absolute. If we advance by stages from one point to another the change is scarcely noticeable, but if we jump suddenly from one to the other, we are aware of entering a different world.

So it is with Greek art, and even if we cannot say that the 4th century is an advance on the 5th, at least the change from one to the other is notable and almost complete. Fresh tendencies come to light which do not appear in the earlier period; new ways of reaching a new ideal open up: the quality and character of art are different from, and almost opposed to, those of the previous century.

That is why, when we seek to define the essence of Greek art, we shall take care not to reject *a priori* examples borrowed from other periods of its history, but shall choose them by preference in the time of its apogee and fullest development. In the 6th century foreign influence is still marked and the workman has scarcely got to work with his tools: in some ways the artist is still a prentice hand with them. Some of his attempts, indeed, were particularly characteristic in vain, since in art more than in anything else one has to judge the creator not by his intention but by what he has actually created. Hence our obligation to seek the real traits of Greek art in its great creations and masterpieces.

These alone will tell us what it is that is specific and original in Greek art—indicate its hall-mark, and show us wherein lies its superiority.

Yet if we stop there the picture will be really incomplete, for however highly we esteem the masterpieces of the 5th century they are not the only masterpieces nor do they represent all that Greek effort has created. Hence, so soon as we have defined, to the best of our ability, the leading qualities of Greek art, and have grasped something of what the masterpieces of the 5th century must have been, we will pass on to the study of later art, and will seek for those new tendencies which reveal themselves and certain of which were to have so great an influence on Roman art and thus a repercussion in the Renaissance and in modern art. Thus completed, this picture will really show us of what the Greeks were capable; we shall find out what art meant to them and exactly what they thought about it.

III

All science, or to speak more generally, all knowledge, presupposes a certain number of elements or data on which the savant or the merely curious exercises his reason. Just as the historian classifies, discusses, and elucidates facts, the philosopher scrutinizes, dissects, and analyzes ideas, and the grammarian studies the forms of words and the laws of language, so does the art critic have a knowledge of monuments of all kinds, buildings, sculptures, paintings, gravings, which, seeing that they are the work of the Greeks, must and can alone shed for him the necessary light on their rôle and on their worth as artists. Theories and dissertations, even though ancient, may be quite useless or misleading when we are trying to get at what beauty was for them; in order to guard against errors of judgment there is only one kind of evidence admissible without question or control and that is or will be the actual work which came, as it were, alive from their hands. Although the material may not have yielded to their will and although they may not have known how to clothe their visions in perfect form, the product of their labours tells us what they desired to do, what they were capable of creating, what their ideals were, and what their weaknesses, and it reveals to us their innermost intentions and the means they employed to translate them into material and plastic form.

Hence it will suffice to have at our disposal a certain number of works of art in which are manifested directly and without intermediaries the creative faculty of the Hellenes, but it will be also an essential condition. Once we have these data before us our task will be to study them and to discover the indications we seek, and it is quite likely that owing either to inability or incapacity we may fail, or that this or that monument under examination will not reveal to us its secret or will yield it up in part only; we shall have but ourselves to blame—our inexperience or our lack of perspicacity. At least we shall have all the elements essential to our science before us; the seed is there, needing only a creative spirit to breathe upon it that it may germinate. With such first principles all is possible, but it goes without saying that without them nothing is possible. If we realize that from such premisses we can draw the necessary logical conclusions, we should also quite clearly understand that without them it is impossible or at least unlikely that we shall arrive at the end in view. In other words, before we can make any deduction we must make certain of the fact or facts which we intend to study and see that they are firmly established.

Since our whole task consists in determining the sense and scrutinizing the worth of the ancient monuments, we must first, in order to avoid as far as possible all chances of error, find out what these facts on which we are to work really are; in short, before we do anything else we must critically examine our sources and see if it is feasible for us, in the 20th century of the Christian era, to comprehend fully and at first hand an ancient work of art.

The problem has its importance because obviously the whole of this study depends on its solution. If the answer is in the affirmative our enquiry will still not have been in vain because it will have consolidated our basic principles and shown us the value of the documents which we shall have to put forward. If it is in the negative, or if it runs the risk of being so, the original question forces itself upon us still more emphatically, because it would be fraudulent deliberately to build on sand and to construct a system on a rotten foundation. Clarity and complete frankness, always praiseworthy, are here absolutely essential.

Can we, then, after the lapse of two thousand years, comprehend the original creations of the Greek artists— which is the indispensable condition for a just appreciation, and essential if we are to draw legitimate deductions from this appreciation ? We must admit, for it is useless to deny it, that the wear and tear of time has done its work, and we must not demand that the entire work of a single artist should have survived to our own day: a few specimens, be they never so scarce or scattered, will suffice, so long as they come to us direct, are definite, and characteristic. This inevitable reservation does not subtract anything from the force of the principal question, which faces us all the more obstinately in that, as we shall see presently, the answer is a difficult one, and in that at first sight it would seem impossible to arrive at a satisfactory solution of the problem.

In order to facilitate its discussion, we shall split up the problem and by passing in review the different categories of works of art we shall see whether we arrive at the same conclusion in each class and each series.

At first sight nothing would seem easier than to represent to ourselves what was the architecture[1] of the Greeks. Its ruins are often extant and, with rare exceptions, there is hardly a single famous monument of antiquity whose site at least and frequently its main lines are not known to us. Occasionally we are even more fortunate, and the Theseum, in which it is supposed we can recognize the Hephæsteum of Pausanias, has only lost its ancient roof. Yet, when we look more closely, we have to confess that appearances are deceptive and that our knowledge is illusory. The Theseum, whose merit should neither be detracted from nor exaggerated, is far from giving a complete idea of Hellenic architecture; it lacks more than the missing marble tiles, for it has lost its polychrome decoration, the greater part of its sculptures, all its interior arrangement, the cult statue which was its raison d'être, the frescoes which embellished its walls, and the votive gifts which filled and adorned the sanctuary; of all this living ensemble there remains but the mute and empty frame. How much the more so is this the case with the most celebrated monuments which, as we know from the universal admiration of the Ancients, were the most beautiful with which they were acquainted! Even if the sculptures taken away by Lord Elgin were still in their places, and, still more to the point, even if the explosion of a Venetian bomb had not disembowelled the Parthenon,[2] should we really have any true idea of this temple which was the most perfect of them all and the one which could have told us most? Here, too, the skeleton survives, and the exterior sculptural decoration is well preserved up to a point despite inevitable mutilations; but if Phidias superintended the building, and if he was indeed the author of this work, there must have existed a subtle and profound harmony between the sanctuary itself and the cult statue— his masterpiece and the masterpiece of Greek art. One or two imperfect miniatures and a few partial replicas allow us to guess at the appearance of the idol, but the idol minus

[1] **XXIII ff.**   [2] **XXXIX, XLIV.**

its attributes and pose, its arms and costume; on the Acropolis we can even lay our hands on the substructure of the old base; but we are ignorant of everything else, of the precise height of the gold and ivory Colossus, the relations which the statue bore to its architectural setting, the lighting, the plastic décor of the building, the wall frescoes, and the manner in which the votive figures were grouped and in which the treasure of Athena was disposed; we have no means of knowing all that which was comprehended between the columns of the prodomus and the opisthodomus. All of which is as much as to say that we are ignorant of almost the entire monument, or, if it be preferred, that we do not know its essentials, since the Greeks, who were skilled and experienced builders, erected their façades as an adjunct to the halls which they limited or concealed—so much so that they are really only explained by their interior: hence if we know nothing of the interior we practically know nothing of the building, because we do not know its real significance nor its raison d'être.

It would be easy to multiply examples: they would all be equally convincing and there would be some which are even more decisive which we could select at will among the numerous monuments of which even less remains to us than of the Parthenon. In many cases, no doubt, modern science has restored the vanished past, reasoning by analogy or basing itself on slender indications, but however ingenious these restorations may be on paper, we can never be sure that they realize their aim, and if we suppose that by some miracle one among them approached the actuality, there would still remain, between the restoration and the once living work, all the difference that lies between the palpitating being and its shadow or reflection.

If we pass on from buildings to sculptures,[1] our enquiry must be directed first towards those original documents which have come down to us from the 5th and 4th centuries—those which must principally engage our attention. To facilitate their examination we can divide them into two distinct groups of decorative schemes and isolated figures. We have preserved, if not in their entirety, at least in fragmentary fashion, the interior ornamentation of a few among the most

[1] **LVIII** ff.

famous temples known to antiquity. Such as, from the beginning of the 5th century, the temples of Ægina, of Zeus at Olympia, the Parthenon, the Erechtheum, the sanctuary of the Wingless Victory, and later on, the temples at Tegea and Magnesia, and the mausoleum at Halicarnassus. No doubt there are many lacunæ in these decorative ensembles; here, the very subject is hardly recognizable and it is still under discussion to-day; there, the details are impossible to discern, limbs are missing, and the skin and bloom of the marble has everywhere disappeared. Despite these blanks and gaps, even if we cannot appraise the work in the form in which the Ancients had it before them, at least we can reconstruct to a certain point the groups of those days from their mutilated remains. Supposing that our patience and perseverance are rewarded, what will be the result of our efforts ? We shall have got to know, more or less, the decoration of one or more buildings; but, however important and celebrated these temples may have been, we may well believe that the reliefs in them were not the original and first-hand work of the great artists of antiquity. Among the temples whose exterior ornament has survived to our day there are some whose decorators remain anonymous: in those instances in which tradition has preserved a name, the question is to determine what was the personal share which the master had in the work of his studio. Let us take the Parthenon for example. It is a much disputed point, and one into which we can hardly enter here, whether the pediments, the friezes and the metopes of the temples are or are not due to Phidias; those critics, however, who are most in favour of the affirmative thesis will never admit—if they have any good sense at all—that we owe to the sculptor anything but the design and the models for the scheme. His pupils may have executed the statues of the pediments and the various bas-reliefs under his direction: we cannot definitely state that a single portion of the work is to be imputed to the artist and, strictly speaking, we have no right to judge the artist himself on this evidence. Not that I do not recognize the rare and sublime beauty which the marbles at the British Museum, and the Athens and Louvre fragments, still retain; but, however precious these sculptures, we cannot deduce from them what Phidias really was, and we should be very easily satisfied

C

and devoid of all healthy critical sense were we to conclude
simply that the work of the master must be even more
beautiful. The inference is quite legitimate but is altogether
too general to teach us anything of the individual character
and genius of the artist; all our efforts would be merely
deception were they to result in so vague and so gratuitous
an affirmation.

Over and above the sanctuaries we possess a considerable
number of funerary sculptures[1] over which we can pass
rapidly, because, whatever their merit, and however precious
they may be for us modern folk, they belong, with rare
exceptions, to purely industrial art, and for the most part the
artists who executed them were simple carvers of marble
among whom, though we are not justified in looking for
artists, we shall find skilled craftsmen. Fortunately we
possess other statues and reliefs which come sometimes from
the great sanctuaries and in which we can see votive pieces
which the pious faithful ordered from renowned sculptors.
The trouble is that all these relics of the past are anonymous.
One original piece of the 4th century alone has come down
to us in part—the Hermes of Praxiteles, slender evidence on
which to judge even the art of the 4th century, since Pausanias,
who alone speaks of it, has not mentioned it among the
celebrated productions of the artist nor included it among
his masterpieces; we can understand his reserve to a certain
extent when we are confronted with the somewhat smooth
flesh and with an art, already almost academic, which has
disconcerted certain archæologists and which carries a
fugitive suggestion of some statue of the imperial period. I
shall not now speak of the insignificant base of Bryaxis nor
of the pedestal of Mantineus. The statues they carried were
the sculptors' work, not the supports, with which they had
nothing to do and which we cannot even say were the product
of their workshops. Bearing in mind the disproportion between the two cases, the relation between the Arcadian bas-
reliefs and the unknown work of the sculptor remains the same
as that between the decoration of the Parthenon and Phidias'
statue: in both cases the original work which alone concerns
us remains a mystery to which we have no clue.[2]

We shall not be surprised at this deceptive result if we

[1] **LXIII-IV.**   [2] See, on these problems, **VI**, vol. i, p. 263.

remember what the Ancients have told us about the work of
the great statue-carvers. Their testimony, which, perhaps,
has been too greatly discredited, is entirely unlike the artistic
judgment of modern folk, but when it is a matter of material
statements and not a question of critical appreciation we have
no right to withhold our credence. And their testimony is
unanimous on this point, that the great masters of the 5th
and even the larger number of those of the 4th century only
occasionally worked in marble: their masterpieces were either
chryselephantine or bronze, both alike having disappeared.
Praxiteles, of whom we spoke above, was definitely an
exception, as were also two or three artists, like Scopas, without, however, any of them, so far as we know, having worked
solely in stone. The others, that is to say the great majority,
were toreutists,[1] which is easily to be understood if we reflect,
as we shall see, presently, on the altogether exceptional facility
of these artists in their work and on the perfection of the process
which insured that they could render in every detail every little
refinement of their model and even the very intentions of
their chisel. And here we are completely baffled, since hardly
a single original has come down to us, not only among the
chryselephantine statues, which is only what we should
expect, but even among the works in metal. We possess a few
originals in bronze of which not one is intact or well preserved,
but which we can legitimately date to the 5th and 4th centuries: not one is signed by an illustrious or even by a known
name, and we are not justified in seeing in any of them the
authentic, individual and certain work of one of the great
masters.

What are we to think of the great decorative painting,[2]
the frescoes of Polygnotus and Micon, the pictures of Parrhasius, Zeuxis, and Apelles? Here the answer can be given more
briefly but with greater peremptoriness. *Etiam periere ruinæ;*
not a single signed work remains which we can definitely
attribute to one of the masters or even to one of his disciples.
We have the walls of the Lesche of Delphi about which Pausanias gives us minute details, infinitely precious: not a trace,
I will not say of the antique work, but of the glaze on which
it was done, is preserved, an irreparable loss when we think
of the fame enjoyed by this creation of the Thasos painter

[1] **CLXXXV,** s.v. "Statuaria ars." [2] **CXV** ff.

and of the crowd of imitations of all kinds which the masterpiece provoked from the moment it saw the light. Elsewhere, in Athens, we scarcely know the site of the Stoa
pœkile; and even if the Pinacotheca of the Propylæa is standing yet, we still know nothing about the gallery which once
garnished its walls.

This is not to say that modern science stands helpless
before these disasters. Carl Robert, an ingenious and able
archæologist, has succeeded in recapturing the order and
spirit, at least, of the frescoes of the Cnidian Lesche by
interpreting Pausanias' description in the light of the industrial
replicas which they may have inspired. He has not given
us and does not attempt to render these two scenes as they
were admired of old with all the grandeur of their design,
the harmony of their proportions and the purity and
simplicity of their colouring. What means have we, then,
to-day, wherewith to gain an idea of antique painting ? It
is not to be doubted that the painters of vases,[1] or at all
events some among them, were inspired by the frescoes
which they may have admired in the sanctuaries, just as
the Limoges enamellers and the Urbino potters imitated the
masterpieces of the great painters of France and Italy in
order that they might provide their clients with a souvenir or
miniature rendering of them. But it has to be remembered
that the potter's field is limited, which obliged the decorators
to select and hence to eliminate many significant details,
while the curvature falsified proportions, sometimes widely
separating, sometimes bringing too close together, the heads
and feet. Finally all the colouring was lost since most
ceramists used reserved and flat tones, and the lecythus
decorators, who used many tones, thought only of riveting
the attention by crude colour combinations, and sought
bright tints rather than truth. The metopes of Thermos,
a few Athenian and Theban stelæ, and the later stelæ of
Pagasæ, provide us with documentation that, in a sense, is
more exact and comes nearer to the original paintings, but
the most perfect and precious of them, such as the monument
of Aristion and the three Theban stones, are not sufficiently
well preserved nor sufficiently decisive and characteristic.
The artisans who worked for the necropoles, like the ceramists,

[1] **CXXIX** ff.

were humble workers, who, having no ambition to be original and thinking before all else of proportion, did not seek to go out of their way to produce a work of art.

Professional education was so perfect and the general taste was so pure that even artists of second rank have contrived to leave behind precious testimony to their ability: how much the more wonderful must have been the glory of the colouring, the perfection of the design, and the execution of a Polygnotus or a Parrhasius, a Zeuxis or an Apelles !

Failing that first-hand testimony which the monuments do not give us, possibly we might feel inclined to seek information from the natural surroundings among which dwelt the artists of ancient Greece, the architects, sculptors and painters. This natural décor has never changed. Though the mountain slopes have become less wooded, their out line remains the same; the same bold, sharply-cut lines define the horizon in the same translucent atmosphere, the same air plays about the valleys of the Cephissus and the Ilissus, and the same sun rises behind Hymettus, and when, at eventide, he disappears behind the hills of Eleusis, the self-same tints of mauve and blue follow one another in the eastern sky. The spectacle is unchanging and there is not a doubt but that its beauty, together with the view of the Spartan plain, of the Delphic Phædriades, and of the Theban Cithæron and the great Thessalian valleys deeply moved the sensitive soul of the Hellenes: that they did feel the spell of these privileged natural surroundings is revealed to us by the discreet avowals which escaped them and by the hymns of gratitude which they addressed to the gods who had cast their lines in " violet-crowned " Athens. Neither can we—modern barbarians—contemplate without emotion the skies to which, even as we do, these famous men turned the regard of countenances on which we would fain look again. On the slopes of the Acropolis there are places where we walk on the naked rock which may have known the footprints of Sophocles and Socrates, Phidias and Alcibiades, of artists and poets, statesmen and philosophers, of the greatest writers and artists known to the pagan world.

Comparisons such as these may be profitable to the moral

ego and productive of long reveries. But do they tell us anything definite about the ancient spirit and ancient art ? And even if it is easy to believe and to prove that the Ancients were really sensitive to the beauty of the surrounding scenery, it by no means follows that we can measure, to-day, the influence that this privileged environment may have exercised on them. And it is not difficult to show that we must beware of exaggerating this environmental influence and that in any case we are not justified in assuming the subject from the décor nor the picture from its frame. Indeed, Greeks still live where their ancestors dwelt before them: and though their material life may be modified or transformed, the aspect of the surrounding nature has not changed, or only very slightly. Hence the same causes ought to act in the same way and produce the same results, and if we claim that Greek art could only have blossomed in this exceptional environment, then contemporary Hellas ought to produce a galaxy of artists inferior in nothing to those of antiquity. Yet nothing of the sort has come to pass, and though we cannot lay it down that nothing of the sort ever will come to pass, at all events there is nothing whatever to justify us in claiming that someday there will be a renaissance of artistic life in this country. Neither is the case of Greece peculiar. Despite the spirit of emulation with which contemporary Italian architects, sculptors and painters endeavour to rival their forbears of the Renaissance, no one could seriously maintain that their work, however admirable it may be now and again, is in any way comparable with the masterpieces of the 15th and 16th centuries. And yet, there too, neither nature nor the land has changed. I am well aware that both in Greece and Italy many accessory causes serve as pretexts to explain this difference between the past and the present, but even if we can thus attenuate or water down reality, we cannot alter the profound nature of things, and the conclusion to which we are driven is both clear and brutal: we can never hope to know the art of the Greeks by approaching it by way of nature —that is to say from the exterior. The most subtle of analyses can never deduce from the environment alone the character of their complex creation which was the result of a number of causes and the fruit of long effort. Thus we have not found here the criterion, the hall-mark which will permit us to obtain a first-hand knowledge of, and to define, antique art.

Is this to say that we must despair of ever attaining what we seek ? That this unknown territory eludes our curiosity and that we must strike out from the empire of science this domain to which our imperfect means do not allow us access ? I do not think so and I believe that, though nothing can replace the sight and study of the masterpieces which have vanished for ever, at least we can get a fairly correct idea of them which, if it is neither complete nor exact in every detail, yet can approach sufficiently close to the reality. Failing absolute certainty, which we can never attain in this world, I believe, and I shall endeavour to show, that we can reach that degree of average certainty with which some of the experimental sciences, such as history, have to be content, and which would appear to serve them with moderate sufficiency.

If we retrace, step by step, the rapid enquiry already undertaken, it is doubtless true, and vexatious, that we do not know a single building of antiquity fundamentally and completely. There is not a temple, a mausoleum, a public or private edifice which presents itself to our view to-day such as it must have appeared to a contemporary of Solon, Pericles or Demosthenes. It would be surprising indeed if over two thousand years could roll by between their civilization and ours without leaving any visible trace of their passage. Still, if the wear and tear of time is always necessarily apparent, is that to say that we cannot by any manner of means figure to ourselves what these things once were, or that we are for-ever forbidden to assume with some little chance of certainty the vanished grandeur from the present state or to postulate the past from the present ?

Above we have alluded more particularly to temples and we said that, despite a fair supply of means of information, neither the Theseum nor the Parthenon is or can be known completely in every detail of structure or decoration. This is true, but on both points we have a certain amount of light and maybe we do know the essentials, after all. Only, we must be resigned to a certain lack of knowledge, inevitable for humanity, and it would be well, or rather it is necessary, that we should know how to interpret such evidence as we do possess.

Hence, where we can learn nothing at first-hand we must make use of methods which will enable us to get as near as may be, and must reason by analogy. We do not know the architectural scheme of the Theseum, and we know very little about that of the Parthenon; but, on the other hand, inscriptions have preserved for us wholly or in part the plans of several antique buildings, such as the temple of Zeus at Livadia, the sanctuary at Delphi, the Arsenal of Philo and the temple at Didymi. These edifices, of which one has entirely disappeared, do not resemble one another in date, arrangement or interior disposition, but they are all the fruit of Greek thought, and the method of execution, the plan, the general arrangement, in short the architectural conception and treatment, would not and could not vary greatly as between one building and another, and we are fully justified in applying to the Theseum and the Parthenon the results of observations suggested by the analysis of these written documents, since it must be readily admitted that there were general laws from which the Athenians to whom we owe these two temples could not escape.

Inscriptions likewise give us the inventory of the treasure preserved in the episthodomus of the Parthenon. However dry the enumeration and however unsatisfying to our curiosity this list may be in some respects, we do at least learn what was the nature of these votive offerings and the manner in which they were arranged in rows and as though by storeys. This store of all manner of articles—a mass of varied and sometimes strange gifts—we can hardly figure to ourselves with exactitude, nor can we see with our eyes its sumptuous and variegated profusion; but we know enough about it to imagine that portion of the sanctuary as a huge depot of goods, among which some, if not all, are known to us with precision. And this detailed view, which other inventories confirm, does not fail to teach us much as to what were Greek sanctuaries in general and the Parthenon in particular.

Furthermore, the means of information about Greek architecture at our disposal are really abundant and guarantee us a relative degree of safety in drawing our conclusions.

This is neither the time nor the place to enumerate them, but we can indicate some at least among the more instructive or, as one says, the more suggestive. There are, firstly, the ruins, scattered as they are, throughout the Hellenic world: although only too often nothing but the foundations of once famous temples remain, we have been able to preserve, thanks to happy excavations, significant portions of walls, pediments and pictorial and sculptural decorations; frequently texts, whether inscriptions or literary, add to this testimony and allow us to see what the aspect of the monument might have been when complete. Even beyond the borders of Greece, the Italian and Sicilian ruins permit instructive comparisons to be made: though we may have to exercise caution in having recourse to them, and though it may not be the case that an example, taken from Pompeii, has an antecedent in Greece, the décor of the Pompeiian cities does, after all, derive from a Hellenic model. So that Vesuvian villas, which are almost intact, shed light on many points and give us the information which we seek in vain elsewhere. Thanks to all these scattered data, and by dint of gleaning wherever we can revealing indications and sources of information, we are able to get a summary idea, yet correct as a whole, of what antique architecture was.

If we pass on to sculpture there is no fear that I shall fail to recognize the force and extent of the objections and reservations that we were obliged to make just now; yet, although it is only too true that we can never know the work of the Greek artists in its integrity, we must not on that account jump to the conclusion that we cannot form any clear idea of it or that it must remain for us a *terra incognita* closed to our researches and for ever removed beyond reach of our curiosity.

I am willing enough to concede that the exterior decoration of the great sanctuaries could not be the actual handiwork of the great masters. It is none the less true that, in certain well-defined instances, these friezes and groups were carried out under their direction and in their studios by pupils or men who worked for them and in the spirit of the master and who had been taught by them, and followed their tradition; thus we are justified in looking for something of the quality inspiring their masterpieces in these secondary, and I might almost say indirect though authentic productions; though these may be but " poor relations " they are yet members of the same family deriving from the same source and drawing their inspiration from the same ideal; the hand of these pupil workers, though less skilled, retains the cunning imparted to it by the master teacher, and that cunning we shall be able to trace even in these lesser productions. Even where the decorative scheme remains anonymous, and in cases in which there is not even a doubtful text to guide us as to the responsible authorship, it is by no means a small thing that we are able to make the acquaintance, albeit imperfectly, of these stone and marble documents. They are, indeed, important pieces of evidence which we can frequently date more or less correctly and which tell us the stage to which the art of modelling had reached at a given period. When we see or can determine what the plastic décor of a notable monument was like, we can safely postulate the degree of perfection which sculpture had achieved at the period in which the building was erected, and this is direct, irrefutable evidence to which no conjecture, no text even, could add anything in certainty.

As for the isolated statues, it is certain that the masterpieces have not been preserved and that, with practically one exception alone, we do not know the authentic and original works of the great masters. Excavation, however, happily yields and continues to unearth sculptures, already numerous and growing more numerous still, which can either be dated with precision or with small likelihood of error. These monuments are unsigned by any great name and represent the average run of sculpture. Common or garden productions of the marble-workers' chisels, they furnish us with the ordinary level of art, or thereabouts. This is evidence taken from among the people who may be somewhat behindhand in the tendencies of the studios and which, in any case, is neither too significant nor too expressive. Thus in one sense this evidence is more precise, if not more valuable. The conclusions we shall draw from the direct and unprejudiced analysis of these works will allow us to get a knowledge of the condition and tendencies of art in the precise period to which these monuments belong. If the investigation is cautious and restrained, as it ought to be, it will yield us modest results with nothing sensational about them, but our conclusions, on the other hand, will be certain, and we ought to place all the more faith in them in that they will be taken at random and will in no way be exceptional.

On the other hand, in many cases we know the titles and have a brief description of masterpieces which have not been preserved. Art criticism properly so-called[1] would seem to have begun with Xenocrates, the disciple of Lysippus, in the first half of the 3rd century B.C., but, over and above the appraisements or descriptions of periegetes and technicians, " lay " writers have transmitted to us the impressions made upon them by works of art: as in our own day there were plenty of the uninitiated in antiquity who considered themselves to be authorities on painting and fancied themselves capable of estimating the merit of a fresco or a picture; but, even in the case of a celebrated piece of sculpture, each one had his own opinion or thought he ought to have one, if it were only to repeat the pronouncement of the connoisseurs. Summary as they may be, all these appreciations, whose echo has come down to us, are not negligible, and, provided we interpret them correctly, we ought to take them into account. Then sometimes we have inscriptions which are silent as to the artistic value of the work but which do give us information about practical details and material conditions. To these documents must be added the replicas and imitations of all kinds, and even interpretations in and translations, into different materials, some idea of which may be had from the renderings, in their own fashion, by the Limoges enamel workers and the Faenza potters of the famous pictures of the Renaissance. When some great master completed a great work the repercussion must have affected every studio, even the workshops of the artisans; its influence on the marble and bronze workers was lively and undying; it was an inexhaustible source of inspiration from which flowed every kind of indirect imitation without counting the early demand for copies by art lovers, which copies were to adorn palaces, villas, libraries and museums, and were especially numerous in the Roman period. The archæologist's task is to trace among the innumerable antique copies which have come down to us those which are to be

[1] **VI**, vol. i, p. 48.

referred to this or that celebrated work and so to reconstruct the prototype; then, by grouping and combining the inferences to give us some idea of the sculptor himself, to discover, if possible, what it was which he contributed to the common stock, of which he himself was the genuine author—in brief, in what consisted his originality and his worth, or, if you will, what was his artistic value.

Thus, by means of inferences and combinations one can build up a complete history of ancient art which is necessarily a work requiring much time and patience but which will lead to definite conclusions if the criticism be sufficiently measured and prudent. I am well aware that much that is arbitrary will enter into certain arguments and that the deductions to be drawn will not all be equally legitimate. It is only too true that for many savants certain affirmations are a matter of fashion or prejudice and that there are writers who, without troubling to think or judge for themselves, repeat without examining them the pronouncements that they have inherited: it is not really of much consequence, because, by acting thus, they themselves lose authority, and science does not suffer from their mediocrity of mind. Maybe these Panurgian sheep are less dangerous, on the whole, than certain great minds who desire to be original at all costs. Such men take a name at random from among the lists of artists which antiquity has transmitted to us; according to some vague epithet with which Pliny or Pausanias may have supplied them, they proceed to make a second selection from the indistinguishable mass of anonymous statues which have come down to us and they proceed shamelessly to attribute a group of works to a master, unknown yesterday and fated to sink back into oblivion again to-morrow: it goes without saying that if they build up new systems and support them with subtle arguments and erudite reasons, they take still greater delight in undermining accepted conclusions which would appear to be based on the most solid foundations. Precious time is lost in defending against these furious onslaughts positions which would appear to be finally won for science, and although this instability sometimes does disservice to the good repute of archæology, we are all the more justified in stating that we ourselves are untouched by it and that France is not the country in which this mental malady and desire for fictitious originality has more particularly raged.[1]

In truth, the historian of antique sculpture must resign himself to a lack of knowledge in many directions. Perhaps I should find it preferable that we should own it frankly and that, for prudence' sake, points of interrogation, in Renan's phrase, should be understood in the margin. This, however, is a question of tact and of a sense of proportion rather than of an objection on principle. I might also wish that the critic would occupy himself less in discussing texts and establishing the value' of testimony and more in first-hand study of those works of art which are preserved; here the prime reality, or if you will, the fact, is the monument, and an authentic piece of sculpture of the 5th century, even if it remains anonymous, is of greater interest to us and can teach us more than inconclusive arguments about a vanished masterpiece of which no certain replica allows us to form a definite picture— provided, that is, that we interrogate our authentic piece of sculpture in the right way. With this reservation, there is nothing to prevent Greek sculpture from being an object of knowledge, if not of science, and it is no vain or sterile task to devote one's efforts to gaining such knowledge.[2]

If we now pass on from sculpture to painting,[3] at first sight it becomes even more difficult, as we have seen above, to get at the facts. At least the Hermes at Olympia is preserved to us; but not a fresco or a picture that has come down to us bears the name of an illustrious master or even of a known artist. It must be recognized that the loss is irreparable, but if we wish to reckon up the extent of this loss, neither must we exaggerate it, and, given that certain fragments of the past have happily survived, we shall endeavour to make the best of them and to extract something from them.

In fact, speaking with a due sense of proportion, the work of the ancient painters is known to us in much the same manner, neither less nor more, as is that of the sculptors. I will mention first among our sources of information inscriptions and literary texts. These are numerous if not always precise, the painter's art having ever appeared to be more accessible to the man in the street than the art of the modeller,

---

[1] On this question see **VI**, vol. i, p. 253.
[2] *Ibid.*, Archæological Methods.   [3] **CXV** ff.

while every writer gloried in demonstrating that he understood it, piqueing himself on possessing superior taste of a delicate and highly refined order. Added to these critical judgments we have the monuments, of which the greater part are replicas, faithful or indirect copies, of vanished masterpieces. The potter who decorated the surface of a vase[1] quite naturally found his stylus or brush giving form to his recollections of great works he had frequently admired: consciously or unconsciously he adapted these memories to the very different field he had to fill; if sometimes he did it instinctively, he did, also, often seek to please his customers who would be pleased to have on modest pieces of pottery some reflection in miniature of an original they could never hope to possess. Funerary stelæ are more original, in a certain sense; but in the nature of things their motifs could neither be many nor greatly varied. Then, here, too, great masters created the models which inspired them and which were imitated though sometimes in a very free manner; one has to be on one's guard, also, not to assume that a simple analogy in motif is necessarily in every case a copy or direct imitation. Thanks to recent discoveries, we do at least know what a painting on marble, on glaze, on wood, and on canvas looked like: though we may not know all the resources of ancient painting we can get an idea of the effects it sought and the effort of which it was capable. Even the frescoes at Pompeii, though they were at one time overestimated, must not be neglected; if we use their testimony with prudence we shall learn much about the repertory and the processes of antique painting.

We shall understand it if we reflect on the effect and the repercussion which the great works exposed in the temples and public monuments must have had on the artists' studios and even in the artisans' booths. A very simple comparison will give us some notion of it. It is enough to think of the impression produced, after the lapse of more than a century, by the compositions with which Giotto and Mantegna covered the churches of Padua which they decorated for the Scrovegni and the Ovetari. Directly they were finished the Arena and the Eremitani frescoes became the great subject of conversation throughout Northern Italy and exercised an influence of which we can still measure the effect to some

[1] **CXXIX ff.**

extent. In Greece, where distances were less and where the
smaller number of artists seem to have formed a more united
family, the completion of important works of art, especially
paintings, were even more notable events and became the
occasion for festivals that were even more thronged, in this
enthusiastic and impressionable environment, and their
influence was both felt more deeply and over a longer period.
Hence there is nothing surprising in the fact that the productions of industrial art, such as painted vases, or even reliefs
and bronzes, should preserve the memory and retain the
reflection of these master compositions. And we have to con-
gratulate ourselves that it was so, because without this sudden
and immediate echo produced by masterpieces, and without
the more gradual repercussion of the shock experienced
by the popular soul and imagination, which might be propagated *ad infinitum*, we should lack our surest means of recon-
structing, by the aid of definite inferences the vanished initial
creation. Doubtless an abyss separates the masterpiece
from the trifling productions which were less an imitation
of it than a memory, yet a relation between them does exist,
a relation which a patient and cautious analysis should permit
us to disentangle; this, if we can achieve it, will be the con-
ducting wire through which we shall get our knowledge, if not
of the work, at all events of the essential spirit of the great
masters.

Thus this triple enquiry carried out in the field of ancient
architecture, sculpture and painting is not destined to be
without results. We cannot achieve a detailed history of
these three arts nor follow them through every phase of their
slow evolution; but at least we can make out the principal
stages, and although the works themselves may elude us we
can distinguish their essential features and their character.
It is obvious that these three domains will not prove equally
fruitful for the particular subject which concerns us and that
it will be preferable for us to draw from two out of these
three sources of investigation. Architecture, no matter how
beautiful the monument nor what the merit or quality perceptible even by uninformed minds, is an art which, if not
more material than the other two, is at least more dependent
on its material. Its prime object is solidity rather than
beauty, and it is designed before all else to shelter and cover

that which the building is to house. Consequently, it cannot be expected to teach us so clearly or decisively as the other two what was the Greek conception of art. Not that we shall not interrogate the temple and portico builders on the secret of the Hellenic spirit—as will be seen in the following pages—but we shall not expect from them the same response nor can we hope that they will teach us what the sculptors and painters can tell us.

Indeed, it is sculpture and painting, the two major arts, which sum up the creative effort of a people in love with beauty, or a people who simply take thought for beauty. This seems so obvious from the outset that it is almost enough to state the proposition for its profound truth to be realized, but I think it will be as well to emphasize the point because of the importance of this fact which cannot be made too clear nor its consequences overstressed.

Sculpture represents beings such as they are in reality: it gives, in an alien material, the illusion of life by means of solids in the three dimensions of height, width, and depth. In truth it is the art of rendering the whole exterior aspect of man and of causing him to appear as he is, no longer in the flesh but in marble and bronze. To achieve this the artist begins by modelling an amorphous lump of clay supported by a solid armature, which, when it is worked and shaped by spatula or fingers, finally assumes the desired appearance. The ideal would be for the clay or wax to be left just as it is fashioned, but the material is too fragile and the work could only be ephemeral. Even in the case of a simple terra cotta it is necessary—unless one is satisfied with something very rough—to mould a first model and to take a cast from it which has to be dried, as often as not after a more or less thorough baking which causes shrinkage and occasionally cracks, all of which operations modify the original model more or less appreciably. Hence it is natural that sculpture should prefer some more perfect process and one which will yield a more reliable result, permitting of the model being more successfully preserved exactly as it was fashioned. This process, obviously, would be bronze-casting, which, when carried out carefully by skilled workers, insures the exact and perfect reproduction of the original model in almost the smallest details. Marble carving, more minute and delicate,

is always or up to a certain point an interpretation, or, if
you will, a translation. The Ancients knew and practised it,
but, with rare exceptions, they held it to be inferior. They
held the toreutists in the highest esteem of all, and in their
eyes these were the masters and the only initiators of plastic
art. Thus for us metal-working will mainly, if not exclusively,
represent the achievement of ancient sculpture.

Of course it is easy to show that metal-working includes
within itself and implies many an art and many an industry of
inferior order which is dependent upon it and which would
never have been conceived without it. Such is glyptic art,[1]
which makes use of hard and precious materials and which
chisels and hollows out intaglios or cuts away from the
upstanding relief of cameos; such, too, is the art of the medal
maker, who makes coins and matrices for currency,[2] or that of
the gold- and silversmith who chisels gold and silver vases,
who sets and incrusts *emblemata* and *protomés* and does
beaten metal work. So, too, the makers of mirrors, lamps
and candelabra, articles made entirely of metal and in which
the same technique is followed. Finally, to mount a stage
higher, bas-reliefs of all kinds, such as those which decorate
funerary stelæ and are carried along the friezes of altars and
temples, although they may arise from a different conception
and are not necessarily later than sculpture in the round,
have the same origin, with certain differences, and belong
to the same art. And it is unnecessary to add that it was the
same with that composite art of which not an example remains
to us to-day, but which, owing to the luxury and refinement of
the means employed, seemed to the Ancients extraordinarily
suited for rendering divine energy; I speak of the great
chryselephantine sculpture: the goldsmith and the bronze-
caster were at their happiest and best in the intricacies of
the different portions which had to be united into a whole,
the complicated adjustment of supports and armatures, the
skilled combination of alloys and colours, in the diligently
sought effects of harmony or contrast in smooth surfaces and
shadowed folds; in subtle mechanical problems and refinements
in the play of light—in all of which the inventive and sensitive
soul of the Hellene took special delight.

Among the Greeks painting, whether the decorations

[1] **CIII-IV.**   [2] **XCVI-CII.**

covering the walls of the porticoes and temples, the votive offerings placed in the sanctuaries or the ordinary small picture, played a rôle and exercised an influence whose importance it is impossible to overrate. It was not without close relations with sculpture, although polychromy, always known, was no longer practised in the great period except with moderation: furthermore, it was necessary and legitimate in this land of strong light; and, in the ordinarily gloomy temples whose interior could only be seen through the open doors, it was essential to make use of vivid paintings and to have recourse to hard and clear-cut tones. Over and above this particular and subordinate use, painting was in evidence everywhere—on the interior and exterior walls of portico and temple, in the lesches where people met together, and in the halls where judgments were given, on funerary monuments and altars, inside the houses, on the furniture and even on the bodies of the most everyday crockery. There needed but a plain surface for this most expressive of all the arts to depict not only the form but the colour of the outside world; on the other hand, although the means employed were simple, the task was a difficult one, and the progress made in technique could not but be slow: the artist's eye and hand had to acquire habit and dexterity, the development of which we cannot follow but which was encouraged by the extraordinary favour of the public. The public loved the painters and competed enthusiastically for their masterpieces, whence the immediate success with which they met and the influence they exercised both in Greece and beyond her borders.

Thus sculpture and painting admirably sum up for us the creative effort of the Hellenes—or can do so. It is in these two major arts that we shall principally seek our examples, and the reason for this is so obvious that we need not insist on it further. It remains only to decide on the nature of the documents of which we shall make use—whether we shall specially seek the replicas or prefer the original and anonymous monuments.

We have seen that we have a mass of small votive objects which date from the 6th, 5th, and 4th centuries, that is to say the actual period in which the masterpieces were a-preparing or were created. These objects consist, for example, of coins,[1]

[1] **XCVI** ff.

a source of knowledge of the first order, which archæologists too often neglect to tap and in which they have only sought reproductions of celebrated groups or statues. Many of these coins can be dated, sometimes with precision, which permits one to estimate the progress of the industry almost from day to day while taking into account the restraining effects, as at Athens, of what may be called official archaicism. The terra cottas[1] and vases[2] are neither public nor State works—except, if you will, certain panathenaic amphoræ—but the humble potters or the koroplastes who modelled and decorated them could not help but be influenced by the great artists from the very fact that they were their contemporaries and that they dwelt at the doors, and as it were, in the very shadow of their studios, and if we know how to identify that influence we should be able to recognize and seize upon it in the productions of the potters. So, too, in the case of the founders who made the small bronzes, the authors of funerary statues,[3] the marble-cutters to whom we owe the mortuary stelæ,[4] and *a fortiori* the decorators of the temples. All these things are contemporaneous, and, albeit in a different degree, they are all animated by the same spirit: we shall find everywhere among them the visible reflection of the great artists and more especially the mark of the influence exercised by their masterpieces.

It is now clear that we shall rather seek out the modest though exact and faithful original documents than indirect and later replicas of celebrated works. These marble reproductions, made at a later date and by the Romans in an alien material, are from the hands of artisans who were incapable of copying with exactitude and who generally imitated rather than copied.[5] The qualities of the original could not but disappear in this transmission through so many intermediaries, and we must put down a great deal to inexperience, awkwardness and ignorance. If we cannot expect the humble decorators of Pompeii to give us any idea of a picture by Parrhasius or Zeuxis, it will be understood that neither can the marble-cutters who worked for the freemen in the times of the Cæsars or even for their masters, give us the originals which they imitated, as often as not, at

---

[1] **CV ff.**   [2] **CXXIX ff.**   [3] **LXIII.**
[4] **LXIV.**   [5] **VI, vol. i, p. 318 ff.**

second or third hand. The most skilled of them, living in
another period, had neither the necessary training of the eye
nor the workshop traditions, and even the aspect of the times
was changed. If we are to construct a history of Greek art
we shall often, for want of something better, have to fall back
on these replicas in which we shall at least find a memory of
the vanished masterpieces—but since what we seek in particular is to get at the essential character and hall-mark
of Greek art, we are more likely to meet with it and to find
it more clear-cut and well-marked in those less pretentious
and more modest productions conceived under the immediate inspiration of and in contact with the great masterpieces. A stricter method obliges us to have if not exclusive
at all events preferential recourse to that contemporary
evidence which alone can give us exact and certain results
and which will enable us to recognize the essence and very
soul of Greek art.

SCHEMA

In order to understand Greek art more is required than the mere contemplation of Greek works of art or the experience of the æsthetic emotions they produce. Admiration, if it is to be justified, demands a knowledge of the spiritual and material necessities which stimulated the artist to create, of his character and his environment and the means of realization at his disposal. Only then has one the right to proclaim the eternal beauty of Greek art and to marvel at the manner in which it has shed its radiance all over the world.

The questions with which we have briefly to deal in this book are the following:

I. The Aim of Art. Art and the City

Art, the social phenomenon, is clearly the reflection of the Hellenic city, its political aspirations, religious beliefs, manners and ranks of life; it is, likewise, their glorification.

II. The Agencies of Realization. Groups and Individuals

The artists who realize this art differ among themselves in ethnic origin, in the regional or local traditions of the schools to which they belong, and in their own personality—so many divergent elements which explain the variety of the aspects of that art.

III. Realization. Technical Problems

These artists learn their craft; they fix the kind, form, type and subject—in a word they determine the mould in which their plastic thought is cast. This is a slow acquisition of technique in which a still awkward hand struggles with its material before it masters it, in which vision, faulty to begin with, gradually becomes perfected.

IV. Characteristic Features of Greek Art. The Evolution of the Ideal

The æsthetics of the Hellenes become revealed in their characteristic traits while this conquest of the material is in progress. For us these traits will be illuminating. Certain among them persist throughout changing times, groups and persons. Others are modified with the centuries, and the ideal evolves in diverse phases.

Conclusion. The Place of Greek Art in the History of Civilization

Having acquainted ourselves with the moving principle of Greek art, its outward appearance and its specific ideal, we shall be able to determine its place in æsthetic evolution—its debt and its reactions to the civilizations which preceded and surrounded it throughout its existence, and that which it gave, in its turn, to the ancient world and to the modern world that has succeeded it.[1]

[1] We shall give in footnotes such references only as are strictly indispensable for the identification of the monuments mentioned in the text, and those which are best known.

PART ONE

THE AIM OF GREEK ART.   ART AND THE CITY

WHAT function did the Greeks assign to art ? Do not let
us seek the answer from the ancient writers, the poets and
philosophers; nor discuss, with Plato and Aristotle, the
nature of the beautiful; and let us beware of losing ourselves,
as they did, and as many modern authors have lost themselves,
among the clouds of metaphysical æsthetics. Let us go
direct to the monuments themselves and seek the answer
from these alone: they will supply us with actual evidence
of what the Greeks asked from their art, and what they
obtained from it.

These monuments support the truth of a formula that
has become banal—that art is the expression of society.
There are certain cases in which this assertion can be contested,
for it is assuredly not absolute; yet in Greece, more than
anywhere else, art does reveal the intimate relation which
links it with the environment out of which it has grown and
from which it takes its particular colour and receives its
mission; art is the humble servant of society as well as its
mirror.

The characters which we shall point out are there from
the beginning and are maintained in all their purity almost
to the close of the 5th century. Then we shall see this social
ideal becoming modified, while the transformation of society
which came about from the 4th century onwards is accompanied by new features which, however, do not oust the older
ones but exist side by side with and attenuate them.

CHAPTER I

THE ARTIST AND THE PUBLIC. TRADITION

THE first thing to be noted is the close collaboration between artist and public. The artist does not seek violently to break his relations with the public or to destroy its visual and mental habits in order to substitute his own personal conceptions; he has no wish to be original at all costs, despising everything that is not his own work. The modern artist, considering himself to be a superior being, takes pride in this rupture with the public which he even maintains as necessary. Only too often there exists between the two a complete absence of spiritual and visual comprehension, of which contemporary exhibitions furnish abundant instances. There was nothing of this kind in Greece: the artist could not, nor did he desire to abandon the language of art common to all, which all might read, in order to substitute for it an unknown idiom.

Nor was there any break with the past, thanks to this maintenance of contact. There was no disconcerting shock in artistic evolution, no sudden abandonment of motif or style for the sake of some entirely new creation springing up from nowhere. On the contrary, Greek art presents an amazing continuity from its beginning to its end. Artists quietly accepted tradition: they did not, as contemporary artists too often do, seek to fight against their predecessors, but rather to push on further by their own exertions along the same road, contributing something to the common effort, as their predecessors had done before them. They had no false pride about what they owed to their predecessors or about acknowledging themselves to be their pupils: τέχναν εἰδότες ἐκ προτέρων, the two Argive sculptors, Eutelidas and Chrysothemis, described themselves in the 6th century. They do not give their paternal names unless they are pupils of their fathers, and the disciples of Pasiteles even substitute their master's name for their own patronymic. Certain artists, who were rather more of innovators, especially when individualism came to be developed in the beginning of the 4th century, prided themselves on having only Nature as their master, but Lysippus, who lays claim to this independence, nevertheless faithfully continues in the tradition of Polyclitus' athletic statuary, and perhaps even in that of Pythagoras of Rhegium;[1] he is but one link in the long chain of sculptural art, and there is not one of his innovations that cannot be seen in embryo before his day. Indeed, maybe there is not a single invention attributed by the Ancients to any one Greek artist which was not anticipated.[2] The rhythm, supposed to have been introduced by Polyclitus in the human body in repose, was already in existence from the beginning of the 5th century from the moment the old straight frontal profile was broken. His square, thick-set proportions and the flattened head of his statues are those of his predecessors of the 6th century, and Polymedes of Argos foreshadowed the Argive master a century before that master's day in his two Kouroi at Delphi.[3]

So is progress achieved as the result of a multiplicity of small accretions. Look at the stiff archaic Kouros![4] It is but a schema of the human body with its arms pressed into its sides, its solidly united legs, its sketchily rendered muscles. Then one leg is advanced—the left; next the arms detach themselves from the trunk and are flexed; the shape of the body and its musculature, at first ill-rendered, become more and more life-like. The straight frontal profile is broken, the weight of the body is now carried on one leg whilst the other is flexed, and attitudes and rhythms, hitherto unknown, become possible. Thus is the way prepared for the perfection of the second half of the 5th century, and for the even more supple rhythms and skilled modelling of the 4th century and the too obvious science of the Hellenists. The entire history of Greek art could be written on a single theme.

For this reason it is very difficult to make clean-cut divisions in this history. Each work, each new style, is linked with those which have gone before and have foreshadowed it; to understand them properly their origins have to be sought very far back and their destiny has to be followed very far. How could one lay claim to know anything

[1] **CLXIV**, p. 39 ff., 126.　　　　[2] **VI**, vol. i, p. 269 ff.
[3] **LXXXIV**, vol. viii, p. 452 ff.　　[4] **LXVIII**.

about the style of Phidias and his originality unless one knows
that it did not appear suddenly with Phidias but was already
in being in the first half of the 5th century ?[1] Or of that of
Polyclitus, unless one linked it up with the workers who
were earlier than the Argive school—with Glaucus and Dionysius,[2] with Ageladas, and even earlier still with Polymedes ?
On the other hand, although the predominant idealism of
the 5th century makes way for a predominant realism towards
the 4th century, it does persist, with its themes and its style,
up till the end in Greek art, and it lasts on to inspire the
Roman artist. Not a form, technical process, or style dies
out entirely; it does but retire into the background there
to survive with somewhat diminished vitality. We must
then notice in every period the persistence of these divers
currents which lend great variety to Greek art under a cloak
of apparent uniformity.

    This may appear monotonous to some. The artist does
not seek to multiply *ad infinitum* the forms in which he clothes
his thought, since he has no desire to be original at all costs
or to break with the public but on the contrary to respond
to its wishes and express its needs—because he desires to
carry on the tradition. A few themes suffice—the naked
athlete, erect, in repose or in violent movement, and the
draped female form; or, in temples, the great unchanging
mythological scenes, and for funerary reliefs the image of
the dead and those near to him; or the stereotyped features
of the gods. In a word, essentially Hellenic themes which
best respond to the needs of their religious and patriotic
life. These themes the artist receives from his predecessors
or else he imitates what his contemporaries are doing, merely
introducing shades of variation. They seem to him good
because they are known to and appreciated by the public,
and he goes on repeating them throughout the centuries.
Look at the hundreds of statues of male nudes, erect or in
repose, which follow one another in succession from the rigid
Kouros of the 6th century up to the last examples of the
series at the decline of Greek art: is it not always the same
image for ever expressing the same idea ? But what nuances
in the attitudes and in the rhythm of the limbs from the
time that the straight frontal profile was broken, towards 500,

---

[1] **LXXVIII**, p. 477 ff.   [2] **LXXIII**, p. 117.

and when a closer study of the muscles took the place of the old conventions ! The artist's originality is not so much in the invention of a new subject as in the perfecting of technique, in the truth to nature of his rendering of the human form, in the harmony of his rhythms, in *symmetria*, the science of the modelling and in the thousand little details which differentiate one work of art from another and introduce a perpetual diversity into the apparent monotony of the same motif, so that it is constantly undergoing evolution. Originality shows itself within the bounds of tradition.

The modern artist, individualistic to excess, tries to be as different as he can from his confrères, and he jealously guards his creations from being copied or imitated by them. The idea of plagiarism, of intellectual and artistic proprietorship, did not exist in Greece. Should someone create a motif or some new detail which the public receives favourably, all imitate it and bring it within the common domain of art. A work of art was not personal but social; a reflection of the community, it remains the property of the community. Any idea of disloyalty never entered their minds and nobody dreamed of claiming a work of art as his personal property. High art motifs passed into industrial art at once, more particularly into vase-painting.[1] And here painters copied from one another; Pamphæus copied from Nicosthenes and Nicosthenes copied the boats of Exekias; Chachrylion imitated the ephebic scenes of Epictetus.[2] There was no barrier of any sort set up against such imitation; on the contrary such was the very spirit, the principle of Greek æsthetics. How many were the imitations of a famous work of art ! The copies of the boy plucking a thorn from his foot, of the Doryphoros and of the Diadumenos, are legion ! And innumerable are the apparently new themes which in reality are adaptations contrived by the addition of some attitude, a change of sex, age or name, or a transposition from the round into relief, or from painting into relief—in a word, by some small detail which, without rendering the prototype unrecognizable, yet lends it new life which will enable it to survive for centuries.[3]

[1] **CXLV**, vol. i, p. 579; iii, p. 628.
[2] **CXLV**, vol. iii, p. 662; **CXLIV**, vol. ix, p. 328.
[3] **VI**, vol. i, p. 318 ff.

CHAPTER II

THE USEFUL AND THE BEAUTIFUL[1]

IT is generally admitted that the Greeks were an artist people; with them good taste and a refined appreciation of the beautiful were not the prerogatives of the élite, but were common to all. "Not a thing that has been dug up in Hellenic soil but has this flower of elegance, this exquisite and sober feeling for harmony, which gives the impression of a race supremely gifted for art."[2] In the humblest monuments of industrial art one feels that the workman is every whit as fully alive to the lines of his vase or the proper adaptation of his decoration as a great painter or sculptor. This notion, however, must not be exaggerated, as has sometimes been done, if we are to avoid hasty generalizations and that lack of fine discrimination combined with realization of complexity which mars so many works on Greek art. Though the average of artistic production in Greece may be much superior to that of other lands, it should be acknowledged frankly that many of the objects dug up in the course of excavations do not justify rapturous admiration. But let us freely admit, since it is the obvious truth, that nowhere else is there so close a relationship between the productions of " high art " and the " minor arts," nor so general a care for the beauty of form and line independently of the value or destination of the object.

Is this instinctive—a natural gift—with the Greeks, or is it the result of especially favourable social conditions ? Here, as throughout science, we are faced with the eternal problem, the question of an innate or an acquired character. Countless anecdotes and innumerable features bear witness to the greater refinement of æsthetic sensibility to be found among the Greeks than anywhere else, a refinement which is responsible for their having outdistanced other ancient peoples, less gifted in this respect than themselves, so that

[1] CLXXXVI-VIII. [2] CX, p. ii.

they were able to impose their own conceptions on such peoples wherever they have come into contact with them, and this before ever they imposed them on Rome and through Rome on the modern world.

Nevertheless, the expression of æsthetic feeling was facilitated by the rôle which the Greeks recognized as belonging to art. For them it is no mere luxury to be enjoyed only by the privileged few, nor is beauty exclusively reserved for rare and costly articles. Art is a necessity linked up with the very existence of the city and the individual and it is always with them in all they do from the smallest to the most important acts of their lives. Beauty as beauty does not exist unto itself but has ever a practical end in view. This principle, whose effects are to be seen in the earliest productions and which is maintained more or less markedly throughout the existence of Greek art, was elevated into a doctrine by the philosophers, and Socrates admits that the agreeable, the good, the true and the beautiful are one. And for him the beautiful is that which is useful, and all practical articles which exactly fulfil their purpose are beautiful. " Think you that the good and the beautiful are not the same ? Know you not that all that is beautiful for any reason is for that same reason good ? Virtue is not good in one case and beautiful in another; so men, likewise, are called good and beautiful, and for the same motives; that which from within the body of man makes beauty to be apparent makes also goodness to be apparent; in fine, all that is useful to men is beautiful and good in relation to the use which can be made of it.—What ! is a basket of manure, then, also a beautiful thing ?—Yes, by Zeus, and a golden shield is ugly from the moment that the one is meet for its use and the other is not . . . So, too, when Socrates said that the beauty of a building consists in its usefulness it seems to me that he was teaching the best principle of building." A cuirass is beautiful when it fits the shape of the body it is to protect and when it allows of the easy movement of the limbs.[1] That which the Greeks admired in the human body such as it is represented in statuary is assuredly the lines and contours and the rhythms of the pose and gestures, but it is also its perfect physical development fitting it for the duties of a citizen who

[1] Xenophon, *Recollections of Socrates*.

has to compete in the exercises of the palæstra and in the
great national games, to be ready to fight against his country's
foes. The beauty of these athletes' bodies lies in the harmonious concordance of their form, their muscles in action,
and the act which they have to accomplish; it varies from
one to another, " as a man who is skilled in racing differs from
a man who is a skilled wrestler; as the beauty of a shield
devised for defence differs completely from the beauty of a
javelin designed to be thrown with force and speed."[1] An
otherwise undecorated vase of harmonious shape which is
well turned, perfectly fired and faultlessly glazed is a work
of art just as is a statue; the potters are as ready to put their
signatures upon it as upon an expensively decorated piece,
and on the same grounds.[2]

When we admire Greek vases,[3] the delicacy of their design
and the elegance of their contours, we sometimes forget that
they contained liquids—oils and wines—and that this was
their true function, which came before delighting the eye.
The Greek, however, has never forgotten that the principal
rôle of industrial art is utility. Unlike modern artisans, he
would never have conceived a piece of furniture whose overcrowded decoration and involved lines render it unfit for use
and which invite the reproach Cochin addressed to his contemporaries when he asked them " not to change the purpose
of things but to remember that a candlestick must be
straight and upright in order to hold a light, and that the
grease-guard of the socket must be concave in order to catch
the running wax and not convex so that it overflows in
cascades onto the candlestick." In Greece the decoration
is not an addition stuck on like a non-essential plating, but
is an integral part of the object and often has a practical
purpose in itself. The beautiful black glaze on vases,
inherited from the Mycenæans,[4] gradually invades more and
more of the surface of the receptacle together with the red-
figure technique; the ceramist appreciated it because it enabled
him to get a fine and delicate design better than with the
earlier incisions, and also for its pictorial qualities, its shades
ranging from black to clear yellow which, according to the

[1] Xenophon, *Recollections of Socrates.*
[2] **CXLIV**, vol. ix, p. 353 ff.   [3] **CXXIX ff.**
[4] **CXLV**, vol. iii, p. 666.

density of the shade, indicate the details of muscles, drapery and hair, and for its warm olive-green tones. But this glaze mainly owes its vogue and its secular use to its technical qualities—the solidity it acquires in the firing and the impermeable surface with which it covers the vase. It is possible that the substitution in the second half of the 6th century of the red for the black figure is the result of practical rather than æsthetic considerations and springs from the desire to give the receptacle greater impermeability, and to restrict those portions which are bare earthenware. The redder colour of the Attic vases, obtained by mixing red ochre with clay, is itself not so much due to a seeking after polychrome effects as to the desire to diminish the porosity of the clay, and to give a better flavour to the wine. The triumph of Attic ceramics, which is to be seen towards the close of the 6th century in all the rival ceramic markets, as, for instance, that of Corinth, arises not so much from the beauty of its shapes and decoration but pre-eminently from commercial considerations—it conserves the liquids better and gives them a better flavour.[1]

On the other hand, for a Greek a statue or a painting is not the product of an entirely disinterested art. It always had some purpose—to represent a divinity and to link that divinity with his or her temple; to honour such divinity by making a votive offering; to commemorate the dead by his presentment and by recording his deeds; to tell and teach the great facts of religion and of national life. " Among the ancients the beautiful is only the high relief of the useful " (Stendhal). The existence of all these works of art is justified solely by their rôle in the social life. The theory of " art for art's sake," the germ of which is possibly to be found in the Hellenistic writers,[2] would have been incomprehensible to Phidias, Polyclitus and their contemporaries. Yet, in no period, not even when art becomes more individualistic and more detached from social life, does the practical aim of art yield place entirely to exclusively æsthetic and emotive considerations. It has often been said that " the foundation of Greek æsthetics is the beautiful harnessed to the service of the useful " (Pottier).

The useful and the beautiful, " high art " and the " minor

---

[1] **CXLV**, vol. iii, pp. 610, 646; **CXLIX**.   [2] **VI**, vol. iii, p. 338.

arts," are not yet divorced from one another. For the Greek there is no gulf dividing the plain earthen undecorated vase which holds wine and oil from the sculpture of Phidias; there is simply a quantitative difference in the formula of beauty and utility of which both are compounded. Knowing that all techniques have their part to play in social life, the artist of the one no more considers that it is derogatory to him to decorate an industrial article than did the Renaissance artists. It is true that Isocrates declares that one must not compare Phidias with the koroplastes or Zeuxis and Parrhasius with painters of ex-votos. But there was not that division which nowadays separates a potter from a painter or a stone-cutter from a sculptor. The ancients, in fact, never clearly distinguished between artists and craftsmen; both belong to the class of manual workers. In primitive times they were despised, but this prejudice disappeared with time except in certain Dorian cities, such as Sparta, where a citizen is forbidden to gain his living by a trade. Solon obliged the Athenians to give evidence of their means of subsistence; Pericles praises work: "It is no shame for any man to acknowledge poverty; but it is shameful not to work to overcome it."[1] Socrates recommends wholesome work to Aristarchus: "Which are the wiser men, those who remain at ease or those who occupy themselves in doing something useful ? Which are more in the right, those who work or those who, without doing anything, deliberate on the means of subsistence ?"

It is essential, if one would understand the fundamental character of Greek art, to take note of this perpetual inter-penetration of two elements which to modern folk appear to be independent or even antagonistic. In the study of ancient ceramics it is erroneous to attribute to its authors thoughts that were above all æsthetic, when they were preoccupied with practical problems both technical and economic. It is an analogous error to study the works of the great sculptors without considering the purpose of the work or the religious or civil idea it contains, in short to eliminate anæsthetic elements. Beauty is not an end in itself in Greece, but a means to an end.

Beauty, for all that, is not neglected; the artist does not

---

[1] Thucydides, ii, 40.

D

allow himself to be subjugated by the needs of social life to such an extent as to leave them masters of the field. His work is not solely useful in the cult of the gods and of the dead, or in the glorification of the city: over and above this it is clothed with beauty. It is just this which distinguishes Greek art from so much other art, such as that of Egypt or of Mesopotamia where the æsthetic aim is subordinate to the social aim. And this secondary importance attaching to beauty is one of the causes—we shall find others—which has prevented these arts from following in the same steps as the art of Greece and from freeing themselves, as Greek art has done, from the old conventions which regulated them despotically up to the very end.

Thanks to its profoundly utilitarian essence, art in Greece, however admirable it became, remains what it has always been and everywhere will be in its beginnings, a language, a means of expressing human thoughts and needs, that communion between men which Tolstoy claims that it should be. The thoughts it materialized in visual forms are highly diverse but they are always comprehended within this limit; it is for the archæologist to understand these forms and read them. What are they ? They are the necessities of the Greek city—its religion, political constitution, social ranks, historical events, and manners.

CHAPTER III

ART AND RELIGION[1]

In its beginnings and for long centuries afterwards art was everywhere the handmaiden of the supernatural. Even before he thought of decorating and beautifying his person and his abode, or of giving concrete form to his æsthetic emotion for the delectation of himself and others, man knew the urgent need to satisfy his instinctive feelings where those mysterious forces were concerned which surrounded him in his terrestrial life as in his death and future existence— forces against which he had to protect himself, which he desired to bend to his own desires and which he reverenced because he feared them.

Go as far back into the past as we may, we see art always penetrated by magic, the primordial and crude form of religion, which inspired the thought of the Magdalenian hunters just as it inspires primitive men today. The theory that art in its origin was bound up with magic is challenged by certain men of erudition, and, indeed, it should not be too exclusive and eliminate æsthetic sentiment altogether, weak though it may have been as yet, which responded to other emotive tendencies of man's nature, but it would seem to be the case that æsthetic needs yielded priority of place to the expression of the more urgent needs of magic. After all, have not most human activities grown up in the shadow of magic and religion before they cast off this mystic tutelage and secured independence by becoming secularized ?

Greek art no more than any other escaped this supernatural bondage.[2] At first, images on tombs did not so much serve to commemorate the dead as to offer necessary support to his soul, as in Egypt; his soul was bound by the magical power of the counterfeit presentment and by the rites which consecrated this effigy. The people of Orchomenos were aware of this when, in order to deliver their land from the wandering

[1] **CXCI-CC.**   [2] **CLXXXVIII; LXIII, p. 3 ff; CXCIX.**

spirit of Acteon which was devastating it, they made a figure of him in bronze and fastened it to the rock by iron clamps. Unhewn and hewn stones, statues, and stelæ are so many material abodes for the soul of the departed. Many among the numerous terra cotta and stone figurines in graves were placed there with this end in view. It may be, as in Egypt, the soul of the dead, that human-headed bird; sometimes it is bearded and helmeted like the warrior it recalls. Or it may be the dead man, that horseman so frequent in the graves of the 8th and 9th centuries, or else a recumbent figure reclining on a banqueting divan.[1] Living by the power of the image in the darkness of the tomb, the dead is surrounded by a band of servitors who prepare his food and carry out the thousand behests necessary to his maintenance and entertainment. Hence those clay statuettes which look like genre representations[2] but which are placed there with a profoundly religious intent—cooks at their oven, launderers at the spring, kneaders of bread and women grinding corn in a mortar, and hairdressers, which recall the analogous images buried in the Egyptian necropoles where their function is the same. All these folk are really alive and really doing the things represented because the image is equivalent to the reality and constrains the reality to be. The dead is thus assured of life in the tomb, a belief which persists in a confused fashion throughout antiquity, even after the later idea of a Hades was grafted on to it. These female and animal figurines placed with their dead or offered as ex-votos to a god are very common in the archaic period. And in the earliest times they also reveal the presence of this belief in magic. They are intended, by the virtue of the image, to cause women to be fruitful and to perpetuate the race—the fountain of Hellenic influence; and to cause cattle and beasts to multiply and bring greater prosperity to their owner. If male images, on the contrary, are rare, it is because man, the master of woman and cattle—to which she was likened of old—desired to avoid any interference with his own person.[3]

Was it not necessary to defend oneself against the powers of evil which surrounded the living and the dead alike? Recourse was had to amulets and talismans of all kinds:

---

[1] **LXIII**, p. 9 ff.   [2] Pottier, BCH, 1900, p. 510; **LXIII**, p. 18.
[3] **CXI**, p. 16.

statues, reliefs, figurines and paintings which represented the
protecting god; prophylactic images such as the eye or the
phallus or hideous Gorgons (Pl. I), and grotesque and ugly
creatures which would cause the adversary to burst out
laughing and thus disarm him. Graves were garnished with
them and they were used to adorn the dwelling-place and the
walls and squares of cities; and people wore them on their
persons—because the magical weapons were just as efficacious
as real ones.

Was not the idol—the statue—the seat (ἕδος) of divine
power, and did it not retain this divine power just as the
funerary statue retained the soul of the dead, thus assuring
the real presence of the divinity amid the faithful ?

These beliefs in fetichism and magic, which were very
lively in the early days of Greek civilization, inspired many
a legend and myth. Pygmalion was not alone in believing
in the life of the goddess he had made. The golden statues
placed before the palace of Alcinous talked, and those carved
by Dædalus walked, while Athena taught the Rhodians to
make the images which one met wandering about the roads;
when the statue of the athlete Theagenes, by Glaucias the
Æginetan, was insulted, it fell on the aggressor and crushed
him, and it was condemned by the Thasians as though it had
been a living person, and thrown into the sea.

We should bear these beliefs in mind when we come to
study Greek art. They explain in part the genesis of certain
genres, such as divine and mortal images, with their use and
their outward appearance. Heracles, kneeling, bends his
bow against the enemy on one of the gates of the walls of
Thasos dating from the first quarter of the 5th century:[1]
he is protecting the city, ready to speed the arrow against
him who would bring evil from without. But close by
Dionysus and his train, turned towards the interior of the
city, bring abundance and prosperity. About the year 448
Pericles made Phidias erect on the summit of the Athens
Acropolis a statue of Athena, armed with lance and buckler
and helmeted, who defends her city. At that period this
was not merely symbolical; it was a reality. The divinity,
incarnate in her image, is present among her adorers and
protects them. Any lese-majesty towards these statues

[1] RA, xi, 1908, p. 25 ff.

was sacrilege, and it was sacrilege for a mortal to wish to join his portrait to that of the goddess, as Phidias did.[1]

How should we ever understand those thousands of terra cotta figurines[2] which fill the sanctuaries, the private dwellings and the graves throughout Greek antiquity unless we bear in mind the ideas, very primitive in their origin, which gave them birth ? Doubtless these ideas became obscured with the passage of time, and the themes, undergoing alteration, developed. An abyss that is not only æsthetic but spiritual would seem to stretch between the charming young woman of Tanagra[3] or Myrina[4] draped in her kilted tunic, and the rude archaic flat figurines or those with " birds' beaks."[5] The artist of the 4th century no longer gives any profound meaning to these images, but he takes delight in reproducing visions which have pleased him; nevertheless, by keeping up the custom he is docilely carrying on the ancient rites.[6]

Maybe it was a superstitious fear which held back for so long the coming of realism in personal portraiture.[7]

*　　*　　*

Independently, however, of magic and superstition, Greek art is still the docile servant of official religion. It keeps this character, which is older in origin than any other, throughout its entire existence, even after the new tendency towards secularization saw the light. It serves the gods and the dead.

The typical creation of Greek art in architecture is not a civil but a religious building. It was towards the temple[8] that all artistic effort converged from the time when, the long experimentation of the 7th and 6th centuries having achieved its object, it found its final form on the Acropolis in the 5th century in the shape of the Doric Parthenon.[9] The ruins of Greece are essentially ruined temples. The Acropoles at Athens,[10] Delphi,[11] and Olympia,[12] are so many sanctuaries.

---

[1] REG, 1920, p. 291 ff.　　[2] CV-XIV.　　[3] CVII.
[4] CXII.　　[5] CXI, Pl. v.　　[6] CX, p. 263 ff.
[7] VI, vol. i, p. 199; ii, p. 368; VII, p. 51.
[8] XXXVI ff.　　[9] XXXIX, XLIV.　　[10] XI-XII.
[11] Fouilles de Delphes (1892–1901); Bourguet's Les ruines de Delphes, 1914.
[12] Olympia. Die Ergebnisse der von dem deutschen Reich veranstalteter Ausgrabung, 1890–97, 5 vols. fol. and 5 maps.

The commercial city of Delos[1] develops under the protection of Apollo, the god of the sacred island. Other buildings, public and private, offer us rarer traces, and our knowledge of the Hellenic dwelling-house[2] in the classical period is mainly based on texts and vase paintings. Built, as they were, of light material, thieves could easily pierce the walls, and simple in design, they were not yet constructed with any luxurious intention. This simplicity is partially explained by an open-air life in the agora and by the clement climate, but it is also in part due to the fact that the religious edifice still monopolized attention. In the 4th century, and especially in Hellenistic times when religious sentiment was in abeyance and man had asserted himself, palaces were built, and sumptuous and durable houses whose ruins survive side by side with those of temples in the Hellenistic and Græco-Roman cities of Delos, Priene[3] and Pergamum.[4]

At first luxury and beauty were entirely reserved for the gods. For the gods it was that the artist, in measure as his hand grew more cunning, successively made use of wood, soft and easily worked stone, and then marble, that his gift might last for ever.[5] It was that he might honour the gods that the architect patiently studied the best proportions to give to his building, the lines of his columns, and the form of his capitals; that the sculptor worked at tympanum, metope and frieze, and that the painter covered with great frescoes the walls of the buildings sacred to the cult. The greatest masters sculped for the cella of the sacred statue; precious ex-votos were heaped up in the interior. Outside, in the temenos, there was a forest of statues, images of the gods and their worshippers, and of victims offered to them, and these were in honour of the city or of private persons. People of small means purchased clay figurines from the koroplastes and brought them to the sanctuary as testimonies to their faith. For many a long day statuary, painting and architecture developed under the ægis of the divinity.

Art's themes were for long exclusively religious. Statuary modelled the body of the divinity and of mortals who offered up their image. Paintings and reliefs recorded the adventures

[1] *Exploration archéologique de Délos.*   [2] **XXXVII, LVII.**
[3] Wiegand's *Priene.*   [4] *Altertümer von Pergamon.*
[5] **LXXVIII,** pp. 3, 21, 101; **LXXIX,** p. 5.

of gods and heroes, perpetuated the acts connected with the cult and the scenes associated with offerings. Even vase painting, although eminently utilitarian, illustrated mythology from the moment that it abandoned first the repertory of the primitive geometric style, then Oriental decoration, to turn by preference to representations of the human figure.[1] But to begin with many of the motifs covering the surfaces of vases had a religious or talismanic value.

Every important act of an individual's life was inspired by the divinity and accompanied by homage. Success was besought from the divinity with offerings, and was thanked for when obtained. The winners in every kind of competition, dramatic or musical—which were cult acts—consecrated their prizes to the divinity and erected commemorative monuments; athletes victorious in combat set up images of themselves in the sanctuary. The faithful placed their own images there, which thus assured them divine protection thanks to the perpetual character of their offering—which was themselves, in plastic form, eternally in the presence of the god.

The gods directed the life of the Hellenic cities; they protected them and they received from them their artistic reward. The Persian wars permitted Athens to become strong and powerful and to build up her great maritime empire; the gods, having given the victory, reaped the fruit. Their temples, destroyed by the Persians in 480, were rebuilt by Pericles with greater beauty than ever, on the Acropolis, in the town and in the Attic countryside, and their decoration exalted the divine power. Athena Polias received the marvellous homage of the Parthenon (inaugurated in 438).[2] One beholds her, there, barely issued from the head of Zeus, confirm her supremacy over Poseidon and take possession of Attica; then, on the frieze, receive the ritual gift which the entire Athenian population brings to her in a long procession. She herself, Phidias' masterpiece, is set up in the centre of the cella (Athena Parthenos, 438); outside, she holds in her hands the helmet and spear no longer needed (Athena Lemnia, about 450), and, near by, she stands sentinel, armed (Athena Enoplos, called Promachos, about 448). On the balustrade of the temple of Athena Nike, the joyous crowd of Victories

[1] CXLV, vol. ii, p. 447, 511.   [2] XXXIX; XLIV.

make a triumphant procession in her honour, bearing her trophy aloft, and bring her a sacrifice as a thank-offering (about 408).

Greek history, seen in the mirror of art, becomes a history of myth, of the gods and heroes who fought the battles of Hellas; human deeds are translated into divine exploits. Contrary to the case of Assyria and Rome, there are few real events before the Hellenistic period, but there are combats between Lapiths and Centaurs, Greek heroes and Amazons or Trojans, and exploits of Theseus and Heracles. It was the Greeks themselves, figuring in this guise, who were the vanquishers of the Barbarians and Persians. They might have vaunted themselves by being actually represented in the doing of these glorious deeds, but they preferred to give the honour to their gods and national heroes, since they only obtained victory by the aid of the Immortals who came and fought at their side. Had they not been seen to take part in person in the mêlée ? Did not Pan appear to the Athenian messenger on the Sparta road before the battle of Marathon, and did not Theseus fight in the ranks of the Athenians with the Attic heroes ?

Thus art was for long only a form of cult. It was an act of faith, a prayer. The frieze of the Panathenæa clearly demonstrates it. On the cella of the Parthenon the long procession is unrolled of the Athenian people in all its unity and diversity; before the assembled gods come priests, magistrates, ambassadors, elders, metics, young girls and ephebi to give to the goddess who is the incarnation of their patria the yellow and violet embroidered peplos, and to thank her for her protection.

The dead whose passage into the beyond brings them near to the gods and raises them to the rank of heroes also claim the veneration of the living. In the tomb they continue in a shadowy existence, or else, pale ghosts, they wander in Hades, in the Elysian Fields or the Isles of the Blest, or, maybe, they are damned, and suffer the punishments of Tartarus. These are contradictory notions, but beliefs do not trouble about logic. The dead must be given an abode, the tomb; this emasculated existence must be maintained by sacrifices, libations and offerings of all kinds placed near by; his soul and his body must be provided with support and protected against the powers of evil. And when the old animistic ideas had become obscured it was necessary to commemorate the dead, recall his memory by an effigy, and set up on his grave a σῆμα. Funerary art ministered to these needs. It built tombs, whose form varies according to time and place, in which the dead was put, surrounded by grave furniture, arms, vases and figurines. It set up a sign on the tomb—a symbolic image of a sphinx or siren, a statue[1] of the dead in his own likeness or in that of a god, a stele[2] which shows him such as he was in his life, a warrior armed, a child playing with a hoop, a countryman giving a locust to his dog, a young woman looking at the jewels with which she will never more adorn herself; or else such as he is in the beyond, seen in his glory, heroic, fêted like a god and the object of a cult on the part of those who survive him.

Religion penetrates even the industrial arts destined to practical ends. It would seem odd, to-day, to paint scenes from the Bible with God, Jesus, the Virgin and the saints, on vases[3] containing perfumes or wine. Yet Greek ceramists decorated their receptacles not only with secular themes such as banquets, ephebic combats and scenes from the gynæceum, but with divine and heroic exploits. This pre-occupation with religion, like the constant feeling for the æsthetic, penetrates the most utilitarian articles because any of them may be consecrated to the cult of the gods or of the dead. The gods, the first craftsmen who created all the crafts, continued to protect them and to be their patrons, and it was only natural that their products should be offered to them. Furthermore, were they not conceived in the likeness of men all of whose needs they shared ? On the relief of the Acropolis (earlier than 480) the master potter in his working garb holds a vase in either hand which he has just turned and which he is offering to Athena, protectress of his work.[4] The sanctuaries did not only receive votive statues and reliefs but articles of furniture, tripods, cauldrons, shields, weapons, earthenware and metal cups and platters, garments— everything which Greek industry knew how to make and which

---

[1] **LXIII.**
[2] **LXII**, vol. i, p. 375; ii, p. 139; **LXIV**; Curtius' *Das griechische Grabrelief*, 1919.
[3] **CXXIX** ff.   [4] **LXXVIII**, p. 365.

could serve to equip the divine dwelling conceived in the image of a human dwelling.[1]

Religion, likewise, is responsible for the spirit in which the artist treats his themes and which changes with the changes in belief. If we follow the history of a divine type we can trace the vicissitudes of the religious sentiment expressing itself in that type. Look, for instance, at the changes brought about by time in the form and features of Apollo, Dionysus, Aphrodite or Eros. What has the Eros of the 5th century, the serious young ephebus, in common with the boy-Loves of the Alexandrian period ? Or the Aphrodite of the 5th century, a vigorous woman chastely clad, with the soft voluptuousness of the naked goddess of Hellenistic times ? What is there in common between the bearded and garbed Dionysus of archaism and the youthful god, nude and effeminate, of the Græco-Romans ? And again between the virile Apollo of early days and the equivocal ephebus of Praxiteles, between the calm impassivity of these divine beings of the 5th century and the dreamy, emotional or even suffering expression which the Hellenists give them ?

Conversely, art reacts on religion. By clothing belief in visible form, giving to the gods a material shape and recounting their adventures, art lends them a clearly defined character and fixes the idea of them. " It is impossible to exaggerate the influence of the iconographic and plastic arts on the life of the soul; one may well say that the whole spiritual life of a people undergoes transformation the moment its ideal is fixed and rendered sensible by means of an image of the gentle features composing that ideal, such as the look of suffering on the face of the patient martyr or the expression of holy resignation " (Darmesteter). Greek art, essentially anthropomorphic, peoples the heavens with gods having all the strength and weaknesses of mankind, and it creates a divine world which is the counterpart of the world terrestrial. As the terrestrial world evolves, so must the divine evolve with it, and the character and function of the gods are modified in keeping with the corresponding modifications in the human sphere. Phidias, said the Ancients, " added something to religion," because, by depicting divine majesty and beauty in his Olympian Zeus, he superlatively characterized the

[1] **CLXXXV**, s.v. "Donarium."

rôle of the lord of Heaven; according to Dion Chrysostom, one recognized in him " the god of peace, supremely gentle, giver of being and of life and all that is good, the father and guardian-saviour of all men." Henceforward, his features, like those of Asclepius, will bear the imprint of goodness; seeing them, the faithful will have a new conception of their divinity. The general tendency which from the 4th century onwards led men's minds towards realism and the weakening of the religious spirit, inspired the artists to produce gods which were yet nearer to men than those of old times; in the Hellenistic period Olympus is no longer inaccessible, and the gods there take part in the humblest of the occupations of mortal existence. Art had a large share in the changes in Greek religion because the image gradually modified man's ideas of heaven.

However thoroughly art in Greece may have been permeated by religion, it was never placed in shackles by it, as it was in Egypt and the East, where dogma not only provided the occasion for the creation and determination of subjects but also oriented æsthetic conceptions, immutably fixed forms, and authorized or forbade technical processes. Was this because Greece never had a theocracy or an all-powerful priestly caste intervening in political affairs and jealous of their prerogatives, and because the service of the gods was one with the service of the free city, which the citizens themselves assumed ? But it was also because the rationalistic spirit of the Greeks was never swamped by mysticism, and because, on the contrary, it gradually freed itself from supernatural tutelage. From the 6th century onwards reason asserted itself to the detriment of belief, and the spirit of free criticism penetrated science and literature; it was then that history was born, which more and more sought truth in psychology and gave up seeking it in supernatural intervention. So, too, the Greek artist came to conceive of art as a work of reason. Fascinated by truth and reality he liberated himself from narrow and tyrannical dogma and established his independence as a creator. Conservatism and routine had small effect in Greece. The panathenaic[1] amphoræ kept up till the 3rd century the archaic image of the goddess, such as she had been conceived by the artists of Pisistratus' day, and the

[1] Braughitsch, *Die Panathenaïsche Preisamphoren ;* **CXLIV,** p. 128 ff.; **XCII,** p. 70 ff.

black-figure process, but these are as much industrial as religious products which were regulated, too, by economic laws. The true artist in Greece never considered himself obliged to give to his divinities an immutable appearance; he sought to modify them by incessant progress; in him the æsthetic sentiment was stronger than the necessities of dogma, and the character of the divine types depended less on ritual tradition than on the artistic exigencies of the period; this becomes obvious if we study the transformations of the Athena of Lindus[1] or of the goddess of Sardes.[2] Pericles' struggle against the religious routine opposed to his projects for the transformation of the Acropolis is surely characteristic, and his triumph was surely the triumph of art itself, because it is to him that we owe the Attic floraison of the second half of the 6th century and the masterpieces of Phidias.

[1] Blinkenberg, " L'image d'Athéna Lindia," *Kgl. Danske Videnskabernes Selskab. Hist. fil. Meddekebser*, 1917.
[2] Radet, REG, 1904, p. 318; 1925, p. 206; *Cybébé*, 1909, p. 104

CHAPTER IV

ART AND THE POLITICAL CONSTITUTION[1]

GREEK cities in certain respects were all alike whether large or small, powerful or weak, oligarchic or democratic, isolated or linked together in a federation, Peloponnesian league or Athenian empire. Being small they cannot be compared with the great empires of Egypt and the East; free, their destinies were confided to a group of citizens or to the whole people, and each individual had an interest in the life of the State; they did not have to submit against their will to a despot who ruled them according to his own will, and even in the times of the Macedonian monarchies they preserved a semblance of political independence unknown to the cities of the Orient. In a Greek city there was no one man in whom all power was concentrated. Even the authority of the kings of Sparta, the last survivors of the old monarchical principle, was more nominal than real, and was under the surveillance of the ephors of the senate. Elsewhere it was either an oligarchy in which the members mutually respected one another, or else, as at Athens and in certain subject and allied towns, a democracy in which the people was sovereign and fearful always lest any one person should raise himself above the rest. The tyrants, imitators of the Lydian Gyges —whose beneficent influence on art, however, cannot be gainsaid, as witness the Athens of the Pisistratidæ—disappeared with the expulsion of Hippias in 510.

From this political conception flow those characteristic features which set up the contrast between the art of Hellenic Greece and of the East and even of Ægean Greece.

Under a monarchy the artist had to do the will of princes and great folk; he recounted their exploits and flattered their vanity, and the official art of the court, usually false and cold, imposed its necessities upon him. He also placed himself at the service of private persons. But he was unable to

[1] **CLXXXIX-XC.**

interest himself sincerely in the national life because neither he nor the citizens to whom he appealed took any active part in it. When the monarchies of Alexander and his successors put an end to independent Greece, one sees the birth of an official art which has broken the link between itself and the aspirations of the community. But, up till then, Greek art is the faithful reflection of national life, and thanks to its glorious past it preserves this character, though in attenuated form, up to the very end; it was never to become enslaved to the monotonous and servile glorification of the monarchy and its entourage which is to be seen in Egypt, Chaldea, Assyria and Persia.

It expresses the collective soul of the city, its pride and its aspirations. Pericles justifies to the Athenian people the works of embellishment which some considered exaggerated: " Very well! it shall be at my expense and no longer at yours; but I alone shall put my name to the dedication of these works about which you complain." At these words the people, either because it admired his magnanimity or because, stirred to emulation, it would not relinquish to him the glory of these fine works, began to cry out more vehemently than ever, and this time to tell him to take from the treasury all that was needed to finance the works, and to spare nothing.[1] The Athenians would not allow a single man to reap the glory of having set up on the Acropolis those masterpieces of architecture and sculpture which illustrate its religion and its patriotism. If they reproached Phidias for the impiety, as the legend has it, of having sculped his portrait and that of Pericles on the buckler of the goddess Parthenos, it was because Athena personified the city which she had led to victory and which she protects always, and because this sculptural homage was paid to her by all and because the divine protection should be extended to all. Had not the artist, by thus linking their individual likenesses with that of the goddess, attempted to turn to his own and his master's profit not merely future fame but especially the divine blessing ?[2]

" Processions and offerings were simply an occasion for

---

[1] Plutarch, *Pericles*.
[2] Deonna, " Le portrait de Phidias sur le bouclier de l'Athéna Parthénos," REG, 1920, p. 291.

the people to glorify its own memory and to admire itself in the beauty of its young men and its elders, to display in the sunshine those strong, agile and disciplined bodies so capable of defending their country."[1] The frieze of the Panathenæa is the evocation of the entire city represented by its magistrates, priests, young men and maidens, its horsemen, ambassadors and metics. "How proud must the Athenian people have been to look upon this noble and splendid likeness of itself which presented to its gaze a sort of ideal mirror, and to have there been able legitimately to recognize itself such as it had been and such as it would wish to be at the greatest moments of its national existence!"[2]

Oriental monarchies with despotic powers and vast territories had a taste for the grandiose and the colossal. Their temples and palaces covered wide surfaces with their complicated plan and numerous halls. They are adorned with long sets of reliefs in which one may see the god, and the king, his earthly representative, in their ordinary occupations of waging war, hunting or indulging in pleasure. The same character is manifested by Ægean Greece in which the Cretan palace exhibits a complexity so foreign to the Hellenic spirit that it gave rise to the legend of the Labyrinth, and in which the dwelling-places of the Achæan princes of Argolis resemble the fortified castles of the feudal middle ages; the frescoes on their walls likewise bear witness to the power of the king, and his servants bring him their offerings.

In Greece everything is on a smaller scale, and the buildings cannot compete in size or magnificence with those of the East or of the Minoan world. The financial resources of the State are less, labour is more scarce since it has not at its disposal for such works the ever-increasing hordes of prisoners of war and slaves, and it cannot impress the forced labour of the citizen. Private individuals, too, are not so wealthy, and since, as in the independent cities, each one keeps an eye on his neighbour's position for fear of tyranny, they cannot nor do they desire to make an insolent display of luxury which the State will at once curb.

The Greek temple, the supreme creation of architecture, is a modest building; its grandeur lies in the harmony of its

---

[1] Boutmy, *Philosophie de l'architecture en Grèce.*
[2] Lechat, **CLXV,** p. 107.

proportions, the careful workmanship, and the beauty of its
decoration. It is true that divine society, modelled on human
society, is subject to a supreme lord, Zeus, but his authority
is limited by that of the other gods who are jealous of his
and of one another's power, and favour this or that city, and set
themselves up in opposition one to another, and there could
be no question of giving one of them a grander home than the
others. There are no colossal temples in the classical period
in Greece proper: they only appear at a later date or on the
confines of the Hellenic world where the Greek spirit is contaminated by foreign ways; in Sicily (Agrigente, Selinonte),
and in Asia Minor (Ephesus),[1] their dimensions excite the
wonder of the Ancients. The columns of the Olympeum,
more than 17 metres in height, are still standing at the foot
of the Acropolis near the Ilisos. A princely work begun by
Antiochus IV Epiphanes of Syria, in 174 B.C., and finished
in A.D. 129 under Hadrian, its dimensions surpass those
hitherto known. But they also reveal how much the spirit
has changed since the times when Pericles set up the Parthenon
in honour of the city's goddess, whose proud silhouette is to
be seen from there, and did not consider that the majesty
of the gods or the piety of the faithful was to be measured
by the material grandeur of their sanctuaries.

Statues larger than life-size are rare, and always represent
gods, who are taller than mortal men—the 6th century
Apollo of the Naxians at Delos and the two Kouroi from
Cape Sunium, probably Dioscuri;[2] for instance, the 4th
century colossal Zeus at Olympia, the work of the Æginetan,
Anaxagoras, which was dedicated by the warriors of Platæa
(479); the Zeus of Phidias (437-432) which was about 14
metres high, and his Athena Parthenos (438), about 12 metres
in height. The Zeus of Tarente and the Colossus of Rhodes
are the largest Greek statues, the next largest being Hadrian's
Zeus at Olympia. But no mortal was allowed to consecrate
an effigy of himself that was larger than the life.

It has been said that the colossal is Asiatic. And, as
a fact, it is in Asia Minor, when the Oriental spirit takes
the offensive in Hellenistic times, that the size of such
works increases. Terra cotta statuettes are no bigger than
38 centimetres at Tanagra; compared with those in Greece

---

[1] **CCX.**   [2] **LXVIII**, pp. 134, 191.

proper the figurines of Asia Minor, especially those made at
Smyrna, are often young statues in size, some of which reach
90 centimetres in height.¹   The Hellenistic schools of sculpture
(Pergamum, Rhodes) also have this taste for the colossal.

None the less, we never find in Greece that excess in which
the vague and indolent spirit of the Far East delights, as
witness the reclining Buddha of Pegu in Burma (62 metres in
length); or the Lungmen Buddha set up against a rocky
precipice on the flanks of the mountain, which is so vast in
size that a tree which has taken root on its head merely looks
like one of the curls of its hair.   These are works as overgrown
in size as the Oriental empires themselves which, at certain
moments, embraced vast regions, but collapsed as quickly
as they were formed.   Nor has Greece anything resembling the
Egyptian Colossi of the times of the Pharaohs.   And, indeed,
it was to glorify a king whose ephemeral power at one moment
united Greece with Asia that an artist suggested to Alexander
that Mount Athos should be hewn into a likeness of himself.

The same thing holds good for funerary art.   After the
Dorian invasion the great vaulted tombs of the Ægean chiefs
were no longer erected.   In the Greek city, where there was
more equality, such a vast and luxurious tomb would have
shocked the dead man's equals no less than his inferiors in
station, suspicious as they were of the dead every whit as
much as they were of the living.   Then, too, as early as in the
Iliad, Achilles suggests to his companions that they shall
not raise too great a tomb over him, but one that is simply
suitable.   Legislation imposed restrictions of this kind more
than once.   Solon forbade too much pomp and ceremony
at funerals: there were to be no lamentations in which the
glories of one's ancestors were vaunted, no sacrifice of a whole
bullock, no huge procession, nor were three garments to be
provided for the corpse.   Later, in the time of Demetrius of
Phalerum (317-307), it was forbidden to have a tomb whose
erection required more than three days' work by ten labourers.
At Nisyrus it was forbidden to erect any monument what-
soever over the dead, an interdict too absolute for it to be
possible to obey it.   Hence the Greek tomb and its decoration
could not but be very simple, and this character is general
whatever the kind of tomb.²   The largest of them grouped

¹ **LXVI-VII.**   ² **LXXXIV,** vol. vii, pp. 58, 62; **LXIII,** p. 96.

together in death a number of citizens, such as the tumulus of the Vourva and Velanidezza families (6th century), and the *soros* of the Marathon warriors (490);[1] yet even these did not equal in size the Mycenæan vaulted tombs, built for one occupant, nor did the earthen mound ever contain great constructions of masonry.

It is again Asiatic Greece that affords examples of funerary monuments of considerable size and luxurious decoration— in the small states of the Hellenized dynasts. In Lycia, the heröon of Trysa develops, in a vast enclosure, its sculptured friezes to a total length of about 108 metres (end of the 3rd century);[2] and at the end of the 5th, or beginning of the 6th century, Xanthus erects the monument known as that of the Nereids in honour of another Lycian chieftain.[3] In the middle of the 4th century, Mausolus (377-358), the powerful prince of Caria, got a " huge tomb of a splendour unsurpassed by any the dead had ever known " (Lucian).[4] These are Greek works, it is true, but they were adapted to Asiatic ideas, and it was Oriental luxury which ordered them.

Whereas the East sought pomp and circumstance, rich embroideries and redundant ornament which betokened power and wealth, Greek genius, whenever it was manifested in its purity and freed from outside influence, rejected this luxury and superabundance and preferred simplicity. The archaic in Greece, up to the end of the 6th century, learning from the East and from Egypt and influenced by their intermediary Ionia, did yield a little to this foreign tendency. The vase painter and the sculptor of Korai[5] of the 6th century liked garments covered with embroidery, painstaking arrangements of minute detail, bracelets, ear-rings and all the luxury of human ornament; they accumulated designs on all their vases[6] as if they loathed to leave an empty space, even filling up their background with superfluous detail. But from 500 onwards, after the rupture with the East and the national reaction that came alike in politics and art, and right up to the time of the Hellenistic monarchies which renewed this severed link and brought about an active return of Orientalism,

---

[1] **LXXXIV**, vol. viii, p. 68; **LXIII**, p. 32.
[2] **LXII**, vol. ii, p. 201.   [3] *Ibid.*, p. 215.
[4] *Ibid.*, p. 321.
[5] **LXXVIII-X**; **LXXXIV**, vol. viii, p. 574.
[6] **CXLIV**, vol. ix.

Hellenic simplicity triumphs: the severe Dorian peplos replaces the more elegant Ionian costume, and all superfluous ornament is rejected, while technique despises minutiæ.[1]

On the one hand force, overweening numbers, the colossal, exaggeration, and luxury. On the other, proportion, simplicity, sobriety. These Hellenic qualities may be instinctive, because the monuments which immediately follow the Dorian invasion (the geometric period and the Attic Dipylon vases)[2] already testify to a spirit quite different from the Ægean; they may have been favoured by the land and its natural features, where all is small and nothing exaggerates or blocks the view and crushes thought; they were favoured by the preponderance of the anthropomorphic conception which brings everything down to the human scale. And they were likewise most certainly favoured by the social environment and the political constitution of the city.

It was of great benefit to the Greek artist to have reacted against the Oriental spirit. He saw beauty, not in material grandeur or riches but in proportion and simplicity. Greek artists did not care for rare and glittering materials such as gold, silver, and precious stones, or for carving Colossi, erecting huge buildings and covering images with sumptuous ornamentation, but sought, rather, to render the harmony of pose, of line, proportions and rhythm in the simple materials within their immediate reach; they demanded beauty from their own æsthetic capacity, not from outside and too facile means. And this is precisely why they have compelled universal admiration.

[1] **LXXVIII**, p. 353.
[2] **CXLIV**, vol. vii, p. 154; **CXLV**, vol. i, p. 212.

CHAPTER V

ART AND HISTORICAL EVENTS

ART, the handmaiden of the city, commemorated the important events of its life—warlike or peaceful enterprises, joyful or sorrowful happenings, national festivals, and all that was of particular interest to the citizen. Whether victory, treaty or national calamity such as the plague, each formed the pretext for a work of art which was at one and the same time an historical document and an act of gratitude or expiation to the gods. History, like religion, is reflected in the mirror of art, and the visitor to such great sanctuaries as Olympia, Delphi, Delos, Dodona,[1] and the Acropolis of Athens, where offerings were accumulated in such profusion, could read it step by step as in a book whose pages were of stone or metal, and thus learn the story of their past.

We modern folk, for whom art is divorced from the national life and artificially participates therein on rare occasions only, too often neglect, when dealing with the past, to note the social fact which gave the artist the opportunity to create his work and which gives to it its particular aspect. For us a sculpture or a picture is no longer anything but the expression of individual phantasy, of the emotion felt by the artist and communicated by him to the beholder. Such art as illustrates national life is cold, official and didactic rather than æsthetic; it does not move us because it corresponds to no sincere emotion in the soul of its creator. How poor in inspiration are the works of art engendered by the war of 1914-18—an event that yet was tremendous in itself and in its consequences! Look at the contrast in the case of the Persian wars (490-449)—as decisive for the continuance of an independent Greece as was the recent war for the continued existence of a Europe seeking to escape the overlordship of an individual—and how those wars exalted the imagination of the artist and inspired him to produce his masterpieces!

---

[1] Carapanos, *Dodone et ses ruines*, 1878.

This was because art, in Greece, was an integral part of national life; being utilitarian, it had to express this national life; the artist himself was a citizen who contributed by his works to the glory of his country.

Fifth-century Greek art would be incomprehensible if we did not link it up with the Persian wars and with the Peloponnesian War (431-404), in which the entire history of this period is summed up. Hardly had they been victorious at Marathon (490) before the Athenians raised their Treasury[1] within the Delphic precincts (Pl. II) with the tithe of their spoil (between 490-480). The Dorian Heracles and the Attic Theseus engage in their exploits on the metopes, and it is the Athenians in their struggle against the Persians who are represented in this mythic guise. Did not the Greek army during the battle occupy a defensive position near a sanctuary sacred to Heracles, and did not Theseus take part in person in the fighting? At Delphi we find another Marathon ex-voto—the bronze group dedicated by the Athenians between 465-460, doubtless as a product of the spoil from the Eurymedon; there we see the triumphant Miltiades[2] surrounded by Apollo, Athena, and various heroes of myth. The project of the first Parthenon was perhaps the fruit of the advent of the democracy which had just overthrown the tyrant (constitution of Clisthenes, about 508), and the second Parthenon, between 490 and 480,[3] was again due to the victory at Marathon. On the coinage, Athena, victorious, now encircles her helmet with a wreath of laurel. At the Athens Poekile, Micon paints the varying fortunes of the battle. It is in three sections and shows the entry into the battle-line of the Platæans, and the general mêlée; the flight of the Persians in the marshes and their pursuit, and the Athenians trying to prevent them from boarding their vessels. Salamis (480) led to the construction of the temple of Aphæa at Ægina[4] in memory of the glorious part the Æginetan fleet had played, and the ornamentation of the pediments, where the Greeks of myth fight against the Trojans under the benevolent regard of Athena. Did not Herodotus say that the taking of Troy was what led up to the Persian wars and the origin

[1] *Fouilles de Delphes*, iv; Bourguet, *Les ruines de Delphes*, p. 96.
[2] Bourguet, p. 40.   [3] **XXXIX.**
[4] Furtwaengler, *Aegina*, 1906.

of the age-long hatred of these two nations one for the other ? The heroes, Ajax and Telamon, who appear on the pediments, fought at Salamis, invoked by the Greeks, and a ship which they sent to Ægina took back the spirits of Æacus and the Æacidæ.

After Platæa (479) Delphi received the triple bronze serpent;[1] an act of gratitude to Apollo, this was likewise a testimony to the union effected against the common enemy, and it was consecrated by all the allies whose name it bears.

While the Greeks were repulsing the Persians in the East, they were also vanquishing the barbarians in the West, in Magna Græcia and Sicily, and this provided fresh occasions for artistic creation—the ex-voto of the Tarentines at Delphi, commemorating their victory over the Messapians and the Peucetians, which was the work of Ageladas; the golden tripod offered by Gelon of Syracuse and his brothers Thrasybulus and Polyzalus, in memory of the victory of Himera over the Carthaginians (480),[2]and many others besides.

Peace, however, was concluded between Athens and Persia (449), as is witnessed by the Lemnian Athena of Phidias offered about 450 by the Athenian colonists of Lemnos. Bareheaded, without her buckler, helmet in hand, and her now idle spear in her left hand, the goddess personifies the city which can now rest from its rude and warlike labours and devote itself to the works of peace. But the Athena " Promachos," set up about 448 between the Propylæa and the Erectheum, is a reminder that it must be a vigilant peace: with her spear at rest, her buckler on her arm, she symbolizes the military power of Athens, constantly augmented by new victories, and ever ready for action. The aigrette of her helmet and the point of her lance glittering in the sunshine, and visible from afar, testify to the world at large that the city is capable of defending her liberties and will defend them dearly.

So, too, must we understand Pericles' Acropolis.[3] It is alike the sanctuary of the local gods and the mirror of the great events of Attic history. The Persian wars which destroyed the temples, also, when victory was achieved, enabled them to be rebuilt with greater beauty than ever

[1] Bourguet, p. 160.   [2] Bourguet, pp. 54, 155, 172.
[3] **CLXV-VI.**

thanks to the wealth this victory brought. On the pediments of the Parthenon[1] Athena springs, full-armed, from the head of Zeus, and disputes the possession of Attica with Poseidon: this is the legendary birth of the city and its progressive domination over the small Attic states, realized by the *synoikismos* of Theseus. On the metopes the Lapiths fight against the Centaurs, the Greeks against the Amazons and Trojans, the gods against the giants: here are all these Athenians who, in the course of their long story, have battled with the enemy to preserve their independence and who now finally consecrate it.[2] On the frieze of the cella the Athenian people, in a long procession symbolizing them as a whole, come to give thanks to the gods who have protected them, and to parade their own triumph. For at the time of the consecration of the Parthenon in 438, Athens, liberated from all her foes, at the head of a vast maritime empire, wealthy, and attracting within her gates from all quarters men who were illustrious in the arts and sciences, had reached the summit of her power.

These were visions of glory and pride, but they were likewise visions full of sadness. The Nike of Pæonius of Mende, set up at Olympia on its high triangular pedestal,[3] descends from heaven to bring victory. We no longer see in her anything but an admirable piece of sculpture in which the two problems of movement and of transparent drapery in motion, already approached as far back as the 6th century, particularly by the Ionians, find their happiest solution. But what bitterness the Spartans must have felt to see her in Attica—if it is true that she recalls the success achieved by the Messenians, their inveterate enemies and the allies of the Athenians, in the affair of Sphacteria (425)! This was a day of dishonour for Sparta, who, for the first time, saw her warriors failing to die to the last man, and shamefully surrendering instead. " Of all the events of this war, this for the Hellenes had been the most unexpected. Because

---

[1] **XXXIX, XLIV, CLXVI.**

[2] Certain scholars—wrongly, in my own opinion—do not see in the oft-repeated Centauromachy, Amazonomachy, etc., any national symbol or profound meaning; the artist likes to depict them simply from an æsthetic point of view because they permit of his endlessly varying his poses, groups and composition. Tarbell, " Centauromachy and Amazonomachy in Greek Art; the Reasons for their Popularity," *Amer. Journ. of Arch.*, 1920, xxiv, p. 226.

[3] *Olympia;* **LXII,** vol. i, p. 457.

it had been believed that neither hunger nor any other extremity could ever have induced the Lacedæmonians to lay down their arms—that they would die rather than surrender, and fight on to the bitter end; it was impossible to believe that those who had laid down their arms were the same as those who were dead."[1] This incident heralds, indeed, the moral decadence of Sparta, and the sad story of the 4th century. This beautiful Nike is the incarnation not so much of a passing victory as of the horrors of that civil war of the Peloponnese which ruined Greece and led up to her coming loss of independence.[2]

And here, Sparta's wounded pride is avenged. Facing the Marathon ex-voto at Delphi was a substantial base supporting thirty-seven bronze statues that represented the gods who inspired success, Lysander crowned with victory, and the leaders who had commanded their naval squadrons. This was the ex-voto of Ægospotami (405).[3] And what a contrast between these two neighbouring monuments, one of which gloriously inaugurates the 5th century whilst the other sadly closes it ! One celebrates the victory of Athens over Persia and her patriotic union with the Hellenes who are to confront the invader, foretells her high political future, the making of her empire and her military, commercial, spiritual and artistic power in the second half of the 5th century; the other recalls Athens' defeat, a city given over to the enemy, and the abandonment of her territories, the end of her political glory, and the odious fratricidal struggles between the Greeks. For those Athenians who passed along the Sacred Way it must have aroused painful memories of the past.

These beautiful works of art, buildings and sculpture, are thus so many historical documents, so many witnesses to the past, ranged along the road to the city. Confronted with them we should not merely admire their beauty, however marvellous that may be; we should also see in them that which, in this constant association of the beautiful and the utilitarian, the Greeks saw in them—historic truth. The goddess, habited in the severe Dorian peplos, sceptre in

[1] Thucydides, iv, 40.
[2] Deonna, *L'éternel présent. Guerre du Péloponnèse* (431–434 *et guerre mondiale* (1914–1918), 1923.
[3] Bourguet, *Les ruines de Delphes*, 1914, p. 41.

her right hand, carries on her left arm the little child, Plutus
(Munich group).[1] He puts out his hand to caress the face of
Eirene, who bends on him a look of maternal tenderness.
It is a work full of charm which heralds the grace of Praxiteles
and which marks an important date in artistic evolution by
evincing a new feeling for humanity, and a more realistic
conception of the form, too long neglected, of a child. Yet
how should we understand this solicitude of the goddess for
the child and his own mute gesture and the horn of plenty
which he holds, unless we interpret literally the names of the
persons in the scene, and unless we know that Peace brings
Wealth and that she owes her protection to this weak and
naked little child ?   Symbolic of peace, this group yet reminds
us of the innumerable ills of war. Chabrias has won the
victory of Naxos (375), the Athenian ships have beaten the
Peloponnesian squadrons of Nicolochus, and the peace of
371 has for the time being put an end to the struggles which
resulted from the Peloponnesian war. Annual sacrifices had
been instituted in honour of Eirene; Peace and the Cephisodotus group were consecrated to her. In Praxiteles' group,
an analogous conception, Hermes carries the infant Dionysus
on his arm (about 340); he has to secure his escape from the
jealousy of Hera and take him to the nymphs who are to bring
him up in secret; he has stopped by the way near a tree, on
which he has hung his chlamys, and he is amusing the child
with a bunch of grapes. Is this simply a mythological
scene ? No, it is to commemorate an alliance between Elis
and Arcadia, symbolized by these gods.[2]

Political events likewise determine the relative importance
of the different art centres and the amount of influence they
exercise. They make possible that marvellous efflorescence
of Attic art in the second half of the 5th century. The
Persian wars had been disastrous for Athens which had
sustained the full shock of the invasion. On the morrow of
Salamis the Athenians returned to a town where everything
was in ruins, both public buildings and private houses; the
countryside had been systematically devastated and there
was wreckage on every side. For a long while they had to
confine themselves to what was most urgent, and that was
not works of art but utilitarian building, such as ramparts

---

[1] **LXII**, vol. ii, p. 180.   [2] *Ibid.*, p. 291.

to shelter them from any fresh attempts, and an enlarged fleet which should teach Persia to respect them, protect the city against a maritime raid such as that of Marathon, and police the allied seas. Nevertheless the disaster proved fruitful, for Athens rose again stronger than ever. She becomes the head of a great maritime empire and has at her disposal financial resources such as she had never known in the old days—tribute paid to her by allies who very soon become her subjects. Once Persia had been finally driven back and peace concluded, she could begin to think of adorning and beautifying herself. The Barbarians had done the best thing possible in ruining everything so completely and wiping the slate clean, for now architects, painters and sculptors had a clear field. Had this not been so, Pericles' contemporaries would have still seen on the Acropolis the old building of the 6th century, the Hekatompedon of the Pisistratidæ with its marble façade and on its pediments the struggle between gods and giants.[1] The Parthenon would not have been the masterpiece of Doric architecture and Phidian sculpture that it was, but the primitive project (of about 506) or the second Parthenon (after 489) whose unfinished drums are incorporated into the north wall of the Acropolis, would have been realized sooner;[2] Pericles would never have conceived his plan for the embellishment of the Acropolis, and that religious conservatism would have triumphed utterly which forced Mnesicles to truncate the south wing of the Propylæa and determined the bizarre orientation of the temple of Athena Nike, and which doubtless stood in the way of the symmetric plan of the Erectheum, that the old sanctuaries should be respected. It may thus be said with some justice that Athens was fortunate in being ruined in 480; left intact, she could but have added a few new buildings to those older ones that were there already.[3]

And while Athens waited for the propitious moment to begin her reconstruction, art was making progress. During the first half of the 5th century it had by no means arrived at casting off old archaic conventions, and its style was somewhat stern and hard. Towards 450 it had reached technical maturity and it was precisely at this moment that Athens

[1] **LXXVIII**, p. 300; **LXXXIV**, vol. viii, p. 552.
[2] **XXXIX**.   [3] **LXXVIII**, p. 424.

found herself able to put her artistic projects into realization. If these projects are beautiful and harmonious in their execution, is it not because the artists had not merely an occasion for creation but had at their disposal from this time forth a perfect technique ? Could the genius of a Phidias, an Ictinus, or a Mnesicles, or of the many artists grouped around these great masters, have manifested itself so clearly and unmistakably, or could it have carried to execution works which their successors looked upon as everlasting models, had these fortunate circumstances not existed ?

It is to the Persian wars, again, that Athens owes her artistic preponderance in the second half of the 5th century; the Barbarians enabled the spread of Attic art to come about. Still of little importance in the 6th century, despite the brilliant dominance of Pisistratus, Athens, by the middle of the 5th century, had become the first city in Greece, taking higher rank even than Sparta. Her political prosperity was the determining factor of her soaring flight in the spheres of commerce, industry, science, literature and art during that brief period which has been called " the century of Pericles." Attic art was mistress of Greece and her dominion was felt everywhere, in the Peloponnese (the temple of Phigalia, built by Ictinus about 420), in Asia Minor in the courts of the little kings of Lycia and Caria, and wherever Hellenic culture had penetrated. The Peloponnesian schools could claim no such success, and the influence of the school of Argos, so flourishing under Polyclitus, did not reach beyond the borders of Greece proper.[1]

But was it not the same in the 7th and 6th centuries? Was not the spread of Ionian art beyond its own geographical boundaries the result of the economic prosperity of Ionia, whose political downfall led to the extinction of her brilliant influence on continental Greece ?

More than anywhere else the prosperity of art in Greece is intrinsically bound up with the country's political vicissitudes just because that art is the expression of the city's life. And this is a fact patent throughout her history. In the Hellenistic period the great centres of artistic activity are no longer in Greece even, but in Asia Minor (Pergamum), in Egypt (Alexandria), and in Syria (Antioch), because inde-

[1] CLXVII.

pendent Greece no longer exists and because political life has shifted eastwards along with the monarchies of Alexander and the diadochoi. Later still, the creative sap has dried up altogether in Greece, and the artist lives on his glorious past because Greece has also lost the outward semblance of liberty and become the docile subject of Rome.

The very choice of themes, denoting a modification of the Greek spirit, sometimes depends on political circumstances. Athens the glorious exalts the god-given victory which enables her to produce so many works of art—witness the Athena Parthenos bearing the Nike on her hand, or the balustrade in which the Nikes form the train of the goddess. At the beginning of the 4th century circumstances have altered. Athens, vanquished in 404, has seen her empire crumble. Her citizens, full of bitterness, are war-weary; their own wealth and that of the state is exhausted, and all long for tranquillity. Nevertheless, by taking advantage of the dissensions bet..een Thebes and Sparta, an attempt is made to regain the lost hegemony, and the peace of 371 enables the second shortlived Athenian empire (civil war of 371-356) to come into being. In order to celebrate it, the group of statuary of Cephisodotus is ordered. But the artist no longer chooses, as his predecessors did, the warlike Nike or Athena the warrior: the theme is a pacific one foretelling that calm and wealth desired by all.

The æsthetic ideal and its vicissitudes are in some measure tributary to historic events. In the 7th to the 6th centuries, Ionia, thanks to her material prosperity, has the main part to play in art.[1] It is in this Greek territory in Asia that the techniques of bronze and marble are built up and developed and that the artist sets himself to solve the problem of drapery. Greece in Europe, particularly Athens of about 560, accepts this beneficent Ionian influence.[2] But round about 500 art sounds a different note.[3] Freeing itself from the minutiæ and elegance sought after in Ionia, it becomes enamoured of simplicity and sobriety, clearly to be perceived in Athens in the Kore of Euthydicus and the head of the Blond Ephebus, which are earlier than 480.[4] The long, trailing dress covered

---

[1] **LXXXIV**, vol. viii, p. 252; **LXXVIII**, p. 168; **CXLV**, vol. ii, p. 486.
[2] **LXXVIII**, pp. 188, 335.   [3] *Ibid.*, p. 353.
[4] **LXXVIII**, pp. 353, 362.

with rich ornamentation which had been borrowed from the
Ionians and which betrays the Asiatic love of luxury rather
than the measured taste of Greece, no longer meets with the
favour it once enjoyed; the ancient national garment, the
so-called Dorian peplos with its simple regular folds is preferred; the manner of hairdressing in which the hair fell in
sheets down the back, with evenly regulated curls detached
from it and hanging over the shoulders, with volutes, corkscrews and complications without number, is replaced by
hair worn short or semi-short, treated with more and more
simplicity. This new tendency is of continental origin and
is that of Peloponnesian art of other days inherited in direct
line from the old Dorian spirit which was already evident in
the 6th century in the Kouroi of Polymedes of Argos and the
metopes at Selinus.[1] Why this change? Was it because
the artists, saturated with Ionianism and having extracted
from it all that they could use with profit, turned away from
it naturally? Or was it due to the necessities of artistic
evolution? Certain scholars, indeed, decline to place this
fact in relation with historical circumstances. And yet was
there not at this very moment a change in political orientation? The East threatens. Darius dreams of conquering
Europe, and makes a beginning with his plans in Thrace,
thus establishing himself at the very doors of Greece. Independent Lydia (546) and Ionia, the natural intermediaries
between European Greece and Asia, are no more, and from
510 their influence is a thing of the past. Ionia, rebelling,
is crushed at the battle of Lade (495), and Miletus succumbs
(494). The misfortunes of their brothers in Asia are painfully
felt by the western Hellenes, and Phrynicus is condemned
to punishment for having revived this sad memory in his
drama, *The Taking of Miletus*. Then come the unfortunate
expedition of Mardonius to Mount Athos, the demand for
homage by sea and land (491), and, finally, open hostilities
—the landing of the Persians at Marathon (490) and the heroic
struggles at Thermopylæ, Salamis (480), and Platæa (479).

Are we to believe that, in Greece, where art is so intimately
bound up with the life of the city, these events left the artist
indifferent or that they merely provided him with the occasion
to create without having any repercussion on his æsthetic

[1] **LXXXIV,** vol. viii, p. 436.

feeling itself, and without giving it a different orientation, turning it away from the East towards Europe and that Dorian land where dwelt great artists such as Callon and Onatas of Ægina, Gorgias of Laconia, and Ageladas of Argos ? Was it not from those lands that the armies of the Peloponnesian confederates were to come and join the Attic forces in a common effort to repulse the alien ? Was there not in art, as in politics, a new consciousness of national feeling and of purely Hellenic qualities which the Dorians of the Peloponnese represented in the highest degree ? The Persian wars did not only enrich the repertory of artistic themes, furnish the occasion for splendid monuments and affirm the artistic dominance of Athens, but likewise confirmed this new direction taken by art from the beginning of the 5th century. Perhaps, had this rupture never taken place, orientalism and Ionianism might have continued to exercise their influence on continental Greece, to the detriment of that robust and healthy strength, that well-proportioned simplicity, and that grace without prettiness, which were to become the dominant features of the great classical period. The question has often been envisaged as to what might have happened if tyranny had succeeded in maintaining itself in the Greek cities instead of being overthrown conclusively at the end of the 6th century when the Pisistratidæ were expelled (510); the supposition has been that these vain and ostentatious tyrants, imitating in a small way the kings of Lydia and the monarchs of the East, would have prepared the way for a Persian victory, accepting it without resistance, and allowing Greece to be reduced to a Persian province. One may put an analogous question in regard to art and ask oneself whether art would not have evolved differently and persisted in its former tracks had relations been maintained with an ever-prosperous Ionia providing Greece with an open door to the Orient.

At the close of the 5th century yet another change comes about. Still almost insensible in figured art it is clearly evident in other spheres. That noble and almost superhuman ideal which had inspired the artist on the morrow of the Greek victories has been shaken; greater interest is taken in reality. Euripides no longer sings, as Æschylus and Sophocles did, the divine force that directs the world, or the human will rising superior to its destiny; he describes the passions which stir

the human heart, and he puts humble folk upon the stage such
as mothers and children, and represents the variety of daily
life. Music becomes more emotive, is a thing of finer shades.
There is now a new note of realism and feeling in the Greek
soul which finds its expression in pictorial and plastic art
in the 4th century, a note that with Scopas and Praxiteles
is emotional and sentimental and sways portraiture in the
direction of individual realism. Is this a natural evolution
leading art towards new resources, or is it the effect of political
circumstance ? The evolution of Christian art presents an
analogous rhythm determined by social events analogous
to those in Greece.[1] What happened in Greece at the close
of the 5th century ? The Peloponnesian war came to an end
with the foundering of the Athenian power (404); this war
put the Hellenic world to fire and sword, and ruined both
the vanquished and the vanquishing states, demoralizing
the Greeks, and weakening their hitherto confident faith in
the traditional gods, and it turned them to seeking passion
and mysticism; the war likewise upset the common life of
the city whose misfortunes developed in them an egoistic
individualism; it encouraged luxury and destroyed the ancient
simplicity.[2] The seeds of realism, emotionalism, voluptuousness and softness which had already manifested themselves
in the art of the 4th century, to reach their culminating point
in Hellenistic times, germinated in the political misfortunes
of the close of the 5th century.

It will be shown how, later still, the monarchic conception
imposed by the Macedonians and their successors introduced
into art quite other characters than those of the days of independent Greece.

To study the evolution of art in Greece is to study the
history of Greece; the archæologist and the historian of art
must of absolute necessity be historians as well.

---

[1] **VI,** vol. iii, p. 261 ff.
[2] Deonna, *L'éternel présent, Guerre du Péloponnèse et guerre mondiale,*
1923.

CHAPTER VI

ART AND SOCIAL RANK[1]

ART reflects the various ranks which made up Hellenic society. It has at its disposal for this nuances whose meaning frequently escapes modern folk, unaccustomed as they are to read works from which they ask nothing beyond æsthetic emotion, but which spoke a social language which was clear as day to the ancients.

This preoccupation with the characterization of the rank which the individual occupied in the city comes out clearly in funerary art. The painters of the geometric vases at the Athens Dipylon (9th to 8th centuries) commemorate the Athenian nobility of the Eupatrids in the execution of their duties as naukrariai, and in the pomp of their funeral ceremonies.[2] In the 6th century a statue of a horseman is erected on the tomb—the dead man as a member of the Athenian class of ἱππεῖς ; a small horseman carved on an Attic stele beneath the image of the dead recalls the same idea. Aristion is the hoplite wearing his heavy armour; Alxenor of Naxos sculps a landed proprietor with his dog and a locust in his hand.[3] Later, the frieze of the Panathenæa groups together in its march-past various representatives of the Athenian people.

What did this social hierarchy consist in ? The Hellenic world comprehended first of all superhuman society with its gods, heroes and semi-heroes; then the dead whose passage into the beyond has made them heroes; finally, in the lowest rank of the scale, those mythical beings still somewhat animal and of the earth, the Satyrs, Sileni, Titans, and Antæus. The society of the living had at its head Greeks of good birth, the citizens who directed the affairs of the city as the Olympians directed heavenly affairs. Below these were the smaller folk—the slaves; beyond the borders of Greece were the

---

[1] **VII**, p. 167.   [2] **LXXXIV**, vol. vii, p. 160.
[3] For these monuments see **LXXXIV**, vol. viii, pp. 360, 603.

E

despised Barbarians who were readily assimilated to the lowest beings in the mythological society.

The artist rendered these social differences by various means. Gods, heroes and the heroicized dead are often taller than mortals, a procedure common to the art of many peoples. On the frieze of Assos (6th century) Heracles towers over those who are aiding in the fight against Triton, and in the banquet scene the cupbearer, close to the reclining guests, is minute.[1] On the Chrysapha stele (6th century)[2] the heroicized dead are receiving the homage of the living— minute doll-like figures. And statues of abnormal size always represent gods, not mortals.

Noble and dignified attitudes are reserved for the gods, for the dead, and for the living of high birth. They are seated majestically on thrones, emblems of power, or they stand erect, facing the spectator. The long persistence of the rule of the frontal pose[3] may have been the result of a social convention, since the ancients attached the idea of dignity to this position. Gods and men, both, seemed proud to testify to their illustrious origin by their magnificent bodies—a leg might be put forward or the arms might make some gesture; as a rule the action is not clearly specified, but is sufficient to render them recognizable. The wounded would not allow their bodies to fail them, and one might say that they anticipated those words of Vespasian: "An emperor should die on his feet." As witness Cresilas' defiant warrior,[4] or the wounded Amazon of Polyclitus (Berlin),[5] bearing pain without betraying weakness and standing firmly, or at the most leaning on their spear or against a pillar. When they are laid low by their suffering, how dignified still is their surrender, such, for instance, as the Niobid of Rome[6] who, her back pierced by Apollo's arrow, has fallen to her knees! A nobility of posture even in agony and death is proper to these superior beings.

---

[1] **LXXXIV**, vol. viii, p. 256.
[2] *Ibid.*, p. 439.   [3] On this law see **CLXXVI**.
[4] Bavai bronze, at the St. Germain museum. Its authenticity, sometimes disputed, is now generally admitted. GBA, 1905; lastly, RA, 1918, i, p. 318; 1921, ii, p. 110; GBA, 1922, i, p. 116; REG, 1916, p. 364.
[5] **LXII**, vol. i, p. 503.
[6] REG, 1908; Sitte, " Zur Niobide der Banca commerciale," *Eranos*, 1909; *Ausonia*, 1907; *Revue ét anciennes*, 1910, p. 325.

But those of lower order do not hesitate to take the most familiar attitudes in which the body carelessly lets itself go without restraint. They crouch on the ground with legs raised or stretched—this is the posture of shameless Satyrs and Sileni, of the young boy, no doubt a serving lad, on the pediment at Olympia (about 460), who, playing mechanically with his foot, watches the preparations for the race between Pelops and Œnomaus.[1] Or they lie down, not in dignified manner on a banqueting divan, but on the ground itself on their stomachs—the figures in the angles of the pediments at Olympia are more likely to be spectators of both sexes of humble rank than river gods and nymphs. They readily cross their legs—an indication of ill manners. The ceramist Douris (Fig. 50) takes us into a school;[2] the masters who are instructing their pupils how to play the lyre and to recite are either seated or stand in simple and decent postures; but in one corner the person sitting on a folding stool with his legs crossed is the school-teacher, the slave who betrays by this breach of manners his lowly origin. On the reliefs of the Ludovisi throne[3] the artist contrasts the severely draped matron with the flute player, a courtesan, naked, who crosses her legs.

The discordant poses, too, which are frequent in vase-painting are felt to be suited to such beings—attitudes which break the rhythm of the body and fling the limbs about at random. Satyrs and Sileni gesticulate and contort their bodies.[4] What a contrast is here between these creatures and the intense action that athletes, such as Myron's Disco-bolus,[5] are sometimes shown in, action which is calculated to bring the body's harmony into full play!

In Myron's group[6] Athena, calm, disdainfully throws away the pipes which deform her features; but, in front of her, Marsyas makes a large gesture of surprise (Fig. 1). In Aristophanes, the Just praises the young Athenians of former days, who were sedate and modest: " When among the masters they sat and did not recline. In the palæstra they sat, their thighs tense and held close together so that nought indecent

[1] **LXII**, vol. i, p. 441.   [2] **CXLVI**, p. 112, fig. 22.
[3] *Antike Denkmäler*, ii, Pl. 6-7; **LXXIII**, p. 202; **LXXIII**, p. 202.
[4] **CXLVI**, p. 87, figs. 14, 15.   [5] **LXII**, vol. i, p. 472.
[6] **CLXIX**, p. 44; **LXII**, vol. i, p. 465.

was visible to those in front of them." The Greeks were very sensitive to the beauty of calm poses, which revealed nobility of person and good upbringing. That which Plato said of

music is appropriate to their figured presentments : " It should seek attitudes and movements that are calm and which maintain harmonious relations between the different parts of the body, fleeing from disordered agitation and the imitation of deformed and ridiculous beings."

FIG. 1. MYRON. ATHENA AND MARSYAS.

Superior beings alone had their form rendered in detail with that perfect musculature patiently fashioned by gymnastic exercises. They were robust and strong with no superfluous flesh on them. The Sileni might be fat even to obesity but a Greek had to cultivate his body and keep it supple and vigorous. The musculature of inferior beings was also ruder and coarser, and the body of Marsyas, by Myron, differs in this way from that of the Diskobolos, just as the form of the Hellenistic Gauls[1] differs from that of the Greeks. In Athens Solon's law made gymnastics obligatory for young men of good family and forbade slaves to exercise in the palæstra. It was doubtless the same in other

FIG. 2. SILENI, ON A VASE BY DOURIS.

Greek cities, and this restriction was abolished only in the time of the last emperors. In the early days it was the sons of wealthy Athenians only who took up gymnastic exercises, hunting, horsemanship and philosophy. The ancient authors

[1] **LXII**, vol. ii, p. 520.

likewise tell us that a well-bred man could be distinguished at once from an artisan by his gait and the nobility of his bearing.

The hair and beard of the superior being was always carefully combed; it always presents this neat and regular character, occasionally too symmetrical in the 5th, and which was rendered more picturesquely in the 4th century, whether it was dressed long, or semi-short or short. But Satyrs and Sileni are given wild and tousled beards and hair; frequently it stands on end.

The straight " Hellenic profile " which imposed itself on Greek art from the beginning of the 5th century, and which is an idealization of nature, is not given indiscriminately to

FIG. 3.   HERACLES FIGHTING ANTÆUS, ON A VASE BY EUPHRONIUS.

all: the artist will not allow the Sileni, the Centaurs or Antæus to have it, whose stubby and turned-up noses are almost animal (Fig. 3).

To be master of oneself, restrain the impulses and hide the stronger feelings, allowing nothing to show in the countenance, was a social convenance to which all superior persons conformed. They had to be impassive, or at all events to be discreet in the display of emotion.[1]   In order to dissimulate it the " archaic smile " of the 6th century imposed its unchanging mask even on the wounded and dying; then the calm serenity of the 5th century gave to all an intentional indifference. Emotion is shown only in slight contractions of the facial muscles. The Rome Niobid[2] falls, her head sinks back,

[1] On expression in Greek art see **VII,** and Girard in REG, 1894, pp. 1, 337; 1895, p. 88; *Monuments grecs,* ii, 1895–7, No. 23-5.
[2] See above, on p. 82.

her eyes are upcast to heaven and she opens her lips to cry out, but pain does not convulse her features; even dying she preserves her dignity and reserve. The Lapiths who fight the Centaurs on the Olympia pediments or on the Parthenon metopes have almost calm expressions; a slight frown alone denotes their choler and the ardour of the fray. But persons belonging to the lower orders of society, divine or human, are not bound by this severe code of manners, nor do they blush to display all kinds of feelings. Fifth-century vase paintings, reliefs and statues show us this difference quite plainly. On the one hand countenances that are almost impassive; on the other features that already betoken passion. On a crater by Euphronius[1] Heracles is shown grappling with Antæus (Fig. 3). The hero's countenance is calm, and only his tight lips and wide eye betray the anger which animates him; his hair and beard are carefully combed; his profile is straight. The giant, on the contrary, with his bristling beard and drooping moustache, his thick brows and corrugated profile, has his mouth open to cry out in anguish; his teeth are bared with pain, and his eyes, showing the whites, betoken approaching death. The common folk are given more realistic and expressive faces. Men of the humbler sort are fighting, and one of them, with a gesture which the artist has copied from the life of the streets, catches hold of his adversary by the pudenda, and makes him howl with pain. Coming out from a too copious indulgence at a feast, they are depicted in the act of vomiting, their faces convulsed. If we look at the Centauromachy pediment at Olympia[2] we shall find there the expression of three grades of society. In the centre Apollo's features are as impassive as his attitude, and allow none of the emotions of the fight to be seen in them. The Lapiths, of noble lineage, have to keep their dignity and control their furious passion, yet one may recognize it by little details—contracted brows and set lips, and, in truth, the brutal head of the youth bitten by a Centaur has nothing in common with that of Apollo. But it is in the faces of the Centaurs that the emotional reaches its maximum intensity. The monsters roar, biting their adversaries in their rage; gloating, they bear off women and youths, and their ugly countenances reflect their tumultuous feelings. This dualism

[1] **CXXIX**, p. 158, Fig. 105.   [2] **LXXII**, vol. i, p. 446.

in expression is pursued throughout Greek art. Even when the emotional comes to be depicted in divinities who have become suffering, it will be shown more intensely in lower beings. On the Pergamum frieze[1] the expression of the giants is more intense than that of their adversaries not merely because they themselves are vanquished but because they are of inferior clay.

In a general way, all that is beautiful is proper to the one sort and all that is ugly to the other. The features of noble Greeks were never to be hideous like those of the Satyrs, Pan and the Sileni, vulgar beings who get drunk and quarrel, depicted by the vase painters. Beauty, harmony, dignity in gesture and pose, care for the person and clothing, calmness of countenance: " What an unmistakable mark is given to mortals by noble birth, distinguishing them from other men !"[2]

Since persons of lower rank, freed from the convenances, are treated in a manner more life-like and more realistic, it was in such folk that the artist could study facial expression, the index of feeling;[3] it was through them that they began to take an interest in lesser folk; in short it was in such types that realism first made its appearance during the thoroughly realistic phase of the 5th century before it had triumphed in the 4th, and particularly in the Hellenistic period, delivering all, even the gods, from a too rigid and circumscribed dignity.

Nevertheless it is sometimes difficult to distinguish the social rank of a figure. In the 6th century B.C. the same types of Kore and Kouros serve indifferently for gods, for the living and for the dead.[4] They can be determined only by the purpose and context of the work and by their attributes. Even in the 5th century they did not at the outset know how to give the gods specific features which should be nobler than those of the already idealized mortal. Are the Doryphoros and Diadumenos[5] of Polyclitus gods or men ? The Munich Zeus[6] certainly has a fine form, but nothing in the countenance specially characterizes godhood. One hesitates before many

[1] **LXXII**, vol. ii, p. 513.   [2] Euripides, *Hecuba*.
[3] **VI**, vol. ii, p. 82; **VII**, p. 169.
[4] See, on primitive indeterminateness, Deonna's "L'indétermination primitive dans l'art grec," *Rev. d'ethnographie et de sociologie*, iii, 1912, p. 22; **VI**, vol. ii, pp. 415.
[5] **LXII**, vol. i, pp. 488, 496.   [6] **LXX**, p. 212.

a statue in which the attributes are not sufficiently precise, and before many an isolated head. Nevertheless Phidias makes a great effort to give to his divine beings a sovereign air distinguishing them from mankind. It would seem that he succeeded better than his predecessors in translating their majesty, no longer so much by attributes, gesture, posture or any such external means, as by the facial features, the soul's reflection. With this master the god-like type began to stand out by its expression from that of even an idealized mortal. But the differentiation was not complete till the 4th century and the school of Praxiteles, who knew how to indicate more exquisitely still the bourne between the two worlds. Soon afterwards the indeterminateness of the old days reappeared under the influence of the realism which depreciated the gods. Asclepius is sometimes no more than a sufficiently common mortal with features lacking in nobility; as in former times it is by his attributes alone, his hair and serpent, that he is to be distinguished, and all moral expression, so finely marked in the 4th century, disappears.[1]

Differentiation between the gods themselves was likewise slow in the making and at the beginning was achieved only by exterior means—beard, hair, and attributes. In the archaism of the 6th century it is difficult, for instance, to distinguish between those gods, whose heads and clothes are the same, depicted in the black-figure vases. On the red-figure vases there is already less uniformity; and even in the absence of attributes Hermes differs from Apollo, although the older gods, Poseidon, Zeus, Hades, Dionysus and Hephæstus, are still capable of being confounded. It was later only that Poseidon acquired the individual characters which distinguish him from Zeus, and often the distinction is very slight; has not Euphranor been reproached for having endowed Poseidon with a nobility which cannot even be surpassed in a Zeus? Asclepius differs from Zeus by nuances in his physiognomy which the artists of the 4th century, masters of expression as they were, knew how to render.

Greek art is aristocratic. For many a long day it never sought to give a complete picture of the social complex and did not interest itself to the same extent in the various classes which made it up. It glorified Greeks of good birth and the

[1] **VII,** p. 188

gods conceived in their likeness, and for them it sought the most beautiful and noble types.   The lower orders might hold the curious regard of the ceramist who was brought close to them by the conditions of his own life; in high art the common people merely accompanied their masters and in the classic period are never treated for their own sake.   It was later on, only, when the ideal had evolved, that the Hellenistic artist sometimes chose them as the unique theme of his studies and accorded them a place equal with the rest.

And yet it was a democratic art, if by that we mean that it is addressed to all, that all may enjoy it and that it is the expression of the ideas and common aspirations of the city.

CHAPTER VII

ART AND MANNERS[1]

THE monuments of pre-Hellenic Greece already have on them pugilists (the Hagia Triada vase with boxers), and acrobats vaulting over a bull (Tiryns fresco, Knossos ivory statuette, gems), showing active muscles; they show that the Ægeans attached a certain importance to bodily exercise and that the subject inspired artists. But it was reserved for Greece to bestow on this culture of the human body a care unknown elsewhere, and to her artists to obtain from it new effects. Gymnastics[2] for the Hellenes were an indispensable preparation for the social life of the soldier-citizen; they moulded body and mind alike, since a strong and noble spirit could exist only in a robust and healthy body. As artists they admired this healthy body, but the æsthetic interest was grafted on to the utilitarian and derived from a social necessity. The Greeks said that it was gymnastics which enabled the Athenians to win Marathon and the Thebans Leuctra. Socrates counselled the young Epigenes to cultivate his neglected body: "What a strange body hast thou, Epigenes! . . . Is that combat valueless to thee whose prize is life, should the Athenians come and propose it? Yet many men, owing to their bad condition, perish in the dangers of war and often at the cost of their honour; many, for the same reason, are taken alive; and others gain a bad reputation, founded on the feebleness of their body, which causes them to pass for cowards. . . . For my part, I think it easier and more agreeable to submit to the fatigues necessary in order to obtain a vigorous body. All is different to him whose body is in good condition from him in whom it is unfit; health and vigour fall to the lot of those whose bodily condition is good; many there are who, by this means, come through a soldier's

[1] CCI ff.
[2] On gymnastics and their results see CLXXXV, s.v. "Gymnastica;" CCIII, CCV-VIII.

dangers with honour; others help their comrades, render
service to their country and achieve fame. Know well that
there is no struggle, no single act of thy life, for which thou wilt
ever repent having trained thy body; indeed, in all the actions
of mankind the body hath its uses, and in every use to which
we put it it is necessary that it should be as fit as may be.
Furthermore, even in those functions in which thou thinkest
it has least part, in those of the mind, who knows but that
great errors are often made in thinking because the body is
indisposed? Bad memory, a laggard mind, sloth and folly
are ofttimes the result of a vicious disposition of our body
injuring the mind to such degree as to make us forget that
which we know. If, on the other hand, the body is healthy,
it is quite certain that there is no risk of a man coming to such
a pass as the result of not having a sound constitution. . . ."[1]

The young men obtained this training of the body in the
gymnasia as the necessary preparation for their duties as
citizens. As early as in the black-figure painting of the 6th
century, but particularly in the red-figure painting of the 5th
century, and on the reliefs, we see them stripping off their
garments, anointing themselves with oil, wrestling together,
throwing the discus and the javelin, and bathing themselves,
and they provide any number of motifs for the Greek artist
who catches them in every position of their bodies, whether
in action or repose. Robust and courageous, but modest
also, they realize Aristophanes'[2] ideal; they have " fresh
complexions, broad shoulders, a reticent tongue, well-covered
buttocks and small pudenda "; they bear no resemblance to
those effeminate and talkative young men, knowing nothing
of such exercises, who have " pale faces, narrow shoulders and
chests, a garrulous tongue, thin buttocks, over-developed
pudenda, and are irresolute in judgment." Does not the
painting on a 6th-century cup[3] bearing the signature of
Phidippus (British Museum) illustrate the words of the comic
poet and the counsels of Socrates? Ephebi are met together
in the palæstra; one of them resembles Epigenes of the
neglected body—he is fat and awkward in his posture; all
about him are his agile and supple companions with their
lissom bodies, seeming to mock at him. Obesity which has

[1] Xenophon's *Recollections of Socrates*.　　[2] *Clouds*, v, 1005.
[3] **CXCIV**, vol. x, p. 368, Fig. 214.

not been dissipated by exercise, and flabby flesh whose muscles it has not hardened, are despised and relegated with one consent to those grotesque creatures the Sileni, to the comic actors who exaggerate it, to slaves to whom gymnastics are forbidden, to barbarians and all whom it is desired to ridicule.

The life of a Greek city included communal ceremonial, usually carried out as an act of homage to the gods, which was both civic as well as religious in character, the divinity being merged in the city which he or she protected. This included solemn processions such as the Panathenæa immortalized by Phidias; and especially competitions in song, dance, music, scenic representation and bodily exercises.[1] These were acts of civic loyalty. Only those who were free men and of Greek nationality might take part in the musical and gymnastic games; slaves and barbarians were strictly excluded during the Greek golden age. A competitor must never have undergone shameful punishment nor have been deprived of his rights as a citizen. To be a competitor at the Olympic Games was the equivalent of recognition of Hellenic nationality. Restricted to a single city (the Panathenæa and Dionysia of Athens), or including all Hellenes (the great Olympic Games), these festivals always required the participation of art, which once more bears witness to its social function. Drama and Attic comedy were not originally purely æsthetic entertainments but acts of patriotic cult, whatever their much discussed genesis—whether funerary or Dionysiac—and they preserved this character, more or less attenuated, throughout antiquity. Was it not in Dionysus' sanctuary that the theatre was set up, and did not all the people have official access to it, as did the ambassadors of colonies and allied States ?

Among the national festivals which have provided the artist with numerous themes there are some which exerted a decisive ·influence on figured art. These are the festivals of which bodily exercise was the main interest, and at which the Greeks rivalled one another in wrestling, foot and chariot racing, armed and unarmed, discus and javelin throwing, and boxing. They had plenty of opportunity at the great games which at regular intervals brought together Hellenes from all over Greece: the Olympic, Pythian, Nemean, and Isthmian

[1] CCV-VI, CCVIII.

Games, as also in local games, such as the Panathenæa.[1]
With their body, which had been trained to be useful to its
owner but more especially to the country, the Greeks did
homage to the gods, showing it off to them in the plenitude
of its strength, ready to serve them as it was ready to serve
the city. And at the beginning those who took part in these
gymnastic competitions were not professionals; athletes did
not devote all their time to training. They were citizens,
from the best families and also from more lowly stock, who
had other daily occupations. Gradually the pride of victory,
the glory it conferred, and the material advantages which
flowed from it, created a class of professional athletes—
somewhat before the time of Plato, according to Galen, and
possibly earlier still.[2]

What advantages did Greek art extract from these
manners and customs ?

In order to run or wrestle the body had to be stripped
of clothing which hindered the free play of the limbs. The
Ægean athletes wore narrow drawers, the masculine garment
of those days, which the Greeks still used in the early centuries.
But the Dorian Cretans and the Lacedæmonians, says Thucydides, set the example of wrestling stark naked; the runner
Orsippus of Megara cast off the διάζωμα to arrive more surely
at his goal in the 15th Olympiad. Soon, stripping completely became general in the games as in the palæstra.
That this stark nakedness aroused no disapprobation was due
to the agelong habit of seeing the body very nearly stripped
on such occasions, preparing opinion for complete nudity, and
it must also have been favoured by the demands of religion
itself that in ritual celebrations the faithful should present
himself naked in token of submission and humility.[3] Such
a custom was not unknown among other ancient peoples,
but nowhere except in Greece has complete nakedness
triumphed in actuality and won its way in art. Here we
really seem to have a characteristic feature of the Greek race
favoured by social circumstances. The Greek had no false
shame in seeing the body stripped, and this distinguished
him from all other ancient peoples. The Ægean Cretan
avoided stripping completely, and the Egyptians, Chaldeans,

---

[1] CLXXXV, *s.v.* " Ludi publici."
[2] *Ibid.*, *s.v.* " Athleta."   [3] CCVII.

Assyrians and Etruscans were thoroughly averse to it except in the case of the lower orders, or of prisoners who were stripped as a humiliation, or in the course of ritual performance. Æsthetic nakedness is so essentially Greek that wherever we find it we may be quite sure there was Hellenic influence at work. And it is from Greece, again, that modern art took it, after the Renaissance rediscovered the obscured tradition, unveiled once more the body hidden by Christian ideas of modesty, and enthusiastically gave itself to the study of human anatomy. Conversely, every time that Greek art underwent Oriental influence this principle was undermined. Ionian art, heir to the art of the Ægeans, and in close contact with the East, does not like it at all; the vase painters of the 6th and 5th centuries, whose origin was not purely Hellenic —as is often indicated by their names—avoided it, preferring drapery, and displaying great ingeniousness in the niceties of its arrangement. Thus Amasis, doubtless a native of Naukratis or Samos, and Nicosthenes, Andocides, Douris, Hieron and Brygus. When they worked for the foreigner, for a Scythian, for instance, Greek artists kept this scruple in mind and hid the privy parts with an opportune piece of drapery. Towards the close of ancient times, when the Oriental spirit triumphed, complete nudity appeared to shock; draperies and fig-leaves—these latter did not appear before the time of Constantine—were the result. Art renounced the Greek conception for many centuries and the nude disappeared—except when the subject absolutely required it (Last Judgment). And when the Renaissance once more came to hold the Greek ideal in honour there was continual opposition between the two tendencies. The beautiful nudes of Michael Angelo scandalized priests and faithful people, and Ammanati confessed, as though to a crime, of having reproduced nude and therefore shameless persons.

The particular note introduced into art by the Greeks was the æsthetic appreciation of the human form in a state of nature as though it had been that of a beautiful animal, strong and agile. If nudity appears among other peoples of antiquity it is never because the artist takes pleasure in it and admires human attitudes and anatomy but because the subject necessitates it. It was the exercises of the palæstra and the national games which taught the Greeks to understand this human beauty, and, long before Cellini, they considered that " the alpha and omega of all art is to be able to draw a nude man or woman."

Although nakedness was actual on certain occasions during the life of a Greek—in the gymnastic exercises—it must not be imagined, however, that the Greeks lived and fought without clothes as we see them depicted in their reliefs, paintings and statues. The æsthetic vision transformed the reality. Nudity became ideal, and a necessity of beauty.

Its use became generalized with time. The black-figure vases (6th century) still show the gods and heroes clothed. Later on, they strip them completely and even Zeus is not excepted. It is instructive, in this connection, to follow the evolution of a single pictured type such as that of Hermes or Dionysus.

Complete nudity was for long the appanage of men, who were obliged by the circumstances of their public life to appear unclothed from time to time. But women took no part in the gymnastic exercises and games; they lived in the gynæceum and busied themselves with domestic duties; they hid the charms of their persons from envious eyes. Feminine nudity is rare in art until the 4th century, and it is there explained by the necessities—usually erotic—of the subject more than by the artist's æsthetic pleasure in rendering her form. In vase-painting the nudes are courtesans, pipe players, dancers, women making their toilet or bathing. A few potters such as Euphronius and Brygus bear witness to a certain predilection for these subjects. Statuary and reliefs, less free in choice of subject than industrial art, have but rare examples to show in the 5th century: there is the Esquiline Venus who is perhaps the diver Hydna,[1] and the Rome Niobid who, in her dying agony, forgets the modest reserve of the young girl and allows her tunic to slip down.[2] On the beautiful reliefs of the Ludovisi throne[3] the sculptor carves a naked pipe player, seated in a bold attitude, and he contrasts the courtesan with the chaste matron. Though there was nothing in masculine nakedness to astonish the Greeks, the nudity of a woman still came as a shock to their

[1] Klein, " Zur sogenannten Aphrodite vom Esquilin " in *Jahresh de k. arch. Instituts in Wien*, x, p. 141.
[2] See above, p. 83.   [3] See above, p. 83.

habits. Most of them disapproved of the education given to young Spartan girls, who were hardly brought up like the boys, appearing naked with them in certain games, and dressing in the short Dorian tunic. They called them φαινομηρίδες, because the folds of the chiton, unsewn, opened when they walked and allowed the upper leg to be seen.

Women gradually caught the contagion, to the point of abandoning the last vestige of drapery and yielding their form completely to the gaze of the artist who came more and more to appreciate its beauty and faithfully to render its specific characters. Apart from the exceptions indicated, woman, whether mortal or Aphrodite, was draped from head to foot in the 6th century and the first half of the 5th. The artists of the second half of the 5th, who brought to perfection the technique of the transparent drapery on which the Ionians had made a tentative beginning in the 6th century, readily clothe the feminine form with diaphanous materials which permitted the body to be seen as though it were nude (pediments of the Parthenon, the Nike of Pæonius of Mende, etc.), and the unknown author (Alcamenes ?) of the Fréjus Aphrodite[1] (Pl. III) uncovers at most the left shoulder and breast. The 4th century went far along the same road. The draperies now slip off the shoulders altogether and only stop at the hips (Aphrodite of Milo, the Praxitelian Aphrodite of Arles, first half of the 4th century).[2] Praxiteles is the first completely to undrape the goddess (Cnidian Aphrodite, middle of the 4th century).[3] " No garment enwraps her. She is nude and completely discovers all her beauties. With one hand alone does she furtively preserve her modesty " (Lucian). This is an innovation of cardinal importance, for Greek art now multiplied nude women, particularly Aphrodites making this gesture of modesty (Pl. IV), preparing to enter the bath, and coming up out of the waves; but there was surprise at first, because the inhabitants of Cos, to whom Praxiteles offered his Aphrodite unveiled, preferred a clothed Aphrodite *severum id ac pudicum arbitrantes* (Pliny). Indeed it must have caused as much astonishment as the hardihood of Michael Angelo when he first dared to disrobe completely the Christ and the Virgin. Even the goddesses gave up their

---

[1] **LXII**, vol. ii, p. 118.   [2] *Ibid.*, vol. ii, pp. 269, 468.
[3] *Ibid.*, p. 273.

modest reserve and their former austerity; they became as naked as the old Oriental goddess of fecundity, as the ancient female idols of the first centuries of pre-Hellenic Greece.

The naked form which was admired was the body moulded and fashioned by gymnastic exercises. The " paidotribes," moulded by gymnastics, recreated the body of the young boy. These gymnastics developed all parts of the body harmoniously without any one profiting to the disadvantage of the rest. It was for the lack of this equilibrium, this proportion, that the professional athletes were reproached, bringing about hypertrophy of a single part while they neglected the varied exercises which would develop the body as a whole. Socrates praises the youth called upon to entertain, by his dancing, the guests at a banquet given by Callias: " No part of his body was inactive; neck, legs, and hands—all were in motion; so should dance anyone who desires to have a supple body." He thus avoids having " stout legs and thin shoulders, like the stadium runners, or stout shoulders and thin legs, like the wrestlers," and " he obtains correct proportions for the whole of his exercised body."[1] " Think you," says Galen, " that I praise running and other exercises which make the body lean ? Not at all; I blame a lack of proportion where-ever I may find it." Alone among the athletes the competitors for the pentathlum who use all their members in turn, possess this desirable balance; and, said Aristotle, " these are the handsomest men because they are both strong and supple at the same time."

The head must not destroy this harmony or attract attention to itself by a too great intensity of thought or feeling. The ideal was a calm and well-balanced intellectual life that was master of the senses—a perfect correspondence between the physical and mental life. The 5th century statues show men who are both apt for the intellectual labours necessitated by the conduct of public and private affairs and for the physical labours entailed by war. Man presented himself to the onlooker confident in his bodily beauty; he seemed to experience the joy of living, of being naked, and having beautiful limbs harmoniously forming a perfect rhythm. This ideal, however, was not always attained, and the pro-fessional athletes, whose bodies were already rendered dis-

[1] Xenophon's *Banquet*.

harmonic owing to some unique exercise, frequently allowed the body to dominate the mind. Euripides was one of the first to combat this abuse of physical exercises, and he proclaims his despite for muscular strength by itself. Athletes had fine bodies without thought; they were statues minus souls. " To eat, drink, sleep, unload the belly, and roll in the mud and dust—such is the athlete's existence," said Galen. Side by side with the beautiful effigies of the complete athlete, there are others in which the artist has not feared to emphasize brutality and the absence of all intellectual life. The head of the ephebus of Tarsus (Constantinople Museum, 5th century)[1] is that of a limited being: such is often the aspect of Heracles, the hero famous for his simpleness and gluttony.[2] The pugilist of the Terme museum[3] (3rd century) and the Roman wrestlers on a Lateran mosaic[4] are nothing but low brutes.

The Greeks had frequent occasion to see youthful and naked bodies and to appreciate their beauty. Artists, people of extremely fine sensibility and feeling, had this love of the living form to a more intense degree than other folk. In the palæstra and the games they could contemplate it in its most diverse aspects, relaxed in repose or the muscles contracted in violent movement. They studied the musculature, attitudes and gestures of this human body when it was vibrating with life, not cold and inert as the bored model presents himself to modern sculptors in their studios, and so they were able to pass on into their work the freshness and spontaneity of the real thing.

This study was imposed on the artists not merely by their æsthetic vision but by social conditions. The champions in the games were proud of their victories which were at the same time a victory for their city. They wanted to perpetuate that memory for ever and they ordered statues of themselves from the artists, and these effigies were set up in the sacred enclosure in never-ending homage to the divinity.[5] These effigies showed the subject as he was, ready for the fray, as he appeared in the arena, or as he was when victorious;

[1] **LXXIII**, p. 125; RA, 1899, ii, p. 19; REG, 1899, p. 453.
[2] Cf. the head in the British Museum, **LXX**, p. 179, Fig. 75.
[3] **LXII**, vol. ii, p. 492.
[4] Helbig, *Guide dans les musées d'archéologie classique de Rome.* Fr. trans. by Toutain, i, p. 524, No. 702.
[5] **CCV**; **CLXXXV**, *s.v.* " Statua, Ludi publici."

they were rarely draped—usually nude. Sometimes they were shown in repose holding some attribute such as the instrument of their victory or the crown or wreath received as prize; sometimes they were shown in violent action, carrying out their exploit, as in Myron's Diskobolos. From the time of the earliest athletic statues of the 6th century at Olympia, namely those of Praxidamas of Ægina and Rhexibius of Opunte, up to the closing period of Greek art, the images of wrestlers, runners and pugilists could be counted by hundreds, because with each returning festival their number increased. The vase-painters, like the sculptors, who watched the ephebus and the man in his prime exercising in the palæstra, did not forget the winning athletes, and they commemorated the runners with stout legs on the panathenaic amphoræ[1] which were given as prizes. Death itself became the pretext for this glorification of the body, because the stele of the dead frequently called to mind that he had once been a champion; he would be represented with the discus, which seemed to form a saint's aureole for his head (Diskophoros stele, Athens, 6th century);[2] or, helmeted, he would be running swiftly in the strange attitude of the archaic race (stele of the Hoplito-dromos, Athens, 6th century).[3]

Peloponnesian art more especially delighted from its inception in athletic statuary. Among the works of a Pytha-goras of Rhegium (first half of the 5th century)[4] one finds practically nothing but figures of athletes; there is not a single isolated statue of a woman, only a few draped male figures and a few legendary or divine subjects. Polyclitus[5] likewise glorifies the athlete's strength by choice.

The civic rôle and the importance of gymnastics gave to Greek art a virile character; just as, in the city, where woman played an obscure and minor part, man for a long time pre-dominated in artistic representations.

Was this man at every stage from his infancy to his old age ? The subjects might well demand such variety. Never-theless, the age preferred by the artist was that in which the young and vigorous man had just reached the plenitude of his

---

[1] Brauchitsch, *Die Panathenäische Preisamphoren;* **XCII,** p. 70; **CXLIV,** vol. x, p. 128.

[2] **LXXXIV,** vol. viii, p. 664.   [3] *Ibid.,* p. 649.

[4] **CLXIV.**   [5] **CLXVII, CLXXI.**

development, having lost the softness and roundness of child-hood, the lankness and awkwardness of early adolescence, yet before maturity could fill him out and make him heavy-looking or age could sap his energies. This was the age of the Apollo and Omphalos[1] (about 460), of the Diskobolos, Dory-phoros, and Diadumenos. These youths, in the full flower of their sixteen to twenty summers, are to be seen every-where, in statues in the round, on reliefs and vase-paintings, and in terra cotta figurines. They are beardless, or at the most their cheeks are furnished with a light down that just begins to show near their ears.[2] Sometimes, although already perfectly muscled, they are even younger and their fourteen years are still impubescent (ephebus No. 698 of the Acropolis, earlier than 480;[3] Polyclitan ephebi). Such is the type which became paramount from the 6th century, which is celebrated by the sculptors of Kouroi and which persists to the very end in Greek art—the wonderful body of healthy youth, with its muscular strength and suppleness that is yet quietly graceful at the same time. Sure of their beauty these ephebi remained modest and full of reserve and control. Look at them as they go past, grave and calm, with head modestly bent, on the frieze of the Panathenæa. They know that they are the city's glory and that its future is with them, but they still maintain their respectful submission to those who have gone before them and who teach them to become useful citizens. They it is who are sung by the poets and praised by the philosophers, and it is they whom the artists eternalize. They are at the age of that most perfect beauty which arouses universal attention—a kind of religious emotion. "Beauty has about it something royal, particularly when, as it was then in Autolycus, it is united with modesty and self-respect. As a light burning brightly in the night-time draws all eyes to it, so did the beauty of Autolycus draw upon him the gaze of all. Not one among the guests who looked upon him but had his soul moved; some fell silent, others made some gesture. . . ." "If, then, I am really beautiful, said Crito-bulus, ' and if I produce on you the same impression produced on me by someone beautiful, I swear by all the gods that I would rather have beauty than a king's power. Indeed, I

---

[1] **LXXII**, vol. i, p. 405.   [2] Xenophon's *Banquet*.
[3] **LXXVIII**, p. 452.

contemplate Clinias with greater pleasure than all that is
most beautiful among men, and I would gladly suffer blindness
to all else than Clinias; night and sleep are accursed because
I can no longer behold him, and I know infinite delight when
day breaks and the sun returns because they will enable me
again to see Clinias."[1]

This preference sometimes became exclusive. From the
6th century the Peloponnesian studios, then, at the beginning
of the 5th century, the Argive school of Ageladas and his
disciples, devoted themselves to the glorification of the
bodies of ephebi more than to any other subject, and Polyclitus, who followed in their footsteps, avoids representing
ripe age. Time accentuated the tendency. There are
plenty of bearded men in the black-figure pottery of the 6th
century; there are less in the red-figure pottery of the 5th
century, in which the invasion of the ephebi, who supplanted
even the gods, is complete.

The artist was haunted by this youthful and athletic
type, and he sought to bring back all forms of human life
to this common æsthetic model. He did not fail to recognize
that both sexes and all ages have each their beauty: "Just
as the child has its beauty, so has the adolescent, the mature
man, and the aged. As witness the Thallophori of Athena,
who are chosen from among the handsome old men as though
to proclaim that beauty belongs to all ages."[2] Nevertheless,
the various stages of life do not interest them so much by
their appropriate features differentiating one from the other,
as by their resemblance to this ideal type; in their eyes the
child and the adolescent foreshadow and prepare for the age
of the ephebus, the mature man prolongs it, and the aged man
preserves its memory in diminished form.

For a long time children interest artists very little. Their
presence was necessary in certain subjects; from the earliest
times the Aphrodite kourotrophos held a child in her arms;
Demeter the maternal cares for it in the Homeric hymn.
On vases and in reliefs the child takes his part in the funeral
scenes of the family, standing on his own small legs or carried
by his mother or a servant. He plays with his dog, a hoop,
or pulls a little cart, or as a small serving lad he accompanies
his master. But the artist for long seems unaware of a

[1] Xenophon's *Banquet*.   [2] *Ibid.*

child's specific form with its rounded contours in which the
muscles do not show, its plumpness and its proportionately
large head. A child is represented as a grown-up person in
miniature. Under the influence of the gymnastic ideal he is
a tiny athlete, an ephebus in little with an ephebus' spare
frame and firm muscles. Thus did 5th-century art conceive
him. On a red-figure vase of severe style[1] at Wurzburg it
is difficult to tell if the figure represents a child who has
just received domestic chastisement with a sandal—whose
imprint remains—or a lover who has been roughly sent flying
by his rival. A few potters, always more realistic than the
sculptors and great painters, do occasionally show some
interest in ages outside the common ideal. Brygus (beginning of the 5th century) draws a small boy playing a pipe
and leaning against a bearded man; or a Satyr chastising
his child with a sandal—and here for the first time one notes
Satyrs of different ages—or a young girl, whose figure looks
to be about fourteen years in age, dancing.[2]—Tentative but
still imperfect efforts in a new direction which sculpture was
only to make at a very much later date. At the close of the
5th century Euripides took pleasure in little children, and
here, as in so many other ways, literature was ahead of plastic
art. In the 4th century, when realism began to assert itself,
Plutus and Dionysus were still no more than accessory to the
groups of Cephisodotus (after 371) and Praxiteles (about
340), in which the interest was centred in the adult figures
of Eirene and Hermes. Yet there is a sensible difference
between the two. Cephisodotus still accords to the child
no more than an indifferent regard; Praxiteles conceives
the head and body with greater truth. In Hellenistic times
the child had definitely conquered his place in art.[3] He was
now reproduced for his own sake, because it gave pleasure
to see him at his games and in his struggles, smiling or put
out; he no longer masquerades in a grown-up body with a
musculature beyond his years, but is shown as he is in all his
gaucherie and indeterminate curves of his body. Roman
art was to go so far as to sculp charming heads of new-born
infants. One cannot attribute the tardiness of this conquest
entirely to the watering-down of the ephebic ideal because

[1] AM, xxx, p. 404.   [2] VI, vol. iii, p. 239.
[3] Ibid., p. 387.

Christian iconography evolved in the same way.[1] In all lands and in every period art began with indeterminate types which lent themselves indifferently to divers uses, and only by degrees differentiated them by giving them their appropriate features.

The body of the full-grown and bearded man is frequently younger than its age; in it one perceives not only the effect of gymnastics which keep it robust and prevent it from putting on flesh, but also of this ephebic ideal.

"When years advance and old age arrives" says an Egyptian text, " weakness and second childhood come, and with each day a new misery falls upon it—the eyes grow dim, the ears close up, and strength ebbs, although the heart continues beating; the lips grow silent, the spirit darkens and yesterday is no longer remembered; the bones are full of pain, all that is good becomes bad, and savour completely vanishes: old age brings misery to a man in all things." This gloomy picture of the miseries of age would have been subscribed to by the Greeks. Achilles might admire the handsome and dignified figure of the elderly Priam seated before him, but Priam himself confesses that the dead body of a young man is always beautiful but that of an old man is repellent. The Greeks symbolized old age in the guise of a decrepit being, ugly and repulsive, which the vigorous athlete, Heracles, vanquishes; it is the λυγρὸν γέρας.

Art avoids the picture of an enfeebled man regretful of his vanished strength and beauty. It is represented but seldom on the funerary lecythi and the stelæ of the 5th century. Death beautified the body; far from perpetuating the memory of its collapse, it gives to it an idealized image; it is no longer what it was at the moment of passing but what it was in former days, what it would wish to be—young and beautiful. It is true that there were, during the classic period, a few realistic representations of old age, particularly in vase-painting. On the kyathos of Pistoxenus,[2] the old Linus is teaching Iphicles, and Geropse, a bent and wrinkled female servant with a scraggy neck, accompanies Heracles—a sketch from the life which testifies to close observation on the part of the potters at a time when sculptors still neglected it. At

---

[1] **VI**, vol. iii, p. 390.
[2] **CXXIX**, p. 178; **CXLIV**, vol. viii, p. 587.

the most one may note on the eastern pediment at Olympia (about 460) the torso of an old man grown meagre in his age, with a fat, soft, creased chest. But more often painters and sculptors rejuvenate their old men, and avoid unsteady poses and flabby or creased flesh. These robust and handsome ancients are to be distinguished only by a stick, by their white hair and beards and their slight baldness. On the frieze of the Panathenæa they have almost youthful bodies.[1] In the 4th century and particularly in Hellenistic times the artist begins to take note of the wear and tear of age; thenceforward he makes any number of images of old and drunken women and of old peasant men and women.[2]

Gods and heroes caught the contagion. Some among them have a perfect right to the bodies of athletes because, like Theseus and Heracles, they had fought against their foes and accomplished great exploits; whereas others among them, such as Apollo and Hermes, had instituted the gymnastic games and were their protectors. But all look as though they had been fashioned and moulded in some heavenly palæstra. This was not yet the period (dating from the 4th century) in which Eros, Dionysus and Apollo became languid and effeminate, with soft and tender bodies, even taking on an equivocal character. Whatever their name or age, all were extremely muscular. In the 5th century Eros is still a vigorous boy, not the lively child of the Hellenists. Hermes and Apollo realize the full beauty of twenty summers. And the gods—Hermes and Dionysus—whom artists delighted to represent as majestic and bearded, in the 6th century, grew young and beardless.

The imagists of neolithic Greece, like all primitives, emphasized the physiological features proper to woman, exaggerating the breasts, the thighs, and the pudenda (example: steatopygous idol at Knossos); the authors of the eneolithic idols of the Cyclades (about 3000–2200 B.C.) even represent the female form in pregnancy, doubtless with the intention of bringing about actual fertility by means of sympathetic magic. Archaic art distinguishes the sexes by colour—reddish brown for men and white for women—by a differently shaped eye, in the paintings on Corinthian vases,[3]

[1] **VI**, vol. iii, p. 239.   [2] *Ibid.*, p. 396.
[3] **CXLV**, vol. ii, p. 508.

and by divers other means. But woman's anatomical characters are still unrecognized by the artist. The Korai of the
6th century have flat chests and narrow, boyish hips. Men
and women alike wear their hair long, and sometimes one is
inclined to hesitate, when faced with isolated heads, as to
which is which. This indeterminateness had not altogether
disappeared in the 5th century; the Bologna head,[1] which
is now recognized as that of the Lemnian Athena of Phidias
(towards 450) was once considered to be masculine. Here,
too, the ephebic ideal exerts its attraction. Female bodies
in the 5th century are large in frame, and the facial features
are virile. The Giustiniani Hestia (towards 460), certainly,
is innocent of all the graces![2] Standing squarely, hand on
hip, she seems more disposed to combat than to smile or
please. When a woman did bare her body, it was thick-set
and robust, with muscles ready for action; the abdomen
was flat, the hips narrow. In the words of Taine, these
women are " strong as horses." Yet some thousand years
or so earlier the plastic appearance of women, at a time
when Cretan naturalism rendered it with astonishing truth,
had been very different. In Greece we have to wait until
the 4th century and Hellenistic times to see the artist not
merely unveil woman completely but represent her specific
features realistically. What a difference is there between
the Esquiline Aphrodite (towards 460)[3] and the Aphrodite
of the sandal of Polycharmus[4] or the stooping Aphrodite of
Diodalses,[5] whose bodies are graceful and voluptuous and
their flesh soft and delicate ![6]

[1] **LXX**, Pl. iii. [2] **LIX**, Pl. 491.
[3] **LXII**, vol. ii, p. 686. [4] *Ibid.*, p. 586.
[5] *Ibid.*, p. 585.
[6] See, on the evolution of the female figure, **VI**, vol iii, pp. 63, 66,
238, 345.

CHAPTER VIII

ART, ITS CIVIC TEACHING. SOCIAL RÔLE OF THE ARTIST

Up to the close of the 5th century art was essentially the expression of the city. It shed beauty all about it, it was true, but its aim was primarily didactic; it did not so much seek to please as to instruct; it addressed itself not so much to the heart or to the emotions, as to the reason and the mind. It tried to inculcate great and noble ideas in the mind of every citizen.

Closely bound up with religion, art was an instruction in theology. It had to inculcate in the people faith in their gods, to teach them the great mystic truths through beauty. Seeing always around him these gods—multiplied by art in the temples and even on vases—who were superhuman and yet so like to man, the Greek understood that they were powerful because they were victorious over monsters and foes, that they were everywhere present, protecting the city and directing human destinies. While it safeguarded its æsthetic independence, art in Greece was a powerful auxiliary of faith; it was " an instruction in theology, a veritable Bible of legend, just as the façades of Gothic cathedrals were an encyclopædia of the ideas of the day " (Boutmy).

It was also a lesson in patriotism. It perpetuated in the sight of all the glory of the mythical and real forebears of the people who had fought to insure for their descendants a strong and prosperous city, and it stimulated them to follow in their steps.[1] These sculptured heroes, these Lapiths overthrowing the Centaurs, and these Greeks of legend vanquishing Amazons and Trojans—Theseus and Heracles triumphing over monsters—seemed to be echoing to all men the valiant counsels which the aged Tyrtæus gave to the Spartans: " It is a fine thing for a brave man to die in the front rank of those who fight for their country. . . . Let

[1] See above, p. 72.

106

each one, standing squarely on his feet, rooted to the ground, and biting his lips, keep firm, his legs, loins and arms well covered by his great buckler. Let each one raise the mighty spear in his right hand, with the terrible plume waving on his helm. Foot to foot, shield against shield, waving plumes mingling and helmets clashing, let the warriors press breast to breast, each sword and spear-point meeting in shock of battle." In their Agora, and standing before the group of Harmodius and Aristogeiton, the Athenians would think of all those who had sacrificed their lives to make Athens free, and as they sang the famous scolia of the Tyrannicides they would vow that they, too, would carry a sword in the branch of myrtle. The many works of art which commemorate the glorious or tragic episodes of Greek history constituted so many appeals to the best in them. Looking at them, their consciousness of their own worth became ever clearer; they took tremendous pride in this race of theirs which was so superior to the despicable barbarians. The monuments confirm Pericles' words: " When you feel its greatness, remember that we owe it to men who, by their courage, their sense of duty and their fear of shame, were leaders in fighting and who, when they thought themselves abandoned by fortune, instead of also depriving their country of the support of their strong right arm, spent themselves generously in carrying out this sacred obligation. By sacrificing their lives to the republic each one of them won undying praise and found the most illustrious sepulture less in the tomb which holds their ashes than in the recollection of their glory by posterity whenever there are deeds to be sung or exploits to be performed."[1]

Pictures of ephebi at exercise on vases, and statues of athletes in the sanctuaries, confirmed in the mind of the Greek this necessity to develop and maintain his bodily strength that he might place it at the service of his country and be ready to defend her in danger, as his forefathers, the gods and heroes, had done before him.

Art, which was the expression of national feeling, at the same time kept its flame alive and brought it to a white heat.

The artist who created pictorial or plastic forms, and the people who furnished him with the occasion for creation,

[1] Thucydides, ii, 41.

knew that they were not working for themselves or their own times alone but for the future glory of their city and their race. Such monuments, unlike great political exploits, were " brilliant testimonials " which, said Pericles, " will insure to us the admiration both of our contemporaries and of posterity. In the time to come we shall be the object of world admiration as we already are to-day." [1] The plan for the embellishment of Athens conceived by Pericles was an æsthetic programme, but it was likewise political. Athens must dominate as much by her beauty as by her commerce and her warlike strength. The people understood this. Malcontents might find the cost exaggerated or disapprove of the employment for luxury building of allied tribute which had aforetime been spent on common defence against the Persians, but Pericles' answer to them was that " this wealth ought to be used for works which, when finished, will be productive of immortal glory." [2] Time has proved him right. If ancient Greece still lives in our thought and in our hearts it is not on account of her warlike exploits, since splendid national victories over the foreigner also call to mind civil and fratricidal strife, but because of the æsthetic and spiritual contribution she has made to the common heritage of the human race. Subject as they are to the vicissitudes of greatness and decadence, States disappear, but knowledge and beauty live for ever.

The part which the artist is called upon to play in Greek society is a natural consequence of this conception of art. He was not merely an " artist," having no personal concern in the destiny of the State, as, often enough, he is in our day. A citizen, he participated in the life of the city, in which he had an essential place. These were not yet the times in which Protogenes, absorbed in his art, went on quietly painting his Satyr while Demetrius Poliorcetes besieged Rhodes. " It is only among us " said Pericles, " that a citizen who remains estranged from national affairs passes not for a lover of quiet but for a man who is of no use." [3] On the contrary, " there are among us men who attend to their own and to the republic's business at the same time, and artisans who have a sufficiently profound knowledge of the interests of the State." [4] How many were the artists who, like Socrates,

---

[1] Thucydides, ii, 41.
[2] Plutarch's *Pericles*.
[3] Thucydides, ii, 41.
[4] *Ibid.*, 40.

who was at once a soldier and a philosopher, and Thucydides, who was a strategist and a historian as well, were both actors in the great events of the Persian wars and competent to celebrate them with enthusiasm! In the 4th century Cephisodotus was a member of the triarchy, and in the 3rd Euboulides was a proxenos and epimeletes in Athens. Foreign artists were readily accorded the title of citizen; statesmen were not afraid to ally themselves with them, and Phocion the strategist married the sister of Cephisodotus. Cities frequently demonstrated their gratitude to artists because they had exalted national life by means of beauty; though Phidias was unfortunate, being persecuted by the enemies of Pericles, others were honoured, and, like the painter Nicias, had a public sepulture on the road to the Academy.

In the Dorian cities their social rôle was less evident than in Athens. The ancient prejudice of the Dorian warriors forbade any free citizen to gain his living by manual labour, so the practice of art was left to pericæci and foreigners. It is true that even in Athens there were a few philosophers who feared that art might distract the citizen from the performance of his prime duty, and so excluded the artist from a Utopian city. Plato—and Aristotle agreed with him—desired that the astynomeus should reprimand those citizens who wished to become artisans and who thus might turn aside from what should be their main preoccupation, virtue and the State. But they could not fail to recognize the educational potentiality of works of art, and, in any case, these were but isolated protests.

CHAPTER IX

TRANSFORMATION IN THE SOCIAL CHARACTER
OF GREEK ART

THE character of Greek art as we have now analyzed it was maintained unimpaired until the 4th century, and the 5th century was the period in which this apotheosis of the religious and national life by art was most marked. But the unhappy rivalry between Athens and Sparta (Peloponnesian war of 431-404) led to the ruin of the Athenian empire and the exhaustion of all Greece, and to the substitution of a monarchy for the governments of the Hellenic free cities. These political changes had their repercussion on art, both in its outward manner and in the part it had hitherto played in the life of the nation. Though the old inspiration was there until the end, it had neither the force nor the exclusive character it possessed in former times, for new tendencies appeared which art was bound to satisfy. These begin to be apparent from the 4th century and produced their full effect in Hellenistic and imperial times.[1]

Independent Greece was no more; Cheronea (228) had seen it crumble. Political power, which had formerly been in the hands of the citizens in oligarchic and democratic cities, was now concentrated in the hands of one man, often a foreigner, who was the absolute ruler of his subjects and dispensed both honours and punishment. A brilliant court was formed about him and this gave the tone to the rest of society. The artist renounced the aspirations of former days that he might win the favour of the prince and his courtiers.

Art ceased to serve the city exclusively and placed herself at the disposal of kings and princes. Phidias had immortalized Athena and the Olympian Zeus, and Polyclitus had celebrated the athletic champions. Lysippus (second quarter of the 4th century, about 300) for his part made innumerable

[1] See above, p. 62 ff.; **VI,** vol. iii, pp. 259, 311; **LXI, LXV, LXIX; LXII,** vol. ii, pp. 173, 443.

images of Alexander whom he elevated to divine rank. He
had the privilege of signing the royal statues while Apelleo
alone was authorized to paint the conqueror's features and
Pyrgoteles to engrave them on precious stones. Here was
something quite new in the history of Greek art—the advent
of the court artist. The prince was glorified by his images
and the recital of his exploits: does not the Pergamum frieze
(towards 180 B.C.) commemorate the wars of the Pergamenian princes against the Galatæ in the mythic guise of a
fight between gods and giants ? Sumptuous buildings, porticoes and stoas were built in the name of the king. Luxury,
love of the colossal and grandiose, pompousness and theatrical
display,[1] the very things Greek art had once avoided, now
appeared, and were distinct features of Pergamenian art.
For the link with the East, long since snapped, was renewed
with the introduction of the new régime, and its tendencies
were once more to influence Hellenic art.

Greece, following in the footsteps of Alexander's conquests, went out beyond her own borders: the barriers between
East and West were now definitely down, and henceforth
there was to be a continual coming and going between them.
Greeks settled in the new cities of Asia Minor, Syria and
Egypt, in Antioch and in Alexandria. They travelled in
lands hitherto hostile or unknown to them, drawn thither
by prospects of gain, by the desire to seek knowledge, or in
search of adventure. Orientals came to Greece and made
their own civilization known at first hand. Commercial
relations developing with more and more success poured
Hellenic productions into the East and Oriental goods into
Greece. There was no longer a hedge between Greeks and
Barbarians; thanks to Alexander and his successors, who
united under their single authority diverse races, a cosmo-
politan era began. The artists, who had once despised the
barbarian, began to get interested in the new races with
whom he was brought into contact and made an effort to
characterize different breeds by their specific features. The
differences between separate schools, so marked in the 5th
century, tended to become obscured from the 4th century
onward. The great masters travelled more. Scopas worked
at Tegea, but also at the Mausoleum of Halicarnassus (to-

[1] See above, p 62.

wards 353) and at Ephesus.[1] There was more effectual give
and take between studios. Art gradually acquired that
international character which was its hall-mark during the
Hellenistic period.

There was a levelling of social classes after Alexander.
In the cities of independent Greece a man had to be a citizen
and to enjoy a citizen's political rights before he could attain
to a position of any influence, and foreigners were kept aloof,
like the slaves. Now a man's origin mattered little. Each
one made his way on his own merits, and the king elevated
or abased men as seemed to him good. Adventurers and
parvenus began to play an important part. Social distinctions which the artist had once conveyed by so many
subtle shades[2] grew less discernible. The gods themselves
did not scruple to take the nonchalant and familiar attitudes
once reserved for the lower orders. In the 5th century the
vase-painters had had a monopoly of familiar and often
trivial scenes; but now, as early as the 4th century, Leochares
represents a slave dealer, and Lysippus a drunken female
pipe player, while the Hellenists made any number of images
of this kind. The high-born Greek no longer monopolized
attention, and the humblest classes of society, the world of
small folk, of keepers of booths, pedlars, peasants, shepherds
and fishermen was opened to the artists in all its variety.
The characters in the mimes of Herondas are those of familiar
life, busybodies, slave-dealers and schoolmasters; in the
mime of the Syracusans, Theocritus puts humble townsfolk
on the stage, and, in his idylls, peasants and shepherds.
Plastic art no longer despised peasants wrinkled with age,
carrying a lamb or driving a cow to market, or noisy and
quarrelsome street urchins.[3]

Thanks, partly, to this intermingling of social classes
formerly quite distinct, and partly to other causes, realism,
which had been confined to the lower orders, now invaded
the whole of art, and we shall see its effects presently.

Individualism, which had been seeking to break its chains
ever since the 4th century, now triumphs. The Greek no
longer takes an active part in the government of his country
as he had done in his free city; hence he no longer concerns

---

[1] **LXII**, vol. ii, pp. 321, 386; **CLIX.**   [2] See above, p. 81.
[3] **LXII**, vol. ii, p. 404.

himself with his country's business, and concentrates his attention on his private affairs. Artists and savants confine themselves to their arts and sciences. They keep apart from the herd and meet together in select circles, a custom which crystallized into its final form in the museum of Alexandria. The philosophers strengthened this tendency; whereas Plato and Aristotle claimed that the common life alone is good, their successors preached withdrawal from mundane, national and family interests and from all attachments which could restrict their personal liberty. Henceforth personal interest alone comes into play, doing away with the ideals of solidarity and patriotism. Certain forms of literature develop which answer to these new tendencies. These forms no longer treat of the collective life of a city or a people but of this or that individual, and biographies in particular become numerous. Man has become of even greater interest than the gods, not merely man, the hero, who vanquished barbarians and monsters, but ordinary man who has done nothing wonderful and has no other merit than that he is.

Hence the individualistic character of art. The artist puts himself at the service of private persons. He seeks the accidental rather than the general. Portraits become numerous; in every genre there is insistence on the characteristic detail which differentiates the models, and on the divergences in age, sex, race or environment.

The artist has become emancipated. From the 4th century onward he has no longer had solely at heart the greatness of his city and the glory of his forbears and his gods; he no longer modestly joins his own efforts to those of all the other citizens in pursuing a common ideal. He has become independent and he is more concerned with producing a personal piece of work than in docilely following a tradition.

The position of the artist begins to grow in dignity with the 4th century, and in the Hellenistic period it becomes higher still. Extravagant prices are paid for his work, and honours are heaped upon him. Princes, who show their enthusiasm for art by bestowing great privileges, themselves sometimes practise the arts, as, for instance, Attala III of Pergamum (198-133). Women, who now occupy themselves with politics, literature and science, take up painting; drawing, which had made its way into the schools in the 4th

F

century, now becomes a regular feature of education and
teaches children to appreciate works of art. Hence the
artist's pride, which is flattered by this general interest—
pride which is betrayed in their works only too often.

The Greek, who now seeks his own good before the glory
of his city, no longer possesses the old simplicity. Although
the State no longer undertakes great artistic schemes revealing
the soul of an entire people, luxury is on the increase among
private persons. Funerary monuments become more and
more sumptuous, and a degree restraining them is issued by
Demetrius of Phalerum (317-307). Official offerings are still
plentiful, but testify rather to the pride and fortune of the
victor than to his gratitude to the gods. Read what Curtius
has to say in his lively sketch of Hellenistic manners: " Now
they neglected everything of public utility, and building was
only concerned with the luxury and ease of a few wealthy
citizens. The rich made a display of their wealth out of
vanity; Athens and its neighbourhood was covered with
palatial dwellings. People gloried in having numbers of
servants, sumptuous teams and equipages, and costly garments
and furniture. . . ."

Having abandoned the manly occupations of a free citizen,
the Greek increasingly sought after pleasure. " Festivals
became the main object in life and were treated with the
greatest gravity as though they constituted the most important business of the community. But the noble ideas
which were at the root of the old Athenian festivals, such
as grateful glorification of the gods and the enthusiastic
cultivation of the most noble arts, were relegated to the
background."[1]

Woman played a great part in this elegant and refined
civilization, a part hitherto unknown. She was no longer
limited to her domestic functions in the gynæceum; she
appeared at court; she interested herself practically in literature and in the arts and sciences, and in politics. She
dominated especially by her beauty and her sensuous attrac-
tions. The cult of Woman dates from the Hellenistic period,
and it was then that the earliest instances of chivalric gallantry
appeared.

This Hellenistic society was voluptuous. The literature

[1] Curtius's *Greek History*.

of the time abounds in erotic and often scabrous writing, and it did not hesitate to modify the ancient myths in this sense. Physical love is the basis of Alexandrian poetry.

Woman invaded art, and in graceful form. The Aphrodite of Cnidus (middle of the 4th century) is still too vigorous, and her nudity remains chaste, but the Hellenistic Aphrodites, the Nymphs and Mænads of the sculptors, and the young women whom the koroplastes of Myrina[1] love to model, appear sensual, of easy virtue, and provocative, rather like the courtesans of the period, and from their form there emanates a disturbingly voluptuous charm. Masculine gesture becomes gallant for their sake. Perseus assists Andromeda to descend from her rock in the manner of a young seigneur assisting a fair lady to alight from her carriage[2] (Pl. V.). The terra cottas of Asia Minor are sometimes over-pretty and affected—a coquettish young woman will be examining her toilette, and another turning to admire the effect of her trailing garments.[3] Woman excites the passions, and her nakedness fans the emotions of the Hellenists.

Olympus did not escape the backwash of this altered Greek mentality. To the grave and austere divinities of the 5th century men now preferred the gods of the senses and passions, Aphrodite and Eros, Dionysus and his train, Satyrs and Mænads—subjects which permitted of the sensuous appeal of the bodies of women and ephebi being emphasized without reserve, and of the passions being stimulated. Aphrodite is a mortal woman, more courtesan than goddess, whose one concern seems to be to enhance her charms by feigning to veil them. Nymphs allow themselves to be caught by Satyrs; recumbent Hermaphrodites set themselves athrill in voluptuous dreaming, or delight to contemplate their own ambiguous forms.

The clean-built form of the athlete is still in favour but no longer exclusively. Instead of making their women and children virile, as in the 5th century, artists now make their young gods effeminate, and bestow on them a soft and sensitive beauty. Praxiteles had already conceived his Apollo, his Eros and his Satyrs thus, and the Hellenists go further still. Hellenistic poetry shows a preference for delicate and youthful countenances with white skin and pink cheeks, and

[1] CXII.   [2] LXII, vol. ii, p. 571.   [3] CX-CXII.

long silken curls. Apollo comes very near to being an Herma-phrodite, and Eros and Dionysus become androgynous in the Myrina terra cottas.

The art of the 5th century tended to bring all ages of life back to the ephebic ideal—children and old men, as well as women, shared in its vigorous qualities. Now that realism has asserted itself, not only does art become interested in the most humble social ranks, in foreigners, in women whose specific features it observes, but it seeks also to characterize the various ages of life, and in Hellenistic art children and old men take on the appearance which is proper to them.

The misfortunes of the Peloponnesian war have caused the Greeks to lose confidence in the gods who were unable to save them. Under the pressure of the scepticism which troubled their spirit, as in all periods of social disintegration, they turned to new gods who stimulated the senses and the passions. The official religion seemed cold and impotent; scepticism grew, and respect for the gods vanished with the vanishing of belief. Myths increasingly became for the artists themes suited to stimulate their virtuosity and their wit; they emptied them of their primitive meaning, and in Hellenistic times they become nothing but a vast repertory from which artists and poets can draw, as artists and poets, without being at the pains to go deeply into what they no longer understand. Allegories, which had hitherto had a serious symbolic meaning which was both sincere and religious, are now graceful themes without any value, in which the ingeniousness, the subtlety and the delicacy of the Hellenist spirit is given full play.

The gods who had already come close to earth in the 4th century now descend still lower from their former high ideality. Hermes covers his face with ashes to frighten the disobedient children of his colleagues. The small Artemis, aged three, pays a visit to Hephæstus' smithy, sits on the knees of Briareus and plucks a handful of hair from his shaggy chest. Eros and Ganymede play at knuckle bones, and Cypris, in order to induce his son to enflame the heart of Medea, has to promise him a pretty toy. Olympus has become a bourgeois household. If art treats of the gods and goddesses, it is to despoil them of their greatness and to bring mytho-logical legend within the compass of the various happenings of everyday existence. Aphrodite is seen at her toilet preparing for the bath; as a mother she covers Eros with kisses and presses him close in her arms; but she also learns to castigate the little rascal who crouches fearfully at her feet.[1]

The art of the 5th century was profoundly religious. Its supreme goal was the temple and the temple's decoration. With the increase of individualism and scepticism it relinquishes the exclusive service of the gods to satisfy also the desires of men. Following the general law of evolution, human activities lose their primitive religious and supernatural character with the passage of time, to become rationa: and humanist. The secularization of art increases from the 4th century. Gods and the dead still receive the time-honoured homage, but they have no monopoly of it—the living also claim their share. They desire larger, moːe substantial and more handsome dwellings. The many ruins of private houses and of Greek cities at Priene, Pergamum and Delos[2] date only from this period. Public life calls for its stoas, porticoes, gymnasia and market-places to be larger, more sumptuous and built of handsome materials. The interiors are decorated with statues, statuettes, paintings, and small pictures. Decorative groups stand out against the green background in the gardens and parks. Goldsmiths' work also becomes secularized and takes on a great importance. Formerly man subordinated himself to the gods; now he is their equal.

In older times art had been the product of the community and chose subjects to be understood by all. Now that it is no longer supported by faith and ancestral patriotism and that it essays before all to be personal and original, there comes a break between the people and art which is now become the domain of the élite; like literature, it no longer expresses the deepest feelings of the popular soul, and, like literature, it often demands considerable erudition of those who would understand it—one of the main characteristics, this, of Hellenistic culture. Inspiration is sought in literature and in erudite works. Mythological legends now begin to be known only at second-hand, through the poets who have sung them, as is the case to-day. The poets are read in order to find

[1] RA, 1903, vol. i, Pl. iii.   [2] See above, p. 55; LVII.

subjects, and the authors of the Anthology praise the artists who have faithfully followed literary descriptions.

Incomprehensible to the public at large, art loses its moral and patriotic character. In former days it affirmed by its grandiose creations the power of the gods and of the patria, and the piety of its citizens. The Pergamum frieze, and the ex voto of Attala,[1] still remind spectators of the courage of the Pergamenians who, under the protection of the gods, vanquished the Galatæ as the Greeks of the 6th century had vanquished the Persians, but these works tend more particularly to glorify the power of the prince who led them.

Art, which has broken its ties with the national and popular life, loses its didactic character; it no longer believes that it has a mission. It seeks above all to please by its beauty, to stimulate the æsthetic sense.

The close relation between the utilitarian and the beautiful is slackened. From the end of the 5th century, despite the protestations of Socrates and of his disciples against pure art, works that are merely beautiful are to be distinguished from those which are merely useful. This dissociation is still more clear in the Hellenistic period, in that elegant, voluptuous literary and learned society which no longer saw beauty in the exact conformity of form with ideal, but in form alone. The Hellenistic poets juggle with words as virtuosi; the artists, likewise, too often find their ideal in skilled technique independent of the subject represented or of its utility. They came to think that " the difficulty overcome is itself a thing of beauty " (Saint-Saëns), and that to please was enough. The theory of art for art's sake is not a modern one; it was born in the Hellenistic period.[2] Nevertheless, as we have said further back, there was never to be a complete divorce between art and the utilitarian; the Greek artist never creates a work whose sole aim is pleasure, æsthetic emotion and beauty. Utility, attenuated, has changed with the changing social circumstances; nevertheless it continues to be adapted to and to serve a transformed city.

[1] LXII, vol. ii, p. 496.   [2] VI, vol. iii, p. 446.

PART TWO

AGENTS FOR THE PRACTICAL APPLICATION OF ARTISTIC AIMS. GROUPS OF ARTISTS AND ARTISTIC PERSONALITIES

THE aim of Greek art having been ascertained we shall now study those agents for its practical application, the artists. Before we sum up the general features common to them all in that they were all Hellenes, we shall examine the variations comprehended in this unity and analyze the differences in spirit due to ethnic origin, social and geographical environment and personality. We shall take these points in the following order:

1. Ethnic groups;
2. Regional and local groups;
3. Artistic individualities.

CHAPTER I

ETHNIC GROUPS

DISTINCTIVE tendencies are to be discerned within the very real unity of Greek art, tendencies which are at times sharply indicated and at others are blended.

The three ethnic groups of Ionians, Dorians, and Attics which constitute the Greek nation each contribute a distinct note whose persistence can be recognized throughout the history of Greek art.

The brilliant Ægean civilization of Crete and the Peloponnese completely collapsed under the assaults of the Dorian peoples towards the 11th century B.C. A new world arose which was inspired with quite a new spirit[1]—the world of Hellenic Greece.

The Dorians,[2] coming from the North, occupied central Greece, crossed the isthmus and settled in the Peloponnese. Soon the whole of Greece, apart from a few districts such as mountainous Arcadia, became subject to them. Arrived at the sea, they embarked upon it and proceeded to conquer the islands which link the Peloponnese with Asia—Cythera, Crete, and Rhodes—and established themselves in the southern portion of Asia Minor which thenceforward bore their name —Doris. The isthmus of Corinth prevented them from reaching the Attic peninsula, and their subsequent efforts to conquer it were in vain. Attica, spared as a result of the legendary sacrifice of King Codrus, preserved its old inhabitants. Athens the hospitable, far from Central Greece and the Peloponnese, welcomed those who fled before the invasion, and this blend of the old populations was to form the Attic nation. Those who had been banished moved on further. Leaving the ports of Attica and Eubœa, under the leadership of their chieftains, they went eastward, landing on the coasts

---

[1] See in this series Jardé's *Formation of the Greek People*.

[2] Neubert, *Die dorische Wanderung*, Stuttgart, 1920; S. Casson, " The Dorian Invasion Reviewed," *The Antiquarian Journal*, 1921, p. 199.

of Asia Minor, and in their turn conquering the earlier possessors; they founded Æolis and Ionia, the latter destined, with her wealthy cities, to become the most powerful of the Greek states on Asiatic soil. This flux of populations, which continued for some time, appears to have come to an end towards the 10th century B.C. From that time forward the Hellenic nation was a constituted entity with its own characteristics. Whether Dorians, Attics or Ionians, all were Greeks, united by the ties of language and religion, and even of race, because the Dorian invaders were nothing but a restricted caste dominating the old population which preserved the same age-old traditions that were kept up in Attica and Ionia.[1]

Nevertheless, the irreducible antagonism between Dorians on the one hand and Ionians and Attics on the other dated from this period, and was to be the cause of many later dissensions, leading to the bloody Peloponnesian war which brought about the downfall of a free Greece. The Athenians knew that they were of different blood; they even forbade the Dorians access to their national sanctuary, the Acropolis; they called to mind their common origin with the Ionians to whom religious and political ties bound them. Had not the descendants of the kings of Attica led the emigrants to Ionia, and did not one of the laws of the Ionian Amphictyony lay it down that each federated city must be governed by a descendant of Codrus ? In the Peloponnesian war the Greek world was divided into two ethnic camps of Peloponnesian Dorians, and Ionians of Athens, the islands and the Asiatic coast. Thucydides constantly emphasizes this racial difference; the proud Dorians were continually recalling their ancient supremacy.[2] " Dorians," said Brasidas, " you go to fight the Ionians of whom you have ever been the conquerors "; and the Corinthians expressed surprise that the Potidæans, native Dorians, should be besieged by Ionians " which is the reverse of what used to be in former times."

This diversity of origin explains the artistic differences dividing these groups. Fundamental in nature, they were accentuated by geographical and social conditions. The Dorians, a warrior caste living uneasily in the midst of a

[1] See below, p. 140.
[2] Deonna, *Guerre du Péloponnèse et guerre mondiale*, 1923, p. 48.

conquered population, were obliged to maintain their ancient
warlike virtues unimpaired in order to insure their predominance in the peninsula. Disdainful of manual labour, they
left commerce, industry and the arts to their subjects. They
were enemies of the sea and their policy was continental.
The Ionians, on the contrary, living as they did on a narrow
strip of coastal territory and inhabiting towns which were
the termini of important lines of communication with the
interior along which flowed the wealth of Asia Minor and
Mesopotamia, were traders, navigators and industrial pro-
ducers, and, being in contact with Asiatic states, they came
to adopt the ideas and the taste of the Orient. The Attics,
whose peninsula is cut up and infertile, early turned to the
commerce and industry of the sea for their livelihood. Midway between the Peloponnese and Ionia, between Ionian
softness and Dorian dourness, they profited by what each
could offer them, reconciled their opposing tendencies, and
by this judicious balance achieved intellectual and artistic
supremacy.

CHAPTER II

IONIAN ART[1]

How brilliant was Ionian civilization up to the time when
Persia conquered the kingdom of Lydia (546)[2] whose
prosperous vassal Ionia had become! The twelve federated
cities, especially the three leading ones, Ephesus, Miletus and
Phocis, grew wealthy through their overland and maritime
trade, and extended their power, founding in the north
trading bases on the Thracian coasts, along the shores of the
Hellespont and the Euxine as far as the furthest point of the
Sea of Azov;[3] in the south they established settlements at
the Nile mouths which had been thrown open to them by
the phil-Hellenic pharaohs Psammetichus (666-612) and
Amasis (570); and in the west they ventured as far afield as
Corsica, Gaul and even Spain. The products of their industry
found their way everywhere. " In the middle of the 6th
century " says Curtius, " Miletus, the mother of eighty
colonies, was the proudest and most powerful of all Hellenic
cities."

Their intellectual flight was no less soaring than their
economic expansion was widespread. Science and literature
blossomed in Ionia when continental Greece, when Athens,
even, was still of no account in the history of science and the
arts. It was here that the main branches of Greek learning
were built up—mathematics and astronomy by Thales of
Miletus, geography by Anaximander of Miletus, philosophy
by Xenophanes of Colophon, Pherecydes and Pythagoras
of Samos, elegy by Callinus of Ephesus, lyric poetry by
Simonides of Amorgus, by Terpander, Alcæus, Sapho of
Lesbos, Mimnermus of Smyrna, and Anacreon of Teos,
morals by Phocylides of Miletus, history by the logographers
and Hecatæus, and fable by Æsop.

[1] **CCIX-X; CCXII-III; LXXXIV**, vol. viii, p. 252; **CXLIV**, vol. ix,
p. 397; **CXLV**, vol. ii, p. 486; **LXXVIII**, p. 168.
[2] **CCXIII.**
[3] **CCXX-I;** Minns, *Scythians and Greeks*, 1913.

It was here that Greek art began its conquests as it emerged from the Hellenic medieval age, a period of barbarism following the Dorian invasion. In the 8th and 7th centuries Ionia is already in the full flood of her artistic activity. Greek texts give us a glimpse of this prosperity and preserve the memory of a number of artists who made their country illustrious. There was the painter Bularchus, whose picture was purchased by Candaulus, king of Lydia, at the end of the 8th century; and the bronze-workers and goldsmiths, Glaucus of Chios, who is said to be the inventor of the art of soldering metals and the author of a crater sent to Delphi towards the year 605 by the Lydian king Alyattes, and Theodorus of Samos, who makes a crater given in 548 to Delphi by Crœsus and a golden vine with grapes of emerald. Among the sculptors were the illustrious family at Chios whose successive representatives in the 6th century were Micciades, Archermus, Bupalus and Athenis. Sumptuous works of art of clever technique pour into the Ionian sanctuaries and are despatched to Greece by the Lydian Mermnadæ, Gyges (687-652), Alyattes (610-561) and Crœsus (561-546), who were anxious to conciliate and win the favour of the gods of the Hellenes for their political enterprises.[1] Private persons rivalled one another in luxury, and Kolæus, about the year 630, consecrates a bronze crater in the Heræum at Samos to commemorate his bold voyage to the columns of Hercules.

The monuments bear even more striking witness to this fruitful activity than the texts. There were painted vases[2] in the metropolitan and colonial workshops, at Miletus, Samos, Rhodes, Naucratis and Cyrene whose exact provenance it is often difficult to determine; and statues and statuettes, reliefs and industrial objects in stone, bronze and terra cotta from the same centres, and especially from the flourishing schools of Miletus, Chios and Samos.[3] They are frequently found very far from their place of manufacture —in the north in the Crimea,[4] in the south in Egypt, and in the west in Italy, Gaul and Spain, brought over by the maritime route and then introduced far into the interior by overland trade routes—the Graechwyl vase (7th century), which is adorned with the Asiatic Potnia Theron, bears

[1] **CCXIII.**   [2] **CXLV**, vol. ii, p. 486; **CXLIV**, vol. ix, p. 377.
[3] **LXXXIV**, vol. viii, p. 252.   [4] **CCXX-I.**

witness to this expansion having extended even to the heart of present-day Switzerland.[1] At the same time architects were building the great temples at Samos, Ephesus and Miletus.

Ionia, which awakened first to art, gave continental Greece fruitful teaching that facilitated progress. It not only gave themes, motifs and technical processes, but æsthetic principles which were to persist long after its own artistic predominance had vanished. Its effects were felt in ceramics, in the industrial arts of Corinth and Attica, and in plastic art, which in Athens from 560 docilely followed the Ionian lead[2] and whose native harshness in the Peloponnese was mellowed by this beneficial contact. It can be said that the main fact of Greek archaism up to the close of the 6th century is the predominance of Ionianism and of its influence on other Greek centres. For the ethnic antagonism indicated a few pages further back had not yet found an echo in art; on the contrary, the Peloponnesian workshops of the 6th century welcomed this influence.[3]

What, then, are the characteristic features of this Ionian art and what exactly is its share in Greek art as a whole ?

Two main causes contributed to give it its special character—the Ægean tradition, and contact with the East. Ionia, thanks to the origin of its inhabitants and to the environment in which its population had developed, was heir to the artistic heritage of the civilization which had flourished before the Dorian invasion, and its art is a survival and a kind of renaissance of Mycenæan art. It was not merely that many ornamental motifs and themes survived but that artistic tendencies persisted, such, for instance, as the taste for naturalism and for floral decoration treated, not in abstract and geometric fashion as in continental Greece, but with truth; and the taste for violent movement and intense life.[4]

The Ionians, living, as they did, at the termini of the caravan routes which brought merchandise across Asia Minor from Cappadocia and the Mesopotamian East, and having maritime relations with the Mediterranean and with the coasts of Phœnicia, Syria and Egypt, received much, likewise, from these ancient civilizations, and it was they

[1] **LXXXVI**, vol. ii, pp. 320, 2.   [2] **LXXVIII**, p. 188.
[3] **CCXI**.   [4] **CXLV**, vol. ii, p. 503; **VI**, vol. iii, p. 107.

who introduced into Greek art that Oriental note perceptible
in the ceramics and industry of the 8th and 7th centuries.
For instance, motifs such as the lotus flower and leaf, the
palmette, ferocious beasts like lions—isolated or fighting
with bulls—fantastic creatures such as the Chimæra—doubtless of Hittite origin—and men with the heads of hares.   And
also certain features of style such as the thick-set proportions
of human beings—of Assyrian inspiration—the nervousness
of complete nudity—which had already been shown by the
Ægeans and which is repugnant to all Orientals—and a
preference for drapery.   Further, certain technical processes
such as hollow bronze casting, borrowed from Egypt by
the Samians Theodorus and Rhœcus.   It was in imitation
of Oriental carpets that the potters covered their vases with
designs as though with a woven and richly polychrome network.   All these contributions, and many others, too, opened
up new perspectives to the Ionian artists who adopted them
to Hellenic taste before they gave them to the rest of Greece.

These two traits, Ægean survivals and Oriental influence,
united with the qualities proper to the Ionians, were never
to be lost by Greek art; restrained during the classic period
of the 5th century, they blossomed out in the Hellenistic
period when Greek art flowed back towards the old centres
in Asia Minor and renewed the link with the East broken
since the time of the Persian wars.[1]

The Ionians' share in the building up of the common
patrimony of Greek art is considerable.   It was they who
initiated artists into the knowledge of the two chief plastic
materials, marble and bronze, which were to serve henceforth for all works which it was desired should be beautiful
and carefully executed and for which limestone, so full of
defects, and over-ductile clay, were abandoned.   Up till
then bronze, outside its employment in industry, was used
only for casting heavy solid figurines, which such a process
condemned to small size.   Hollow casting, borrowed from
Egypt by Rhœcus and Theodorus of Samos, henceforth
permitted the conception of large light statues in which
only a minimum of metal was employed, and authorized freer
poses impossible in stone.   If we recall that the greater part
of the classic masterpieces were bronzes and that some of

[1] **VI**, vol. iii, p. 107.

the best artists, Myron, Polyclitus and Lysippus, were bronze-workers, we shall understand the enormous importance of this gain. And if the Peloponnesian studios preferred this material even to marble for representing athletes, it is to be remembered that they owed the technique to their enemies, the Ionians.

Continental Greece, other than Attica, is poor in statuary marble, but the islands possess rich beds, and the marble of Naxos, and especially of Paros, surpasses in beauty that of Hymettus or Pentelicus.[1] The crude island image-makers of the eneolithic civilization of the Cyclades had already carved their funerary idols in marble; and later on the Ægean sculptors used it for the lion heads of Knossos and Delphi. But it belonged to the Ionians to understand and to make others understand the æsthetic value of this material. It renewed architecture. Byzes, a Naxian, replaced the old terra cotta temple tiles by tiles of marble from his isle. His example was followed, although the old process was kept up even in the 5th century, to the time of the Parthenon. The practice of carving the details of the higher portions of a building in marble (metopes of the Hekatompedos, first quarter of the 6th century) was begun. In 536-525 the Alcmæonidæ built the façade of the temple of Apollo at Delphi of Parian marble; and it was of marble that the Pisistratidæ, their jealous rivals, made the sculptured entablatures, friezes and pediments of the Hekatompedos in Athens which was transformed about 520. Although limestone is still used for important buildings in the first half of the 5th century (temples of Ægina and Olympia), one realizes, nevertheless, that marble is coming to be regarded as the most handsome material for architecture, not only for the details of ornament, such as pediments, metopes, gargoyles, and cymas, but for the building as a whole, and the buildings of Pericles' Acropolis— the Parthenon, the temple of Athena Nike, and the Propylæa —are an " ideal crystallized in Pentelic marble."

The Ionians appreciated in statuary the beauty of marble with its homogeneous grain and smooth surfaces which are so well suited to represent the human body, more especially the soft and delicate tissues of woman; they know that its hardness not only insures a longer life to the work of art

[1] **LXXXIV**, vol. viii, p. 141.

but enjoins on the artist less hasty and more detailed and exact work than limestone demands, causing him to study form with closer attention. They carve, with consummate knowledge of the resources of marble, statues of Korai,[1] young women elegantly dressed, covered with jewels and embroideries, and the naked bodies of Kouroi.[2] Thanks to them we know that the choice of material in a work of art is important in itself, having its own beauty which can be adapted more or less harmoniously to the subject. Polychromy, necessary in order to hide the imperfections of limestone, completed the statues; toned down, it softened the whiteness of marble to a flesh tint by a light "ganosis."[3] It became increasingly clear that materials have their specific qualities, demanding different treatment. All this the Greeks owed to the Ionians, who put them on the right road.

The Ionian artist created typical forms. He made fashionable the costume of the Korai—a long short-sleeved linen chiton which was caught up in the hand, and a himation which crossed the chest obliquely—a costume full of grace, made more elegant by its embroideries, and falling into light, close folds, bespeaking a very different spirit from that shown by the severe Dorian chiton. He adopted the long, narrow stele known as Ionic, surmounted by an acroterium in the form of a palmette which held the single image of the dead, standing erect. In architecture, the

FIG. 4. IONIC COLUMN OF THE TEMPLE OF EPHESUS, 6TH CENTURY.

Ionic order[4] has a good title to that name, because it was an Ionian creation formed partly from old Mycenæan elements and partly from elements borrowed from the East. Elegance and luxury are more sought after in it than strength, and are evident in the general proportions and in the slenderness of the columns and the graceful volutes of the capitals (Fig. 4). Its ornamentation is not limited,

[1] **LXXVIII-IX.**   [2] **LXVIII.**
[3] **LXXXIV,** vol. viii, p. 211; **LXXVIII,** p. 316.
[4] **XLVI-LII; XXXVI,** p. 91; JDAI, 1920, 15, p. 1 ff.

as in the Doric, to the frames of the metopes and pediments, but there are mouldings, palmettes, *rais de cœur*, and beads without number, and even the bases of the capitals are sculptured (Ephesus, 6th century).[1] The plan is not so rigorous as in the Doric; there is a certain easy-going

FIG. 5.   PRIMITIVE IONIC
CAPITAL (DELOS).

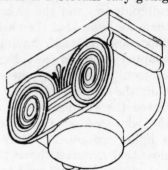

FIG. 6.   PRIMITIVE IONIC
CAPITAL (ATHENS).

nonchalance in the long frieze which runs as far as the building can carry it and whose prolixity contrasts with the rigid alternation of the Doric triglyphs and metopes—all so many traits characterizing this order and betokening a different spirit from that animating continental Greece.   At the end of the 6th century the Ionic order is definitely constituted.   The

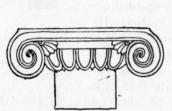

FIG. 7.   CAPITAL OF THE COLUMN
OF THE NAXIANS (DELPHI),
6TH CENTURY.

FIG. 8.   ARCHAIC IONIC
CAPITAL (DELOS). 6TH
CENTURY.

capital has developed and the examples found on the Acropolis in Athens and at Delos give it in almost its final form.[2] The volutes, formerly separated, with an almost vertical stem, are united in an elegant curve tending towards the horizontal (Figs. 5-9).

[1] **CCX; LXXXIV,** vol. viii, p. 321.   [2] **XXXVI,** p. 100.

Greece is not yet completely conquered, however. Born in Ionia, this order is confined to that region. The 6th-century continental artists undergo Ionian influence and carve isolated capitals which terminate the pedestals of statues, and crown their funerary stelæ with volutes (example: Hoplitodromus stele, Athens).[1] The architects of the Hekatompedon transformed by the Pisistratidæ at the end of the 6th century adopt the principle of the continuous frieze—if it be true that the fragments of reliefs in the Acropolis museum, of which the most beautiful shows a man in a chariot and the bust of Hermes,[2] belong to a frieze that ran round the cella of the peripteral Doric temple, and which frieze would thus be a prototype of that of the Panathenæa. But these are only details. The Doric, though it was already influenced, still reigned supreme on the continent. The Treasury of the Siphnians, that Ionic gem of the second half of the 6th century at Delphi,[3] does not constitute an exception because it was built by Ionian architects for an insular Greek city the affinities of whose art were with Asiatic Greece. We have to wait till the second half of the 5th century to see the Ionic order win

FIG. 9. ARCHAIC IONIC CAPITAL (ATHENS), 6TH CENTURY.

its citizenship in Greece proper. It achieved this progressively, thanks to Phidias and his collaborators. The Parthenon, begun in 447 and completed in 431, but inaugurated in the year 438, already betrays a certain yielding in the Doric spirit, because the Ionian influence[4] is manifest in the presence of the frieze round the cella, in the more abundant and luxurious ornament of palmettes, cyma, and rows of bead on the border of the metopes, and in the number of the columns of the façade—eight instead of the six ordinarily present in a Doric temple.

This still weak influence is definitely shown almost simultaneously in a neighbouring building. In the Propylæa

---

[1] **LXXXIV**, vol. viii, p. 649.   [2] *Ibid.*, p. 652.
[3] **LXXXIV**, vol. viii, p. 363; Bourguet, *Les ruines de Delphes*, p. 65.
[4] **XL.**

(437-432) Mnesicles associates two rows of interior Ionic columns with the Doric columns of the façade, and the two systems of construction are now juxtaposed. Still hidden in the interior, the Ionic order is employed for the first time overtly and alone in the small amphiprostyle temple of Athena Nike, built about 435. Finally the Erechtheum (420-407) testifies that it has been definitely accepted by Greek architects for a big architectural scheme. It now becomes the successful rival of the Doric. More elegant, more luxurious, it responds better to the new needs of luxury and wealth which appear from the close of the 5th century. It was to multiply its effects until the time came when it found a rival, in its turn, in the Corinthian capital,[1] which was more deeply sculptured and still more luxurious (Fig. 19). Created in the second half of the 5th century, possibly by Callimachus, this was at first hidden in the interior (temple at Phigalia, about 420; tholos at Epidaurus, first quarter of the 4th century), and it was not used in complete ensembles, which were at first restrained, till the second half of the 4th century (monument of Lysi-crates, 335-4), to come into its own in the Græco-Roman period. For the rest, it does not constitute an order, strictly speaking; it is simply a variant of the Ionic capital which had no repercussion on the system of proportions of the building. There are only two orders in Greece, each responding to one of the main tendencies of the Greek spirit, the one strong, severe and virile, the other graceful, charming and more feminine. Adopted by continental Greece, the Ionic influenced the Doric and transmitted to it some of its elements. We have noted this in the Parthenon and in the Propylæa. The principle of the frieze is also applied to the Hephæsteum (called the Theseum, 437-432, exterior frieze), to the temple at Cape Sunium, and to the temple at Phigalia (about 420) built by the architect of the Parthenon, Ictinus. The latter unites within itself three conceptions, for though the ensemble is Doric, there is an Ionic colonnade in the interior, and an Ionic frieze, and even a single Corinthian capital, the earliest example known. The three types are grouped in a skilful hierarchy, which corresponds well with chronology: the Doric is still supreme, but the Ionic has invaded the interior, and the Corinthian is preparing for its future conquest.

[1] LIII-V ; JDAI, 1921, 36, p. 44.

Conversely, Ionic, when it came into contact with Doric, took from it certain principles, more particularly its regularity of plan which henceforward becomes common to both orders.

One motif that was destined to come into favour and is known later as a " Caryatid "[1]—that which employs a woman's form as an architectural support—was created in Ionia; the beautiful Korai of the Erechtheum (towards 415) had as their ancestresses the Caryatid at Tralles (about 450),[2] those of the treasuries of Cnidus and of Siphnus at Delphi (6th century),[3] and the small figures which support the archaic fountain basins of Ionian style. The masculine Doric genius, whose massive columns stripped of all ornament betoken a geometrical spirit, would never have conceived this elegant feminine column.

The continuous Ionic frieze contrasts with the alternation of the Doric triglyphs and metopes. The temple at Assos (6th century)[4] may already unite the two principles, but we have to wait till the second half of the 5th century and the coming of the buildings already mentioned before we see sculptural decoration resorting to both simultaneously

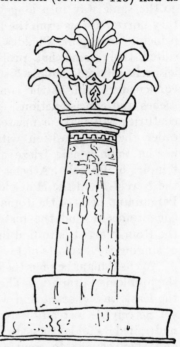

Fig. 10.   Funerary stele on an Attic lecythus of the 5th century.   The terminal acanthus foreshadows the coming of the Corinthian capital.

in the same building, though with a different disposition— that is to say, when the Doric and Ionic begin to blend. These two elements, indeed, issue from a different spirit. The Doric frieze,[5] which Ægean art had already inaugurated,

---

[1] **XLVII**; JDAI, 1920, 35, p. 113.   [2] MP, x, 1903, Pl. ii-iii.
[3] **LXXXIV**, vol. viii, p. 385; Bourguet, *Les ruines de Delphes*, p. 66.
[4] **LXXXIV**, vol. viii, p. 256; Sartiaux, RA, 1913–14.
[5] **XXXIX-XLV.**

perfectly expresses the Dorian spirit in love with symmetry, regularity and rhythmical alternation, and liking a limited field. The principle of the metope is not special to architecture; vase-painting early uses this rectangular field in which the elements of the subject can be inscribed with logic and clarity. The Ionians preferred, on their temples and on the bodies of their vases, a long band on which the motifs all go the same way in a long indefinite procession;[1] doubtless they borrowed this from the East, because it is the decorative principle of Egypt, Chaldea, Assyria, and the Hittites. It suited their somewhat prolix and discursive spirit which leisurely sets out endless histories on these bands instead of condensing them, as the continentals do, in a few clear-cut scenes and concise actions. The artists of the 5th and 4th centuries will make a masterpiece of it when they come to order their composition with greater rigour—for example, in the Panathenaic frieze and those of the Theseum, the temples of Phigalia, Athena Nike, Trysa, the monument of the Nereids, and the Mausoleum; the Hellenistic sculptors of Pergamum, heirs of the Ionians on their own soil, unwind the Gigantomachy and the history of Telephus, and, later on, the Roman artist is to find in the frieze the happy possibility of singing the exploits of his history.

To the Ionians belongs the honour of having first approached the problem of drapery. They understood its beauty of which the East was ignorant and which continental Greece had not yet perceived; instead of treating it as a rigid carapace they multiplied its folds; they studied it in its relation to the figure, and they sought to render its transparency; finally, they realized that each must have its proper value and be united in a balanced harmony. True, the results were not yet perfect, but at least they had caught a glimpse of its various æsthetic necessities.

They had a feeling for the beauty of the human form which they rendered, not with the brutal strength of the Dorians, but with delicacy and sensuous appreciation. What a difference there is between the insular Kouroi[2] with their elegant and occasionally precious form (Kouroi at Melos and Tenea, 6th century) and those of Polymedes of Argos (6th century), sometimes known as " burden bearers "; between

[1] LIX.   [2] LXVIII.

the Korai of the Acropolis (6th century), dainty and delicate,[1] and the heavy Athena of the metope at Selinus (6th century)![2] The musculature may be wanting in precision, the skeleton in firmness, and the flesh may be soft and plump, but the silhouette is generally graceful and pleasing to the eye.

This human form that they appreciated was more especially the form of woman. Ionian civilization, brilliant and sensuous, softened by contact with the Orient, preferred gentle and peaceable forms to the more robust and angular form of man.

The Ionian spirit communicated to Greek art the instinctive feeling for grace, elegance and charm which the Dorians lacked. It is revealed in the poses with their occasionally somewhat mannered and affected gesture, in the arrangement of the many fine folds of drapery which ripple over the bodies of the Korai, in anatomical details such as hands with slender fingers, sometimes a trifle curved at the tips, the slender arched foot, and the soft modelling of the statues which avoids the hard and angular plane surfaces so common in Peloponnesian sculpture, and which is often a veritable caress for the eyes.[3]

The Ionian spirit inspired Greek art with the desire to please, to be smiling and gracious. It seeks a pleasant expression, turning up the corners of the mouth and eyes, and the " archaic smile," sometimes exaggerated and artificially amiable, soon came to light up with its gaiety even the melancholy Peloponnesian countenances. It brought polychromy into vase-painting—doubtless necessary in order to translate approximately the vivid colours of the carpets and embroideries imitated by the potters, but also responding to this native gaiety. Black, white, brown, red, yellow and blue make bright patches on the pale slip of the pot, and this bright note which the Corinthians tried to imitate was in strong contrast with the sombre colours of the Attic vases.[4]

The realism which the Ionians seem to have inherited from the Ægeans is attested by numerous details and by a closer observation of life than is to be found in continental Greece.[5] The sculptor, instead of carving the eye as an almond, indicates the conjunctival sac at the internal angle; he does not leave the upper lid absolutely smooth when the eye is open, but

[1] **LXXVIII-IX.** [2] **LXXXIV**, vol. viii, p. 487. [3] **LXXVIII**, p. 339. [4] **CXLIV**, vol. ix, p. 440. [5] **CXLV**, vol. ii, pp. 507-11.

incises a small fold on it. The continental vase-painters differentiate man from woman by the shape of the eyes, round for men and oval for women; the Ionians, more exact, avoid this convention for the same reason that they paint the skin of both men and women white, because the continental contrast of black and white is not true to nature.

The Ionians preserved the Ægean love of nature when continental Greece, under the Dorian influence, eliminated everything that was not human, and it has been said that they were the "landscape artists of antiquity." When this note appears sporadically in the Attic art of the 5th century, especially in pottery, and when, at the end of the 4th century, the uniform background of reliefs begins to carry picturesque details, it is, in fact, a renaissance of this old spirit.

The violent action and the impetuosity of the composition on the Ionian vases and reliefs has often been remarked; this desire for life inspired the sculptor Archermus of Chios in his flying Nike, posed in the attitude of the archaic runner, ancestress of the beautiful Nike of Pæonius of Mende, also an Ionian; it foreshadows the effort to represent action in the red-figure pottery, the reliefs, and the statuary of the 5th century.

These features persist throughout Greek art. The Ionian spirit did not die with the fall of independent Ionia and with the artistic dominance of Peloponnesian ideas at the beginning of the 5th century. It was maintained in the later works of Ionian provenance such as the reliefs of the heröon at Trysa (end of the 5th century),[1] and the reliefs and statues of the Nereids' monument at Zanthus (end of 5th or beginning of 4th century).[2] The good qualities and the faults of the Ionians are to be seen in these monuments—a flowing, superficial, prolix and discursive style which wanders over long friezes, but that is also graceful, delicate, informed with a sense of the picturesque and full of realistic detail observed from life contrasting with the abstract quality of continental art, of the love of violent action, and of drapery in movement, billowing and fluttering in the wind and allowing the body to be seen through its transparency. In Greece proper, artists of Ionian extraction keep up this tradition. Pæonius of Mende finally solves the problem of transparent

[1] **LXII**, vol. ii, p. 202.   [2] *Ibid.*, p. 216.

and flowing drapery on a body in action in his beautiful Nike
at Olympia (towards 423). Agoracritus, in Phidias' entourage,
is a native of Paros. Attic artists, such as Calamis and Callimachus, are related to the Ionians by their efforts after grace
and delicacy, and the mysterious smile of the Sosandra of
Calamis is a dim reflection of the old smile of the Korai. The
Doric Parthenon makes concessions to Ionian elegance, and
Phidias or Ictinus gives it, by way of ornament, the sculptured
band of the continuous frieze.[1] And in the pediments the
marvellous statues of draped women in transparent chitons,
the " Parcæ," Iris, and the Nike, are the culminating point
of long years of effort by the Ionian sculptors. Wall-painting
in the hands of Polygnotus of Thasos and vase-painting
in the 5th century likewise assimilated much that came from
Greece in Asia.

In the 4th century Praxiteles is the sculptor of woman
and of delicate youthful bodies; in order to translate their
tender and sensuous forms he resorts to the caressing surface
of white and translucent marble rather than to bronze; to the
lips of his Satyr in repose he gives a gentle smile; and it has
been justly said that the rarer qualities of his technique
are traceable to his Ionian predecessors. Scopas of Paros,
who was to bring new life to plastic art by importing emotion
into his attitudes and faces, realizes the goal to which the
Ionian art of the 6th century had already been tending.

Finally, Hellenistic art, which abandons Greece proper to
flow back towards the great centres of Greece in Asia, once
more gives free rein to tendencies which the classical art
of the 5th century had repressed; which explains a great
deal of its particular character and the many analogies it
presents with Ionian art in the 6th century, and also with
ancient Ægean art.[2] It finds again on Asiatic soil the qualities
which had never been lost and which, thanks to a finer
technique, will be expressed with new precision—poignant
realism, exuberant and violent action, and feeling for nature
and historic truth. The Hellenistic period, it has been
justly said (Willamowitz-Moellendorf), " was really nothing
but a continuation of Ionianism."

Archaistic art[3] copies the works of the 6th century which

---

[1] **XL.**   [2] **VI,** vol. iii, pp. 61, 107.
[3] **LXII,** vol. ii, p. 643; **XCII.**

are pleasing to it not only because of their antiquity but in the mannerism of their gesture and smiles, and the clever conventional folds of their drapery; the form and style dear to the Ionians persists in this archaistic art.

Ionianism, then, is one of the elements in Greek art which lasts as long as it does itself. The expression of the amiable people of Greece in Asia, it likewise responds at all times to certain artistic temperaments, and certain periods whole-heartedly enamoured of grace, delicacy, realism and the picturesque. Doubtless it has its faults; it sacrifices too much to detail, to decoration, to the luxury of ornament and the minutiæ of hair and drapery; it slurs over any study of anatomy, and the body is too often plump and boneless; sometimes it is guilty of mannerism and over-prettiness; it is prolix and wanting in the Dorian conciseness. Greece, when it went to the school of Ionianism, yet had the intelligence to select only what might prove profitable and to reject all that was exaggerated. Greek art owes it a great deal—forms, subjects, new processes come from the East, the use of marble and bronze and the judicious knowledge of their properties and their technique, together with the æsthetic study of drapery, the comprehension of human beauty and especially the beauty of woman, the feeling for grace, sensuousness and softness and the taste for realism which struggles successfully against the tendency of continental Greece to be too schematic and abstract.

Without denying the great influence which Ionia exerted on the Greek spirit and on Greek art, we must recognize that other influences also made themselves felt and that these were necessary in order to counterbalance the others and to give to Greek art the harmony of perfect equilibrium. Any exclusive thesis would be false because it would not take into account the complexity of the phenomena. It is an exaggeration to see the exclusive mark of Ionian genius in all the archaic work of the 6th century; " pan-Ionianism " is as unwarranted as " pan-Babylonianism," " pan-Elamism," the " Ægean mirage," or as the one-time " Hindu mirage " or " Oriental mirage." The Ionians have a sufficiently goodly share in this art to render it unnecessary that it should be exaggerated.

CHAPTER III

DORIAN ART[1]

FLOURISHING though Ionia was, the Peloponnese from the 8th to the 6th century had prosperous studios[2] in the great cities of Corinth under the Bacchiadæ and Cypselidæ (627-629), of Argos, Sicyon and Sparta which played an important political rôle, whose commerce (with the exception of Sparta) rivalled that of the Ionians, and which founded distant colonies and exported the products of their industrial arts, more especially their pottery and worked metals. Corinth and Sicyon even wrongly prided themselves on having invented painting and on having seen its earliest progress, in the time of Craton, Cleanthes and Aregon.

If we go into the relative correctness of the terms " Ionian art " and " Dorian art," in so far as they are the expression of two ethnic groups, we cannot but recognize that the artistic products of archaic Greece reveal, according to the place of their origin, two very distinct tendencies. The field of expansion of Ionianism is Greece in Asia, the islands, and the countries reached by Ionian trade; on the other hand, those which originate from districts under Dorian domination, such as the Peloponnese, Crete, Sicily, and Græcia Magna, present undeniable affinities with one another of a quite different character; for example, the torso of Eleutherna, the goddess of Prinias and the figurines of Præsus, in Crete; the torso of Tegea, the Agemo statue, the Chrysapha relief, and the Kouroi of Polymedes of Argos, in the Peloponnese; and the metopes of Selinus in Sicily[3] present a contrast with the statues of the Branchidæ and of Samos, and the insular Kouroi and Korai. The vase-painting of continental Greece differs, in special features, from that of oriental Greece even when it is inspired from thence, as in the case of Corinth.[4]

---

[1] **CCXI.**   [2] **LXXXIV**, vol. viii, p. 436; **CXLIV**, vol. ix, p. 569.
[3] See, for these monuments, **LXXXIV**, vol. viii, pp. 431, 439, 450, 452, 483; **CCXII**, p. 161.
[4] **CXLIV**, vol. ix, p. 569; **CXLV**, vol. ii, p. 416.

Are the Dorian invaders responsible for these differences ? They used to be credited with too great a share in the matter, and the discoveries of the Ægean civilization, showing a quite other spirit, accentuated still further the divergence between the prehistoric world and the Hellenic world constituted by the conquest. A more careful study has permitted the recognition of the numerous links which bind one period to the other,[1] and a realization that the newcomers had not been able to make a clean sweep of the past. Texts remind us that the Dorians, few in number, and a warrior caste which despised manual labour, had to leave to the ancient population which they had enslaved and thrown back into barbarism, the practice of the arts and industries, and to utilize the products their subjects manufactured for their use. Is not the artistic and spiritual predominance of the Ionians, who were no other than the descendants of the old Ægean populations, likewise an argument ? Hence the question had to be faced as to whether there really was a " Dorian " art, and sometimes the answer has been given in the negative—which is going too far. There is no Dorian art in the sense of an art practised by the conquerors themselves, but there is a Dorian art practised for them, which, while it carried on the techniques and motifs that had degenerated as a result of the invasion and the disturbances following it, was constrained, in order to please the conquerors, to bend itself to their taste and to bear the impress of their spirit— a spirit quite different from that which animated Ægean and Ionian Greece.

Long before the final conquest, this change in spirit was in progress. The Dorians constituted the last of those migrations which descended from central Europe to conquer the Hellenic peninsula, the islands, and the coasts of Asia Minor, and they had been preceded by the Achæans who on more than one occasion settled in Crete and the Peloponnese, and whose coming constituted the final phase of the Ægean civilization known as the Mycenæan. The differences which were already present in Ægean art result from these ethnic differences. The Cretan palace, conceived on the model of an Asiatic palace in the East with its irregular plan and its numerous halls, is in strong contrast with the Trojan and

[1] **CCXI.**

Peloponnesian megaron, which comes from the North and is small and logical, and is to be found in its most perfect type at Mycenæ and Tiryns (Fig. 11).[1]   Asia and Europe are already contrasted within the bounds of a single unity, just as, later on, the Dorian newcomers, having finally brought the Ægean culture to ruin, will present a contrast to the Ionians albeit constituting with them a single nation.

The Dorian spirit is made manifest in architecture.[2] Assuredly the " Doric " temple (Fig. 12) is no more a Dorian creation than the " Gothic " cathedral is a creation of the

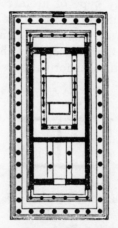

FIG. 11.   MEGARON AT
TIRYNS.

FIG. 12.   PLAN OF THE
PARTHENON.

Goths, the Dorians having found its constituent elements already in existence on their arrival and having accepted them.   The Doric temple (Pl. VI) in effect is almost the integral copy of the Mycenæan megaron whose plan it reproduces[3]—longer than it is wide, with the interior of the nave divided by columns (Fig. 11), its exterior arrangement of columns *in antis*, as a façade, the form of the columns and their capitals, the upper portions with their triglyphs and metopes,[4] and perhaps even the double coping of the roof.[5] As the megaron was, the earliest temple is built of wood and baked clay.   The main difference consists in its purpose.

[1] **XXXVII**, pp. 48, 103.
[2] **XXXVI-XLV.**
[3] **XXXVII**, p. 87; **XXXVI**, p. 7.
[4] **XLI-III, XLV.**
[5] **XXXVII**, p. 52.

The palace, which already held the cult objects, quite naturally became the abode of the god in a society which was no longer monarchic, and the oldest temples in Tiryns, Mycenæ, on the Athens Acropolis, in Troy and other places were built on the sites of the Mycenæan megarons. Gradually the primitive plan grew more intricate by the addition of columns on the outside and developed into the peripteral type, which quite likely had antecedents in pre-Hellenic Greece.[1] But although this type of building was not created by the Dorians it is thoroughly " Doric " in spirit, and for a long while was the only type of architecture in continental Greece—before the Ionic order found its way there and took root; it contrasts with the Ionic just as the Mycenæan megaron does with the Cretan palace. Its characters are those which are to be found in other forms of Peloponnesian art.

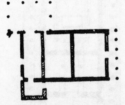

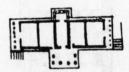

FIG. 13. PLAN OF THE ERECHTHEUM.   FIG. 14. PRIMITIVE PROJECT FOR THE ERECHTHEUM.

The plan of the Ionic temple is less precise and homogeneous, and more complex, as was the case with the Cretan palace. The Erechtheum (420-407), left asymmetrical (Fig. 13) when, apparently, it was intended to be symmetrical (Fig. 14) in the primitive project which was not carried out,[2] includes several juxtaposed cellas at different levels, and projecting portions, and the small temple of Athena Nike is quite different. There is every possible and conceivable variety. The Doric building, on the contrary, is obedient to a rigid plan as a complete construction, and the small variations are confined to details which do not affect the general scheme, such as the interior disposition of the columns or the number that go round the cella. It is a unique whole whose essential

[1] **XXXVII,** p. 87; Theuer, *Der griechisch-dorische Peripteraltempel. Ein Beitrag zur antiken Proportionslehre,* Berlin, 1918.

[2] Against this hypothesis of Dörpfeld, Weller, AJA, xxv, 1921, p. 130; Rodenwaldt, *Neue Jahrbücher,* 1921, p. 1; Dörpfeld, *ibid.,* p. 433.

parts are immediately recognizable and are logically to be
deduced from one another.

There is the same precision in their figured art. In con-
tradistinction to the Ionians, they like restricted and limited
fields in which a subject is inscribed which is often as concise
as a laconic word, and the principle of the rectangular metope[1]
appeared to be preferable to the continuous frieze for this
reason (Fig. 15). The decoration of triangular pediments is
likewise essentially Dorian. The Ionians are often content
with a bony framework that is merely approximate and lacking
in cohesion. The continental
Greeks manifest a more scrupulous regard for exactitude
and approach more nearly to
truth in human delineation.
Even their earliest works,
despite their awkwardnesses,
strikingly betoken this desire.
Perhaps this was why the
Corinthians were the first to
introduce the process of incision in vase-painting, quickly
copied by their rivals, which
enabled them to indicate in
detail with the burin the internal features of the muscles
instead of leaving a mere
opaque silhouette or leaving
a few parts unpainted.[2]

FIG. 15. RHODIAN VASE OF GEO-
METRIC STYLE. DECORATION IN
METOPES.

Symmetry, rhythm, balance, alternation and antithesis—
these are the characteristics of the Peloponnesians in contrast
with those of the Ionians. The Ionians make their animals
and people follow one another in the same direction on their
zones with no reason why they should ever stop, except the
limits of the surface to be decorated; there is no essential
beginning or end, and no centre. The Peloponnesians prefer
a central subject, on either side of which their composition
is made to balance, a principle which appears to be of European
origin in contrast with the Oriental principle of the zone.

[1] **XLI-XLIII, XLV.**
[2] **CXLIV,** vol. ix, p. 436; **CXLV,** vol. ii, pp. 429, 437.

The earliest monuments in painting, the geometric vases of the Attic Dipylon, already testify to this tendency. The ceramists of Corinth and Athens may adopt the circular zone under Oriental and Ionian influence, but they sometimes conceive it differently—their animals and groups of persons will confront one another and the procession will be divided into symmetrical portions which break the monotonous continuity. Each metope alternates its smooth or sculptured surface with the vertical lines of neighbouring triglyphs. In their pediments, once the tentative period is past, from the end of the 6th century, a rigorous symmetry constrains each figure in a wing exactly to correspond with an opposite number in the other wing, and the composition is divided in two by a central motif.

Number is the directing force in Dorian art—alternation of triglyphs and metopes above the architrave, balanced figures in vase and pediment compositions opposed isolated figures, or binary or ternary groups—these are the effects of a mathematical conception of art and of a geometrical way of looking at things.

This spirit is abstract. The brilliant naturalism of the Ægeans, their love of flowers and of the terrestrial and marine fauna, of the picturesque, of life in all its forms—this has vanished, and the Ionians alone preserve a dim memory of it. The Dorians substitute for it an abstract and geometrical vision of reality. The pottery which is found everywhere in the Greece of the 11th to the 8th centuries and of which the Dipylon of Athens presents the most highly developed types, is called "geometric,"[1] because its decoration consists almost exclusively of combinations of lines; floral motifs are rare, and if they occur are always stylised and well nigh unrecognizable. Continental Greece preserves this character through many centuries; although Ionia sometimes treats floral motifs picturesquely, the vases of Corinth, Chalcis, and Attica schematize them and the change is invariably to a purely decorative form. The Doric temple is no more nor less than a composite arrangement of purely geometrical lines from which any living form is banished, except in the portions reserved for decoration such as pediments, metopes and acroteria. Embellishments borrowed from the floral kingdom, such as

[1] **CXLIV**, vol. vii; **CXLV**, vol. i, p. 212.

palmettes or volutes, which still preserve a suggestion of the palm or the lotus—as in the Ionic order—there are few or none.

There is likewise less suppleness in the lines of the Doric. The curves beloved of Ægean art, no doubt because they approach more nearly to reality, disappear almost entirely to be replaced by rigid straight lines. The Ionians manifest in their drapery a desire to break up its uniformity by minute criss-crossed and oblique folds; the Dorians conceive drapery geometrically, and the skirt of their women in the Dorian peplos forms straight parallel folds like the fluting on a column.

If Ionian art is generous, prolix, and is fond of ornament, luxury, and occasionally of tinsel, continental Greece manifests a remarkable desire for simplicity and sobriety. It disdains the redundant and reduces accessories to the minimum. The Doric temple seems naked by comparison with the Ionic; the one multiplies the mouldings of its bases, gracefully curls the volutes of its capitals, chisels bands of *rais de cœur*, bead, and palmettes, and covers every available space with reliefs; the other resorts only to pure lines and their harmonious combination. Continental vase-painting renounces, for the first time, in the Corinth workshops,[1] the overcrowded ornament which covers the fields as with a network, and the primitive " horror of an empty space " maintained by the imitation of Oriental carpets and embroideries. There is a beginning of comprehension that beauty does not lie in complication but in simplicity, and the subject stands out alone on a naked background. A few vases of the Ionian cycle (Rhodes, style II)[2] really seem to denote by this feature an influence come from the West. In sculpture there are no gewgaws, elaborately dressed heads, displays of jewels, or multitudes of minute folds, but a massive treatment, and drapery in which folds are barely if at all indicated. The fine Ionian costume is a luxurious shimmer of colours and embroideries, and it determines the abundant intersecting lines calculated to inspire a sculptor; the Dorian peplos, the national dress, is a very simple woollen shirt which lends itself ill to such detail and which hangs straight.[3]

[1] **CXLV**, vol. ix, p. 614; **CXLV**, vol. ii, p. 450.
[2] **CXLIV**, vol. ix, p. 428.   [3] **CCI, CCII, CCIV.**

The Ionians are enamoured of grace and delicacy; the continentals pursue strength. The proportions of the Ionian canon may be stumpy in imitation of Assyria, but the flesh tissues are soft and lacking in substance—flabby. Here, on the contrary, are bodies strongly made, with powerful frames and firm muscles, and tissues that are hard to the touch. This character is even exaggerated and tends towards brutality. Heracles and Perseus on the metopes of Selinus,[1] and the Kouroi of Polymedes of Argos are typical " strong men." This strength is tense and ready for action like the strength of the Dorians themselves who were ever on the defensive in a conquered land. There is no smile on these countenances, and the straight mouths, like sword-gashes, are grim, whereas the Ionians brighten the features of their statues with a smile.

Enamoured of vigour, the continentals love the masculine body such as gymnastics toughly fashion it. The athlete, in his muscular nudity, is more pleasing to them than woman with her soft tissues, or than drapery—whereas the Ionians show precisely the opposite qualities.

The Dorians likewise prefer bronze. Its sombre colour is better adapted than fair marbles to the masculine figure tanned in the open air of the palæstra; this material seems to them more virile, and makes the silhouette stand out better in its sober main lines without drawing the eye to the petty details which the polychromy of marble tends to emphasize. The great Peloponnesian artists are all bronze-workers, and the Argive-Sicyonian school makes this material its speciality.

These features which are revealed in the archaic are perpetuated on Dorian soil throughout the history of Greek art. Polymedes of Argos lives again in Ageladas and his disciples, and again in Polyclitus, whose athletes have the same strong square frame, the same flattened head as the old Kouroi. In these workshops there will always be a preference for bronze, a love for the masculine body and its solid frame, a tendency to sobriety, simplicity and the instinctive seeking after number, which determines a study of the rhythm so dear to the 5th century. Peloponnesian art, likewise, will ever preserve, in so far as it is not softened by contact with Ionian

[1] **LXXXIV**, vol. viii, pp. 487, 488.

or Attic art, the harshness, the too austere severity and the schematic quality still to be seen in the statuary of Polyclitus and his pupils. Ionian art runs the risk of being effeminate and arch; Peloponnesian art, unadulterated, is too rough. Fortunately neither the one nor the other remained isolated but each penetrated the other, and their respective qualities were welded into one to the great benefit of Greek art.

CHAPTER IV

RECONCILIATION OF THE TWO TENDENCIES

THESE two tendencies mutually influence even while they are in opposition to one another. The Corinth potters have already gone to the school of Ionianism;[1] continental art gets from it a rich repertory of motifs, and the statuary's art itself is becoming softened by the contact. There has been a tendency to exaggerate this influence and to see nothing but Ionian characters in the Chrysapha reliefs, the Spartan base, and the Cretan and Sicilian sculptures; it has been said that even in the 5th century Polyclitus has lost the primitive solid frame of the Dorians, that he descends from the Ionian sculptors such as Bathycles of Magnesia, who came to the Peloponnese in the 6th century to initiate it.[2] One may admit a less extreme thesis which, while recognizing this undeniable influence, yet allows the Peloponnesian studios to keep their characteristic features.

Conversely, we may trace Western infiltration in the Ionia of the 6th century. In Greek Egypt, Orientals and Occidentals rub shoulders and Æginetans are cheek by jowl with Ionians; the ceramics of Naucratis undergo the influence of Corinthian ware and borrow from it the process of incision,[3] while the pottery of Rhodes, imitating the Peloponnesian ware, gets rid of the encumbering motifs on the field of its vases.[4]

Towards 500, political circumstances being to some extent responsible, Ionianism declines, and Peloponnesian art becomes dominant. The workshops of Argos and Ægina have at their head masters whose fame carries far. In their turn they are to exercise a fruitful influence on Greek art.

Greek art owes all its qualities to this reconciliation. It has been said that " Greece is simply the antithesis of the Dorian and the Ionian " (Renan); it has been claimed that

[1] **CXLIV**, vol. ix, p. 569.　　　[2] **CCXI**.
[3] **CXLIV**, vol. ix, p. 394.　　　[4] *Ibid.*, p. 428.

" Ionia on one hand, and Athens on the other, appear as two poles between which the Greek spirit fluctuates " (Pottier). On the contrary, classic Greek art is the harmonious union of qualities proper to them both. It could hardly come about in the extreme parts of Ionia and the Peloponnese; it was consummated in a land situate midway between, whose spirit is nicely balanced between the Dorian and the Ionian spirit, and whose art, likewise, is a happy mean—Attica.

CHAPTER V

ATTIC ART

ATTICA gave herself to the practice of the arts at a very early stage, and the "geometric" period foreshadows her future successes.[1] Geometric decoration, instinctive with all primitive peoples and placed once more in honour or brought in by the invaders, was in Attica erected into a veritable æsthetic system. The large vases of the Dipylon of the 8th century astonish us not only by the material difficulties overcome in their firing but also by their skilled composition in decoration, by no means of an arbitrary character, which was regulated by a definite system. One cannot but recognize this quality despite the naïve design which is still barbaric and conventional. Ceramic industry, in close relation with economic prosperity, remains one of the principal branches of production;[2] it was to develop the beautiful Attic style of the black-figure vases (6th century) after passing through the proto-Attic stage and the Attic-Corinthian phase imbued with Oriental influence; then the advent of the red-figure style (end of the 6th century) was to foreshadow the ceramic masterpieces of the 5th century. The qualities of design peculiar to the Attics was clearly revealed at the earliest stage. By the technical skill of their manufacture, the qualities of style and the efficient maintenance of a flourishing trade, Attic ceramics gradually imposed its wares on Greek and foreign markets[3] and in the course of the 6th century eliminated its rivals such as the Corinthians, whose best period was over and who ceased to manufacture painted vases somewhere between 480 and 460.

"Doric" architecture did not take any special forms in Attica; the monuments earlier than 480 have disappeared, wrecked by the Persian invasion. But their decorations, preserved in part, such as the votive and funerary statues

[1] **LXXXIV,** vol. vii, p. 160; Poulsen, *Die Dipylongräber und die Dipylonvasen.*
[2] **CXXIX** ff.   [3] **CXLIX.**

and reliefs found in the débris, permit us to trace from their earliest phase the characteristic features manifested by Attic genius in sculpture and confirmed by the data provided by pottery.

It has sometimes been said that Attic art in its earliest period was indistinguishable from Doric art, and together with it can be contrasted, as a single unity, with the art of Greece in Asia. We can no more accept this confusion of identity than we can admit the pan-Ionic thesis which would annihilate distinctively Peloponnesian characters. The oldest sculptural works[1]—for we need only mention the crude idols of the Dipylon in order that they may not be overlooked—the pediments in soft stone of the Acropolis (end of the 7th and beginning of the 6th centuries), and the earliest marble statues (second quarter of the 6th century), differ from the Ionian and Peloponnesian works at the same time that they resemble them; from its beginnings Attic art occupies a happy mean between these extreme tendencies; it links the desire for grace and elegance manifested in the one to the effort to obtain strength and precision shown by the other. To characterize these Attic works we cannot do better than quote the words of a very fine connoisseur of primitive Attic sculpture: " Placed side by side with the Selinus metopes the people on the ancient pediments of the Acropolis, even the most monstrous, appear almost elegant; at least the vigour of their nude bodies has not that extreme heaviness and stiffness which distinguishes their Sicilian contemporaries. And what a difference in their physiognomy ! The countenances of the triple Typhon breathe amenity, and the joy of living, together with a desire to please; they have a frank expression and a light and happy smile; they are far removed from the air of inflexible severity which hardens the eyes, compresses the lips and clenches the jaw of Heracles or Perseus." In the Ionian reliefs of Assos, what strikes us is the effeminacy, the backboneless character of the bodies despite the savagery of the scene. " Very different is the nature revealed in the contemporary Attic sculptors: they have more sap and vitality, greater firmness of hand and a more frank manner of reaching their goal; and even their visible preference for solid construction and strong frames,

[1] **LXXII, LXXVIII-IX, LXXXIX-XC, XCIV.**

for robustness rather than finesse in form, leads one to think that, despite their racial affinities, they are less closely related to the Ionians than to the Dorians."[1]

Vase-painting reveals the same dualism. Ionia exerted on it its influence from a very early period, and taught it to use floral decoration, bands of animals, and more particularly to show a preference for illustrating mythological scenes. But others of its qualities are Peloponnesian—its symmetry, antithetic groups, ever growing exclusive preference for the human form, love of the nude and muscular figure, sobriety, and clarity which sometimes amounts to dryness. The black-figure vases of the 6th century, the crater of Ergotimus and Clitias,[2] the later works of Amasis and Exekias clearly testify that these tendencies are present in colour as well as in form.[3] It was by going to the school of the Dorian race " that the Ionians of Attica won that balance, that sane proportion which has become so significant an element of their genius " (Pottier).

Black-figure vase-painting, disengaging itself from fruitful foreign influences, Ionian and Corinthian, more and more asserted its originality. Sculpture followed a parallel road. It learned much that was valuable from Ionia. This influence, still timid about 560, became dominant under the government of Pisistratus and his sons, who followed an islands and an Asiatic continental policy, and it reached its apogee between 540 and 510, to lose all its active power about 500. It is to this period that the smiling Korai of the Acropolis belong, some of them carved by Ionian artists, the rest imitated from them by native sculptors. Attic art was transformed: it had got from the Ionians the knowledge of working in marble with its soft and supple modelling, the rendering of drapery, elegance, grace and charm, all of which was to tone down the still somewhat harsh quality of primitive Atticism.[4]

From about the year 500, however, the Attic artist turned his regard towards the Peloponnesian studios, whose influence manifests itself in sculpture as in ceramics (red-figure vases of Euphronius and Douris). He gained new qualities from this schooling. He learned from the Dorians a better appreciation of bronze for the reproduction of the human figure,

---

[1] Lechat, **LXXVIII**, p. 136. [2] **CXLIV**, vol. x, p. 137.
[3] **CXLV**, vol. iii, p. 612 ff. [4] **LXXVIII, LXXIX.**

especially the body of the athlete; he ceased to devote himself
to minutiæ and an exaggerated care for details, and gave up
seeking after a sometimes affected elegance, to cultivate
instead sobriety and simplicity of drapery and hair; he
abandoned the now stereotyped smile for a grave expression
of countenance that had been manifested in Peloponnesian
sculpture from the earliest times; he straightened up the
receding forehead of the Ionian heads (Fig. 16) till he had
achieved the vertical " Hellenic " profile (Fig. 17) already
aimed at in the old Peloponnesian work; in his technique he
acquired a more exact rendering of such details of the human
body as the eyes and muscles.[1]

FIG. 16.   RECEDING PROFILE   FIG. 17.   " HELLENIC "   PROFILE
ON A 6TH-CENTURY IONIAN   ON A LECYTHUS OF THE MIDDLE
VASE.   OF THE 5TH CENTURY.

Thenceforth the Attic artist was to blend in one harmonious
and original whole his own native qualities and those he owed
to the Ionians and the Dorians.   Exaggerated grace, elegance
and sweetness on the one hand, and a too hard and tense
strength on the other, were to be toned down to a grace which
did not degenerate into affectation, a sweetness that was not
effeminacy and a strength that avoided roughness.   Atticism
shows these qualities from the first half of the 5th century
and preserves them throughout its existence.   These, allowing for the differences of time and temperament, are the
qualities of Phidias and Praxiteles.   Now Ionian and now
Dorian traits come uppermost, according to the individual
artist and his training, and we can distinguish two tendencies,

[1] **LXXVIII**, p. 384.

developing simultaneously, an Attic-Ionian, manifested in Calamis and Callimachus, and an Attic-Dorian, manifested in Phidias. But these are merely nuances which shade into the complete whole.[1]

Athens achieved dominance by this reconciliation of diverse characters and also through happy political circumstances. Her merchant fleet, protected by the navy, exported the products of her ceramic industry far and wide. The Corinthians, who had got into a rut of routine, did not realise what tremendous progress would be achieved by the Attic invention of red-figure decoration at the close of the 6th century; they saw their own industry decline, driven off the markets by Attic vases, in the first quarter of the 5th century, and this was one of the reasons for the hostility between Athens and Corinth, which was to lead to the outbreak of the Peloponnesian war.

The artistic fame of Athens began to grow from the first half of the 5th century. In the second half of this century she was the intellectual and artistic centre of Greece, drawing artists from all parts. Ionia no longer existed as an independent centre; a few of her artists continued to practise their art in Greece in Asia, in particular for the Lycian and Carian dynasts, but they came under the influence of the Attic masters and reflected the style of Phidias, and many of them came to Athens. The Peloponnese itself, which possessed the flourishing Argive school, witnessed Polyclitus softening his too severe style by contact with Phidian art. A pleiad of Athenian artists radiated the fame of their city by working in the Peloponnese, at Phigalia, Olympia, and in the isles and in Asia Minor. Everywhere, those works which were really Attic, or were inspired by them, celebrate the glory of the city which Pericles justifiably held up to the admiration of the world.

Doubtless from the 4th century the distinctions between the different schools grew less marked owing to the greater interpenetration that now went on; doubtless, too, with the coming of the Hellenistic monarchies, other art centres competed with Athens and took away her lead, for her creative vein had petered out and she lived on her glorious past. Yet Attic art was preserved from the Hellenistic excesses of

[1] **LXXVIII**, p. 351.

emotion and exaggerated musculature manifest in the Asia Minor schools, thanks to its nice feeling for proportion. Up to the end the Attic artists remained faithful to the old ideal which produced the masterpieces of Phidias and Praxiteles, and it was they who taught the Romans to admire it.

CHAPTER VI

LOCAL SCHOOLS

THESE three great ethnic divisions were subdivided in their turn into smaller groups. These were the studios and schools whose character differed according to locality, and which marked with their more or less original imprint the products of the industrial arts and of sculpture.

Their rôle was especially important in archaic times. By the 5th century the artist, freed from the constraint of the old conventions, was expressing his own individuality; but before that time the studio tradition and the stylistic processes handed down from father to son, from master to pupil, in the same environment, thus constituting a traditional discipline, took precedence of individual artistic characterization. In the Ionian art of the 6th century, one can distinguish the ceramic workshops of the Cyclades, of Rhodes, of Naucratis and of Cyrene; the sculptural studios of Chios, of Miletus and of Samos; and in Peloponnesian art the pottery of Corinth, of Argos and Sicyon, and the sculptural schools of Argos, Laconia and Ægina. Beneath the features common to the ethnic group, the expert seeks to determine the more individual details which separate one local school from another. Insular Ionian art reveals different qualities from those manifest on the Asiatic coast: in statuary it likes attenuated proportions, inherited, maybe, from the Ægeans, whereas the statuary art of Asia, influenced by the East, prefers stockiness.

Confronted by works of uncertain provenance, one often hesitates to attribute them to this centre rather than that. In fact, the schools were frequently interrelated, and even by the 6th century spoke a kind of common dialect. Certain scholars for this reason contest the existence of regional schools, putting forward by way of argument the numberless collaborations between Attic, Æginetan and Peloponnesian artists; they claim that there is no ground for setting up distinctions in the first half of the 5th century between the features of the sculptures of Argive, Sicyonian and Æginetan schools, that, on the contrary, there is a remarkable uniformity of style and a general unification.[1] Assuredly, it was an error to multiply these regional groups to excess, to go so far as to create certain fictitious schools on the strength of mistaken criteria such as provenance, quality of the material and details of style which a closer examination has shown to be non-existent (for example, a Naxos school of the 6th century founded on the use of Naxian marble, and a Northern Greek school), and to seek subtle nuances which often existed nowhere but in the mind of the archæologist.[2] Both these points of view are extremist, but mere suppression of the reality of local groups will not solve the difficulties. The Æginetan ideal is not that of the Attics, and although the Peloponnese turns Attic sculpture into a new direction at the beginning of the 5th century, it is yet hardly possible to confound the ephebus of Ligourio,[3] a work by one of the successors of the Argive sculptor Ageladas, with ephebus No. 698 of the Acropolis, conceived, perhaps, by the Athenian Critius.[4] For the rest, does not the school of Argus show a remarkable continuity of style from Polymedes (6th century) up to the time of the disciples of Polyclitus ?

What is undoubtedly true is that the distinction between the regional schools grows less with the passage of time. The work of unification already begun in the 6th century was pursued in the first half of the 5th century and renders these differences less and less perceptible; in the second half of this century one can no longer distinguish any schools except the Attic which Phidias and his disciples render illustrious, and the Argive-Sicyonian represented by Polyclitus and his successors. Even these two are mutually interpenetrated, because, though there may be something Dorian in Phidias, there is also something Attic in Polyclitus and more especially in those who carried on his tradition in the 4th century. Regional differences become more and more blotted out in the 4th century, and art takes on an international character. None the less, one still perceives slight differences of style between the schools of Pergamum, of Rhodes, of Antioch

---

[1] **LXXIII**, p. 23 ff.
[2] **VI**, vol. i, p. 413.
[3] **LXII**, vol. i, p. 322.
[4] **LXXVIII**, p. 452.

and of Alexandria, and an ideal that is very different from the ideal of the Attic school.

For these regional schools a personal school was now to be substituted, that is to say the æsthetic ideal and stylistic processes inaugurated by an original artist which are docilely followed by his disciples. Phidias and Polyclitus, doubtless, are traditionalists, but they are likewise powerful geniuses whose personal style impresses itself on the one hand on Attic art and on the other on the Argive art of the second half of the 5th century and even of subsequent centuries. In the 4th century Praxiteles, Scopas and Lysippus are also heads of schools whose influence, concurrently with that of their earlier rivals, we can follow up to the very end in Greek art.

CHAPTER VII

ARTISTIC INDIVIDUALITIES[1]

THE personality of the individual artist must also be taken into account in this analysis of the differences between schools. Texts, and their own signatures, have often given us their names. Sometimes the pride of the creative artist is naïvely shown: "Alxenor the Naxian made it; behold it!" (6th-century stele).[2] They rivalled one another in skill, and Euthymides, the vase-painter, proclaims of his own work that Euphronius never did anything better (first quarter of the 5th century).[3]

In the 6th century there are plenty of names—need we recall the Chios family comprising Micciades, Archermus, Bupalus and Athenis,[4] and others as well? We cannot deny them their originality. But it is to be found mainly in the application of some new technical process or in the happy choice of a motif. Archermus of Chios invents the type of the winged Victory, or, rather, adapts an old Oriental theme to the goddess; Glaucus of Chios, according to the Ancients, invented iron soldering; Rhœcus and Theodorus of Samos introduced from Egypt hollow bronze-casting. They perfected the effects sought by their predecessors, working out in closer detail the study of drapery and anatomy, and Cimon of Cleonæ was better at rendering folds, transparent drapery, and foreshortening than those who had gone before him.

But individual style had not yet asserted itself. Their work pre-eminently reflected the studio tradition, showing the family likeness it bore to the work of the local or national school, and no individual talent stands out from the uniformity of the mass.

The individual artist's personality grew in stature in the 5th century, whether in painting, sculpture or pottery; obvious differences in style and execution now correspond

[1] **CLIII** ff. [2] **LXXXIV**, vol. viii, p. 360.
[3] **CXLIV**, vol. x, p. 391. [4] **LXXXIV**, vol. viii, p. 298.

with differences in name. Calamis, Myron, Callimachus and Phidias in sculpture; Euphronius, Douris and Brygus in vase-painting, to quote only a few names at random, cannot be confounded the one with the other. Individual temperament now begins to play its part, whereas previously art had progressed chiefly by the collective effort of workshops. From the 5th century the history of art begins to be that which hitherto it has not been and which it has been nowhere else in antiquity, a history of artistic individualities which modify its development according to their will. Neither Egypt nor Mesopotamia can make such a claim: it is one among the many titles to glory possessed by the Greek artist that he could impress his own strong personality on art.

From this date, while we distinguish in works of art the features belonging to this or that ethnic or local group, we must endeavour to discover these individual differences. A difficult study, in the uncertain state of our knowledge, on which scholars have often wasted much ingeniousness and subtlety in vain.[1] Too often they have attempted to define the style of a master, of whom nothing is known but his name and a list of his works, by the aid of anonymous monuments or later copies of vanished originals ! They have even gone so far as to manufacture complete artists who have never existed except as phantoms of their own fancy, and this to reconcile the contradictory data of texts and monuments, so that Alcamenes the Older, Calamis the Younger, and Scopas the Elder have been called forth from the void only to be chased back again in the end by common sense.

And how uncertain is our knowledge of the artists who really did exist and whose works won the admiration of the Ancients ! What do we know of Calamis, of Callimachus, of Alcamenes, and of many other artists of repute ? Even Phidias' personality is hard to disentangle from that of his pupils. How very rare are those plastic originals about which no doubt whatever exists and which permit us to ascertain with absolute certainty the style of a master ! Though the Hermes of Olympia really appears to have been carved by Praxiteles himself, we only have copies of Myron and Polyclitus. What actually was the share of Phidias in

[1] VI, vol. i, p. 263 ff.

the Parthenon, of Scopas at Tegea and in the Mausoleum at Halicarnassus ? Not a single copy can be definitely attributed to Pythagoras of Rhegium, to Calamis, Callimachus, Alcamenes, or to numberless others, and the reconstruction of their artistic activity is but a tissue of hypotheses, some of which are plausible while the others are doomed almost as they appear. This deceptive study, like the study of regional schools, should teach the expert caution, and with even better reason. He is justified in trying to characterize the personal style of the masters so long as he does not attempt —as is too often done—to pass off fragile hypotheses as actual truth, and so long as he does not obscure and complicate the history of Greek art. How much time has been wasted in testing these hypotheses—and then in destroying them ! In the effort to be too precise the history of Greek artists becomes untruthful. Further, it is not the individual who matters so much as his work; the thoughts and emotions revealed by the monuments themselves are more interesting than the personality of those who created them or than the somewhat peurile satisfaction of having attributed a certain piece of work to a given artist.

Yet we perceive that there was great variety among these artistic temperaments. Some are more bound by tradition than others; while they achieve progress they continue to follow docilely in the way traced for them by their predecessors. Phidias and Polyclitus are traditionalists *par excellence* who carry to its culminating point an earlier ideal slowly elaborated by such men as Hegias and Ageladas. In taste, Calamis and Callimachus are heirs to the Ionian spirit, and carry on the work of the 6th-century sculptors. A few, in their technical routine, persevere in antiquated practices, and somewhere about 415 the sculptor of one of the Caryatids of the Erechtheum models a back according to the process of his 6th-century ancestor.[1] Among vase painters, some look towards the past and some towards the future. The differences between the two pediments at Ægina (about 470), between the Parthenon metopes (about 442-440), are not the result of chronological discrepancy but proceed from a difference in the age and temperament of the authors, of whom some, who are old, maintain the style in vogue in

[1] **LXXVIII**, p. 493.

their youth, whilst others, who are younger, exhibit new tendencies.

There are, as a fact, some spirits who are greater innovators than others, and who seek fresh paths. In the 5th century such were Pythagoras of Rhegium[1] and Myron,[2] masters of action and of violent and quick movement, which they import into isolated statues from reliefs and figurines.

There are some who are enamoured of calm and repose. It is they who complete the development of the old statuary type of the immobile archaic Kouros and Kore. In these images the muscles are slack, and the weight of the body rests on one leg, the arms make but simple and slow gestures such as that of the athlete placing the victor's crown on his head, or pouring into his hand the oil with which he is about to anoint his body, or knotting about his temples the fillet of victory. The severe Dorian peplos covers the women with its vertical folds. Such was the ideal of Phidias, who yet interested himself also in light arrangements of moving drapery and in bold gestures, and such, in particular, is the ideal of Polyclitus and of Praxiteles. Polyclitus' ephebi, and his very rare women, exhibit only the smallest degree of action. How calm are the Doryphoros, the Diadumenos, and the Westmacott ephebus![3] The Ancients claimed that Polyclitus invented the walking attitude, in which the body's weight rests on one leg whilst the other, in the rear, and poised on the ball of the foot, appears to be on the point of moving forward. In reality this is not action but a means of varying the rhythm of a body in repose—of which the Argive master, moreover, was not the inventor. In the Panathenaic procession the actors slowly advance towards the temple entrance where the presentation of the peplos to Athena takes place, giving the impression of tranquillity and of enduring life about which there is nothing fugitive. Praxiteles resorts even to nonchalant and languid attitudes in which the body, no longer supporting itself, leans its weight on a pillar.

Quite different is the desire of Pythagoras of Rhegium and of Myron. They seek the accidental, the pose that is fugitive and unstable. The athlete straining his body to throw the discus, Silenus flinging up legs and arms in a disordered

---

[1] CLXIV.   [2] CLXIX.   [3] LXX, p. 250.

gesture of surprise, and the pugilist raising his fist to strike the brutal blow, show the mobile variety of reality; this desire contrasts by its ardent energy with the slight nuances in the state of repose at which their confrères aim, and with that apparent monotony for which the Ancients reproached Polyclitus, whose statues, they said, are *pœne ad unum exemplum*.

Then there are idealists who abstract from reality the permanent and durable features irrespective of the accidental, such as, again, Phidias and Polyclitus.   Others are more realistic, such as Myron and Pythagoras who catch the fleeting action and are led to a closer observation of nature.   They testify to it in the details of the human body; they render the hair, the tendons and veins more scrupulously; they are more anxious to reproduce nature faithfully than to embellish it according to some preconceived ideal.   Pythagoras already seeks to render the signs of passion, of pain and of age in his faces.   That is why, when art finally developed in a realistic direction, at the beginning of the 4th century, later artists claimed him as their precursor.

There are artists who imprison the soul, or a thought, in stone.   Phidias' countenances, however calm they may be, are not inert; they seem to be plunged in profound reverie; the spiritual sculptor gives a soul to his ephebi and to his maidens who advance gravely along the Panathenaic frieze, as he has given a soul to his gods, and to his Olympian Zeus. But with Polyclitus and Myron the body takes precedence over the mind; these artists had no other thought than to render the human body in its most beautiful aspect, without troubling to ennoble it with an intelligence.

According to their tastes and their places of origin individual artists lean towards Ionian delicacy, Attic charm, or Peloponnesian strength and severity.   Some prefer the naked figure of man and his solid musculature.   Polyclitus creates nothing but athletic statues, and the Amazon is an exception among his works.   Pythagoras, likewise, chose male figures, avoided drapery and the representation of woman.   Lysippus was of this line, with his athletes and his statues of Heracles. Others, on the contrary, liked the supple and sensuous female figure, and drapery which offers so many possibilities of beauty in its folds and by its contrast with human flesh; such was

Praxiteles. Witness, for example, the vase-painting of the beginning of the 5th century—with Oltus it was almost always draped figures; with Brygus the muscles were indicated less exactly than with Euphronius, because feminine nudity attracted him more.

There were artists whose interests were rather with earth than with the gods, who made a study of the living body rather than dreamed of conceiving superhuman images of divinities—Pythagoras of Rhegium and Polyclitus, for example. Their ideal was above all human, and they form a contrast with Phidias whose imagination flees from the real to dwell in the realm of the Olympians with Athena and Zeus and the rest.

How diverse are all these individualities beneath their apparent uniformity! The variety results from different causes, from personal temperament and taste, from age, and even from the ethnic origin of the individual. In vase-painting, the foreign potters preferred drapery to complete nudity— a reminiscence of Oriental ideas of modesty unknown to the Greeks. The rank of the artist also enters into this question, and that is partly why potters are more realistic than sculptors, because, being artisans of humble extraction, they are closer to the people and less embarrassed in their productions by social convenances.

Thus we must take note of individual variants which, perceptible at every period, introduce into art, however homogeneous it may be, the complexity and subtle shades of difference proper to life. They are responsible for artists such as Lycius and Styppax[1] being realists during the height of 5th-century idealism; and, later on, for Attic idealism carrying on in its classical manner in the face of the realism and triumphant emotionalism of the Hellenists; they explain the continuities of style; they foreshadow the still obscure tendencies destined to become paramount later, the various currents which run right through the history of Greek art, now distinct, and now in a mingled stream.

[1] **LXII**, vol. ii, p. 128.

PART THREE

REALIZATION. TECHNICAL PROBLEMS

How will the artist realize his thought ? On the morrow of the Dorian invasions he was back, in technique, in native barbarism. His material forced strange conventions on him— the conventions of art's earliest beginnings—and these he had to get rid of gradually, in measure as he became more skilled. He had to educate his vision and establish an exact correspondence between this vision, which perceived, the hand that worked, and the material to be manipulated. He had to solve problems of anatomy, drapery, pose, foreshortening, perspective, modelling and composition. These difficulties were overcome in stages; each age brought some fresh progress. This apprenticeship in technical methods which would make it possible for him to realize an æsthetic ideal constitutes an essential chapter of the history of Greek art; as we come to see how the artist finally bent to his will the rebellious material which at first resisted all his efforts to master it, and as we find out what chiefly engaged his attention, plastically and pictorially, we shall come to understand what those characteristic features of Hellenic art really are which we shall note individually later on.

This education did not come to the Greek from without; he had to master it himself. Soon he had overtaken his predecessors and his contemporaries and he opened up a wide road of progress for art. He grappled with problems which at the very most had been glanced at by other minds prior to his day, such as pose, rhythm, muscles in repose and in action, drapery, the principles of composition, of foreshortening and perspective and so on—acquisitions which to-day seem banal but which were then all quite new. Modern art, which profits by them, owes them to those Greek masters who, by long effort and experiment, urged on by their sense of reality and their æsthetic feeling, solved these problems once and for all.

And what are these problems ?

Firstly: The constitution of the several branches of art; and in each of them a definition of the forms and typical themes which were to become the moulds of thought.

Secondly: The choice of the materials to be used and which were to be the vehicles of thought.

Thirdly: The acquisition of the grammar of art, at first incorrectly and then perfectly; the knowledge of how to transcribe the human body in its thousand details, the drapery which covers it, and the life proper to it; the constitution of the syntax of art, that is to say, the raising of it from detail to the co-ordination of its parts with a view of building up an æsthetic synthesis; and a careful examination of rhythm, *symmetria*, harmony, composition, and modifications of reality by action, atmosphere and so forth.

Towards 450-445 (the date of the Doryphoros of Polyclitus and of many of the celebrated works of Phidias, such as the Athena Lemnia, about 450, and the Athena Promachos, about 448) this patiently experimental stage was finished. The few naïvetés which still persisted in the time of those who went just before (beginning of the 5th century) had disappeared. It only remained finally to solve the problems of pictorial modelling, of linear and aerial perspective, and to introduce nuances testifying to a modified ideal. The great artists of the second half of the 5th century had merely to practise and perfect their knowledge and to rub off the edge of extreme novelty—to make it, as it were, instinctive and natural; those of the 4th century and of Hellenistic times could add nothing to it that was essential, and were to contribute simply a few unimportant modifications.

CHAPTER I

THE VARIOUS BRANCHES OF ART AND THE CHOICE OF MATERIAL

THE Greeks created original forms personal to themselves in every branch of art—in architecture, painting, sculpture and the industrial arts.

They created for their divinity a dwelling—the temple[1]— quite unknown to the Ægeans, whose sacred places were caves, high-places, and chapels within their palaces. In continental Greece they made use of the Mycenæan megaron which became the Doric temple; in Greece in Asia maybe they also took some elements of the Doric temple from pre-Hellenic buildings, and there were others that they got from the East. But these borrowed elements were so thoroughly transformed and adapted that both the Doric and Ionic orders were genuinely Greek creations. The elaboration of this creation was complete by the 6th century. The Doric temple, built at first of wood and brick and then, from the end of the 7th century, of stone, had refined its too heavy forms, and had succeeded in achieving the best relation between its various parts, such as columns and entablatures, the harmony of its lines, and the distribution of polychromy and ornament. Henceforth slight modifications only are possible, for example in the echinus whose curve became more and more upright.[2] The capitals at Ægina (towards 470),[3] Delphi (Treasury of the Athenians, about 485), already classic, foreshadow those of the Parthenon (447-38). The Parthenon marks the apogee of the Doric; later architects could only introduce nuances, or contaminations, frequently unfortunately, which betrayed exhaustion.

The Ionic column, for its part, also evolving from wood to stone, built up its floral ornament, straightened the volutes

[1] **XXIII** ff.
[2] " Évolution du chapiteau dorique depuis le viie siècle," **JOAI**, xix-xx, 1919, p. 167.
[3] Furtwaengler, *Aegina*, 1906.

of its capital which at Delos and at the Acropolis at Athens
(end of the 6th century) already foreshadow that of the Erechtheum (420-407) (Fig. 18). This provides the typical example
of this architectural order, henceforth to be the rival of the
Doric on the Continent.[1]

The Corinthian capital, which, although its elements may
be sought in earlier times, appeared first in the temple at
Phigalia (about 420), does not constitute an order properly
speaking, being really only a variant of the Ionic. It was to be
preferred, at a later period, in which growing luxury replaced
the old sobriety, because it was richer than the Ionic and
especially than the Doric (Fig. 19).

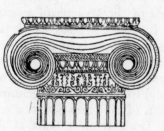

FIG. 18. IONIC CAPITAL IN
THE ERECHTHEUM.

FIG. 19. CORINTHIAN CAPITAL OF
THE THOLOS AT EPIDAURUS, BE-
GINNING OF THE 4TH CENTURY.

These three forms are characteristic of Greek architecture
and reveal to us the æsthetic thought of the Greeks. Born
of cult necessities, they are adapted to such various uses as
funerary edifices, fountains, stoas and markets among public
buildings, and to private dwelling-houses. We find the
principle of the Doric or Ionic colonnade and entablature
everywhere.

The other buildings which realize architectural ideas,[2]
such as graves and utilitarian structures, ramparts, aqueducts
and ports, are less typical and do not call for notice.

The Doric temple provides fields for decoration: the
triangle of the pediment and the rectangle of the metopes
at first called for painting (terra cotta metopes at Thermos,
6th century), then relief and carving in the round. Fresh

[1] See above, p. 130.   [2] **XXIII** ff.

problems were set the artist, who could not seek models in
the Oriental or pre-Hellenic arts, in which such decoration
was unknown, although the Ægeans had a knowledge of the
principle of alternation between metope and triglyph.   And
we shall see what were the solutions arrived at after some
experimental efforts.[1] On these fields, as on the sculptured
frieze borrowed from the East, the artist was to record the
exploits of gods and heroes and to glorify religion and the city.

Both the Ægeans and the Greeks of the geometric period
were ignorant of statuary in the round and knew figurines
only. The earliest representations of human beings and
animals of large size appeared only about the 7th century,
and thenceforward they were to multiply. Was the artist
influenced by seeing Egyptian statues ?   Perhaps the innovation was necessitated by the very conditions of social life.
The anthropomorphic god, in effect, had to live in his temple;
just as his dwelling is analogous to the dwelling of a human
being, so his effigy had to be conceived at least on the same
scale as that of mortal man. The custom of consecrating
images of victors in the national games, and of raising portraits
over the grave of the dead, likewise forced the artist to increase
the size of the divine images.

The statue fulfilled a multitude of purposes. Gods and
heroes were placed in the cella of the temple, in the empty
pediments, and were erected in the open air. On graves[2] it
was an image of the dead or an allegorical symbol, a lion or
a siren. Mortal men offered themselves as ex votos to the
divinity or commemorated some official event celebrated by
the city. Later on, statues were used decoratively in houses
and gardens. All of which supplied the artist with so many
opportunities for creative production.

But the modelling of figurines[3] in different materials
such as clay or bronze, which, at a lower cost, did duty for
the same purpose, was still continued: there were figurines
as offerings in the sanctuaries, figurines placed in graves,
figurines in connection with the domestic cult, and, much
later, decorative figurines. Produced by industrial art, they
yet retain a clear reflection of high art, and this is even more
surely reflected in the charming Tanagra and Myrina statuettes
than in later marble copies. Humble as the material may be,

[1] *Cf.* further on, p. 251.   [2] **LXIII.**   [3] **CV** ff.

are they not originals which preserve the thought of the modeller intact ?

Metopes, friezes, pediments, funerary stelæ, official and private ex voto, decree headings—all provided so many surfaces to be decorated. If some of these presented an immutable rectangle, triangle, or band, others provided forms which developed with time and which gave greater opportunities for variety to the artist. It was impossible to inscribe more than a single erect figure in profile on the tall narrow slab which was the form of the 6th-century Ionian stele. In the 5th century a wider stele was preferred, which terminated in a pediment with acroteria; on this less limited field there could be a larger number of different attitudes and the number of figures carried could be increased. In the 4th century architectural decoration has become of greater importance and the pediment is advanced, antæ limit it at the sides, and the stele takes on the appearance of a naiskos, in the interior of which the figures stand out in high relief, very nearly in the round. Great masters were not too proud to carve these industrial works, and the beautiful stele of Aristonautes (Athens Museum, first half of the 4th century) might be from the hand of Scopas himself.[1]

Painting on a large scale,[2] rendered illustrious by Polygnotus, Micon, Panainus, Zeuxis, Apelles, Parrhasius and many another, has left not a trace, and we can only get a glimpse of what it was through the medium of industrial works such as painted stelæ, terra cotta ex votos, tomb decoration, and, more particularly, vase-painting.[3] Done in fresco, in distemper, and occasionally in encaustic, its rôle was pre-eminently architectural; it was employed in the beginning for ornamenting the wall surfaces of religious and public buildings, before it came to contribute to the decoration of private dwellings about the close of the 5th century, and before it quitted the surfaces of walls for the small picture (4th century).

All these various forms of art are closely interrelated, and they all reflect the general characters of Greek æsthetics. In some, progress may have been more rapid than in others; painting and drawing were in advance of sculpture in the round, and, from the geometric Dipylon period, when sculptors

---

[1] **LXIV ; LXII,** vol. i, p. 255; ii, pp. 145, 372.
[2] **CXV** ff.   [3] **CXXIX** ff.

were carving rude ivory figurines, painters had already become capable of composing complex scenes on big vases. This advance was kept up throughout the story of Greek art. The vase designers and painters made the first experiments, created the motifs and made use of the technical methods which were later adopted by sculptors and bronze-workers; it was they, likewise, who made the first attempts at foreshortening, perspective, modelling, and chiaroscuro, and, finally, who introduced realism of view into art.

There was always interpenetration between the different branches. Sculptors and painters borrow mutually. The industrial art of the makers of stelæ and ex votos, of the figurine modellers and vase-painters, followed, at a distance, the lessons of fresco and sculpture. It is necessary to understand this reciprocal action, as also to take note of the relations which bound artists and writers together. The same spirit runs through all the productions of Greek thought.

Does the artist prefer one of these forms above the others ? Important as painting may be, sculpture[1] takes precedence of it. The surfaces available for decoration by painting are few and exiguous. They consist of the walls of sanctuaries, public buildings, assembly halls (Lesche of Cnidus, at Delphi, decorated by Polygnotus), and stoas (the Athens Poekile, painted by Polygnotus, Micon, and Panainus); then, when art had become secularized, those of private dwellings (decoration of the house of Alcibiades by Agatharchus at the end of the 5th century); and also those of funerary stelæ and vaults which were left to industrial craftsmen. There was not much point in enriching and brightening buildings by painting in a country like Greece, with its clement skies, where people lived in the open air. Furthermore, paintings are ephemeral, a failing in the eyes of the Greeks who sought to make their works of art lasting. Painted funerary stelæ are rare by comparison with those that were sculptured. It would even seem that sculpture came to take the place of painting in the course of a natural development. Although the ancient metopes at Thermos (6th century) are still of painted terra cotta, necessitated by a wooden entablature, the later stone temple adopts metopes of smooth or sculptured stone. The opportunities of sculpture were on a different scale. It was used every-

[1] **LVIII ff.**

where.   Statues and reliefs were incorporated into a building just as painting was, and they were used to decorate pediments, metopes and friezes.   But they were also set up in hundreds in the open, in the temenos, and in public squares, and they needed no protection because they were durable by nature. But more profound causes reinforced those that were due to material circumstances.   In northern lands the atmosphere is humid, outlines are blurred, colours vivid and varied, and every hue has a gamut of shades from very light to very dark, corresponding with the change of hour and the alteration of light.   In the brilliant light of the south the outlines of things stand out in that limpid atmosphere with surprising sharpness, hills and mountains looking as though their edges had been cut out; but there is little variety in the colouring; the sea is a deep blue, but the details of the landscape are lost in one uniform tint.   The south is luminous but its colour is to seek. Thus the Greek, coming under the influence of the country, must have been instinctively drawn to prefer line to colour, and sculpture to painting.   Sculpture, likewise, is more in harmony with the Greek rationalistic mentality, because line, which is abstract, is more intellectual than colour, which appeals to the senses rather than to the mind.   This is why even painting itself is linear among the Greeks; it is a coloured drawing with very clear, sharp contours and firm, clean lines: it is the painting of a sculptor not of a colourist.   Line is what the painter seeks as his supreme aim in art; is not the rivalry of Protogenes and Apelles characteristic, each one endeavouring with all the ingenuity at his command to outdo the other in fineness of line ?   For a long while the colours are flat, because modelling and chiaroscuro are recent acquisitions.

The material, by its specific qualities, exercises a great influence on a work of art.   The Greek artist reveals his æsthetic ideas by his choice of the material he works in by preference.   Evolution in the process of time causes him to give up soft materials for harder ones.   At first his hand, still uncertain, fashions statues and temples out of wood. Stone comes next; easily worked limestone is used in Doric buildings from the 7th century, as in the earliest sculptures on the Acropolis in Athens (end of the 7th and beginning of the 6th century).[1]   It is not a favourable medium for a work

[1] **LXXII, LXXVIII, LXXX, LXXXIX-XC, XCIV-V.**

of art owing to its defects and its lack of homogeneousness
in texture which tempt the artist to a rough and slipshod
mode of work. Marble takes its place;[1] statuary yields its
earliest example of marble in the second quarter of the 6th
century (Moscophoros of the Acropolis);[2] the Alcmeonidæ
use it for the façade of the temple at Delphi (536-515) and,
about 520, the Athens Pisistratidæ employ it in the enlarged
Hekatompedon. In the 5th century the temples of Aphæa
at Ægina, and of Zeus at Olympia, are still of limestone
which the architect uses according to his resources. But the
Parthenon and the Attic temples are of Pentelic marble, and
marble henceforth is the material which the artist holds most
beautiful and most worthy of him both in sculpture and
architecture.

The Greeks alone understood the beauty of marble.
No other land of antiquity attached such importance to the
choice of plastic material, and they carved indifferently in
granite, in the hard diorite of Egypt, and the sandstone and
rough limestone of Cyprus and Etruria. After the experiments of the Ionians[3] the Greek made his final choice; everywhere he adopts marble, whether he has it to his hand or is
obliged to send for it from afar. He asks from it that his
work shall endure, that it shall prove resistant to his chisel,
because the stone must be neither too easy, like clay, nor too
rebellious, like granite, but should exercise the hand of the
artist without tiring it, and permit him to gouge with that
minute detail and precision which limestone and wood forbid.
He also asks from it the beauty of its homogeneous texture
and fine grain, the smooth surfaces it offers to the eye, its
whiteness, and, in the warm Parian marble, its translucency.
Since the supreme aim of art was to reproduce the human
form, the artist realized that marble was specially suited for
rendering flesh, particularly the smooth flesh of woman, and
to give the illusion that it was alive, and that is why the
Ionians, who were pioneers in its use, carved their smiling
Korai in marble, just as, later on, Praxiteles, that master
of women's and youths' figures, preferred marble to bronze.

---

[1] **CLXXXV**, *s.v.* "Sculptura;" **LXXXIV**, vol. viii, p. 161; **LXXVIII**,
pp. 101, 127.

[2] **LXXVIII**, pp. 129, 135.

[3] See above, p. 128.

Bronze[1] was known from very early days, but the Ægeans never modelled big statues and their figurines are always cast solid. Abandoning the old process of sphyrelata, in which hammered plates of metal are riveted to a " bridge " of wood, Rhœcus and Theodorus of Samos, towards the middle of the 6th century, introduced hollow casting from Egypt and gave to Greece a new technique which was destined to bring fresh life into plastic art. Large hollow-cast bronze statues became common, and some of the greatest Greek artists, Pythagoras, Myron, Polyclitus, Phidias and Lysippus were bronze-workers. Bronze renders the artist's ideas more faithfully than marble; it perpetuates without the smallest alteration the clay model in whose easily and quickly worked plastic substance the artist shaped his thought; it avoids that rough preparatory reduction of the stone by which the model risks alteration; it permits a boldness of pose impossible in stone; like marble, it endures; it allows of minutely detailed work being done at will with the burin; finally, its sombre tone and polished surface admirably render the masculine body—the athlete's body tanned by exercise—and it makes a sharper silhouette than marble.[2]

Marble and bronze are the two principal plastic materials of Greece. Chryselephantine statuary, of very early origin, inspires masterpieces such as the Athena Parthenos and the Olympian Zeus. But its high cost restricted its use to the rare occasions on which an exceptional testimony to the piety of the faithful was to be offered to the gods, and when the statue itself was to serve as a monetary reserve. Difficult in technique, fragile, and demanding constant upkeep and repair, it runs counter to Greek taste which seeks endurance, homogeneity and sincerity in a work of art, and which marvels at this rich outward appearance that hides a miserable interior. " On the outside," exclaims Lucian, " it is Poseidon, trident in hand; it is Zeus all bright with gold and ivory. But look within: levers, wedges, iron bars, nails traversing the machine from one part to another, bolts, pitch, dust and other things equally shocking to the view—that is what you will find there."

In the Hellenistic period technique became more and more refined; the artist brought hard materials into use, and the

[1] CLXXXV, s.v. " Statuaria Ars."   [2] LXXXIV, vol. viii, p. 172.

growing luxuriousness drove him to choose rare and shining stone. Statues and statuettes were sculped in crystal, chalcedony, topaz and glass; images of negroes or of Serapis of the infernal regions were carved in dark basalt, in black marble, or in dark-coloured rocks; porphyry, which had begun to come into use in the second century B.C., was employed to imitate Satyrs ruddy with wine. Materials of different colours were used together, thus obtaining a rich natural polychromy of which chryselephantine statuary had provided an earlier example. Realism, which transformed the types of former days, introduced a greater variety into the use of statuary material which it was desired should imitate nature more closely.

The artist modelled figurines in clay[1] which were a cheap substitute for marble and bronze statues, and also vases that were less costly than those of metal. Cyprus, Etruria and Rome readily demanded large statues of it, but Greece only rarely practised this kind of statuary, in archaic times and in the closing period of her existence.[2] In temples, the ornament of the high parts such as acroteria, gargoyles and antefixæ, was carried out in terra cotta when the building was still of wood or limestone, but this yields place gradually to marble. Economic circumstances occasionally dictate an earthen statue, or even a plaster one, such, for example, as that made by Theocosmus of Megara during the Peloponnesian war. But the artist early recognized that clay, which is too ductile, held out no promise of progress, that it becomes deformed in the baking and that his intentions may be betrayed, that it is too humble an agent for the magnification of gods and men. Nevertheless, during Hellenistic times and in order to supply the wants of a private clientele avid for luxury and pleasure—princes who loved ostentation, and towns that kept up a mutual rivalry—it was necessary to produce much and to produce rapidly whilst at the same time satisfying at a small cost the new taste which attached greater importance to external brilliancy and to appearances than to sincerity. Clay, which could be rapidly worked, and whose first cost is insignificant, was in high favour, and one even sees a genuine renaissance of plastic art in clay, which flourished in archaic times but which the classic age had

[1] CV ff.　　　　　　　　　　　　[2] LXVI-VII.

abandoned. Soft limestone, which had not been employed since the 6th century, also came into use; stucco and plaster were used to render certain details, for modelling reliefs and statues, and the busts of poets and celebrated writers adorning libraries and studios were often of this material. Even wax itself was used in statuary.

The choice of material is thus guided by profound reasons which bring out the general characters of Greek art. Endurance was demanded of the material. The temple, the everlasting abode of the god; the statue, the substitute for divine or mortal man, must resist the attacks of time and insure to the divinity a perpetual homage, to the faithful his constant benediction and protection, and to the author imperishable glory. Thanks to the desire for perfection, that hardness was asked for from the material which was calculated to exercise the artist's hand and permit him to realize fresh and unceasing progress, instead of holding him back in consequence of an easy routine such as that practised in Cyprus and Etruria, where the too soft material renders such technical education impossible. Beauty is also required of it, because the material was appreciated for its own sake even when unworked: the architect leaves his walls bare without plaster; are not the walls in the Propylæa beautiful in themselves, in their marble, and in the precision with which the stone is arranged? That is why polychromy retreats as marble appears.[1] The wooden and limestone temples, and statues in soft stone, are entirely covered with a coat of variegated colour, but the buildings and statues in marble now show only a discreet polychromy which is partial and not total; the flesh of the statue keeps its hue of the marble which is at the most warmed up by " ganosis." Homogeneity is also demanded. The statue is entirely of marble or entirely of bronze, and gold and ivory figures are the exception. At most, a few details such as the eyes, the curls of the hair, ornaments, swords, lances and cuirasses are occasionally added in some other material. Sincerity, likewise, is required. The material presents itself such as it really is, and there is no attempt to deceive the eye. The gilding and silvering of terra cotta figurines is a more recent Hellenistic and Roman process. The Egyptians and Ægeans in their architecture

[1] **LXXVIII,** pp. 79, 316.

and ceramics had already imitated stone in painting, but this delusive expedient had to wait until the Hellenistic and Roman period for its revival. These details reveal the feeling for proportion and fittingness in Greek art. Very precious or very rare materials are not employed, but, on the other hand, neither is the use of too common materials, such as clay, admitted; marble and bronze constituted a happy mean.

The artist for a long while attempted to carve his statue free-hand from the stone, without the aid of a model.[1] This appeared later. The sculptors of the pediments at Olympia would appear to have used small models conceived as reliefs, and the authors of the pediments at Epidaurus (4th century)[2] and of the Korai of the Erechtheum, reproduced large and carefully executed models. Whereas bronze-casting secures the immediate and exact reproduction of the clay model, the sculptor is obliged to reduce to it slowly in stone, and to interpose this preparatory work between the first crystallization of his inspiration and the final result. But the Greek artist undertook all stages of the work himself; he did not give himself over to the marble-carver who, in modern art, shapes the block, and points it up, leaving to the creator the final touches only. These intermediaries and mathematical pointing are not employed in Greece before the Hellenistic period;[3] the work of art retains a freshness and sincerity which such processes can but impair.

There is a mutual reaction of materials. Bronze and marble techniques exert a reciprocal influence on one another; clay working, essential for the model, can be recognized in the bronze statues and sometimes even in the stone; and, possibly, at the beginning the processes of wood sculpture, exercised some influence on the appearance of images carved in soft stone and marble.[4]

The artist, having chosen the form of art he will practise, the material he will work in, goes on to realize his subject: he has to transcribe the human body, which is his ideal, either in repose or in action, nude or draped, isolated or in a group.

[1] **CLXXXV**, *s.v.* " Sculptura."
[2] **LXII**, vol. ii, p. 195.
[3] Furtwaengler, *Statuencopien in Altertum*; **VI**, vol. i, p. 333.
[4] **VI**, vol. ii, p. 265.

H

Many problems now confront him whose solution he found only after long experimental effort. They are as follow:

1. Pose;
2. Anatomy;
3. Drapery;
4. Co-ordination of parts: synthetic view, rhythm, *symmetria*, harmony, proportion;
5. Modification in the appearance of the object due to distance and atmosphere: foreshortening, perspective, modelling, chiaroscuro;
6. Composition: groups, etc.

CHAPTER II

POSE

THE human being has got to be posed, to be given some kind of attitude, and his external contour—his general silhouette—has to be traced before the rendering of his muscles or drapery can be attempted, or before consideration can be given to the question of grouping him with his compeers.

The most ancient Greek plastic works[1] are the ivory idols found in the Dipylon tombs at Athens (9th to 8th centuries) and the crude bell-shaped clay statuettes of Bœotia. Their barbaric quality is surprising when we know that, many centuries earlier, Ægean artists had known how to render the human body with truth and boldness in poses full of action, in the round (Knossos acrobat), in relief (the Boxers' Vase from Haghia Triada), and in line (frescoes); that they had already observed human anatomy very closely (Knossos torso), and such details as veins and nails (Knossos acrobat).

The Dorian invasion had plunged art into native barbarism again, throwing it back some thousands of years—almost to the point to which Neolithic peoples had brought it (before 3000 B.C.). Is there very much difference between the statuettes of the Attic Dipylon and those yielded by the eneolithic horizons at Phæstos and Knossos, or the eneolithic idols of the Cyclades ? The body is merely silhouetted without any interior detail, is rigid and lifeless with the arms stretched down the sides, and undetached from the body, and the legs unseparated. This schema belongs to all art in its earliest stages, whether ancient or modern. The nearest relatives of the first Greek sculptures are the statues made by the present populations of Africa or Oceania. Art everywhere felt the same constraints and had to submit to the same conventions; beginning with crude uniformity it only gradually differentiated its productions according to race

[1] **LXXXIV**, vol. vii, p. 142.

and country. Yet it was these shapeless dolls that fore-shadowed Hellenic perfection (Fig. 20).

What did the artist desire to convey when he made such figures ? His intention was not to show the human body such as it really is, representing its muscles, drapery, expression and varied poses truthfully. These were not only problems too hard for his rudimentary knowledge to solve, but they had no interest for him. Art everywhere began as a writing; in it the image was but an ideogram of the human body. It sufficed that the spectator should recognize the very simple idea it was intended to express. This was sometimes the notion of a god re-ceiving homage, protecting human beings, or present in his sanctuary where his statue was set up, or in the grave where the figurine was deposited; or the notion of the faithful who offered his own effigy as an ex voto. Or else it was the idea of a goddess whose fruitful and maternal character was emphasized by showing her holding her breasts in her hands or carrying an infant in her arms.

Fig. 20. Detail of proto-Attic hydria of Ana-latus, 8th Century.

The image seemed to say to him who contemplated it: I am the god, I am the faithful, I am the dead. For this there was no need for complicated poses or exact details; an inert silhouette, the simplest of gestures—a schema, in short—sufficed to evoke the idea.

The types were indeterminate. The same external pre-sentment served indifferently for gods and mortals, for the living and the dead. The intentions of the donor determined the sense to be given to the image, to the cult statue, the effigy of the dead, or the ex voto of a worshipper. Up to the end of the 6th century, the Kouroi[1] and Korai[2] repeated the same type, and it was external details alone, such as the circumstance of their discovery in a sanctuary or on a tomb, or else inscriptions, which permitted them to be denominated with some degree of accuracy as Apollo or the mortal deceased,

[1] LXVIII.   [2] LXXVIII-IX.

as Aphrodite or the feminine worshipper. This general
indeterminateness of the earliest times still persisted, in part,
up to the 5th century.[1]

One great technical rule inflexibly regulates all primitive
art, and the art of Greece is no exception. This is the rule of
" frontality."[2] It obliged the sculptor
to conceive his statue in such manner
as to be viewed exclusively from the
front, and it caused him to stereotype
the figure in a rigid attitude in such
fashion that a vertical plane cuts it in
two symmetrical halves, and, passing
through the root of the nose, the
mouth, the umbilicus, and the pudenda,
undergoes deviation neither to the
right nor the left. In this vertical
plane there is no flexure, no torsion,
no inclination of the torso, except
from before or behind. It is impossible under such conditions to give
life to a statue, to render those
thousand modifications of form that
action brings to the body, or to engage
it in common action with other figures.
This immobile body remained what it
had been at the beginning, an ideogram, a geometrical abstraction. The
only movement possible is one that
does not disturb this inflexible torso
and pelvis—action which bends the
arms in a forward, backward, or sideways direction, or that moves the
legs, one of which is advanced. But
this movement entails no such repercussion on the muscles as ought to be
present (Fig. 21).

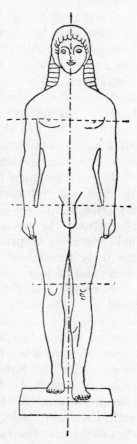

FIG. 21. FRONTALITY.
TENEA KOUROS.

The gestures are lacking in expression, as with all primitives. The artist does not know what to do with these arms

[1] Deonna, "L'indétermination primitive et la différenciation progressive," *Rev. d'Ethnographie et de Sociologie*, 1912, iii, p. 22; **VI,**
vol. ii, p. 415.

[2] **CLXXVI,** p. 9; **VI,** vol. ii, p. 167.

and legs, and the image stands as gawkishly before him as a present-day peasant in front of a camera. Its arms hang by its sides, or it crosses them on its chest; it does not yet know how to look easy and natural or how to evince life in its attitude by some significant action which would break the monotony.

Plastic art is still ignorant of how to give some meaning to these inert limbs or to make them express an action or a thought—a problem which the 5th century will have the honour of solving. Up till that period gesture is almost meaningless. The arms hang by the sides or are advanced slightly, and sometimes the hands hold some attribute. That is all. Drawing and relief, and the statues that issue from drawing, alone had the knowledge at the time to co-ordinate arms and legs in some definite movement, and this was because they were governed by other rules.

It was a technical constraint which embarrassed the artist. He had not yet arrived even at mastering his obstinate material, and it was the material which mastered the hand of the artist. He was afraid of breaking his stone if he tried bold gestures; he prudently kept the arms undetached from the body throughout their length, thus getting support for them, and he joins the legs together.

None the less, the artist achieved some progress as time went on. Gradually the arms became detached, till at last only a light tenon united the hand to the sides, and might even be absent, leaving the hand free. The rigid arm flexes at the elbow as it is advanced. The Ptōon Kouros, the Piombino Apollo, the last-comers in this series (end of the 6th century)[1] testify to the progress accomplished. The legs also are separated. One is put forward, timidly to begin with, then more boldly. It is always the left leg; the only exceptions are the rare statues conceived as pendants, in which alternate legs are symmetrically advanced (Pl. VII.). One asks oneself the reason for this monotony, all the more curious that it is in opposition to the prescriptions of Greek religion, in which the left is unlucky. An imitation of Egyptian statues has been suggested, since these always advance the left leg. It is possible, however, that it is a

---

[1] **LXVIII**, p. 157, No. 31; p. 274, No. 102.

question of a spontaneous feature of primitive art both in Greece and in Egypt.[1]

In the course of this evolution the greater or lesser skill of the artist, and the material employed, introduce slight variants; bronze, for example, permitting greater freedom of gesture than marble.

Within these narrow limits Greek artists seek such diversity as is permissible. The number of poses can be but few. The erect human type comprises two series. One was the youth, nearly always completely nude, rarely clothed (the Samos statues,[2] and statues of the Acropolis), advancing the left leg: his arms are glued to his sides or are slightly advanced, usually without holding any attribute, and with the fist closed. The other was the female figure draped in the Dorian peplos or the Ionian chiton and himation; her arms hang inert or one hand gathers up the folds of her dress while the other holds some offering.[3] These, with slight variations in clothing, the pose of the arms, or the attributes, are the two chosen types the artist repeats up to the end of the 6th century, and which he tirelessly multiplies because they can be adapted indifferently to any purpose, the nude male doing equally well as a god, as the dead, or as the faithful, and the draped female figure serving as well for a goddess as for a worshipper. These are the two types to-day known under the only generic names which would cover them all—Kouroi,[4] that is " youths," and Korai, that is " maidens."[5]

The draped human figure seated on a throne—the emblem of dignity of gods, highborn mortals, and the heroized dead—is less frequent.[6] A straight torso, conjoint legs, and arms generally lying flat along the thighs, compasses this attitude (Fig. 22). It was not to acquire the suppleness and the nuances proper to life before the first quarter of the 5th century, when Endœus—if he is really the author—carved the Athena of the Acropolis museum (about 479).[7]

[1] Deonna, " L'influence égyptienne sur l'attitude du type statuaire debout dans l'archaïsme grec," *Festgabe für O. Blümner*, 1914, p. 102.
[2] Curtius, AM, 1906, Pl. x.
[3] **LXXXIV**, vol. viii, p. 631.
[4] **LXVIII**.   [5] **LXXVIII-IX.**
[6] Möbius, " Die Darstellung des sitzenden Menschen in der antiken Kunst," *Diss*, Marburg, 1921; *cf.* AA, 1921, 36, p. 266.
[7] **LXXIX**, p. 445.

There were also, here and there, a few animal statues—horses and dogs.

These types are to be found from one end of Greece to the other, from Ionia to Sicily. But the horseman, more rare, is almost entirely limited to Attica, where he characterized the social rank of the Athenian ἱππεῖς.[1]

FIG. 22. STATUE OF CHARES, BRITISH MUSEUM, 5TH CENTURY. THE ARCHAIC SEATED TYPE.

These were the few statuary types realized by the artist from the early days up to the end of the 6th century. This monotony itself had its uses. Since he did not have to dissipate his efforts on attitudes and movements which were forbidden to him by frontality, the artist could turn his attention to other problems such as anatomy and drapery, and, imperfect as his understanding of them still was, it enabled him later on to realize the human figure correctly in detail and as a whole. This limitation was a very good thing for him, because he was capable of freeing himself from it precisely at the moment when, at the beginning of the 5th century, it was becoming a hindrance to him, and when, his hand and his vision being sure, and having gradually corrected the old-time errors, he was ready to pass on to further investigations and attempts.

Attitudes are more or less free and correct according as to whether the medium was drawing or sculpture in the round; drawing was ahead of plastic art because it had not had the same technical difficulties to overcome. It is, indeed, easier to trace bold gestures on a plane surface than to render them in volume in an intractable material. Though the Dipylon image-makers only knew how to make lifeless dolls with arms glued to their sides and conjoined legs, the vase-painters could already animate their figures, naïve though these might be, introducing action and movement. Relief shared in this advance made by drawing and which was maintained throughout the story of Greek art, being especially

[1] **LXXXIV**, vol. viii, p. 634.

marked in the formative period or up to about the end of the 6th century. While the painter painted on the bodies of his vases and the sculptor cut in his reliefs the most animated scenes of violent combat with figures in the most complicated attitudes, the statuary, who conceived his statue frontally, clung to his ancient schema in which the figure is frozen into the most utter immobility.

Despite his greater freedom the draughtsman, too, has to submit to certain universal conventions which prevent the exact reproduction of reality. The projection of volume in its various aspects in a single plane entails foreshortening. The artist was still incapable of reducing volume to this single plane.[1] Furthermore, his mind refuses to admit it. What he wishes to render is not reality accidentally modified by pose, environment or atmosphere, but reality as it actually is, constituted by its entire elements. In movement, certain parts may be hidden by certain other parts; the chest seen from the side may become narrower than when viewed from the front and both pectorals may not be visible; the eye, seen in profile, is likewise diminished in size. But the artist has no intention of perpetuating these temporary illusions; each part, on the contrary, must be given in its most characteristic aspect, the one which shows it most clearly and at its largest. The body seen from the front entails some difficult foreshortening, as, for example, of the nose and the feet. Placed in profile, however, the face is quite clear and the general silhouette emphasizes the incurved waist, the salient buttocks and the sinuosities of the legs. The image is thus clearer and its execution made more easy. That is why, in reliefs and paintings, with very few exceptions denoting bold but still faulty attempts, human figures up to the end of the 6th century are placed in profile, as it were filing past the spectator.

Nevertheless, certain details of this silhouette have to be rendered full-face, always with the intention of making them more comprehensible and avoiding foreshortening—the large, open, almond-shaped eye, for example, and the chest showing both pectorals. The figure as a whole is thus a mosaic of elements seen under different aspects, some in profile and others full-face, an unreal mixture to be found

[1] **CLXXX.**

in all inexperienced art and which serves for all kinds of forms, living or otherwise. The Egyptian and Eastern artist maintained this convention to the very end, and only made timid efforts to free himself from it; the Greek artist, by inventing foreshortening, was to get rid of it altogether.

Statuary, conceived so as to be viewed from the front, could only represent the human body in complete repose; frontality prohibited all action. Yet the artists of the first half of the 5th century pushed their study of movement very far; the Ægina warrior, falling backwards, is an amazingly bold "snapshot"; the art of Myron and Pythagoras is enamoured of violent action, as was the vase-painting of Euphronius, Douris, and Phintias at the same period. Whence came this new possibility for plastic art? It came from drawing and the conventions of drawing.

These, in effect, also regulate certain works done in the round, in which the artist expresses a movement, some

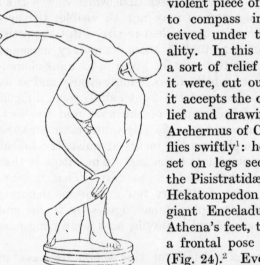

violent piece of action impossible to compass in a statue conceived under the rule of frontality. In this case the statue is a sort of relief with contours, as it were, cut out, that is to say it accepts the conventions of relief and drawing. The Nike of Archermus of Chios (6th century) flies swiftly[1]: her torso is frontal set on legs seen in profile. In the Pisistratidæ pediments of the Hekatompedon in Athens the giant Enceladus, overthrown at Athena's feet, twists his torso to a frontal pose on legs in profile (Fig. 24).[2] Even in the 5th cen-

FIG. 23. MYRON'S DISKOBOLOS.

tury the sculptor will not have succeeded entirely in ridding himself of this convention, and the Diskobolos of Myron (about 450) is an example of this persisting constraint (Fig. 23). But it is thus through the intermediation of drawing that action makes its way into modelling in the round. Without

[1] **LXXXIV**, vol. viii. p. 300.　　　　[2] *Ibid.*, p. 553.

such help, it could never have got beyond the lifeless figure. Further, representation in profile, inherent in drawing, tends to favour grouping and the common action of several figures, and modelling in the round which, in frontal statues, was capable only of setting people up, awkwardly, in a row, profits by it.

Statues in the round thus derive from two different origins: one class is conceived frontally and in repose; the other in action, as a projection. From the first are derived all those works throughout Greek art which show the human figure not in action but relaxed in tranquillity, and the

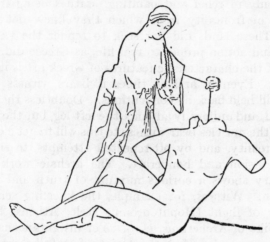

FIG. 24. PISISTRATIDÆ PEDIMENT OF THE HEKATOMPEDON IN ATHENS. ATHENA AND ENCELADUS.

ancient Kouroi of the 6th century are the direct ancestors of the 5th-century calm effigies of athletes, as also of the nonchalant ephebi of Praxiteles. The second, the statuary of action, governed by the rules of drawing, inspires small archaic bronzes, pediment statues, and isolated statues (Nike of Archermus) in the 6th century. The work of all those Greek artists who love violent action, such as Pythagoras and Myron in the 5th century, and, much later, Agasias with his fighting warrior (1st century B.C.),[1] can claim descent from it. It is a mistake to suppose that the bold gesture and the angry manner of the Tyrannicides (477) mark

[1] **LXII,** vol. ii, p. 672.

progress from the peaceable attitude of ephebus No. 698 of the Acropolis.[1] These two works, very nearly contemporaneous, belong to two distinct series which evolved independently of one another. Myron's claim to the glory of having created the instantaneous pose is also only a late invention, because violent action existed before his day; he did no more than to import into large isolated statues what had hitherto been especially limited to relief, pediment figures and small bronzes.

Nevertheless, action in statues in the round is an innovation made by Greek art. In Egypt and Mesopotamia it appears only in relief and painting, statues being frozen in the calm of frontality from which they knew not how to escape. These lands did not seek to render the variety of attitude and action proper to real life, as Greece did.

One of the characteristic features of Greek art is its desire for truth. Even in archaic times it bears witness to this, though still held back by conventions. Doubtless the statues are frontal, and uniformly advance the left leg, but the interior details of the muscles bear witness to this will to get closer and closer to reality, and by oft-repeated attempts, to eliminate errors of vision and handcraft. The archaic work of the 6th century shows a curious mixture of truth and illogical convention. Witness, for example, the kneeling schema of a race or of flight (Hoplitodromus stele, Athens; Sambon bronze, Nike of Archermus, etc.). Yet instantaneous photography has revealed that the Greeks faithfully copied one phase of a leap, the moment in which the jumper, clearing the obstacle, tucks his legs under him. Accustomed to the sights of the palæstra and the games, they noted a swift attitude which our modern eyes, unused to these scenes, for long failed to recognize.[2]

This innate feeling for reality triumphed at the close of the 6th century. The artist, whose hand had become more skilled, now rebelled against the conventional vision of former days, and he substituted for it a correct view of reality. He gave up the old supports of his primitive inexperience which had served their purpose but which, as he persevered, only hindered him.

[1] **LXXVIII**, pp. 438, 452.
[2] Deonna, "L'archéologue et le photographue," RA, 1922, xvi, p. 85.

Towards 500 the old rule of frontality ceased to exercise its despotic sway. It became apparent to the Greeks that these petrified dummy-like figures were unnatural, and that real life entailed a thousand flexures and torsions, that the plane passing through the middle of a figure is rarely vertical but curved and broken according to the attitude taken, that the body does not rest uniformly on both legs but sometimes on one and sometimes on the other, and that as a result one hip is raised higher than the other; that the two feet are not necessarily glued to the ground; and that the head is not always presented full-face to the spectator. As witness an ephebus' head in the Acropolis museum, earlier than 480, called the Blond Ephebus[1] because of the traces of colour still to be seen in the hair, or the Sulker, because of the severe, even morose, expression of the mouth. Although detached from its trunk it demonstrated that this body was no longer frontal, because it is bent and turned to the right. Or witness ephebus 698 of the Acropolis museum,[2] very nearly contemporaneous with it (Fig. 25): the weight of the body is carried on one leg, and the other is flexed, while the body is slightly turned. Frontality is broken by such little changes, and the vertical plane that aforetime divided the body in two symmetrical halves now undergoes much torsion. And this is big with consequence. Because

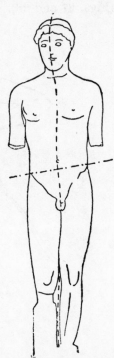

FIG. 25. EPHEBUS 698 OF THE ACROPOLIS (ATHENS). THE FRONTALITY IS BROKEN.

it means that variety of attitude, carrying with it variety of subject, is introduced into the monotonous series of Kouroi and Korai of the 6th century. Legs, heads and trunks, liberated from the old ankylosis, are now to unbend in all directions. These are no longer indeterminate figures, as of old, for whom a generic name sufficed; they are individualities each one of whom accomplishes a definite act

[1] **LXXVIII**, p. 382.   [2] *Ibid.*, p. 452.

in a particular attitude. Should we attribute this innovation to some bold master, perhaps to the ancient Ageladas of Argos,[1] whose example was soon followed by the rest ? One is more fain to believe that this was necessary progress, and that it was realized by the common efforts of the generation of artists working in the first quarter of the 5th century (Figs. 27 and 28). This breach in frontality, in effect, would

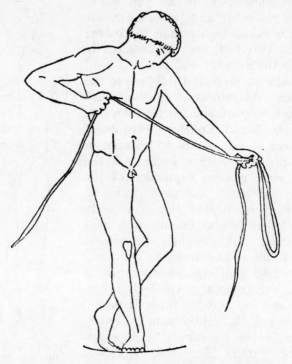

FIG. 26. EPHEBUS ON A CUP ATTRIBUTED TO ONESIMUS.

seem to be an inevitable stage in artistic evolution, because we note it also in Christian art as it emerges from the Romanesque period.[2]

The Greek was the only artist in all antiquity to break this frontality. His confrères of Egypt and the East were no more able to free themselves from this constraint than in drawing they could achieve that other Greek conquest,

[1] **LXII**, vol. i, p. 316.   [2] **VI**, vol. iii. p. 157.

so intimately linked with it, the ability to foreshorten. For thousands of years they acquiesced in this frontality rule, which did not disappear for good before the year 500. When Roman art, which was heir to the art of Greece, declined and began in the third century A.D. to sink gradually back into barbarism, frontality reappeared: figures lost their

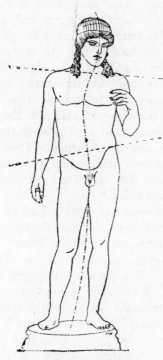 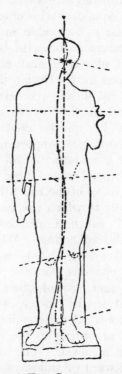

FIG. 27. POMPEII APOLLO, NAPLES MUSEUM. COPY OF AN ORIGINAL OF ABOUT 450 B.C.

FIG. 28. THE STEPHANUS ATHLETE. COPY (END OF 1ST CENTURY B.C.) OF AN ORIGINAL OF THE 5TH CENTURY, VILLA ALBANI, ROME.

suppleness and once more were presented full-face, and legs became stiff; this was an instinctive return to those archaic conventions from which artists with such pains had freed themselves. Even in the height of the Greek classical period one finds sporadic examples of frontality: it sufficed for the artist to be inexperienced for him to come under its sway, so inherent is it in the early stages of art in every land and in every age.[1]

Hardly noticeable at first, the raising of one hip asserts itself more and more in a whole series of works (Figs. 25 to 29), both marbles and bronzes, posterior to 480: for example, the Selinus ephebus, Albani ephebus, the ephebus of the Olympeum in Athens, the Sciarra ephebus, Ligourio ephebus, the Apollo of the omphalos, etc.[2] This movement is particularly noticeable in the nude masculine figure, but one perceives it likewise beneath the feminine draperies. The skirt of certain statues of the first half of the 5th century, draped in the Dorian peplos, falls in stiff folds, in rigorously vertical fluting (the Hestia Giustiniani), but the artist soon found in the breaking of frontality a happy occasion to vary his effects, contrasting, with the old straight fluted folds on the supporting leg, drapery that is stretched tight over the advanced and flexed leg, and the Athenas of Phidias (Athena Lemnia, about 450; Athena Parthenos, 438), and the Korai of the Erechtheum (about 415) show the harmonious results to which this experimentation led.[3]

It can be understood that another convention had to go at the same time. Why need it always be the left leg that is advanced ? This was not in accordance with nature. So the ephebus No. 698 of the Acropolis advanced his right leg, and several other figures of this period advanced the right leg by choice, as though in reaction against the old custom. Complete liberty of the limbs, at the artist's will, and according to the requirements of his subject, had now been achieved. The leg may now be flexed in a forward, backward or sideways direction. All these variants of pose are to be found, the 5th-century artists choosing among them freely. The foot of the flexed leg may rest flat on the ground, a pose found throughout the 5th century, especially in the Phidian statues. The Argive school is rather prone to place the bent leg behind the other, and this pose is a favourite with Polyclitus. Gradually the foot comes to rest more and more lightly on the ground, and often it only just touches it with the tips of the toes. Pliny attributes the invention of this attitude to Polyclitus; it existed, however, long before his day and is due to his forerunners at the beginning of the

[1] **VI**, vol. ii, p. 167.   [2] **LXXIII**, p. 62.   [3] *Ibid.*, p. 153.

5th century. This schema is already that of the statue
which surmounted the base of Smikythus at Olympia (about
460), a work by Glaucus and Dionysius of Argos;[1] the im-
prints, in fact, prove that the left foot was placed flat and
that the right, flexed to the rear, barely touched the ground.
A charming figurine at the Louvre[2] illustrates this attitude
(Fig. 29). The body is supported on the
left leg with the foot flat on the ground,
but the right leg, flexed posteriorly, only
touches the ground with the tips of the
toes. Is this really, as it has been said,
the attitude of walking beloved of Polyclitus ? Is it not rather much more an
attitude of repose, but treated with greater
suppleness ?

The arms of the Korai and Kouroi hung
by their sides or were slightly raised, holding some attribute or the folds of the
drapery. These were but a few stereotyped
gestures without meaning. But now there
is variety in all its thousand shades—the
arms are bent in all directions according
to the requirements of the subject and the
necessities of rhythm.

Despite this great freedom in pose, the
artist concerns himself particularly in establishing a rhythmic relation between the
movements of arms and legs. This is a
new feature of realism while it is also an
æsthetic effort to achieve harmony. In
nature there is a cross-correspondence of
alternately moving limbs: when the right
arm swings forward the left leg is at the

FIG. 29. BRONZE
FIGURINE, IN THE
LOUVRE. FIRST
HALF OF THE 5TH
CENTURY.

rear; the movement of an opposing lower limb responds
to that of the upper limb. The imagists of the 6th century
did not trouble themselves about this alternation except
in certain Korai to whose forward left leg there corresponds a right arm which is stretched forward. Now
this " chiasmos " becomes the rule: the arm and leg movements of either side of the body are opposed, balanced

---

[1] **LXXIII,** p. 117.   [2] *Ibid.,* p. 119; MP, i, p. 110.

in such a way that if we want to find the correspondence we must look for it diagonally (Figs. 30-31). Was Pythagoras of Rhegium, who came to the fore about 490, the first to apply this chiasmos deliberately ?[1] The Valentini torso attributed to him[2] advanced the right shoulder relatively to the left, and the left knee relatively to the right. In ephebus 692 of the Athens Acropolis (earlier than 480),[3] the movement of the right arm to the rear balanced that of the left leg to the front. At the same time the parts involved in action and inaction cross from above downwards, and from below upwards, the typical formula of Polyclitian art : in the Doryphoros, the active right leg supporting the body's weight corresponds with the left arm carrying the spear, and the passive left

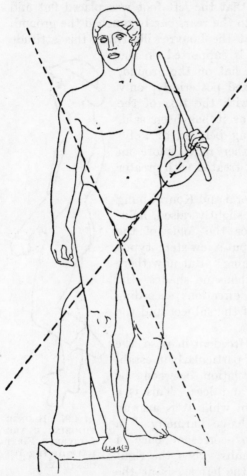

FIG. 30. THE DORYPHOROS OF POLYCLITUS. CHIASMOS.

leg, flexed, corresponds with the right arm which hangs inert. Chiasmos is not regularly observed till towards the middle of the 5th century. In the first half of this century many works escape its sway, such as the Ægina statues, the Tyrannicides, and the Marsyas of Myron, which advance

[1] CLXIV, p. 54.   [2] Ibid., p. 57.   [3] LXXVIII, p. 458.

arms and legs on the same side of the body. It is not
observed in figure drawing, or in reliefs, and consequently
it is not observed in work in the round that is derived
from them (example: Opper-
mann Heracles):[1] arms and
legs advance or are with-
drawn to the rear on the
same side, which is necessitated by the frontal position
of the shoulders and thorax,
in order to avoid foreshortening and contortion of the
lower part of the body.[2]

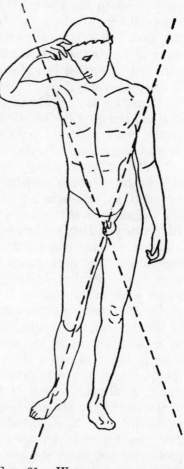

In the old 6th-century
schema the line of the shoulders is horizontal and rigorously parallel with that of
the hips; when frontality is
broken they are often op-
posed one to the other, one
raised and the other lowered.
The Orestes of the Naples
group,[3] and the Stephanus
athlete[4] lean their weight on
the left leg, and the hip on
this side is the higher; the
line of the shoulders, however, is still almost horizontal.
But the Polyclitian statues
are examples of the inverse
obliquity of these two lines.

The torso is turned in all
directions according to the
requirements of the subject,   FIG. 31. WESTMACOTT EPHEBUS,
and the gestures of arms and   BRITISH MUSEUM. KYNISKOS OF
legs modify its former uni-   POLYCLITUS (?). CHIASMOS.
form appearance. The Diskobolos of Myron, and the Louvre
Pugilist[5] retain nothing whatever of the ancient naïveté.

[1] LXII, vol. i, p. 284.   [2] CLXIV, p. 54, note 3.
[3] LXII, vol. ii, p. 662.   [4] Ibid., p. 661.
[5] CLXIV, p. 107.

The head no longer looks straight in front, but is turned to the right or the left, or it looks backwards or is bent forward or inclined to one side, and these various movements may be combined as in the Petrograd Eros[1] which lifts its curly head to the right. What progress has been made in accomplishing all these varieties in pose and attitude during the first half of the 5th century, thanks to the abandonment of frontality ! The stiffness of Kouroi and Korai has vanished: the artist henceforth can reproduce all the complex freedom of reality.

Parallel with this abandonment of frontality in statuary, drawing acquired the knowledge of foreshortening,[2] the result of the same desire to represent reality as it is, thanks to closer observation. Formerly the artist adroitly evaded the difficulty of transcribing the alterations in the forms of objects on a plane surface. Isolated attempts, of which 6th-century vase-painting shows naïve examples, become more common and come to a head from the beginning of the 5th century. They are helped by the new red-figure technique which, appearing about 520,[3] supplants the old black-figure technique. The dark image of the light background of the vase was generally obtained by the cast shadow method,[4] which gave faithful silhouettes of figures in profile but not of foreshortened or three-quarter poses; the interior details of the musculature could only be indicated approximately by incision and often incorrectly. Now that the image was done in light colour on the vase, a new precision was within the power of the draughtsman. And how interesting was this gradual achievement of foreshortening which the vases of the end of the 6th and beginning of the 5th century allow us to follow ! Each detail merits attentive examination. The eye, for example, for long seen full-face in a head in profile, is for the first time correctly drawn by Onesimus. Torsos seen frontally are no longer set on legs in profile, but bend in all directions, forward and backward, and are seen in three-quarter and back views. There was faulty draughtsmanship, of course, for a long time, but this was gradually eliminated and Greek drawing came to have at its

[1] LXXIII, p. 80.　　　　　　　　　　　　[2] CLXXX.
[3] CXLIV, vol. x, p. 345; CXXXIX.
[4] CXLV, pp. 576, 674; Pottier, REG, 1898, p. 355.

disposal a means of expression which was a title of glory because other artists of antiquity, remaining in their old rut, never sought to acquire it except under Hellenic influence.

Statuary, already freed from frontality, also gained by this conquest of foreshortening, at all events those classes of statuary which comprise images deriving from drawing. The Athena of the Ægina pediments is still obedient to the old conventions: although placed full-face, her feet are in profile in order that they may be seen in all their amplitude, and that foreshortening may be avoided. These are the final reminiscences of archaic awkwardness. The conventions shackling both kinds of statuary disappear; whether in repose or in action the statue is no longer obedient to different principles, and truth alone is sought in both.

Thus art threw off the shackles of former days from the beginning of the 5th century, and abandoned the schemas which had stood between it and reality. Variety succeeds monotony. It is no longer a matter of three or four unalterable plastic types, but of figures in attitudes of every conceivable shade of variety—ephebi erect and in repose, differentiated from one another by the play of their limbs, crowning themselves with wreaths, encircling their heads with the victor's chaplet, carrying a spear or a flagon of oil with which to anoint themselves; there are figures performing the most varied movements, from the most leisurely to the most rapid; figures seated at ease and without any of the stiffness of the Branchidæ.[1] Henceforth it is impossible to enumerate all the different themes; it is sufficient to realize how promising a road is opened up before the artist in both sculpture and drawing by these two immense steps forward achieved almost simultaneously—the breaking of frontality and the practice of foreshortening.

In 5th-century statuary the erect human form is always active, even while in repose. Even without any definite action and while allowing the arms to hang inert, it is nevertheless carried braced, on one leg, when the other is flexed, and it balances itself without any extraneous support. It is as though there were a secret desire to retain that mastery of self, that high dignity, which is characteristic of classic art. Together with inferior beings of easier manners, it is

[1] **LXXXIV**, vol. viii, p. 268.

the wounded and dying alone who seek some aid for their
failing force, as, for example, the Philoctetes of Pythagoras
of Rhegium (Valentini torso),[1] the wounded man of Cresilas
(Bavai bronze),[2] and the Amazon of Polyclitus (Berlin
Amazon)[3] (Fig. 32). Very few are the poses that betoken
a certain *laisser-aller* or bodily abandon. It is true that
on a Peithinus cup (first quarter of the 5th century) one
sees an erect ephebus leaning carelessly on a stick, one leg

flexed to the rear and his hand on his hip,[4]
and, in reliefs from the 6th century, figures
in an analogous attitude (funerary stelæ
of Orchomenos at Naples). In the Panathenaic frieze the old men lean on sticks.
But in the round one can cite but few
examples—the Doria Pamphili Aphrodite
of Phidian style,[5] and the so-called Nar-
cissus,[6] a funerary statue of the end of the
5th century, leaning against a pillar.

In the 4th century sculpture in the
round adopts this as a general principle,
to the point of making it a typical attitude
of that period. Praxiteles made it his and
derived from it the rhythm of his statues.
The Apollo Sauroctonos (Fig. 33) leans his
left arm against the tree up which the little
beast climbs which he is about to pierce

FIG. 32. THE
BERLIN AMAZON.
POLYCLITUS.

with his arrow; the Satyr, laughing (Fig. 34),
leans his elbow on a tree-trunk, just as the
Hermes does who holds the infant Dionysus

on his arm (Fig. 35). By raising or lowering this support,
and by leaning the elbow, the raised or the lowered hand,
even the shoulder, against it, the artist gets a series of new
effects.[7]

The figure, rigid and vertical in its lines as conceived by
the imagists of the 6th century, flexed its silhouette and made
it sinuous in the 5th century when the frontality convention
was broken and one hip was raised. In the 4th century,
thanks to the support, the hip makes a gradually greater

[1] **CLXIV**, p. 57.   [2] GBA, 1905, p. 204.
[3] **LXII**, vol. i, p. 503.   [4] **CXXXVI**, Pl. xxv.
[5] RM, 1901, Pl. i-ii.   [6] **LXIII**, p. 130.
[7] **CLIX, CLXII, CLXXII**; **LXII**, vol. ii, p. 253.

salient and the curve of the external line is accordingly accentuated till the curve described from the shoulders to the ankles becomes serpentine. The centre of gravity is displaced; the vertical line passing through the middle of the head tends to fall no longer, as in the 5th century, straight

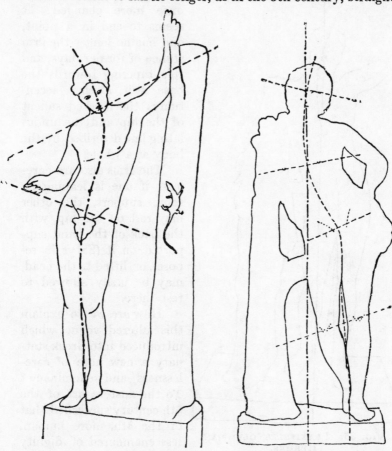

FIG. 33. APOLLO SAUROCTONOS
OF PRAXITELES.

FIG. 34. SATYR IN REPOSE
OF PRAXITELES.

to the feet, or between the feet, but outside the body altogether, a detail to be noted already in vase-paintings of the Meidias cycle. The human form no longer balances itself; take away the support and it must collapse.

In the 5th century, as the feet supported the body naturally, the legs could not be crossed. Now that there are external supports, the movement of the legs becomes quite free: one foot may be advanced in front of the other (Sauroctonos, Satyr in repose), or one leg may cross the other (Satyr playing the flute, in the Louvre, School of Praxiteles).[1]

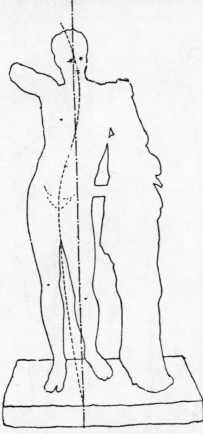

FIG. 35. PRAXITELES' OLYMPIAN
                HERMES.

The general silhouette is once more changed: it seems to end in a point, and has no longer the firm stance of former days, and this tapering towards the base still further accentuates the marked salient of the hip and the undulating line described by the body as a whole.

The arms also are careless; if one is leaning on some support, the other may rest on the hip, with the back of the hand supported on it (Satyr in repose), or, lifted to the head, may be lazily allowed to rest there.

How are we to explain this altered vogue which introduced into Greek statuary a new note of carelessness and effeminacy? To the austere art of the 5th century succeeded that of the 4th, more human, less enamoured of dignity than of sweetness and sensuousness. The attitudes of the 5th century, though natural, still betray a suspicion of effort and tension; the easy attitudes of a body that is relaxed and that is content to be alive without seeking action, were neglected, though equally real and human. His attention diverted from action by sad political events and by the Athenian disaster which

[1] **LXII**, vol. ii, p. 452.

resulted from the Peloponnesian war, and then by the Macedonian conquest, the artist, like the citizen, turns his back on effort and seeks repose. Are we, however, to regard this as due to historical influences rather than simply to the instinctive development of art itself? Did not the artist choose this more supple and graceful rhythm simply because he had at his disposal new resources enabling him to vary his ancient schemas? Christian art, as a matter of fact, presents the same change. The 13th-century sculptor broke the frontality of the Romanesque statues just as his Greek predecessors at the beginning of the 5th century broke the frontal pose of the Kouroi and Korai; then, towards the 14th century, as in the 4th century B.C., one hip is raised, even exaggeratedly, and from an analogous desire for a more supple line. Young girls and young women found this a graceful pose, and this raising of one hip, fashionable from about 1240, became universal towards 1300, to such a point, indeed, as to give the historian, as in Greece, a chronological criterion. This is not, as was once imagined, because this appearance is required by the curve of ivory; it is a necessary stage in the spontaneous development of sculpture, and Greece gives us the proof of it.[1] In antiquity Greece alone arrived at this stage which flows logically from the breaking of the frontal pose: Hindu art borrowed this raising of one hip from the Praxitelian tradition; it even exaggerated it to excess in its images which sometimes " bend into an arc the outline of their body " (Foucher).

The sculptors of the 4th century, the disciples of Praxiteles, and the figurine modellers who, at Tanagra,[2] reflect the grace of the Attic master, sought simple, easy, careless poses inspired by real life in its calm and relaxed moments. But art at that very time became emotional, and so we also get attitudes bespeaking passion or pain, and gestures of ecstasy—heads lifted to heaven, and the heroes and the Maenad of Scopas.[3] Nevertheless the old schemas were not abandoned and the Polyclitian rhythm persists, for example, in the athletic statuary of Lysippus (Agias of Delphi, Apoxyomenos).[4]

[1] **VI**, vol. iii, p. 262. [2] **CVII, CX-XI.**
[3] **CLIX**, p. 36; **CLXX**; JDAI, 1918, xxxiii, p. 38.
[4] **CLX, CLXVIII.**

The Hellenists did not introduce such characteristic innovations as those of the 5th and 4th centuries, despite their desire to renew art; the poses of the human body not being infinite in number, their predecessors had had the lion's share. They carried on the earlier creations in a different spirit which we shall characterize later, and varied them in many subtle ways. However, we must note their predilection for complicated attitudes, for difficult and skilful

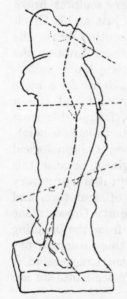

rhythms which raise knotty problems to be solved in statics and musculature and permit the artist to display his virtuosity—often, likewise, his subtlety. At Myrina[1] the terra cotta figurines show this predilection for contorted attitudes. If, during a long period, the artist rendered the flexion of the torso on the pelvis somewhat awkwardly (up to the Parthenon),[2] now he affected those attitudes in which the body twists itself round on the axis of one leg (Fig. 36). The Callipygis Venus,[3] the Satyr looking at his own tail,[4] the Hermaphrodite of the mirror,[5] twist themselves about to see themselves from behind; the young woman would see how her dress falls at the back;[6] the sleeping Hermaphrodite on his couch stirs and turns in the excite-

FIG. 36. DANCING MÆNAD. BERLIN.

ment of his voluptuous dream.[7] Exaggerating the emotion of the 4th century, we now get passionate action, and limbs twisted in pain (Laocoon). And in tranquil poses we get graceful, pleasing or sensual attitudes, and Aphrodites, Nymphs and Satyrs. In the course of their efforts to produce them the artists do not always avoid preciosity and mannerism or grace that is both studied and arch. At Myrina, Eros curves his arm over his head with the smile of a ballet dancer;[8] the Naples Dionysus[9]

[1] CXII. [2] CLXXVI, p. 569.
[3] LXXXVI, vol. i, p. 328.
[4] RA, 1903, i, p. 386; CLXII, p. 207; CLXIII, p. 49.
[5] CLXII, p. 270; RA, 1903, i, p. 386.
[6] CXI, Pl. xxii, 511. [7] LXXXVI, vol. i, pp. 153, 371.
[8] CXI, Pl. xxi. [9] LXII, vol. ii, p. 453.

delicately lifts his finger, inclines his head, and bestows his favours on the public.[1]

But how can we enumerate the variety of Hellenistic art ? The complexity of life itself is now the theme and no longer certain limited and codified types of it, as in the 5th century, and even in the 4th century. Even the chiasmos of the limbs is sometimes abandoned whose regular observance had become almost a convention, since it is impossible to bend nature invariably to this rigid law; it is often abandoned in figures in action; the crouching man of Cythera (Athens Museum)[2] advanced his left arm and his left leg, and the whole of the right side of his body is drawn back; in a series of Pergamene works action is entirely confined to one side of the body (ex voto of Attalus, the Venice Gaul, the Aix Persian, etc.).[3]

Looking back at the distance travelled from the formless Dipylon idols and the crude mannikins of the geometric vases, and entirely from the point of view of the problems of pose, one realizes how great have been the acquisitions, made with rigorous logic, and how vastly superior the Greek artist is to his fellow-craftsmen of other lands incapable of making progress without his assistance. Following the same road up to the end of the 6th century, he then breaks suddenly with them and he sees before him a marvellous future. He begins by ridding himself of frontality: thenceforth the variety of subjects, attitudes and rhythms is infinite, and there is the chance of solving the problem of foreshortening in drawing, and of introducing action into statuary instead of limiting it to repose or to a few unalterable schemas that are incorrect withal. He has finished with conventions and gives himself up to the close study of reality. In Egyptian art, although it covers a longer total period, by thousands of years, than Greek art, frontality remains to the end and imposes on statuary analogous schemas to those of the 6th century in Greece—enthroned Pharaohs and gods, and immobile and lifeless erect figures; foreshortening is unknown, and the same conventions replace it as did duty in Greece— the union of limbs seen full-face with those seen in profile. The Greek artist had a feeling for the real, and a desire to

---

[1] **VI,** vol. iii, p. 369.   [2] REG, 1901, p. 125; AA, 1921, 36, p. 333.
[3] **LXII,** vol. ii, p. 500.

get ever closer to truth, a love of the life animating that human body which he observed in all its varied attitudes; he had æsthetic feeling, too, an understanding of the beauty of form whether in action or repose. All these qualities enabled him to break the fetters of those poses which for ever bound the art of other antique peoples, and, through the intermediation of Rome, to facilitate the task of the modern artist.

CHAPTER III

ANATOMY[1]

ANATOMY was being studied at the same time as pose; the artist wished to acquire a knowledge of the internal structures as well as of the outer form. The human body which he had occasion to observe in many different poses interested him also on account of its architecture, the play of the limbs, the articulations and muscles both in repose and in action. He began by independently analyzing its multiple details such as the pectoral muscles, abdomen, hair, eyes, mouth, kneecap, etc.—by studying its grammar before he considered it as a whole, that is to say before he knew how to establish the correct relation between its different parts or the reciprocal repercussions for a given subject and a given attitude.

This, too, was an original conquest. The art of such other antique peoples as might have inspired Greece had no more scrutinized anatomical truth than it had understood the variety and verity of human attitudes. For them the details of the body are always conventionally or approximately rendered. Egypt took no heed of such precision; Chaldæa had made but a few rare attempts to achieve it—praiseworthy, none the less, at such a remote epoch, and it has been remarked that in some of its works of art " the broad modelling of the shoulders, and the chest which breathes beneath the drapery, would not come amiss to a Greek Jupiter of the ancient style !" (Heuzey). The Assyrian human form seems to be firmly built, with tense muscles, until you look more closely, when it is seen that this is schematic exaggeration done with the idea of giving an impression of strength rather than a close study of the living model. In Cyprus and in Etruria the plump balloon-like bodies have no internal armature.

The Pre-Hellenes who dwelt on Greek soil are an exception

[1] **CLXXVI-VII; VI,** vol. iii.

to this general mediocrity. At Knossos the torso in relief of a prince, the arm in stucco holding a rhyton, and the ivory acrobat, possess a musculature both strong and correct, in which the artist goes so far as to indicate the veins in the arm and the finger-nails. The vigorous boxers on the Haghia Triada vase were already muscled like Greek athletes. Was it from these old Ægeans that the Greeks got alike their passion for gymnastic exercises and their knowledge of muscles, preserved by the natives who were subjugated by the newly arrived Dorians ? Yet the Ægeans had been unable to develop this germ. Allying to their anthropomorphism, as they did, those other religious conceptions of dendrolatry, phytolatry and zoolatry, they did not make large statues, and their realism concerned itself less with man than with plant and animal life. The Dorian conquerors drew the attention of the artist to human anatomy because their anthropomorphism eliminated everything else; then, too, they were driven by the very conditions of their life, for ever on their guard, to give great importance to physical education in private and public life; they developed the athletic games after which the victors, who had triumphed by the strength of their muscles, consecrated their effigies.

The Greeks studied anatomy as artists, not as students of science; the sight of beautiful limbs and their harmonious play awakened æsthetic emotion in them; one might almost hear them say, as later the Renaissance artist: " You will derive pleasure from drawing the vertebræ because they are magnificent; then you will draw the bone which is placed between the two branches: it is very beautiful."

But for the Greeks it was a living not a morbid anatomy. For long they never studied the skeleton or the écorché. They observed the living model, not immobilized in a studio but in the free rough-and-tumble of gymnasia and stadium, and out of doors under the eye of them all in the multifarious movements inseparable from daily life. They saw it in the open air, tanned by the sun, silhouetted against the sky, the relief of its surface emphasized by the changing light. Active life in its thousands of varied aspects was for long the sole inspiration of the artist. Such aid as is given by the studio with its poses taken to order, fatiguing and frigidly immobilizing the body, or of science with its scalpel excavating among muscles and flaccid flesh, was not yet his. Even in repose the figures do not appear to be posing but to be reality rendered in stone. It is only with Praxiteles that we begin to get the impression of a model who has posed for the artist in the calm of the studio; this artist was the first to supply examples of those poses which are not instinctive but which have been dictated; he was to be the forerunner of that academic art which developed among the Hellenists. It was by viewing the living body that the artist moulded himself, and by viewing the masterpieces of great artists, and studying their writings on the "canons" of art (for example, those of Polyclitus), and on proportions. From the 4th century the practice of taking life casts, begun by Lysistratus, the brother of Lysippus, and of taking casts from statues, also facilitated his task by multiplying correct models.

Sculptors were the principal authors of progress in anatomy, though painters may have been responsible for the greatest advance in poses. Certainly drawing does not give the artist the same facilities in this domain. The figures on the black-figure vases, posed in profile and projected on a plane surface by means of the cast shadow method, were for long nothing but silhouettes with sufficiently correct contours, satisfying the eye, but whose interior details were negligently rendered or incorrect, imposed by the conventions inherent in drawing. Neither was the use of a burin to incise the outlines of muscles on this opaque image very favourable. It was modelling in the round that made and kept the lead here, up to the time when the substitution of the red-figure vase with its light ground for the figure itself, the use of a brush instead of a burin, the interior delineation by means of varying densities of glaze—a method which did not appear in the earlier red-figure vases and which seems to have come in with Chachrylion—and the knowledge of how to foreshorten which enabled the body to be drawn in the most varied muscular poses, all combined to enable the ceramist to follow closely the progress accomplished in statuary.

It was a laborious and patient study[1] because the artist started from almost complete ignorance. The oldest examples

[1] **VI**, vol. iii, p. 131.

of Hellenic sculpture, the ivory idols of the Attic Dipylon, render only the external contours of the human body and are in no way superior to the eneolithic idols of the Cyclades, though these were over two thousand years earlier. In fact, up to the close of the 6th century, the silhouette might be correct, in statuary and in vase-drawing, whilst the interior details were often quite wrong; many of these bodies appear to be innocent of internal structures, being round and as though blown up like a balloon, or else present a smooth surface. Progress was rapid or slow according to the individual talent of the artist and his ethnic origin—whether he was Ionian or Dorian, the Dorians from the earliest times being more anxious than the Ionians to seek anatomical truth. If we compare with these early naïve works the ephebic statues of Polyclitus, whose anatomy, although synthetized, is perfect, or those of the Hellenistic period with their subtlety, marking the extreme point of development, we see how great have been the acquisitions during this period of a few centuries.

The anatomical problems the artist had to solve are many and various.

The primitive readily omitted details which seem to us essential—such as mouth, nose, arms, legs, etc.—but which to him seemed useless if the human schema was sufficiently recognizable without them. Now, however, every detail is to be observed, and then translated in the most precise fashion because it is there in reality. The first effort, then, consisted in remarking the presence of bones beneath the skin, of muscles, tendons, veins and the multiple features of the living body, often scarcely perceptible. Then these have to be repeated in the body of stone, first those which are most easily seen, and the more important, then the smaller ones, because everything did not attract the attention of the artist at one and the same time, and their presence or absence sometimes serves as a chronological criterion; for instance, the serratus magnus muscle on the side is not indicated before the Æginetan art of the first quarter of the 5th century, and if it is sometimes missing later it is due to the youth of the subject (example: the basalt ephebus of the Palatine).

In the earliest statues of the 6th century[1] the vertical

[1] See for such details, **VI,** vol. iii, p. 158; **LXVIII,** p. 65.

and uninflected line of the back is separated from the vertical line of the legs by the swelling of the buttocks. In the Naucratis or Rhodes Kouroi[1] the reverse of the statuette— its hair, back, and thighs—form an almost plane surface. Soon the vertebral column begins to take a curve; at first hardly perceptible, the curvature gradually increases and the back loses its primitive plank-like aspect. To the swelling of the buttocks, at first scarcely projecting and gradually becoming more rounded, is opposed the growing curvature of the shoulder-blades. On the other side of the figure the chest and the abdomen begin by being quite straight; the slight swell of the pectorals and lower abdomen is hardly distinguishable. The earliest statues, seen in profile, thus present two perceptibly vertical and parallel lines, and one can very nearly square them between two upright planks, one placed in front and the other behind[2] (Fig. 37, Plate VIII). With time this parallelism disappears and the dorsal curve becomes opposed to the pectoral and abdominal curve. Although the thickness of the chest does not at first equal that of the pelvis with the protruding buttocks of the archaic ideal, yet since the pectorals develop and the back incurves more and more, balance is established between the upper and lower portions of the trunk.

Seen from the front the 6th-century Kouroi are slender in build, with the sides curving in beneath the armpits, strong shoulders, and sloping hips without any projections (Fig. 38, Plate VIII). The torso may be bounded on either side by two regular and opposed curves (Fig. 39, Plate VIII). Soon the artist comes to perceive the projection of the iliac bone and indicates it. Still rare in the 6th century, this detail becomes constant in the 5th, and is exaggerated in Argive athletic statuary. The inguinal folds, indicated by two lines of varying length which depart obliquely from the pubis, do not reach the hip-joint, and lose themselves in the swelling of the lower abdomen and the thigh before they come to be carried further. Rectilinear at first, they end by describing a slight curve which becomes more and more accentuated and transforms itself eventually into a broken angular line: this is the well-marked schema of the 5th-century statues. The abdomen, formerly ending in an angle of which the

[1] **LXVIII**, pp. 232, 243.   [2] **CLXXVII.**

I

pubis was the apex, now, in the ephebi of the 5th century, describes in this region an elliptical curve. In nature the linea alba passing through the umbilicus descends as far as the pudenda and divides into two portions the rectus abdominis. The three tendinous markings of the rectus muscle divide it into four aponeuroses, the lower intersection coming exactly where the umbilicus is situated, and the uppermost coming below the pectoral muscles. The external borders of the right and left rectus determine the lines separating this from the external oblique muscle. The sculptor of the 6th century experienced considerable difficulty in understanding how these muscles were disposed. At first he ignored them completely, and the abdomen is merely a smooth surface with a hole in it where the navel comes midway between the two pectorals and the inguinal folds. He begins by indicating the lower border of the thoracic cage beneath the pectorals by an incised angle, and when he came to observe this he also added the linea alba, tracing it as far down as the umbilicus. In the first quarter of the 5th century this line is sometimes carried down as far as the pubis, a detail rare in reality, which is seen in Æginetan work, in the Treasury of the Athenians, and in vases of the severe style; on certain 5th-century vases it may even be shown by two parallel lines, a more precise convention for rendering this furrow.

The artist next takes note of the divisions of the abdomen below the thoracic angle. But his observation is faulty to start with (Fig. 40); he does not clearly recognize the aponeuroses separated by the three intersecting tendinous markings; he gets their number wrong; he exaggerates it, and divides the abdomen by five parallel lines (Orchomenos Kouros), by four (Sunium Kouros, Moscophoros), and then by three. And how odd it makes the abdomen look, as if scored across by lines of music! The thoracic cage, beginning with an abrupt angle, curves in at the apex, widens, and is confounded with the upper portion of the rectus. The sides of this curve are at first arrested fairly high up, then descend as far as the pubis, as they do in reality. In the latest Kouroi of the 6th century the external borders of the rectus are elongated to a point in the direction of the pubis, and the rectus is only divided by two lines determining

three divisions. This is the most developed stage and this
tripartite division remains in the art of the 5th century.[1]

These minute analyses, of which we give only a few
examples, are necessary if we are to understand the sum
total of the work done by the 6th-century artists. We shall
appreciate better by what laborious tentative experimentation they arrived at the stage of observing and rendering
the multiple details of human structure. The inevitable
initial errors are corrected one by one, and convention yields
place to truth.

They had likewise to situate these details in their proper
place in the body as a whole, neither too high up nor too

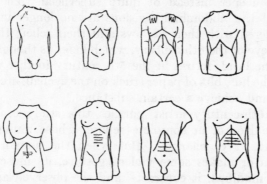

Fig. 40. 6th-century Kouroi. (*Cf.* **LXVIII**, p. 77, Pl. iv.)

low down. The artist went wrong on this point for a long
time: in particular the pectorals and the ears are often too
high, the former in line with the armpits.

Next, these details have to be given their correct dimensions proportionately to the other parts of the body. The
eye is enormous, and the neck out of all proportion both in
archaic drawing and sculpture.[2]

Finally the details must be rendered in their correct
form and not according to some convention. But at first
the artist reduced them to geometrical schemas—a triangle
for the torso, the head, the eye, the foot, and the nose; a
rectangle, a pillar or a *cloche* for the body; an acute angle
for the pectorals and a lozenge for the knee-cap.[3] He

[1] **LXVIII**, p. 76. [2] **VI**, vol. ii, pp. 154, 155, 267.
[3] *Ibid.*, p. 142.

schematizes them. Look at the ear:[1] it lends itself to curious stylizations resembling a snail's shell, or the volute of an Ionic capital (Sunium Kouros). Or look at the hair:[2] it formed bead, godroons, whorls, corkscrews and volutes. How strange are the decorative renderings of the hair of the Rampin head,[3] of the Sunium Kouros and the Acropolis Korai (6th century)![4] Gradually the sinuous contours of real life, the appearance of reality, has to be substituted for these schemas and for this ornamental conception.

At the same time the linear markings, which look as though the anatomical details had been drawn on the marble, have to be replaced by genuine modelling, which gradually becomes deeper instead of quite superficial. The thoracic arch and the abdominal divisions are no longer incised but are rendered with their hollows and their relief; the exophthalmic eye of the 6th century, which looks as though starting out of the head, retires in the 5th century further under the brows; the lids, bits of paper stuck on the eyeball, are detached from it and achieve a certain substance.[5]

The 6th-century artist pursues this study especially in his male Kouroi in complete repose, whose musculature is inert and never changes. But when the human figure is in action or makes some violent gesture, its musculature is thereby modified, it contracts, and the observed appearance no longer holds good. " Is it not by modelling your works on living beings " said Socrates, " that you make your statues appear animate ?—Exactly. And, as our different attitudes cause the play of certain muscles of our body, upwards or downwards, so that some are contracted and some stretched, some wrung and some relaxed, is it not by expressing these efforts that you give greater truth and verisimilitude to your works ?—Precisely."[6] This alteration in the musculature and limbs caused by movement sets the archaic artist a difficult problem which for long he could not solve. In the frontal statue the trunk seen from the front is immobile; the gestures of arms and legs in no way affect it. The muscles remain inert in a body that is in action.

---

[1] **VI**, vol. iii, p. 154; **LXVIII**, pp. 91, 96, Pl. vi.
[2] **VI**, vol. iii, p. 157; **LXVIII**, p. 100.
[3] **LXXXIV**, vol. viii, p. 641.   [4] **LXXIX**, p. 197.
[5] **VI**, vol. iii, p. 208.
[6] Xenophon's *Recollections of Socrates*.

Look at the Acropolis Triton;[1] the muscles of arms and trunk ought to stand out as a result of the effort of the struggle, but they merely show rounded, unbroken and horizontal surfaces without any real modelling. The arm of a combatant (Acropolis torso, prior to 480)[2] rests tranquilly on the shoulder of his adversary instead of itself contracting and leaving an impress on the other's flesh, and the frontal torso in no way feels the repercussion. The Moscophoros carries a calf: he raises his arms to the height of his chest to hold the animal's feet, but the weight of the burden is not reflected in his shoulders, and the muscles of the trunk are rendered precisely as though the arms hung by his sides. The movement remains localized in the limb that makes it, no matter how violent the action, and it is not propagated throughout the body as it should be.

And how maladroit they are when they come to couple the different portions of the body affected by movement, making the whole move as one piece, like the carapace of a crustacean, with the joints as rigid as mechanical hinges, and with the heads of such figures as are looking backwards slewed round, practically back to front, like a windvane on a steeple, and with the frontal torso fitted on to the pelvis in profile much as a rigid cuirass might be (the Enceladus of the Hekatompedon pediment, Athens)! Displacements are neither accurately observed nor correctly rendered. In the Corcyra Gigantomachy (6th century), despite the torsion of the trunk, the axis of the umbilicus is not sufficiently displaced towards the right.[3]

Frontality is broken towards 500, and, with its abandonment, statues will acquire freedom and ease of movement. The solution of the problem, however, is still too fresh for there to be nothing left of the old naïveté; the torso, when it is rendered in action, still bears traces of its early ankylosis for a long time to come, and it betrays the difficulty experienced by the sculptor in establishing correct junction with the rest of the body. In the Tyrannicides group (477–476)[1] the shoulders and trunk still participate inadequately in the violent action of the arms and legs. The faulty junction is perceptible in the fallen figures of the

---

[1] **LXXVIII,** p. 37.
[2] *Ibid.,* p. 405.
[3] RA, 1911, ii, p. 1.
[4] **LXXVIII,** p. 438.

Ægina and Olympia pediments, in the Heracles with the Bull of a metope at Olympia, in Myron's Diskobolos, in the Boy plucking a Thorn from his Foot, in which the navel is placed quite incorrectly. Even in the Doryphoros of Polyclitus the flexion of the trunk, though slight, has not all the ease and freedom to be desired (about 445). Only in the Parthenon is the natural junction of torso and pelvis, and the true concordance between the play of the limbs and the joints[1] achieved by Phidias (Fig. 41). Indeed, difficulties of this kind reappear whenever art goes back to the inexperience of its beginnings; for instance, we can see the same maljunction of torso and legs in the frontal seated figures of certain Flavian reliefs.

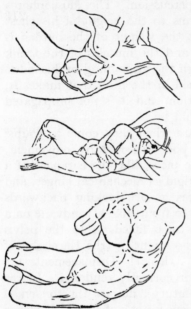

FIG. 41. RECLINING FIGURES OF THE ÆGINA AND PARTHENON PEDIMENTS.

If musculature has to be adapted to the movement made, it has also to be adapted to the subject chosen. The body of the adult man is not the same as that of the adolescent. The 6th-century artist makes no difference in his stone people, bringing them all within a mean age, such variants as there are resulting from the æsthetic tendencies proper to this or that school or studio. Furthermore, types are still in that indeterminate stage usual in the earliest phases of art; the artist does not know how to transcribe the specific characters of man, of woman, or of the various human ages, and the dominance of the athletic ideal imposes on all, young and old, an analogous appearance. From the beginning of the 5th century, however, he tries to render the differences in musculature according to age, social station, and individual peculiarities. About 480 the Acropolis ephebus No. 692[2] has the

[1] **CLXXVI**, p. 69; **CLXIV**, p. 66.   [2] **LXXVIII**, p. 458.

body of a youth of sixteen years or thereabouts, with the appropriate flowing lines and slimness of build, whereas his contemporaneous comrade, ephebus No. 698,[1] has already the sturdy breadth of shoulder of a small athlete. In the Panathenaic frieze, Poseidon, of ripe age, has stouter muscles than Apollo. The task of the 5th-century artist was to give to each individual his appropriate anatomy, and to understand these subtle differences. As we know, however, it was not till the 4th century and later that art became thoroughly realistic, rendering with scrupulous fidelity the anatomical forms of the child, the woman and the old man; it is still limited in the 5th by its idealism and obsessed by the body of the ephebus.

This patient study of anatomical detail was pursued throughout the 6th century. From the first quarter of the 5th it has very nearly achieved its end. The artist, such as he of Ægina, has a good knowledge of the human body and there are only a few small details to be perfected. For example, he modifies the shape of the eye towards the middle of the 5th century, knowing that the two lids do not join in an abrupt angle at the outer extremity, but that the upper lid slightly overrides the lower. He establishes a better relation between different parts in action. His predecessors were absorbed in the grammar of the body in repose; he seeks synthesis and the co-ordination of details in attitudes that have become infinitely varied since the abandonment of frontality. Towards 450 the last traces of inexperience have gone; the artist has now but to put his knowledge into practice, to familiarize himself with it till it becomes instinctive, and also to bring ease and subtlety into it.

Fifth-century musculature is exact, often dry, even to excess. Happy in his possession of its secrets, the sculptor seeks to put his knowledge to the proof and occasionally he exaggerates in his expression of it—as witness the torso of the Heracles with the Hind in the Treasury of the Athenians (Delphi, between 490 and 485);[2] it looks almost like an écorché, or a rigid shell taken as a cast from the body (Fig. 42). This character is only attenuated by degrees in the second half of the 5th century, especially in the Attic art of Phidias, but the sharpness of delineation

---

[1] **LXXVIII**, p. 452.　　　　　　　　[2] *Ibid.*, p. 414.

and the precision remain characteristic features to which the statues of Polyclitus bear witness.

This musculature is reduced to its broad divisions; it is treated in large planes, almost geometrically. It does not pretend to render every detail; following the ideal of the day, it synthetized and generalized. But the transitions from one plane to another are still somewhat hard in quality; the Doryphoros and the other ephebi of Polyclitus are instances of this.

FIG. 42. METOPE OF THE TREASURY OF THE ATHENIANS, DELPHI.

Nevertheless, convention is not entirely eliminated in the 5th century. Short and semi-short hair for men, and occasionally for women, has succeeded the long hair, falling in a sheet down the back, with a few symmetrical curls detached from it and disposed over the shoulders on either side. The hair is now sober and simple, without the embellishments and minutiæ of the 6th century, and no longer incised but modelled. All the same, it has not yet the picturesque quality nor the variety of real life; its curls are too schematic—whorls in several rows framing the countenance, or spirals resembling a carpenter's woodshavings, volutes, and short locks each one identical with its neighbour; they cover the head far too regularly; their mass does not adapt itself to the cranium naturally and sometimes looks like an artificial cap (the Tyrannicides); the curls are too regular, too well dressed and combed. The Ancients praised Pythagoras of Rhegium for having rendered hair more realistically than his predecessors;[1] Phidias bestows more elasticity that Polyclitus on his short and tumbled locks which are already modelled pictorially. Nevertheless, hair, throughout the 5th century, preserves, like musculature, a monumental and architectonic character.

The artist of the 4th century, inheriting from his predecessor the precise knowledge of anatomical detail, has no more errors to rectify, but he can still conceive the æsthetic

[1] **CLXIV,** p. 41.

transcription of the human body in quite a different fashion, bringing to his version subtlety and variety. Hitherto the sculptor has concerned himself mainly with the athlete, and this ideal has even modified other types of figure. The 4th-century artist concerns himself, rather, with the differences between the sexes, and between various ages and environments; he seeks to render the delicacy, grace and sensuous quality of the bodies of women, adolescents and children, and the feminine ideal now softens even the masculine figure (Apollino, Sauroctonos). He wants to soften the frigidity of a mathematical and ornamental modelling; his transitions between the planes of the statuary body are more frequent and more skilfully effected. In order to achieve this he utilizes more freely than his predecessor the resources of painting, which, from the close of the 5th century, devotes its attention to modelling, to chiaroscuro, light and shade, and atmosphere. Henceforward sculptors will look at things pictorially. Formerly the human frame has been shown as it really is, with its general anatomy correctly transcribed; now, in the 4th century, it is represented as it appears to be in its accidental variations by means of attenuations of the brusque transitions from one plane to another, and by the play of light and shade on the salients and depressions of its modelling. Greater realism is desired, and the chance effect is welcomed. The hair is no longer a mass of symmetrical curls, each one of which is identical with the rest, but every lock of hair is now treated individually by the artist. It is irregular, untamed locks of all sizes tumbling over one another (Apoxyomenos of Lysippus),[1] and here and there one is allowed to escape and encroach on the forehead and neck. The mass of the hair is deeply sculped in order to retain shadow and set up contrast with the high lights of the salient portions. Hair as treated by Praxiteles (Olympian Hermes, Eubouleus[2]), Scopas (Tegea heads),[3] and Lysippus (Agias)[4] is picturesque and pictorial.

The Hellenists developed these tendencies. They gave greater precision to the anatomical differences between the sexes and different ages, and to the differentiation of social, intellectual and moral status; they loved to transcribe the

[1] **CLX**, Fig. 6.
[3] **XLIX**, Figs. 3-4.
[2] **LXX**, Pl. xvi; **CLIX**.
[4] **CLX**, Fig. 2.

plump bodies of babies or the withered flesh of old women and fishermen, and they observed a thousand gradations in the gamut running from one of these extremes to the other. They did not shrink from rendering physiological and patho-logical defects—especially was this the case with the modellers of terra cotta figurines.[1] On this point, as on others, 5th-century art was idealistic; knowing the form and position of the different parts of the body, it gave to musculature a general and abstract character which was the same for all; the 4th century brought in greater diversity; but it belonged to the Hellenists to render the thousand and one differences with a precision that was often pitiless, and with all the complexity of life itself.

Hitherto artists had studied the living body exclusively; now they sought information from the doctors who, from the time of the first Ptolemies, had, like Herophilus and Erasistratus, already practised dissection. Scientific anatomy henceforth was included in the education of an artist. And it modified the aspect of the work they accomplished. They often betray a too exact knowledge of anatomy. They loved to exaggerate musculature that could be detailed at leisure. When we look at the body of the Marsyas bound to his tree of punishment,[2] we realize that the sculptor has not a scrap of sympathy for the suffering of his Silenus but that what particularly intrigued him was the skeletal frame so curiously indicated beneath the skin. It has often been made a reproach to the Borghese combatant[3] that he looks like an écorché—is more of an anatomical model than a work of art; one feels that the musculature of the athlete, hardened in the sun, has become a sort of cuirass of which each detail is chiselled, and that his energetic attitude has been calculated with the purpose of showing the play of his muscles; and this precision begins to get too learned, too deliberate, and somewhat boring in its excessive exactitude. The muscles swell into veritable mountains. In the 5th century Heracles was a man of strength, but not exaggeratedly so: in the Farnese statue[4] he has become the strong man of the circus, and this excessive musculature is a Hellenistic trait of which there are a number of samples in the Pergamum

[1] **CXI**, p. 95.   [2] **LXII**, vol. ii, p. 547.
[3] *Ibid.*, p. 673.   [4] *Ibid.*, p. 427.

frieze. The anatomy is tortured, bombastic and declamatory; it is a schoolmen's science, and it degenerates into an affair of studio formulas. Hellenistic work has no longer the sincerity and freshness of the 5th-century sculptures, of a time when the artist got his anatomical knowledge exclusively from the living model which he could observe going through its exercises under his very eyes.

CHAPTER IV

DRAPERY

THE Greek artist also grappled with the problem of clothing, and by its solution he made himself master of a new means of expression. The Egyptian with his rigid drawers and his transparent tunic and the Chaldæan made only timid efforts in this genre, and their knowledge was limited to conventional folds; the Assyrian buried his figures under robes over-burdened with embroidery, looking as though they were of cardboard. The material, in the art of these lands, remains a garment which covers the body, either less or more; it had no æsthetic value for them. The Greek alone comprehended that beauty was to be achieved by means of the stuff of which a garment is made, of its folds and its adaptation to or its contrast with the body that is partially or wholly dissimulated by it. Enamoured of the real, he was to seek to render this stuff with increasing fidelity, adapting it to the personality and to the movements of the figure, and deepening its folds, and he was to do away with the conventional schemas which persisted up to the end in the art of these other lands. Drapery became for him, like pose and like anatomy, an indispensable element of statuary and drawing.

Greek clothing certainly lent itself to this experimental study.[1] It was no longer the sewn costume of the Ægean ladies,[2] the simple masculine drawers of the Ægeans and Egyptians, or the heavy woollen *kaunakes* of the Chaldæans. It was a piece of stuff, soft and ample, which had no well-defined form. Whether chiton, himation or chlamys, it was suspended from the shoulders and fell freely, and by its own weight it determined its folds which were many or few, heavy or fine, according to whether the garment was the woollen Dorian peplos or the linen Ionian chiton. The movements of the body which modified their folds, or the presence or absence of a girdle, imported into them infinite variety.

[1] CCI, CCIV.　　　　　　　　　　　　　　　[2] CCII.

220

According to the place and the weather the Greek dress presented differences in the manner of its adjustment, but it always preserved this character of freedom, so eminently æsthetic, which we find again to-day among certain peoples of Asia and Africa for whom dress material is a drapery, as it was for the Greeks, and not, as with our modern selves, a fitted garment.

The Greek artist got from drapery the possibility of new subjects. How many of his works, statues and drawings, show a figure putting on a garment, disrobing, or occupied in some way over the toilet ! The Korai of the 6th century gather up in the left hand their trailing tunics; Hera draws back her veil to show herself to her mystic spouse, Zeus: (metope of the Heræum at Selinus, prior to 450;[1] Panathenaic frieze); the Herculaneum dancers (about 460)[2] repeat the old archaic gesture, or fasten the peplos on their shoulder, as the Artemis of Gabii does, later (4th century).[3] In the Parthenon an ephebus is putting on his tunic as it might be a shirt, another is having his girdle fastened by a little serving lad, and the Aphrodite of Cnidus allows her last veil to slip from off her.

The artist studied musculature chiefly in the masculine body; drapery he studies principally in his female figures. For if man actually stripped in the palæstra and for the gymnastic competitions, woman never appeared unveiled in ordinary daily life. These social differences determined two artistic series which in archaic art are entirely distinct. In the 6th century the nude Kouros contrasts with the draped Kore; there are few draped men and few nude women, and this dualism persists to the 5th century. It was in transcribing in art the feminine form in which they delighted that the Ionians became pioneers in the close study of the problems of drapery, whilst the Peloponnesian Greeks who preferred masculine strength concentrated on the study of the human muscles.

The following are the problems that the artist has to solve in regard to drapery:[4] he must observe and render truthfully the material itself, whether quiescent or in movement, together with its plane surfaces and its folds, and the modifica-

---

[1] **LXII**, vol. i, p. 413.   [2] *Ibid.*, p. 424.   [3] *Ibid.*, vol. ii, p. 283.
[4] See, for these details, **VI**, vol. iii, p. 125 ff.

tions it undergoes as a result of body movements and wind; he must establish a correct correlation between this drapery and the figure it covers; he must also get an understanding of its expressive beauty and value and of its spiritual and moral significance.

At the outset folds were often neglected, and the stuff enveloped the body like a sheath, without a single furrow to vary its uniformity (statue of Nicandra, at Delos, statues at Eleutherna, at Tegea,[1] etc., 6th century). But in the course of the 6th century, in statuary, and in painting in which Cimon of Cleonæ is reputed to be the first to have studied folds (*in veste rugas et sinus invenit*), the artist's attention is arrested by the folds of the garment. These are still highly conventional—as were anatomical details: they may be undulating furrows, grooves, lines in relief, flutings and swallow's tails which give the stuff just as ornamental, decorative and unreal a character as that given to hair or anatomical features. In the Acropolis Museum in Athens many statues of Korai,[2] the relief showing a figure mounting into a chariot, dating from the early years of the 5th century,[3] and the Kore of Euthydicus, prior to 480,[4] all bear witness that the period of such conventions is over, and that truth was now being sought. This task was pursued and carried to its conclusion in the first half of the 5th century.

A fold consists of a raised portion and a hollow. The artist at first failed to recognize these two elements and he painted or incised a simple line on the surface of the stone (Chrysapha relief, Samos Hera, Samian statues of the Acropolis, seated statue of Chares, 6th century).[5] As time went on the fold acquired some body and substance and was modelled; but, throughout the 6th century, it retained this superficial character on the surface of the marble, which we already remarked in the delineation of muscles (Acropolis Korai). From the close of the 6th and the beginning of the 5th centuries, the fold bit deeper into the material; the flat folds, looking as though they had been crushed in the process of being ironed, and which were usual with the Korai, now disappear; they become deep and substantial in the figures

[1] **LXXXIV**, vol. viii, pp. 148, 430. [2] **LXXVIII**, p. 358, etc.
[3] *Ibid.*, p. 408. [4] *Ibid.*, p. 353.
[5] **LXXXIV**, vol. viii, pp. 146, 273, 295-7, 439.

wearing the Dorian peplos in the first half of the 5th century, and they hold shadow in their cavities, allowing the light to play on the salient portions.

The artist, now that he has a knowledge of the variety possible in folds, chooses those which please him most, and which give the best æsthetic effect, and a study of vase-painting from the beginning of the 5th century, as a study of plastic art at the same period, will yield evidence of this attentive and refined experimentation. We shall find drapery with wide, sober folds largely spaced, as, for instance, in the vase-painting of Hieron, and in statuary in the series of female figures draped in the Dorian peplos;[1] we shall find drapery with numerous very fine folds, either straight or undulating, often rendered with a certain mannerism, as, for example, by Brygus. Finally, we shall find in every period the variants corresponding with the taste and temperament of individuals, some of whom prefer simplicity and mass effects, whilst others prefer elegance, suppleness and the refinements of detail; variants which also correspond with what is fitting in the subject, because drapery is to become a means of expressing the spiritual and moral status of the figure it covers. Compare, for instance, the little sinuous folds which ripple like water over the bodies of the Victories accompanying the goddess on the balustrade of the temple of Athena Nike,[2] with the wide, straight folds of the Korai of the Erechtheum or of Athena Parthenos.

The artist finds plenty of resources in the direction given to these folds; he was already interested in it in the 6th century; these tentative experiments have achieved their object by the 5th century, and are now more consciously undertaken. Certain works betray delight in the vertical and the parallel. In the 6th century the Samos Hera (Fig. 43),[3] the Samian statues of the Acropolis[4] and the feminine bronze of Lusoi[5] have the parallel folds of their chiton directed vertically downwards. In the 5th century, the Auriga of Delphi,[6] the Hestia Giustiniani (Pl. IX), and the series of women draped in the Dorian peplos (Herculaneum Dancers, Aphrodite of Dodona, etc.),[7] and a large number of red-

---

[1] **LXXIII**, p. 153.   [2] **LXII**, vol. ii, p. 104.
[3] **LXXXIV**, vol. viii. p. 146.   [4] *Ibid.*, pp. 295-297.
[5] *Ibid.*, p. 453.   [6] *Fouilles de Delphes.*   [7] BCH, xv, Pl. 9.

figure vase-paintings, are examples of it. From this predilection there results an impression of tranquillity and strength. One thinks, as one sees them, of the fluting on Doric columns that support the architrave without flinching. These statues have

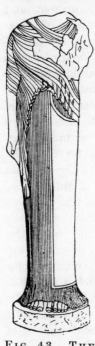

an architectural stability. It is the type beloved of the 5th century, enamoured of calm and serenity, and conceiving statuary as a living architecture.

Elsewhere oblique and transversal folds cross, overlap and cut one another; this results in quite different effects of grace and suppleness, besides greater variety. These are the folds, in the 5th century, seen in the " Parcæ " of the Parthenon, in the Aphrodite known as the " Fréjus,"[1] of the Nike of Pæonius (after 425), and of many other figures. The 4th century shows a preference for this conception, which is more realistic and more human; it is the conception of the Praxitelian drapery, of the Mausoleum statues,[2] and of the graceful Tanagra figurines.[3]

The artist is interested not merely in the form and direction of the folds but in the stuff itself, which, by its quality and the contrast of its smooth surfaces with those that are variously creased, provides him with several new effects. The sculptors of the 6th-century Korai already contrasted

FIG. 43. THE SAMOS HERA (LOUVRE), 6TH CENTURY.

the vertical folds of the chiton with the oblique folds of the himation, and the large folds of the latter with the fine folds of the cotton chiton. From the end of the 6th century, and in the 5th, the painters of red-figure vases testify to the amount of experimentation of this sort that was going on; they contrasted the fine undulations of the *kolpos* with the straight folds of the skirt, and the naked simplicity of the heavy mantle with the numerous creasings of the light tunic. In the feminine statues draped in the Dorian peplos the sculptor alternates the smooth surfaces of the *apoptygma*, the semicircle of the *kolpos*, with the vertical lines of the

[1] **LXII,** vol. ii, p. 119.　　　[2] *Ibid.*, p. 321.　　　[3] **CVII.**

skirt; in the Tralles Caryatid (about 450),[1] the heavy mantle, barely grooved by a few oblique strokes, is associated with the straight lines of the chiton. In the Fréjus Aphrodite the chiton, with a number of small oblique folds, clings to the body in front, and at the side it falls in substantial severe vertical folds. From this time forward there is an infinite variety in the combinations.

It is to be understood, too, that drapery is an entity in itself, having substance and necessary direction. The 6th century already provides a few timid attempts in Ionian and Attic-Ionian sculpture. In the Korai of the Delphic pediment (second half of the 6th century),[2] as in the Kore of Antenor[3] (about 510), the thin edges of the stuff are hollowed out from underneath and not merely worked from above; they take on a look of airiness and of movement. In Kore No. 594 of the Acropolis,[4] the ampler folds of the himation are no longer flattened on to themselves, but already stand out, ready to balance themselves naturally. This innovation is accentuated in the first quarter of the 5th century. The himation of Kore No. 688,[5] a little earlier than 480, has the substance of a woollen stuff, which stands away from the neck. Henceforth progress is rapid. Doubtless a certain awkwardness sometimes still persists, for example in the Olympian statues (about 460), in which the drapery, which looks as if it were made of cardboard, is glued too closely to the body. But the women draped in the Dorian peplos, distributed throughout the 5th century, bear witness that the artist, once he has grasped the necessity of detaching the stuff from the body, quickly finds the correct solution of the problem. From this point of view one may compare the old Korai of the 6th century with the Hestia Giustiniani (about 460), and with the Herculaneum Dancers, or with the more highly evolved Korai of the Erechtheum (about 415): on one hand the stuff is conventionally rendered, on the other it lives, has the proper substance, and is really modelled.

And then came the realization that the stuff has weight. From clinging to the loins of the Ionian Korai, being insinuated between their legs, with its folds departing in

[1] MP, 1903, Pl. ii-iii. [2] BCH, 1901, p. 457.
[3] **LXXIX**, p. 338. [4] **LXXVIII**, p. 222.
[5] *Ibid.*, pp. 358, 410, 413.

impossible directions, it gradually comes to fall perpendicularly and to obey the laws of gravitation when there is nothing
to interfere with their action. We shall see later that even
in 450 or thereabouts the last mistakes of this kind had not
yet entirely disappeared (relief of the Athena of the pillar,
Acropolis Museum).[1]

To unite the drapery harmoniously with the body without
sacrificing one to the other was a problem that the 6th-century
artist failed to grasp, but that the artist of the first half of
the 5th century made great efforts to solve, though it was
not till about 450 that a correct solution was found. A
certain awkwardness persisted after the conventional naïvetés
had gone. The bodies of the Hestia Giustiniani, of the
Herculaneum Dancers, and of the Auriga at Delphi, are not
perceptible beneath the stiff fluted sheath of their skirts;
but in other contemporaneous works, and particularly in the
later sculptures of the 5th century, the folds of the dress,
while retaining their substance and correct direction, are
adapted to the forms they cover, permitting the contours
of the hips and the flexed leg to be perceived.

The artist, seeking to unite the body and its drapery,
found two solutions—a drapery that was transparent and a
drapery that was opaque, according to the importance he
gave to the figure itself or to its garment, and according to
whether he observed the precedent principles of the substance
and weight of the stuff.

The first was not an exclusively Hellenic creation. Egypt
had had these figures in which the stuff of the drapery " exists,
one might say, only in the imagination " (Winckelmann).
The Chaldæans sometimes allow the body to be seen beneath
its clinging robe. " Nothing is more surprising," said old
Perrault, with reason, " than to see a piece of stuff, instead
of falling straight as is the natural way of all bodies possessing weight, clinging tightly to the whole length of a
leg that is bent backwards." Transparent drapery is technical in its origin: the attention of the primitive artist is at
first attracted by the human body, and he only considers the
question of its clothing later; hence the drapery is sacrificed
and comes as an afterthought. The transparent drapery of
drawing in the 5th century is sometimes to be explained by

[1] **LXXVIII**, p. 467.

a technical expedient[1] which modern artists have used (David, for example): the artist draws the nude body and clothes it afterwards, whence the transparent quality of the drapery which allows the silhouette to appear through it. Still rare in the earliest red-figure vases, this process later became frequent, for example with Douris, Hieron and Brygus. The ancients attributed to Polygnotus the honour of having first represented transparent drapery in ordinary painting; the modern critic knows that the 5th-century Thasian master was no innovator in this matter and that he had had predecessors among painters and sculptors for many a long day.[2] From the morrow of the Dorian invasion and up to the 6th century, artists had indeed carved and modelled statues and statuettes in which the body at first sight seems quite nude, and in which the drapery is only discernible on examination. This is sometimes merely painted on (Dipylon idols; flat terra cotta figurines with " bird's beak "),[3] and sometimes indicated by a few lines incised or shown in relief on the naked body (Moscophoros, Cyprus Kouros).[4] With the passage of time, folds achieved substance and are better rendered, but the stuff continues, none the less, to stick to the form; it is moulded on the back and hips of the Korai, and it allows the male pudenda to project (Cyprus Kouros, Kouros No. 633 of the Acropolis);[5] the hand which gathers up the skirt on one side ought to stretch the material tight between the legs, but the stuff indiscreetly insinuates itself around and between them (Korai of the Acropolis, relief of Hermes and the Charities, Acropolis).[6] Sometimes even the hair appears beneath the stuff (Kore).[7] The red-figure vases of Epictetus (end of the 6th century) show analogous details.[8]

Following a general law of evolution,[9] technical expedients involuntarily become deliberate efforts after beauty in subsequent periods. The Ionian artists of the 6th century, when they moulded the form of the body beneath the stuff, may have already transformed into definite æsthetic effort that

[1] **CXLV**, vol. iii, pp. 862, 956.   [2] *Ibid.*, p. 1068.
[3] **LXXXIV**, vol. vii, p. 142; **CXI**, Pl. v.
[4] **LXVIII**, p. 237; **LXXVIII**, p. 106.
[5] **LXXXIX**, p. 56.   [6] **LXXIX**, p. 443.
[7] BCH, 1899, p. 221.   [8] **CXLV**, vol. iii, p. 890.
[9] **VI**, vol. ii, p. 337.

which at first had been merely inexperience. The problem, however, was not completely solved till later, in the second half of the 5th century, in the Parthenon, in the marbles of Phidias and his imitators. Drapery, as transparent as though it were wet, ripples in a number of minutely fine folds over the body, of which nothing, however, remains hidden. It is impossible to improve on this. Hebe and the " Parcæ " of the east pediment, and Iris of the west pediment, are masterpieces in this genre. They inspired the numerous sculptors who, since the Parthenon, repeat the principle of this transparent drapery: *e.g.*, the Nike of Pæonius of Mende (after 425), the Aphrodite called the " Fréjus," the Victories of the balustrade of the temple of Athena Nike (about 408), the Xanthus Nereids[1] (end of the 5th century), the acroteria at Delos.[2] What a difference from the drapery painted or drawn on the bodies of the primitives, or from the sticky drapery of the 6th-century Ionians, all as unreal as they can be ! The stuff now has its proper value, creases into folds, follows the movements of the body, and is agitated by the least action, but, owing to its lightness and transparency, which it seems to owe to its texture, and also to the breeze which causes it to cling to the skin in figures in movement (Nike of Pæonius, Iris of the Parthenon), it leaves the human being all its beauty, and is calculated less to dissimulate the form than to emphasize it. Its effects may be criticized from the rational point of view; it may seem illogical, despite this virtuosity, that the dress should be so diaphanous and cling everywhere; one finds it a little difficult to believe in these goddesses clothed in wet materials. However conventional this process may be in principle, its realization is henceforth conceived with truth and naturalism. Up to the end, Greek art testifies to this taste for transparent draperies. To quote a few examples taken at random, there are, in the 5th century, the Vienna Kore[3] and its derivatives, one of the Thessalians of the Lysippian group at Delphi,[4] the feminine torso from the Tegea pediments;[5] and, in the Hellenistic period, the group of Niobe and her daughter,[6] and the Aphrodite with the sword, from Epidaurus.[7]

---

[1] **LXII**, vol. ii, p. 228.   [2] *Ibid.*, p. 191.
[3] **CLXII**, p. 362; **CLXIII**, p. 15.
[4] *Fouilles de Delphes*, iv, Pl. lxv; **CLX**, Fig. 3, Sisyphus i.
[5] BCH, 1901, Pl. vi.   [6] **LXII**, vol. ii, p. 538.   [7] *Ibid.*, p. 463.

The opaque drapery which completely hides the body under a rigid and geometrical cope was also, in its inception, a happy expedient which avoided the difficulty of musculature, and not an æsthetic choice: the statue dedicated by Nicandra of Delos,[1] the Auxerre statuette[2] in the Louvre, the Treasury of the Sicyonians at Delphi,[3] and numerous figures on the black-figure vases, illustrated this appearance in the 6th century. The 5th century recognized an æsthetic value in this heavy drapery with its large and sparsely placed folds, beneath which the body disappears, and of this type we have the thick himation of the Tralles Caryatid (about 450),[4] and of the Berlin female figure;[5] also the chlamys of the so-called Phocion (Hermes) at the Vatican;[6] and, in the 4th century, that of the Thessalians at Delphi[7] and of the Tralles ephebus[8] pensively leaning against a pillar.

The stuff of drapery may be transparent and finely creased, when it is graceful, delicate and sensuous in quality; or it may be opaque and yielding only large smooth surfaces, when it evokes calm and a repose of body and mind.

There is also a mean between these two contrasting tendencies: the body may be allowed to show whenever the material permits it by its natural play and its texture; whereas it is hidden wherever, in reality, the thickness of the stuff or its way of falling would hide it. The long series of women draped in the Dorian peplos show the progress achieved in this effort to arrive at a just balance; the Hestia Giustiniani (about 460) is still covered up in a rigid tunic like a carapace, but elsewhere the leg put forward and the swelling chest stretch the material, and the Korai of the Erechtheum (about 415) show the harmonious result when this reconciliation is definitely effected.

The human body and its drapery, whilst each has artistic independence, must also lend one another mutual aid and bring out one another's values. The folds of the stuff, with its vertical, oblique, and curved lines all directed the same way, or cutting each other, contrast with the smooth surfaces of the naked skin which are enhanced by its proximity.

---

[1] **LXXXIV**, vol. viii, p. 148.   [2] RA, 1908, i, Pl. x.
[3] **LXXXIV**, vol. viii, p. 454.   [4] MP, 1903, Pl. ii-iii.
[5] **LXIII**, p. 116; **LXXIV**, No. 1518.
[6] **LXXXVI**, vol. i, p. 511.
[7] BCH, 1899, p. 468, Pl. xxv.   [8] MP, x, 1903, Pl. iv-v.

This, the artist of the 6th century who veils the body of his female figures and completely strips his male ones, does not yet understand. He only rarely associated nudity with drapery (Naples stele);[1] he does not yet throw drapery over the arms or round the loins with a solely æsthetic aim, that it may serve to throw up the figure. The chlamys that Aristogiton carries over his arm in the Tyrannicides group (477-6) is required by the subject: the assassin uses it as a buckler to protect his young friend Harmodius who advances against the tyrant, sword raised. However, the vase painter has already adopted the use of drapery for this æsthetic end; the masters of the red-figure work frequently hang a chlamys over the arm of their ephebi in order to provide a background which will throw up their nude strength. This aim is distinctly perceptible in the pediments at Olympia

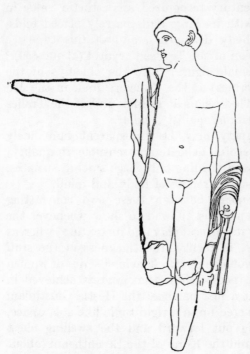

Fig. 44. East pediment at Olympia. Apollo.

(about 460): the chlamys that falls over the shoulder at the back and on the arm of Œnomaus and Apollo (Fig. 44), and the drapery around the hips and legs of Zeus, and the figures reclining in the angles, have no other purpose than to form a contrast by their folds with the unbroken surface of the flesh. The Parthenon supplies marvellous examples of this (Fig. 45). Doubtless the metopes carved by the older sculptors, whose artistic education had not felt the Phidian

[1] **LXX,** vol. i, p. 256, Fig. 125.

influence, disdained drapery; their drily modelled musculature is nude, and the grounds against which the Centaurs
and Lapiths stand out are somewhat empty. But how very
different are the metopes in which we recognize the teachings
of the Attic master ! Look at that one in which the young
Lapith is in the act of striking a wounded Centaur on the
back: the ephebic body, carried forward by an impetuous
movement, detaches itself in its smooth nudity from the large
circular folds of the mantle which falls at the back—a nudity
that stands out as a light figure from the coloured ground
of the material.[1] What pur-
pose is served by the drapery
on which the Dionysus of the
east pediment reclines unless
it be to throw up his form ?
Or what by that of the ample
drapery with its deep folds,
thrown negligently on the
tree-trunk at the side of the
Hermes carrying the infant
Dionysus, in the Praxitelian
group at Olympia ? What
purpose, again, is served by
the rugose animal's skin of
the Praxitelian Satyrs,[2] which
crosses their chests ? The
stuff of drapery serves less
and less its primitive pur-

Fig. 45. Detail of the North
Frieze of the Parthenon.

pose of clothing, and increasingly becomes a means for the
realization of beauty.

The same contrasting effect between one figure and
another is to be observed. The vase-painters and the 6th-
century relief sculptors occasionally associated nude figures
with others that were draped, but this was more often due
to the necessities of the subject than to any æsthetic purpose.
In the Pisistratidæ pediment,[3] though Athena is clothed
whilst the giant Enceladus at her feet is nude, that is because
she is a goddess and because art still eliminated feminine
nudity, whereas it sought after masculine nudity (about

---

[1] **XXXIX; LXII,** vol. ii, p. 15, Fig. 4.
[2] **LXII,** vol. ii, pp. 289-290.   [3] **LXXXIV,** vol. viii, p. 553.

520-510). But from the 5th century artists liked to alternate, on vases and in reliefs, and in pediments, draped figures with nude ones, and at Olympia the nude Œnomaus and Pelops are framed on either side by the semi-nude Zeus and by Sterope and Hippodamia draped in the Dorian peplos.

The problem of adapting drapery not only to the shape of the body but to its movements, and of observing and rendering the modifications these movements cause in the drapery, did not preoccupy the artist until the 5th century, and did not until then obtain a satisfactory interpretation. Nothing in the foldless chiton, stuck fast to the body, in the statue of Nike by Archermus, betokens the rapidity of flight. The draughtsman was better able to try and get his drapery to float than the sculptor who was obsessed with the fear of a breakage. Yet how stiff is this drapery[1] still— it looks like a rigid pipe—behind the galloping horseman on an Ionian vase ! The draughtsman even envisages the complicated movements of torsion: on the " Nola " amphora in the British Museum (6th century) an oblique fold, traced on the leg of a woman, indicates that she is turning. In a marble torso of a woman at Delphi (6th century), though the curls of the hair fall inert, the garment is already slightly blown by the wind.[2] From the beginning of the 5th century such essays are multiplied. It is true that the drapery of Aristogiton falls vertically from his arm, despite the energy of his movement; but the folds of the drapery of Victories 690 and 490 of the Acropolis are deviated from the straight by the flight of the goddesses.[3] In the severe style red-figure vase-painting the artist seeks to adapt the movement of drapery to that of the body, and in Hieron's work the solution of the problem appears to be expressed correctly for the first time. Brygus likes drapery blown out on the breeze. This is more faithfully rendered by Euphronius, more rigidly by Chachrylion, and more schematically in the cycle of Epictetus. Then come the beautiful draperies of Polygnotus, a master of fresco, imitated by the ceramists. Progressing steadily, they achieved, after 450, perfect accord between the swing of the drapery and the action to which it is due. In Phidias'

[1] BCH, 1892, p. 259; **LXXXIV,** vol. viii, p. 300.
[2] **LXXXIV,** vol. viii, p. 571.
[3] **LXXVIII,** p. 395; **LXXIX,** p. 380.

Parthenon, in the Theseum, at Phigalia (about 420), in the Nike of Pæonius (after 425), in the temple of Athena Nike, the drapery, agitated by the wind, or by running or fighting, twists this way and that, clinging against the body or fluttering in the wind, reinforcing the action of the figure by emphasizing its effort and its direction, while at the same time it throws up human nudity by the contrast formed with its folds (Fig. 46). To bring out movement, folds are frequently twisted into spirals and whorls; these are already to be seen on vases in the style of Brygus, as, later on, they are to be seen in the cycle of Meidias; in sculpture they are particularly frequent in the Parthenon (Hebe), at Phigalia, in the temple of Athena Nike, in the Nereids' monument from Xanthus, and at the heröon at Trysa. Become conventional, they persist in art, and the Hellenistic Telephus reliefs at Pergamum[1] (2nd century B.C.), and the neo-Attic reliefs,[2] supply numerous examples.

FIG. 46. FRIEZE OF THE MAUSOLEUM AT HALICARNASSUS (355-350 B.C.): DETAIL.

This agitation of drapery even becomes artificial[3] from the second half of the 5th century, and, already in the Parthenon, is not always necessitated by the action. Sometimes an exterior puff of wind swells out the drapery of a body in repose. Already perceptible in the reliefs of the temple of Athena Nike at Phigalia, this feature is later developed, and it seems that the breeze—or even a violent wind—blows in the studio of the sculptor. In a Hellenistic Myrina terra cotta, Aphrodite is seated tranquilly on the swan, but her garment bellies out behind her; on a Roman

[1] **LXII,** vol. ii, p. 527.   [2] Hauser, *Neu-attische Reliefs.*
[3] **VI,** vol. iii, p. 268.

relief the chlamys of a horseman, whose horse is only walking, flutters in the wind. In the Mausoleum, the drapery of the Delian Artemis with the Hind,[1] is blown in the direction in which she is going, as though the wind were pushing her from behind. Certain 5th-century statues even present an unexpected agitation, difficult to explain, an experiment full of danger which may lead to reasonless gusts of wind in the manner of Bernini. The drapery floats in different directions as though blown by contrary winds. In the Doria Pamphili Aphrodite and in a whole group of Attic works later than the Parthenon, the drapery is quiescent on the upper portion of the body and agitated at its feet.[2] Hermes stands erect in front of the chariot of Echelus and Basilia (relief of the beginning of the 4th century),[3] and the wind coming from behind blows his garment in the direction they are going, but an opposite wind blows the feminine draperies out behind.

Artists had come to love drapery for itself, for its infinite plastic variety, and they had somewhat lost sight of its harmonious union with the human body which had been finally realized after long experimental efforts. From the 4th century it sometimes engrosses the artist's attention to the detriment of everything else: in certain Praxitelian statues, in the Tanagra terra cottas, the main thing for their authors is the play of the drapery with its large or fine, oblique or vertical folds, and the grouping and contrasting of them. However skilfully it may be treated, the body sometimes seems as though reduced to the rôle of a support for the drapery. And finally, in Roman times, an artist was to represent a piece of drapery cleverly disposed on a throne empty of its divine image.

Drapery became more than a means of æsthetic expression, more than a sensuous delight for the eyes; it became a psychological element, a means of transcribing the intimate self, its rank, sex and even thoughts, with the same authority as the pose or the countenance. Vase-painters understood this from the end of the 6th century and the beginning of the 5th,[4] before the sculptors and modellers. They made the drapery of courtesans and of the frenzied Mænads boil and

---

[1] *Proceedings* of the Acad. des Inscript., 1907, p. 367.
[2] **VI**, vol. ii, p. 459; vol. iii, p. 271, note 2.
[3] **LXII**, vol. ii, p. 190.   [4] **CXLV**, vol. iii, p. 861.

swirl in a thousand folds (Fig. 47); they contrasted this with
the calm perpendicularity of the Dorian peplos in which
matrons and goddesses are clothed; they rendered broadly
the plane surfaces of the himation of sturdy ephebi. Then
they all began with one accord to try to adapt drapery to the
moral character of the person portrayed. Look at the celebrated relief of Eleusis (about 450).[1] The vigorous nude body
of Triptolemus, emphasized by the drapery which serves as
background, is contrasted
with the two draped
goddesses who stand on
either side of him. De-
meter wears a severe
peplos, with rigid grooves,
which suits the gravity
of the maternal and sor-
rowing goddess. But a
chiton with supple folds,
and himation liberally
draped, accentuate the
youthful character of her
daughter Cora. On the
east end of the Parthenon
the grave and majestic
drapery of the Eleu-
sinian goddesses, seated,
in the left wing, is quite
different from the supple

FIG. 47. MÆNADS. DETAIL ON A CUP
BY HIERON (BERLIN).

transparent drapery of
Dione and Aphrodite (" Parcæ "). The 4th century introduced still further subtleties into this expressive drapery,
and the products of the Tanagra modellers[2] show drapery
rendering the most diverse meanings, and the most subtle
interpretations of the inner self.[3]

Drapery in the 6th century was still unreal, conventional
and decorative; in the 5th century it is truthful, but it often
preserves that same character of somewhat artificial regularity
and abstraction that we have already noted in the musculature
of the time, and a too rigorous symmetry: in the Berlin
Amazon (Polyclitus), for example, the folds on the right

[1] **LXII,** vol. ii, p. 141.　　　[2] **CVII.**　　　[3] **VI,** vol. iii, p. 268.

exactly correspond with those on the left side. Drapery is above all architectural, and tends to emphasize the effects of stability and repose. On female figures the parallel folds of the Dorian peplos are directed perpendicularly, like the flutings of a living column; the Hestia Giustiniani and the Herculaneum Dancers exaggerate this feature, which becomes softened in the second half of the 5th century. But the 4th century and the Hellenists introduce the same note of realism and picturesqueness as they did in musculature. They seek to imitate more exactly the thousand little accidents of a real piece of stuff. The chlamys of the Olympian Hermes is thrown negligently on the trunk of the tree, the folds crease, intercross and pile up under the arm of the god; here and there light undulations wrinkle the woollen tissue, and the artist pushes his care for detail so far as to indicate the hole made in the stuff by the pin which served to hold it. The realism is such that a savant, to whom the first photographs of this statue were shown, exclaimed: " It is very fine, but why, when they took the photograph, did they leave that cloak hanging there ?" What suppleness and what virtuosity is there in these beautiful draperies of the Mausolus statue,[1] and what refined observation ! To get closer to nature and to vary the aspect of the stuff, the sculptor cuts with parallel striations the folds determined by the gestures of the figure: these are the creases left in the material as a result of being folded up in a chest. This feature also appears at Delphi on the statue of one of the Thessalians,[2] and in Pergamenian plastic work. Differences in tissues are indicated, such as the impression given by a light and silky stuff (Delos statue),[3] and the transparency of a silk himation on a chiton of thicker material.[4] Thus drapery loses all its dryness, and is treated more and more pictorially.

[1] **LXII,** vol. ii, p. 339; **LXIII,** p. 256.
[2] BCH, 1899, p. 463; **VI,** vol. iii, p. 267.
[3] BCH, 1907, p. 407; **LXIII,** p. 299.
[4] **VI,** vol. iii, p. 320.

THE ANALYTIC AND SYNTHETIC VIEW. HARMONY, RHYTHM, " SYMMETRIA," PROPORTION, COMPOSITION[1]

THE artist, through this patient education, learned to render truthfully attitude, musculature, and drapery, and their correct reciprocal relations. He examined their infinite variety and drew therefrom æsthetic effects hitherto undreamed of. But he had to make further progress and unite all these elements into one faithful yet harmonious whole.

The human mind does not at the outset rise to synthesis. The child and the primitive are attracted by details. The former remarks, in a man, his hat and his pipe; the man of lowly culture gives his attention to analogous futilities. The individual education of the artist, as the general evolution of art, begins by this stage of analytic perception, and only in the course of time rises to the synthesis that neglects superfluous and minute detail and establishes the proper correlation between all the parts of a whole—an organic unity in place of a sum of disparate parts. The Greek artist, prior to 500, justified those words of Delacroix: " To know how to sacrifice to the whole is great art of which novices are ignorant; they want to put in everything."

It was the minutiæ which attracted the artist. The authors of the dreadful ivory dolls of the Dipylon (9th century)[2] were still incapable of correctly representing the body anatomically, but they did not neglect to put in the meander which runs along the *polos* of the goddess, a purely accessory element. This love of detail, though general, is more evident in some regions and in some artists than in others. Peloponnesian art, more sober and more robust by nature than Ionian art, is not so prone to multiply trumpery trifles; none the less, it, too, squandered time on detailing the hair, line by line, in putting in every hair on the pubis, and

---

[1] **VI**, vol. ii, p. 453; vol. iii.   [2] **LXXXIV**, vol. vii, p. 142.

there is, as it were, a discordance between this minute work and the massive build of the Kouros of Polymedes of Argos (6th century).[1] The Ionian sculptors abandoned themselves unreservedly to this debauch of detail, to which they were urged by their innate desire to please, their coquetry, and their love of luxury. The drapery of the Korai is covered with minute pleats and embroideries. But the hair, in particular, provided the artist with the happy occasion to display his instinctive taste. The hairs of a head defy enumeration, and so, too, do the modes of arranging it in spirals, waves, whorls, diaper and bead! There are a hundred fashions of tiring it with circlets and diadems! And then the ears cry out for cunningly chiselled ear-rings, and the arms for bracelets. This is due to a desire to make the figure look elegant, no doubt, but it is also due to an instinctive love of detail for its own sake, that by its means a pretty ornament or a decorative motif may be contrived. The Rampin head,[2] with its minutely executed hair contrasting with the broader work on the face, and a masculine head at Delos[3] are significant in this connection. In the Sunium Kouros,[4] whose gigantesque size should have called for a sober method of execution, the artist, on the contrary, refines the curve of the ear, transforms the cartilages into a kind of Ionic capital, and erects on the forehead an amazing assemblage of whorls looking for all the world like fossil ammonites. Hence the expert who studies archaic art must not shrink from spending time on details; he must do as the artist did then, and so get at his ideas.

This detail, however, was detrimental to the ensemble. The artist did not yet know how to establish the proper accord between the different parts which each individually claimed his attention. He made a number of mistakes in anatomy before he arrived at rendering each part in its proper size, its correct position, and in relation with the attitude assumed. This was partly due to a lack of observation and fluency of technique, but it was also due to his predominant habit of looking at things analytically. Thence came his errors in the logical linking up of different organic parts, which he would

[1] **LXXXIV**, vol. viii, p. 454.
[2] **LXXXIV**, vol. viii, p. 641; **LXXVIII**, p. 197.
[3] BCH, v, 1881, Pl. xi; **LXXVIII**, p. 185.   [4] **LXVIII**, p. 135.

allow to contradict one another—eyes placed frontally in a head in profile, and a frontal torso on legs seen sideways. He did not free himself from these errors till he substituted the truth of the whole for the truth of separate parts, and this was when sculpture gave up frontality and when drawing had learned to foreshorten.

Numerous examples of this faulty co-ordination can be quoted in the 6th century and in the first half of the 5th, although from 500 the artist gradually freed himself from his errors by a closer observation of reality.

The drapery sticks to the loins of the Acropolis Korai (6th century); it clings between their legs, although the left hand stretches the stuff and the left leg is put forward: it ought here to form a rigid plane surface. The artist did not trouble himself about this correlation between his drapery and the form and movements of the body. See, on the contrary, how, a century later (about 420), the sculptor of the Phigalian frieze stretches the stuff tight across the legs of an Amazon who is moving quickly, so that it seems like to tear.[1] In one Kore the folds of the himation are oblique when they ought to fall perpendicularly; one cannot suppose that they have swung rearwards owing to a forward movement, because the statue is immobile; the artist, in his desire to break the monotony of parallel folds, has not asked himself whether this was true to nature.

None the less there was correct observation from this time forward. On a metope of the Treasury of the Sicyonians at Delphi, the mantle of Europa,[2] folded in four and placed over the arm, falls vertically; on a metope of Temple F at Selinus[3] the drapery of the overthrown giant falls plumb straight, as does that of Kore No. 687 of the Acropolis.[4]

Such errors, however, appear sporadically in the 5th century. The chlamys of Aristogiton, inert, does not follow the energetic movement of the body when it ought to be swung out by the resistance of the air to his swift oncoming movement. Later on the chlamys of the Apollo Belvedere[5] (4th century) is also artificial, and this is doubtless due to a clumsy addition to the original bronze by the Roman copyist.

---

[1] **LXII**, vol. ii, p. 159.   [2] **LXXXIV**, vol. viii, p. 461.
[3] *Ibid.*, p. 493.   [4] **LXXVIII**, p. 236.
[5] **LXII**, vol. ii, p. 317; RA, 1904, ii, p. 225.

On a cup by Chachrylion the two points of the himation thrown over the shoulders come together at the bottom instead of falling straight. And on the Acropolis relief (about 450) the chiton of the Athena wrongly called the " Mourning," who is leaning forward, falls impossibly slant-wise (Fig. 48).

The same is true of anatomy. The neck of the Acropolis bull, in soft stone (6th century), being considerably arched, the skin here ought to be tightly stretched, but it is all wrinkled. The scales on the body of Triton do not participate in the movement of his nether parts, but form a rigid cuirass without a crease.[1] The hand of a man, fighting, rests placidly on the shoulder of his enemy, in an Acropolis group, instead of grasping it as one feels it should.

FIG 48. RELIEF OF THE ATHENA OF THE PILLAR, ATHENS.

In the composite monsters the join between the two disparate elements is bizarre. On a Bœotian vase in relief (7th century)[2] the Gorgon is a human being to which there has simply been added on the hinder parts of a horse with no organic connection; the composition of the archaic Centaur is of the same order. On an Attic-Corinthian vase Triton has an entire human body to which is fastened a fish's tail which one would say was artificial.

Each single element of the body is treated separately, for itself alone, with no regard for its neighbouring elements. The hair is too often independent of the shape and pose of the head. The hair of the Blond Ephebus (before 480),[3] regularly combed, ought to fall away from the point of departure of the two tresses, as had been learned later by the author of the Apollo of the Omphalos. But the tresses do not follow the

[1] **LXXVIII**, pp. 36, 75, 406.   [2] BCH, 1898, Pl. v.
[3] **LXXVIII**, p. 362.

movement. Those of the Nike of Archermus, in full flight, keep quite rigid. How many figures bend their heads without their locks following suit and falling perpendicularly, as they should—in the 6th century the Hoplitodromos of the Athens stele,[1] in the first half of the 5th century the Spinario, the Barberini Girl Runner, the goddesses of the Eleusis relief, one of the reclining figures at Ægina, and Achilles on a red-figure vase. There is no harmonious transition between the cranium and the hair upon it in the numerous heads of the early 5th century; the hair of Harmodius forms an independent cap of thick fur. In Polyclitus' Doryphoros the nipples are still stuck on like bits of ornamentation, without any connection with the surrounding skin. The movement is localized in a single limb and has no repercussion throughout the body, and when the trunk is turned its relation to the legs is faulty. In the Doryphoros there is still a certain want of mutual easiness and naturalness between the different parts of the body.

There is the same want of accord in poses; on an Ionian relief there is a galloping stag, but the dog that is biting its belly is shown in repose; on a Palakastro terra cotta relief (6th century), the chariot has started, but the warrior appears to be getting into it from a stationary position.[2]

These errors, frequent in archaic work, and rarer in the 5th century, are general, nevertheless; they appear in all periods when the artist, either clumsy or careless, does not closely observe reality and fails to recognize the mutual relations between parts. For instance, in a group of Dionysus and a Satyr, Dionysus, in repose, leans on the Satyr who is moving forward. Many centuries earlier, in Ægean art, the bull borne on the sarcophagus of Haghia Triada is in the conventional flying gallop attitude. And, in the 13th century in France, the sculptor of an ivory descent from the cross makes the same mistake over the hair as the author of the Spinario.

About 500, however, the Greek artist realized that this minute regard for detail was peurile and that beauty lies above all in sobriety; the aim of art was no longer to pile up detail but to get the maximum effect from the simplest of means. The Kore of Euthydicus and the Blond Ephebus

[1] **LXXXIV**, vol. viii, p. 649.   [2] **VI**, vol. ii, pp. 457-458.

reveal in Attica this new spirit that had come under the
influence of Dorian art in which it had already for some time
been visible. Doubtless artists, according to their individual
temperaments, were still to squander their time picking away at
hair and drapery, broadly treated by others, and in accumulat-
ing embellishments; Attic art, from 500, was to show a dual
tendency in which an Attic-Dorian influence, enamoured of
simplicity and severe strength, and an Attic-Ionian influence,
carrying on the Ionian tradition of the 6th century, and
showing a preference for the refinements of technique,[1] flow
as two currents in one bed; but these are mere subtle distinctions, and the day of detail beloved for its own sake and
without thought for co-ordination, of analysis which never
leads to synthesis, was past and gone.

It was realized now that beauty lies in a mutually logical
and harmonious concord of parts, that a work of art is not
a mosaic of independent fragments but that from the outset
it must be set about with its ultimate unity in view, and that
each part reacts on every other part and is itself subject to
this reaction. The aim of the artist was now the unity of his
work and the correct adaptation of its detail to the whole and
of that whole to some given situation. The earlier faults were
finally to vanish, and if a few of them persisted into the first
half of the 5th century, and if the work occasionally betrayed
a slight want of ease and naturalness in the union of its various
elements, it is because truth cannot be achieved all at once,
and the eye and the hand of the artist must have time
to get accustomed to it. He was learning to manage the
necessary transitions between one element and another, and
drapery and hair now fall according to the law of gravity or
follow the inflections of the figure, whilst action has its repercussion throughout the body, and the muscles change
according to the attitudes taken.

This effort to achieve unity is asserted by the rhythm[2]
that occupied the main attention of artists from the beginning
of the 5th century. According to Diogenes Laërtius, who
doubtless is repeating Antigonus of Carystus (3rd century),
who, in turn, was inspired by Xenocrates of Sicyon, Pythagoras of Rhegium, who began to work about 490, was the first
to display this rhythmic feeling in statuary.[3] This was the

---

[1] **LXXVIII**, pp. 353, 387.   [2] **CLXXIX.**   [3] **CLXIV**, p. 39.

moment when, as a result of liberation from the frontal convention, new problems were being faced by the artist. Rhythm, or "eurhythmy"—the two terms mean the same thing—is the æsthetic impression produced on the spectator by the correct concordance of the parts of a whole, their perfect and harmonious accord which comes from the adaptation of the pose, the gestures, and the musculature to the subject and the action, and from the proper relations between figure and drapery. Rhythm varies with the temperament and artistic feeling of the artist; it is simple in the Polyclitian images, which Pliny reproaches with being nearly all conceived on the same model; and it is more complex and subtle in Lysippian work; it is full of movement in Myron and Pythagoras, and tranquil in Phidias and Praxiteles. But whatever it be, it is essential from this time forth, and it becomes an indispensable condition for any work of art. Diogenes Laërtius, repeating from one of his predecessors, praises Pythagoras of Rhegium also for having been the first to display the feeling for *symmetria*,[1] in which Myron and Lysippus excel, and for a legitimate conformity of form and proportion to subject, pose, and action.

The unity and beauty of a work of art also depend on its proportions and on the numerical relation of the parts to one another. Had not number, at a very early date, already regulated architecture, in which, once the temple had been constituted, one of the chief cares had been to determine the most harmonious relations of the constituent parts to the building, the relation of the column to the entablature, of its diameter to its height, and the interval separating one from another ? According to the legend, the Samian artists Rhœcus and Theodorus had made a statue of which each of them had independently carved one half, the two being then put together;[2] does not such a method of working presuppose, together with obedience to the frontal convention, the application of a precise system of measurements ? Thenceforward there were "canons," that is to say "a system of measurements which must be such that one can determine the dimensions of a single part from the whole, or of the whole from one of its parts" (Guillaume). To work out with exactitude what such systems were is a difficult task for

---

[1] **CLXIV**, pp. 46, 50. [2] **LXXXIV**, vol. viii, p. 711.

scholars; they should bear in mind that these canons were more often than not in the eye of the artist rather than a matter for his callipers, that they were rather an æsthetic approximation than a rigorously mathematical code.[1] If the effort to achieve proportion was pursued in Greek art from the archaic period, both in statuary and architecture, it became of dominant importance in the 5th century, just because the artist was then passing from the analytical view of things to the synthetic and so could consciously establish the relations of parts to a whole. Polyclitus codified the principles of his Argive predecessors, basing on them a precise formula, and demonstrating their laws in a treatise whose existence is attested by Galen. His Doryphoros, for the Ancients, embodied these principles, and it was called the "Canon," the rule, the formula (χάνων).[2] Polyclitus would build the entire human body with his module, probably the dactylos, because this body is a living architecture, governed by number, as is inanimate architecture. "That which is well" he said, "depends on infinitely subtle distinctions and is the result of agreement between many numbers." This idea is in full harmony with the spirit of the 5th century which proclaimed the necessity for harmony and for the co-ordination of parts in a logical whole.

According to their individual taste, different artists living in the same period might adopt different rules of proportion, and the same artist might not always keep to one. In the severe style red-figure pottery Peithinus loved figures that were gracile and delicate; Heiron preferred slimmer figures than did Douris; Oltus made his shorter than any master of the period; Euphronius in his early days shows thick-set proportions which he was later to make more elegant, while Douris uses both kinds simultaneously.

Despite individual preferences, one can follow throughout Greek art the vicissitudes of two systems of proportion, the one slim and tall, the other short.[3] Ægean art loved the tall, spindle-like figure with a pinched-in waist and slender limbs, perhaps in imitation of the Egyptian.[4] After the wreck of Mycenæan civilization, and after the "Hellenic Mediæval Age" which followed it, when the earliest crude monuments

---

[1] **IX**, p. 234.
[3] **VI**, vol. ii, pp. 206, 242.
[2] **LXII**, vol. i, p. 490.
[4] **CXLV**, vol. iii, p. 621.

appear, we get the slender strangulated human form of the
Dipylon vases and the ivory statuettes of the same provenance,
and this continued to be the æsthetic model generally in
vogue up to the 6th century, as witness the many small
bronzes and vase-paintings in which the figures are nine or
even ten heads in height.   Certain scholars consider that this
canon is inherited from the Mycenæans and that it is a
tendency proper to the European spirit represented by the
Dorian invaders.   But must we not also attribute some share
in this to instinctive feeling, to the primitive and barbaric
effort after elegance, since this preference for an elongated
body is also shown in the numerous small Etruscan bronzes,
and, many centuries later, in our Romanesque art ?

The Attics accepted this canon in the 6th century.
Although the Attic-Corinthian vases had formerly shown a
height of only four or five heads for the human figure, this
grew to eight or nine, and even more in the black-figure vases,
and the average in the time of Nicosthenes was from six to
seven.[1] Sculpture, too, carved slender bodies for its Korai
following on the squat figures in soft stone, and thus returned
to the old tradition, inherited, so it is said, from the Mycenæans.   The first half of the 5th century maintained these
slender proportions.[2]   We see this elegance in the figures of
Pythagoras of Rhegium, such as in the Louvre Pollux[3]—if we
are to admit that it can be attributed to this master; in the
Auriga at Delphi, in the Apollo of the Omphalos, and in a
number of other sculptures.   After a reaction in the time
of Phidias, this canon is again placed in honour in the 4th
century by Praxiteles, Lysippus, Scopas and Euphranor.   The
statues of Lysippus, his Apoxyomenos and his Agias, have
very long trunks, a very small head, and are about eight heads
in height.[4]   In the Sicyonian school this canon takes the
place of the thick-set canon of Polyclitus.   Certain Hellenistic
works, especially the terra cottas of Asia Minor, of Myrina,[5]
and the figures in relief on 3rd-century mirrors,[6] elongate the
body to exaggeration, and in the Roman period the affectedly
slender Victories of the Farnese stuccos[7] reach a point where

[1] **CXLV**, vol. iii, p. 624.   [2] *Ibid.*, pp. 1091, 1095, 1107.
[3] **CLXIV**, pp. 108, 119.
[4] BCH, 1899, p. 448; RA, 1909, i, p. 72.   [5] **CXII.**
[6] BCH, 1884, Pl. xv-xvi.
[7] Gusman, *L'art décoratif à Rome*, Pl.

this tendency becomes almost a caricature of the figure. Speaking generally, although this taste is proper to the Attics who preserve it to the end with a few momentary eclipses,[1] it is not peculiar to them, as is proved by the monuments quoted from other regions.

But from very early times there was another ideal which evinced a preference for short, square figures giving the impression of strength rather than elegance. It used to be considered proper to the Dorians, and the opposite ideal to the Ionians. Pottier says we should rather put it the other way about. Whereas the continental and island Greeks inherited from the Mycenæans their taste for elongated figures, the Ionians, in contact with Asiatic art, preferred shorter proportions, as is witnessed by their vase-paintings, the sarcophagi of Clazomenæ, and by their reliefs. This canon spread from Ionia into eastern Greece, inspiring the massive Kouroi of Polymedes of Argos (less than seven heads in height), the Eleutherna torso, the small Cretan bronzes, and the Corinthian and Attic-Corinthian vases.[2] It was this system of proportions that became that of the Argive school of the 6th and 5th centuries; after Polymedes, it was applied to their work by Ageladas and his disciples, such as Dionysius and Glaucus (Ligourio ephebus), and finally by Polyclitus. The last-named artist imposed this conception on art for a long time; he gave to the human body a thick-set shape with short torso and legs, wide hips, and square head, and a look of powerful strength.[3] This canon spread beyond the Peloponnese, and was adopted by certain Attic vase-painters of the end of the 5th century, even by the Attic sculptor Phidias and by his disciples, who nevertheless tempered this strength with the innate grace and elegance of the Attics. If the statues of Phidias, and still more so those of Polyclitus, appear to our modern view a little too massive, it is because, thanks to the intermediation of the Romans and of the Renaissance, we have adopted, rather, the elegant canon of Praxiteles and of Lysippus.[4]

We may see in Greece, within the boundaries of a single country, an alternation of long and short proportions, which

---

[1] BCH, 1899, p. 448.
[2] **CXLV**, vol. ii, p. 509; iii, pp. 622, 623, 624.
[3] BCH, 1900, p. 456; RA, 1909, i, p. 50.   [4] RA, 1895, ii, p. 22.

is to be found, as a matter of fact, in the history of all art. To the heavy and squat Attic work in soft stone (end of the 7th and beginning of the 6th centuries) succeeded the elegant and affected insular Korai (second half of the 6th century); Phidias reduced the elongated proportions in vogue before his time, but Praxiteles restored them to honour. In the Argive-Sicyonian school, though Polyclitus carried on the ancient tradition, Lysippus modified this too square and squat system.

Nevertheless we notice a general tendency to lengthen proportions, towards elegance. The columns of the earliest Doric temples (example: Corinth)[1] are squat, the echinus of the capital seems crushed under the weight of the abacus, and the entablature is enormous. Gradually the column is lengthened, becoming slenderer, the curve of the echinus is straightened and the height of the entablature diminished. When the Doric order attained, in the Parthenon, a perfection which is already disturbed by alterations in an Ionian sense, the satisfaction of this desire for elegance and slimness came to be sought elsewhere. The Ionic order, hitherto confined to Greece in Asia, took root on the continent and provided there its first architectural examples (Propylæa, temple of Athena Nike, Erechtheum) whose tall, slender columns, less heavy entablature, and ornament richer than that of the sober Doric, are so pleasing.[2]

This tendency to unity not only affects the isolated human figure but figures in common action. The group develops in the same manner from something analytically seen to something seen synthetically. How did the artist carry out a group in the early days ? We must distinguish, as we did earlier, between works conceived in the round to be seen from the front and those which derive from drawing and from relief, the first being governed by the rules of volume and the others by those of drawing—of projection on to a plane surface. It is relatively easier in drawing and relief, in which the side-view predominates, to group a number of figures with a satisfactory regard for truth; doubtless the lack of knowledge of foreshortening leads to odd conventions, but the draughtsman does not meet with the obstacle that faces the modeller in the round—that rigorous rule of frontality which forces the sculptor to make his statue face the

[1] **XXXVIII**, vol. vii, pp. 373, 420.   [2] See above, p. 131 ff.

spectator without allowing him a single flexion, and which hinders all organic connection.[1] It was in drawing that groups first evolved in which combatants confront and are entwined with one another, and it was drawing that inspired them in statuary in the round (pediments of the Acropolis, 7th and 6th centuries).

A primitive method of grouping, in the round and even in drawing, instinctive in children and in inexperienced adults in ancient and modern times, consists in juxtaposing two or more figures face to face, each one being conceived by itself and sufficing unto itself. The art of Egypt and Asia never got beyond this stage, nor did any art that did not follow the progressive course pursued in Greece. The Hellenic artist adopted this method of grouping to begin with, and the link by which he sought to unite these supernumeraries set up in a row like so many ninepins is extremely naïve. The figures in a 7th-century Præsus terra cotta,[2] and Dermys and Citylus on the Tanagra stele,[3] are petrified in their frontality, each one encircling the shoulder of the other with one arm, and, in order to conform to the rules of symmetry, advance each a leg, the right on one side and the left on the other—an awkward connection in which, moreover, the gesture is localized and has no effect on the rest of the body which remains in complete repose.

There were other queer conventions as well. Sometimes the bodies are stuck together like the Siamese Twins (Cypriot terra cottas), and sometimes the other elements of the group are painted or modelled in relief on one of the figures. Women, dancing round in a circle, are painted on the dress of the Bœotian geometrical idols;[4] a dancing girl is modelled on the robe of Artemis in a 6th-century terra cotta from Corcyra;[5] there is a winged Eros in relief on the breast of a seated Aphrodite in a 5th-century statuette in terra cotta from Camarina.[6] The group is thus reduced to a single figure on which the others are projected, which gets over the necessity of treating them in the round. This convenient expedient persisted for a long time, and the Hecateum of Alcamenes,[7] where the circle of dancing women dance round

[1] See above, p. 181.   [2] CCXII, p. 166.
[3] LXXXIV, vol. viii, p. 521.   [4] LXXXIV, vol. vii, p. 150.
[5] BCH, 1891, Pl. vii, p. 71.   [6] MA, 14, pp. 869-870, Fig. 74.
[7] JOAI, 1910, p. 87; REA, 1911, p. 144.

the divine triple body, shows that it was still being employed, although consciously and with greater skill. To sum up, union was sought by means of still faulty gesture or by conventional artifices.

The group properly so-called, where there is a real connection proceeding from the nature of the subject, a correct repercussion of the constituent parts on the whole, is a victory for Greek art won simultaneously in drawing and in sculpture in the round. It resulted from the progress realized at the beginning of the 5th century—the breaking-down of the frontal convention, the knowledge of foreshortening and of anatomy, and the desire for co-ordination. It is essential, for a plastic group to be possible and to conform to reality, that the figures should be capable of bending in all directions in natural and not conventional attitudes which shall connect one with another; it is essential that these movements should involve correct anatomical repercussions, and it is essential, too, that over and above this physical truth there should be spiritual unity—that there should be an inner as well as an outer bond.

It has been said that the first genuine plastic group is that in the west pediment at Olympia. But this Centauromachy is conceived according to the principle of relief in which grouping is easier than in the round. Real progress in grouping had already been revealed, before this, in the Tyrannicides of Critius and Nesiotes (477-476).[1] If there was still a certain awkwardness in the junction of torso and pelvis, in the too lifeless drapery, and in the transmission of the action throughout the body, there was now at last a more subtle bond. With his extended arm covered with the cloak, Aristogiton protects, as with a shield, his young friend Harmodius who is advancing on the tyrant: the two figures become inseparable—the gesture of the one is a consequence of the gesture made by the other.

In contemporaneous vase‑painting certain ceramists already bear witness to great skill in grouping, while others show rather a lack of it: if Douris often juxtaposes figures in the old way, Euphronius knows how to link up attitudes correctly, for example that of Silenus and Hermes walking with arms entwined.[2] The genuine group is in existence

[1] **LXXVIII**, p. 448. [2] JOAI, 1900, iii, p. 125.

from the first quarter of the 5th century; it is very quickly perfected in the sense of a closer and more correct co-ordination of its constituent elements.

It occasionally retains the earliest principle of juxta-position where it is intended to be seen only from the front, particularly when it is to be set up against a wall. In such groups movement and action are generally slight or non-existent: the members of the group are living beings, tranquilly posed before the spectator and united in no more than a common idea. The east pediment at Olympia (about 460), the ex voto of the Athenians at Delphi (about 460),[1] that of the Thessalians at Delphi (4th century),[2] show statues placed side by side but independent of one another. There are also two ephebi side by side, and a young man and a young woman (in the groups known as Orestes and Pylades, and Orestes and Electra),[3] who fraternally link arms, but with an ease unattainable by the old image-maker of the Dermys and Citylus. If there is violent action, the images are conceived as in a relief and are governed by the rules of drawing as formerly: such, for instance, is the group of Athena and Marsyas by Myron.

Note the different conceptions in the two Olympia pediments. In one (east pediment), the statues, full-face and in repose, are simply set up side by side. This absence of connection has been mistakenly criticized, since it results from the nature of the subject. The sacrifice is being prepared; all, in the invisible presence of Zeus, hold themselves quite still, waiting in a religious silence: there is no action, it is a calm that is absolute. In the west pediment, on the contrary, there is a furious mêlée in which Centaurs and Lapiths grapple with one another; here there are knots of two and three fighters, conceived in the manner of a relief rather than as statues in the round.

A statuary group designed to be seen from all sides and not only from the front, of which no part is sacrificed to any other part no matter whence it is viewed—the group that is a group in volume and not deprived of its depth—comes later still. Seen from the side, the Tyrannicides and the earlier aligned sets of figures are defective in one aspect in

[1] Bourguet, *Les ruines de Delphes*, p. 40. [2] *Ibid.*, p. 195.
[3] **LXII**, vol. ii, p. 662.

which certain parts are mutually covered, and they have
no thickness. But we can walk all round the Florence
Boxers (4th century),[1] the Child with the Goose by Boethus
(2nd century),[2] and get a satisfactory view from a number
of points. In Hellenistic times the principles of perspective
were applied even to groups, in which the constituent elements
were disposed in different planes (Niobids group, punishment
of Dirce, etc.).[3] To arrive at this point Greek art had to
familiarize itself with volume and perspective, new acquisitions that will be noted later. This was the culminating
point of the synthetic effort, of the desire to subordinate
the parts to the whole, whereas hitherto there had always
remained some lacuna.

Later on, when Roman art was declining to its technical
decadence (3rd century A.D.), and in its provincial productions

FIG. 49. PEDIMENT OF THE HYDRA. END OF THE 7TH CENTURY.
ATHENS ACROPOLIS.

at all times, we find this primitive simple juxtaposition in
statues and reliefs: the figures are presented full-face, stiffened
in the frontality that has once more got the upper hand, and
with no connection between them.

The same development is to be seen in the composition
of pediments, that is to say in more complex grouping.
The designer experienced considerable difficulty in furnishing
this triangular field before he finally arrived at a happy and
harmonious solution.[4] The technical exigencies of this empty
space, in the beginning, were despotic. In order to fill them
without exerting any effort of imagination, artists resorted
to a display of the coils of serpentine monsters such as
Tritopator, Triton, and Hydra (Acropolis, soft stone pediments of the end of the 7th and beginning of the 6th century),

---

[1] **LXII,** vol. ii, p. 592.   [2] *Ibid.*, p. 603.   [3] *Ibid.*, p. 535.
[4] **LXXVII,** p. 40; **LXXVIII,** pp. 25, 43-44, 49.

which they trailed and looped so as to fill the angles and empty spaces (Fig. 49). The figures were gradually diminished in size as they approached the corners, so that they might be fitted into the diminishing space, and no effort was made to bring their height into natural relation with their actions, and, in the Hydra pediment,[1] Iolaus, erect, is quite small. The poses were governed by the exigencies of the field: Europa on a metope of the Treasury of the Sicyonians at Delphi,[2] the Hoplitodromos on an Attic stele,[3] the horses in Heracles' chariot in the Hydra pediment, bend their heads simply and solely because there is not sufficient

FIG. 50. DETAIL ON A CUP BY DOURIS (BERLIN MUSEUM).

space for them to be carried erect. The theme might even be modified by the frame. In the legend, the sea monster grips Heracles by the heel, but in the Hydra pediment the creature is placed far away from the hero because there is not enough room for it to be put close to him. Gradually the artist frees himself from this technical constraint; he realizes that his subject should not be despotically governed by its frame but that it should be disposed therein easily and naturally, with a central point and symmetrically balanced wings, and that some bond is required between the constituent elements of the whole. In short,

---

[1] **LXXVIII,** p. 24. [2] **LXXXIV,** vol. viii, p. 461.
[3] *Ibid.*, p. 649.

it begins to be borne in upon him that the composition of a pediment is subject to laws of its own, and he sets himself to learn them.

In the earlier pediments the wings were not symmetrically balanced; the motifs were unequally distributed, and one

FIG. 51. PEDIMENT OF THE CORFU TEMPLE, 6TH CENTURY.

side might be overcrowded while the other was sparsely furnished or almost empty.   Progress in this was realized in the second half of the 6th century.   The pediment of the Treasury of the Megarians,[1] of the Corfu temple[2] (Fig. 51), and of the Hekatompedon of the Pisistratidæ[3] already shows, as the centre of gravity of the composition, such a central

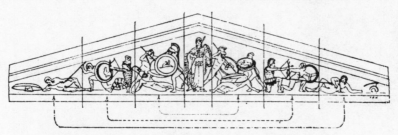

FIG. 52.   WEST PEDIMENT OF TEMPLE OF APHÆA, ÆGINA,
ABOUT 475.

figure—the Gorgon, or Athena—and corresponding groups on either side.   This principle of exact compensation was undoubtedly Dorian in its provenance, and it was to remain one of the principles regulating Greek art up to the end. The first half of the 5th century is mathematical in its

[1] *Olympia*, 1890-1897.   [2] RA, 1911, ii, p. 1; 1914, ii, p. 130.
[3] **LXXVIII**, p. 306.

rigorous observance of this symmetry: the central figure is almost like the needle of a balance at Ægina (Fig. 52) and at Olympia (Figs. 53 and 54), and each wing repeats, almost exactly, the disposition of the figures in the other. This can be somewhat monotonous. Yet the progress made is undeniable: the pediment now has the unity, balance and

FIG. 53. WEST PEDIMENT AT OLYMPIA, ABOUT 460.

equilibrium indispensable to it, instead of the former disorder. And this conception is well adapted to the architectural frame, because henceforth the sculpture will be governed by the number and rhythm that inspire the entire building. What a happy relation there is between the statues of the Œnomaus pediment (Olympia) and the perpendicular lines of the triglyphs and of the columns whose lines they seem

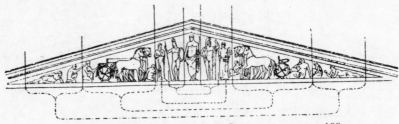

FIG. 54. EAST PEDIMENT AT OLYMPIA, ABOUT 460.

to continue ! Unity is also realized by the common action participated in by all the figures distributed equally from one end of the pediment to the other. In the soft stone pediments of the Acropolis one side may be entirely occupied by a single impassive spectator of large dimensions (Tritopator), whilst the fight is concentrated in the other wing; there is no equilibrium. But now the ingredients of equal action to left and right of the centre figure are prescribed with the nicety of a chemical formula. Movement and repose, likewise, are logically distributed. In the centre is set the calm figure of the god—Athena at Ægina, Apollo or Zeus at Olympia; in the corners are extended inert dying figures (Ægina), or tranquil spectators (Olympia). Between the extremities are energetic groups of fighters, the most violent action being disposed nearest to the centre. In order to accentuate the finished character of the composition, the figures in the corners are sometimes looking round at the centre and curiously watching what is going on (Olympia); or they may face the centre; they thus appear to lead the attention of the spectator towards this point and deliberately to prevent it from straying beyond the limits of the rigorous frame. The centre motif and the reclining figures in the corners constitute the terms and stops of the composition— a sort of sculptural punctuation.

The progressive lowering of the coping in the 5th century necessitated, as had already been the case in the 6th, the placing of erect figures towards the centre, the tallest being exactly in the middle, and then, in either wing, as the corner was approached, first stooping, then kneeling, and finally reclining figures. These poses no longer look as though they had been dictated by the frame, but appear as if they were the natural consequence of the subject itself and of the necessities of the action. In the centre may be the god, Athena, Zeus or Apollo, of superhuman stature, as is fitting for divine beings; on either side, the warriors, erect, then the archers, kneeling to take aim, and the wounded whose agonies bring them low, and seated servitors, and, finally, in the corners, the dying and the dead, and careless spectators. The sculptor takes great pains, too, to treat his subject in groups, and to unite these groups to one another in such a way as to achieve a perfect decorative continuity from one end of the pediment to the other. This is still to seek at Ægina: there, the figures in the round are conceived as isolated entities placed in juxtaposition; they confront one another in the fight but without any organic link, and there is no grouping, in the strict sense of the word. In the Olympia Centauromachy we have connection and grouping; the figures press close together and the eye runs over the arabesque they form without being arrested by a single gap.

Material and spiritual unity has been acquired in the first half of the 5th century. In the Parthenon, Phidias adds nothing to these fundamental principles; he contents himself with softening the former too rigid application of them and with bringing more subtlety to this unity (Fig. 55). He respects the rule of symmetry, but he relieves it of its schematic character; the isolated figures and the groups always correspond with one another in the two wings but without being almost replicas of their opposite numbers; there is analogy in their disposal, their mass, their attitudes, but there is no longer identity. There is always a central motif, but instead of being a single upright figure as immobile as a stay supporting the roof-tree, he has a group whose members, in differing poses, leave empty spaces between them (Zeus seated, and Athena standing erect before him,

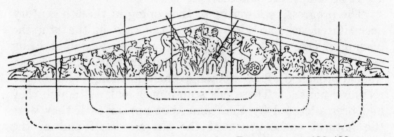

FIG. 55. WEST PEDIMENT OF THE PARTHENON, 439-433.

east pediment), or are symmetrically placed (Poseidon and Athena erect and starting suddenly back from one another, west pediment). The frame and its limits are less material. In this triangle, symbolic of the vault of heaven, the miracle of the divine birth, at which the gods and heroes of myth are present, is accomplished in the period between day and night, between the quadrigas of Helios and Selene. The composition is no longer so rigorously punctuated. Helios and Selene, driving their quadrigas, rise from the waist up from the tympanum—a manifest borrowing from the great painting of Polygnotus—and, directing all the movement from left to right, cause it to describe a sort of trajectory.

Although the Roman artist was the disciple of the Greeks, he sometimes neglected these rules which had been taught by experience and æsthetic feeling; he did not shrink from placing a smaller figure in the centre; he did not necessarily observe the regular decrease in height of the figures; he freely employed motifs to fill up and furnish the corners, and his floating lemniscus is reminiscent of the convenient coils of the older serpents. Thanks to his carelessness and slackness and his blunter sense of equilibrium and composition, he often repeated the archaic expedients that classical masters had abandoned.

FIG. 56. PERSEUS AND THE GORGON, SELINUS, 6TH CENTURY.

The composition of metopes lends itself to a like examination.[1] The artist gradually learned what were the best principles to guide him in furnishing this rectangular frame, of which Oriental art could give him no examples. At first he hesitated—now

FIG. 57. HERACLES AND ATLAS, METOPE AT OLYMPIA, ABOUT 460.

crowding it with figures and attributes (quadriga, Perseus and the Gorgon, Heracles and the Cercopes, Selinus temple, 6th century;[2] the Argosy, metope of the Treasury of the Sicyonians at Delphi);[3] now leaving the field too empty, only putting into it a single figure. As with the pediments, he distributes his elements badly, filling the whole of the right by the huge figure of the Gorgon and only leaving a limited space for Perseus and Athena (metope at Selinus) (Fig. 56). Sometimes there is overmuch action, and sometimes there is none at all.

There is no bond between the different metopes, each one having its independent subject. The figures are sometimes

[1] **LXXVII**, p. 45.   [2] **LXXXIV**, vol. viii, p. 483.   [3] *Ibid.*, p. 459.

almost in the round, sometimes they are also facing the
spectator, and the Selinus quadriga comes right at one.   The
artist finally realized his errors.   This limited field lent itself
to the display of a couple of figures engaged in a definite
action, in opposing and balanced attitudes.   The action is
broken up into a series of analogous episodes, which, by
their likeness to one another, establish the necessary bond
between the different metopes, and by their differing poses
and lines, obviate monotony (Centauromachy of the Parthenon).   There is a correspondence of similitude or of opposition between the perpendicular lines of the triglyphs and

FIG. 58.   HERACLES CLEANING THE
AUGEAN STABLE, METOPE AT
OLYMPIA, ABOUT 460.

FIG. 59.   HERACLES AND THE
AMAZON, METOPE AT SELINUS,
5TH CENTURY.

columns and the lines of the metopes as given by the poses
of the figures they contain; these lines may be vertical (the
metope of Heracles and Atlas, Olympia) (Fig. 57); diagonal
(metopes of Heracles cleaning the Augean stable, Heracles
and the Cretan Bull, Olympia) (Fig. 58);[1] and oblique (metope
of Temple E at Selinus, Heracles and the Amazon) (Fig. 59),
etc.   This new science of composition works out a solution
of the problems facing it, as was done with the pediments,
during the first half of the 5th century, and here, too, Phidias,
in the Parthenon, had merely to refine and give greater
subtlety to the work of his predecessors.

[1] **LXII,** vol. i, p. 429.

There was the same study of considered and ordered composition in the frieze,[1] which had been pursued in the Ionian, Corinthian, and Attic-Corinthian vases with their circular zones, and in archaic buildings (Temple of Assos, Treasury of Cnidus, relief on the Harpies Tomb, etc.) up to the period of the classical monuments of the second half of the 5th century (Panathenaic frieze, friezes in the temple of Athena Nike, in the Theseum, at Phigalia, Sunium, etc.). On funerary and votive reliefs and in vase-paintings we shall remark the increasingly logical, harmonious and well thought out principles of composition, and the adaptation of the theme to the field to be decorated, whether it be medallion, metope, circular zone, or the corresponding sides of a vase;

Fig. 60. The Harpies tomb: detail (British Museum),
6th Century.

and the transformation of the " epic " narrative spirit of the 6th century into the " dramatic " spirit of the 5th, this last proceeding from the same desire for synthesis as inspired Attic drama.[2]

These analyses are of the greatest use in helping us to grasp the essence and aims of Greek art. Whether it is a matter of pose, anatomy, drapery or composition, these principles all spring from one source, a spirit endeavouring to achieve, with a growing exactitude of observation, increasingly perfect unity and synthesis in which details have their logical and at the same time their harmonious place. Those purely exterior expedients of former days, which gave to a work of art an appearance of unity, are abandoned, and the

[1] **LXXVII**, p. 47.   [2] **CXLV**, vol. iii, p. 830.

old rule of "isokephaly,"[1] which kept the heads in a relief at the same level no matter what their attitude or their height (Fig. 60), is no more than a memory, because it was not truth but an arbitrary procedure, a technical necessity, thanks to which the frame dictated the subject.

[1] **LXXXIV,** vol. viii, p. 699.

DISTANCE AND ATMOSPHERE AS THEY AFFECT THE APPEARANCE OF THINGS. CHIAROSCURO, MODELLING, PERSPECTIVE [1]

THE authors of modern works of art designed for interior decoration need not take into account the effect these will produce in the open air, and, only too often, those which are seen in the open, on the façades of buildings and in public squares, are defective because their authors failed to allow for the repercussions on them of their atmospheric environment. There was nothing of this sort in Greece for many a long day. Sculpture, if we except cult statues and a few reliefs in temple cellas, was meant to be seen in the full outdoor light, being set up in sacred enclosures, on tombs and on the façades of temples. From this arose certain optical necessities which early attracted the artist's attention.

If he came gradually to select more and more hard and homogeneous material, did not one of the causes lie in his desire to make his work last longer, exposed as it was to the elements ? The Greek climate is clement but does not preserve woodwork like that of Egypt, and it must have become apparent at an early date that wood was not a suitable material for statues and temples.

Buildings and sculptures were painted. Was not this partly in order to preserve this corruptible woodwork, and then to tone down the whiteness of stone and emphasize the modelling and details which the strong southern light effaced ? It is true that the complete polychromy of the earliest times later became partial only, when artists realized the beauty of marble (6th century), and then it no longer hid the material under a coat of badigeon, as had been the case with wood and soft stone, but was used sparingly, and " ganosis," the light wax polish applied to skin surfaces, was never given up.

In architecture the purpose of fluting on columns was not

[1] **VI**, vol. iii, p. 423; **CXV** ff.

only to direct the eye upwards and to dissimulate the joins of the drums, but to hold shadow in the hollows and to catch the light on the ridges; the angular columns are stronger in order to avoid seeming slender owing to their isolation; the entire peristasis leans inwards, because, were the columns of the cella strictly straight, the building would look as though opening outwards; in the Parthenon the lines of the stylobate are not absolutely horizontal, but slightly incurved in order to combat the illusion of concavity.[1] And there were other optical refinements besides.

The sculptor took into account the position his statues would occupy. Destined to be placed high up on a temple or on a pedestal, their necessary visual deformations were prepared in advance. A characteristic if doubtful anecdote tells of a competition between Phidias and his pupil Alcamenes: the prize was about to be given to Alcamenes, whose statue seemed the more beautiful, whereas that by Phidias was not thought much of, because its open lips and its high nostrils gave a silly expression to the face; but once the two statues were placed in position, it was seen that these deformations were deliberate, that the faults disappeared and were transformed into beauty. The sculptors of the temple of Aphæa (Ægina) did their work as though their warriors were to remain at eye-level and even as though the spectators' view should dominate the plinth on which they are placed. But as early as the 6th century the imperfections of the Sphinx at Delphi,[2] whose head seems too large, must have been greatly minimized by its six metres of height on the top of an Ionic column. The folds of the dress of a young Amazon on the Epidaurus pediment (4th century) seem rather coarse; this is because we see them at too close quarters when the sculptors were quite justified in securing radiating shadows since the statue was to have been seen from below, and far off. Was the oncos of the tragic mask a trick of the light, as has sometimes been thought? Such examples are plentiful.[3] Rodin rightly remarked that the ancients avoided dryness and succeeded in preventing their statues from having hard outlines against the sky by arbitrarily reinforcing their curves and making them more emphatic than in the living model, so that the light played better on these broadened surfaces.

[1] **LVI.**   [2] Bourguet, *Les ruines de Delphes*, p. 127.   [3] **VII,** p. 38.

To give, in drawing, volume to a body instead of reducing it to a simple linear projection, to note the play of light and shade on it, and to render comprehensibly the successive planes of the objects from those that are nearest to those that are farthest off, and to cause these to melt into the atmosphere—these are all problems which to-day seem easy of solution, but which the Greeks took a long time to solve.

The primitive artist makes no pretence of translating the illusion of volume and the depth of planes to a plane surface as though he were opening a window on to nature. He shows objects in their logical, and not in their optical reality—not as they seem to be, deformed by their position and by the light. " How many people there are," said Perrault, " who would like one to make the distant figures stand out as strongly and in as great a detail as those that are in the foreground, so that they can be better seen—who would gladly let the painter off all his trouble in composing his picture and diminishing the figures according to their planes, but especially who would like one not to put any shadow in a face, particularly in the portraits of those whom they love."[1]   Such cases are known in all periods: a lady reproaches the painter for having indicated the shadow cast by her nose, or a Pasha wants the scarlet of his fez to be uniformly brilliant. What difficulties the impressionists met with before they could get people to accept shadows that were violet or green and not black, flesh-tints that varied with the lighting ! In all lands people are very slow in learning to see with the observing eye in drawing the play of changing light and distance.

Beyond the borders of Greece attempts in this direction were few and far between, and suffered eventual eclipse. There was already a genuine feeling for the modelling of the body in the Magdalenians' paintings, but these were by no means the products of an art in its infancy. In Egypt the curious attempts at realism in the time of Akhenaton got the length of putting the back of figures in shadow, and directing a ray of light on the thigh of a young girl. There is a Mycenæan fresco which sought to render modelling by hatching. Occasionally, too, there is a timid attempt at perspective in the pottery of Susa, in Egyptian frescoes, and Assyrian reliefs. And on a Mycenæan vase showing a stag

[1] **VI**, vol. iii, pp. 57, 423.

hunt the painter indicates the leg of the hunter on the animal's body in order to show that it is in a different plane.

The Greek artist, like all others, began by tracing silhouettes without substance, by avoiding any foreshortening and replacing it by naïve conventions that are universal, by putting things in the same plane and by neglecting all play of light and shade. But he was to out-distance his fellow-workers in other lands and here, too, to be an innovator. If he did not achieve his aim until very late, this was partly, perhaps, because Greek art is decorative first and foremost,[1] and because for a long time it would seem strange to him to desire volume, depth and light on a plane surface which he had to treat as such without attempting to deceive the eye; perhaps, too, because he had a preference for colour-drawing and purity of line, of which vase-painting provides so many fine examples. Is there not a certain analogy here between Greek and Japanese art ?

The severe style red-figure pottery (end of the 6th and beginning of the 5th centuries) timidly attempted the study of modelling objects, light and shade; the various shades of the glaze, running from a deep black to a light yellow, according to how much it was diluted, enabled the painter to get varying degrees of light and shade for the delineation of muscles, hair and drapery. These vase-painters are able to express the light playing on the fluting of a column (Brygus) and to model the cheek of Troïlus or the folds of Demeter's and Hermes' garments (Cora carried off by Hades, middle of the 5th century). There was also another method: a number of small hatchings show the convexity of a shield (cup by Onesimus). Sotades shades by fine hatchings and curves the ovoid tomb of Glaucus and Polyeidus.[2] In a painting illustrating the myth of Cadmus and the Dragon, shading is done by hatchings and by alternating thick and fine strokes; the same line, according to whether it begins in shadow or passes into full light to re-enter a dark zone, is first full, then thin to the point of being scarcely visible. On a 450 scyphos from Eleusis, broad clear-cut patches of a different colour between fine lines indicate shadows, and

---

[1] **CLI, CLII.**
[2] Smith, *Catalogue of the Greek Vases in the British Museum*, 1895, p. 391, No. 5.

the succession of hollows and salients in folds. These essays,[1] isolated among the early masters, become frequent in the vases of Polyclitian style in the middle of the 5th century; the lecythi with white backgrounds of the end of the 5th century and beginning of the 4th also show modelling by means of hatching. The Ficorini cist of the 3rd century is a characteristic example of this method. Then the Hellenistic vase-painters occasionally seek to render volume and its nuances by painting certain portions over in rose colour.[2]

The vase-painters also take note of cast shadows. The blue-violet mantle of an old man, standing at a deathbed, throws a violet shadow on his feet (5th-century white background lecythus). On a Nola red-figure vase vertical strokes emphasize the contours of the material and indicate the shadow cast by the fall of the drapery; on an engraved mirror in the British Museum the artist shows by hatching the differing light and shade due to the form of objects, their planes, and the diminished light falling on one body owing to another coming between it and the light. Thus artists give up using uniformly monochromatic surfaces from the middle of the 5th century; they take pains to render the volume of objects, the play of light and shade on them, and the shadows they cast with their varying tones.

Once these ideas had been grasped they became general. The Cortona Muse;[3] the Græco-Roman paintings[4] at Delos, Herculaneum and Pompeii, with their skilled modelling despite their industrial mediocrity, show us how painting developed some time later. In certain paintings at Pompeii and in the Fayûm, the painters had arrived at breaking the line and the continuity of contour by methods resembling those of the modern impressionists, *tachistes* and *pointillistes* : the evolution of antique painting would appear to have followed the same road that modern painting has followed since medieval days when, starting out from a linear drawing, it, likewise, progressively acquired volume, modelling and variation of light. Did not Giotto, like the Greek ceramist, still consider it unnecessary to represent cast shadows ?

A related experimental study is that of perspective, the visual modification of objects according to the planes they

---

occupy.[1] It was long unknown in Greece, as elsewhere, and Greek artists resorted to conventions universal in art where its resources are not known. Figures in different planes are superposed, or else their feet are placed on the same lines and their size is not reduced by distance; nor do the lines yet converge as they are more distant from the spectator. Occasionally, even, we get an inverted perspective: frequent with children and primitives, this expedient was already known to the Palæolithic artists, who, in a group of bulls seen in profile, make the second head larger than the first; it is also used in Byzantine art and in Western medieval art; even Giotto still used it, one of his paintings showing

FIG. 61. CRATER FROM ORVIETO (PARIS).

a man, who is coming down a staircase, larger in size than the man who is in front of him. In Greece, too, profiles override one another, the furthest off being the largest (proto-Attic vase), and the warrior in the second plane being made larger than the one in the first (black-figure vase).

But from the 6th century there were naïve attempts at perspective on Ionian, Corinthian and Attic vases. For instance, on an Ionian vase from Eleusis, women are seated facing one another: the legs of the chairs rest on the ground line, which is wavy, the two not being quite at the same height; between them, a man, erect, shown in profile, is at a lower level; there is here a curious desire to indicate different

[1] **VI,** vol. ii, Table, *s.v.*; vol. iii, pp. 137, 437.

planes.[1] The red-figure vases of the beginning of the 5th century multiply these attempts, which come to a head in the Polygnotian perspective, with background and figures seen in depth masking one another and disposed at varying heights (Figs. 61 and 62).[2] On a white lecythus a funerary monument is seen in perspective in the second plane; elsewhere it may be an altar whose lines vanish; Meidias likes figures partly hidden by the ground; they are ranged in two or three tiers on the buckler of the Parthenos by Phidias; on a mirror in the British Museum, of the beginning of the 4th century, the engraver indicates the different planes, though still with a certain amount of awkwardness, it is true.[3] We even meet with essays at ceiling perspective on vases in the Meidian style; there is a basin on which the

FIG. 62. BATTLE OF THE AMAZONS. ARYBALLUS AT NAPLES.

throne of Zeus looks as though one saw it from below, as if the artist who had copied the Parthenon pediment had represented it such as he saw it from below.

The draughtsman at first achieved perspective with the only means at his disposal, foreshortening, diminution in the size of objects, and different levels. But once he was equipped with the knowledge of modelling and chiaroscuro he was able to add to these linear means the resources of aerial perspective and the modifications in light and colour brought about in objects by distance.

Greek artists formulated these principles. In the second half of the 5th century, Agatharchus of Samos[4] developed the art of optical illusion when he painted the earliest theatre

---

[1] **CXLV,** vol. ii, 455-56, 569.   [2] *Ibid.,* iii, p. 1052.
[3] CRAI, 1905, p. 137; BCH, 1899, p. 325; *Congrès d'Athènes,* 1905, p. 180; **CXLV,** vol. iii, p. 1099; JHS, 1907, p. 4.
[4] **CXXIV;** Six, "Agatharchus," JHS, 1920, p. 180.

décors at Athens; he is said to have invented the perspective due to the play of light and shade and a special contrast in colours. Then came Apollodorus the skiagrapher, who, says Plutarch, " proceeded by diminishing and attenuating his tones." The word " skiagraphy " really designates the art of perspective and not that of shadow and modelling, but these problems are all closely related because the principal means of achieving perspective in several planes is the employment of diminishing shades.

Relief profited by these pictorial gains in the 4th century, and more especially in Hellenistic times. The sculptor, who could also utilize the differing salients of the stone, gives depth and distance and develops the experiment already timidly sketched out by Phidias in the Panathenaic frieze (examples: sarcophagus of Alexander,[1] Tralles relief,[2] in the Constantinople museum, etc.). But the final solution of the spatial problem in sculpture is furnished by Augustinian art and its "illusionist" style. On the silver vases of the treasure of Boscoreale, the relief passes from the almost round to the simple silhouette sketched on the background, the figures are grouped in depth, and the modelling seeks to render the effects of light and shade.[3]

Yet, very soon afterwards, Roman art abandoned these conquests which had been so patiently won; it went back, in the triumphal arch of Claudius, the Antonine and Trajan columns, and on tombs, to the old method of figures superposed in height. At that time the method may have been deliberate, but soon it became unconscious again, in measure as art went downhill to its decadence and forgot, in its growing lack of technical skill, the way by which it had climbed to its fullest expression.

Sculpture, in the course of time, had acquired volume and substance. In the archaic work of the 7th and 6th centuries, details, such as drapery folds, facial features, and muscles, were incised rather than modelled, sculptors merely scratching the surface of their marble. The eyes were goggling and ready to jump out of their sockets, and the brows did not overhang to protect them. Gradually details penetrated right

[1] **LXII**, vol. ii, p. 404.
[2] RA, 1903, ii, p. 397; 1906, vii, 225; 1908, xi, p. 9; BCH, 1908, p. 526.
[3] Strong, *Roman Sculpture*, 1907.

into the stone; they were not merely drawn on the surface, but modelled with their proper depth and thickness. Thus in Antenor's Kore[1] (about 510), and then in that of Euthydicus,[2] and in the head of the " Blond Ephebus " of the Acropolis (before 480),[3] the eyes retire beneath the brows, and the lids are no longer stuck on the eyeballs like bits of paper, but stand out from them; the folds of the garment acquire depth and are no longer flattened on the body. The progress made in this direction was regular and rapid, and concerned every part of the whole.

Relief began by being very flat, a simple silhouette with sharp contours, sometimes obtained by the same expedient of a cast shadow as was used in contemporaneous vase painting (relief of the Dioscuri, at Sparta;[4] Naucratis relief).[5]

Statues were often very flat, like boards (Nicandra of Delos, the Auxerre statuette); conceived to be seen frontally, they lacked depth and substance. A few works, in which the body is a regular cylinder (Samos Hera),[6] do, however, already reveal the desire to render volume. We cannot recognize in this appearance the hypothetical influence of wood-carving on a squared or rounded log; rather are these the instinctive necessary forms that are the same for all art in its beginnings. The 5th century preserves the memory of them. Seen in profile, the Diskobolos of Myron still lacks substance. But directly the frontality convention was broken with, the artist began to treat the sides and reverse of his statues with the attention he at first gave exclusively to the front, and the statue then gets its correct volume,[7] and we can look at it from all sides. The group, as we have seen, did not make this conquest, achieved by isolated statues in the 5th century, until the 4th.[8]

In archaic work the various planes join up in sharp angles or ridges, the transition between them being faulty; there is none of that modelling which, said Rodin, is "a caress for the eyes." These sculptures look as though they had been hacked out in wood with an axe and worked over with a carpenter's gouge. An ingenious theory recognizes in this

---

[1] **LXXVIII**, p. 245. [2] *Ibid.*, p. 353. [3] *Ibid.*, p. 362.
[4] **LXXXIV**, vol. viii, p. 442.
[5] *Annual of the British School at Athens*, v, Pl. ix; **VI**, vol. ii, p. 304.
[6] **LXXXIV**, vol. viii, p. 146.
[7] **CLXXVII**. [8] See above, p. 250.

appearance the influence of a wood technique on works in soft stone and marble. In reality it is a question of a general expedient, independent of the material employed and necessitated by lack of technical experience, just as lack of substance arises out of the frontal conception. The 5th century softened these angles and asperities: the sides of the statue no longer join in a right angle like the faces of a quarried block, but increasingly subtle transitions are sought. Nevertheless, something still persists, now and again, of this earlier harshness, even up to the time of Polyclitus' work.

Statuary early borrowed from painting its attitudes and motifs. In the second half of the 5th century it went further and began to treat stone by pictorial methods, by carving the drapery of its figures, and by giving a softer modelling to its heads, of which the pediments and the frieze of the Parthenon afford numerous examples. None the less, silhouettes are still sharp in the 5th century, and planes are precise, even somewhat dry, especially in the Argive art of Polyclitus and his disciples. What the great masters of the 4th century, Praxiteles, Scopas, and Lysippus[1] did was to make the light and shade play softly on the surfaces and in the hollows of the marble, as Phidias—without rival as a marble-worker—had already tried to do, and to treat stone in the fashion of a painter, transposing pictorial modelling into plastic art, and giving to this art new resources which had been opened up to it by the chiaroscuro experimented in by Apollodorus, Zeuxis and Parrhasius. Henceforth contours that are too clear-cut are repudiated, and soft transitions are favoured, and great pains are taken to get the statues bathed in the atmosphere. These were the qualities the ancients admired in the Cnidian with her " humid and brilliant look " (Lucian), and that we still recognize when we speak of the Praxitelian charm and *morbidezza*. The hair of the Olympian Hermes (Plate X) contrasts its mass of wayward locks with the polished surface of the flesh; the transition between the almost effaced lower lid to the plane of the cheek is extraordinarily delicate; the contours lose their precision in a modelling that is light as air and insubstantial as mist. It was this pictorial conception of marble that the ancients doubtless had in view when they attributed

---

[1] See above, p. 217; **VI**, vol. iii, p. 423.

to Lysippus these words: "Hitherto men had been represented as they are, but he shows them to us as they seem to be," that is to say, no longer in the precision of attitude and anatomy alone, but as these are modified by the effects of lighting.

What a difference there is between the head known as the Eubouleus (National Museum, Athens),[1] sometimes attributed to Praxiteles himself, but more probably by one of his disciples, and the head of the Doryphoros, even with a Phidian head already influenced by painting; between these and the other, statuary had evolved in the direction of an altogether pictorial modelling that certain Hellenistic sculptors were to exaggerate, especially those who carried on the Praxitelian tradition (Plate XI); thanks to their *sfumato*, their veritable transposition of chiaroscuro into the round, they seem almost to have been painted by some Leonardo da Vinci, or some ancient Prud'hon (heads of the Leconsfield, Aphrodite[2] and Meleager,[3] etc.).

The Hellenists also applied to plastic art the principles of perspective, and by disposing their figures in several planes, and ranging them at different levels, they sought to bring new life into the old methods of composition: that kind of group known as the " picturesque " is one of the most daring innovations of Hellenistic art (Farnese Bull, etc.).[4] The moment had come in which the various genres run into one another, in which literature itself becomes the rival of painting and plastic.[5]

---

[1] **CLIX**, p. 93.   [2] **LXX**, Pl. xvii, p. 344.   [3] *Ibid.*, Pl. xv.
[4] **LXII**, vol. ii, p. 535.   [5] **VI**, vol. iii, p. 426 ff.

PART FOUR

THE IDEAL AND ITS EVOLUTION

THUS far this book has shown what the Greek artist tried to do and what technical means he had at his disposal for achieving his aims. As we went along we made a note of the general principles guiding him in his effort and which give a particular character to the Greek artistic ideal. In the following pages we shall indicate just in what that ideal consisted, and mark the chronological stages of its evolution.

CHAPTER I

SOME ASPECTS OF THE GREEK IDEAL

" By man are all things measured " (Protagoras). Ancient and modern peoples, young and old, see in natural phenomena themselves, dress these in their own form, and dower them with their own thoughts. Perhaps this instinctive anthropomorphism[1] was stronger in the Greeks than in any other peoples, or at all events they transformed it into a conscious principle of their spiritual and emotive life, and it made an indelible impress on their civilization.

The Ægeans had not yet precisely figured to themselves the appearance of their gods. For them the supernatural powers dwelt in stones, trees, plants, animals, and stars as much as in the human form; these had no need of a temple resembling the house of a mortal man, for their cult was rendered to them in enclosures in the open, and in chapels attached to the royal palaces. Ægean artists regarded nature—the fauna and flora—with curious eyes; they represented with great truth the energy of a galloping bull or the maternal affection of a wild goat suckling its kids; they adorned their vases with crocus, lily, seaweed, shells, and cuttlefish. No doubt they took an interest in the body of man, which they admired in its slender silhouette, muscular power, and energetic action (Knossos acrobat, Boxers vase from Haghia Triada), but they did not pay him their exclusive attention. They had a wide and sincere comprehension of nature, and it is this that gives to their art, sometimes so modern in its style, its great attraction.[2]

The Hellenes brought in quite another spirit. Everything converges on man who is their one and only interest, and who was thenceforth to exercise a despotic sway over thought and over art. It was a fruitful despotism because it obliged

[1] **IX**, p. 137.
[2] **CCII**; **VI**, vol. iii, p. 59; Glotz, *The Ægean Civilization*, 1923 (Engl. trans., 1925).

them to study more closely this man, hitherto confounded
with nature and now set up alone on his pedestal, and to
know him perfectly in his physical and psychological form,
in his social relations and his reactions on the world around
him.　But anthropomorphism limited the view of the Greeks
and turned them away for many a long day from those other
aspects of inanimate and animate nature which they only
sought after having achieved perfect knowledge of man.

All gods now were men, doubtless bigger and more
powerful, more beautiful than ordinary mortals, yet clothed
in human form and acting and thinking like men, and, from
Homer's time, subject to the terrestrial passions of joy and
pain.　This, for the artist, was a great advantage.　The
world of the gods was not for him an unknown and mysterious
land to which he could penetrate only by a great imaginative
effort and which would drive him to create strange beings;
he daily saw this world all about him.　The gods were men
who bore divine appellations.　Mythology, which told of their
adventures, was but a projection into the celestial sphere
of human exploits.　Myth and reality, the divine and the
earthly, are all one in the mind of the painter, the architect,
and the sculptor.

Indeterminateness of type is common to all art in its
infancy.　But in Greece it was confirmed by the dominant
anthropomorphism.　In the archaic period it is impossible
at first sight to distinguish between a god and a mortal, and
the 6th-century Kouros serves equally well for an Apollo
or one of the Dioscuri as for a commemorative image of the
dead or the ex voto of one of the faithful; the Kore serves
as well for Artemis or Aphrodite as for a priestess or an
image of the faithful or of the dead.[1]　There is the same
difficulty in the art of the 5th century when it had arrived
at its maturity.　Confronted with a statue, one often hesitates to say whether it is that of god or mortal: is the Doryphoros of Polyclitus an ephebus who is a victor in the games,
a hero such as Achilles, or a funerary image ?　And is the
Vaison Diadumenos an athlete or an Apollo ?

Once art has become humanized (from the 4th century),
with what facility the gods descend from heaven to earth to
take part in the humblest occupations of daily life !　Aphro-

---

[1] See above, p. 180.

dite is just a woman, bathing, arching her back beneath the
stream of water that Eros pours over her, or loosing her
sandal; or, surprised by Pan, defending herself from his
attack (Delos group); Apollo is merely a youth tormenting
a lizard.

And with what facility, likewise, man becomes a god,
represented with the features of a Hermes or an Apollo,
whose attributes he assumes![1]

Divine exploits are with little trouble identified with
those of the Greeks themselves, and the symbol is a veil for
reality. The gods who struggle against the giants, Heracles
and Theseus, accomplishing their exploits, in subjects that art
never tires of repeating and with which the walls of temples
and the sides of vases are covered, are, as we saw farther
back,[2] the Greeks who were victorious over their enemies
and especially over the Persian. Projected into heaven by
anthropomorphic ideas these adventures come back to the
earth whence they were inspired.

The god who is assimilated to the most powerful of
mortal men can no longer be contented with his former
holy places. He requires a fine dwelling for himself alone,
a chief's residence, and not a mere palace annexe. Thus
came into being the Greek temple which is not the place
of assembly of the faithful but the private mansion of the
god. Thus it is quite natural that this temple should carry
on the form of a king's palace—of the Mycenæan megaron.
Anthropomorphism rendered this substitution necessary, and
excavation has shown, at Mycenæ, at Tiryns, at Troy, and
on the Acropolis in Athens, that the archaic temple was
raised on the very site of the Mycenæan palace.[3]

The god, in his corporeal semblance, mingles with men,
held within his stone or metal effigy by the magic virtue of
art, by the power of rite and sacrifice. He is there in the
house, in the cella of the temple; he is everywhere that his
protection is needed, in the sacred enclosure, in the public
square, in the dwelling-house and on the tomb.

In his temple he must be entertained as a man, fed by
means of sacrifices, clothed and provided with furniture
through offerings. We can see in his temple, stored among
the age-old ex votos, everything that industry created to

[1] **LXIII**, p. 315. [2] *Cf.* p. 57. [3] *Cf.* p. 142.

help mortals maintain life—cauldrons, tripods, seats, beds, and arms.[1] Religion, which accepted indifferently as a gift a statue or a roasting-spit, thus usefully maintained in being the union of industrial with Fine Arts.[2] The " Treasuries," small sacred buildings built round the temple or the dwelling of the cult statue, were the store-houses of the god. The Parthenon is nothing but a magnificent treasury (the venerated Xoanon, doubtless restored just after the Persian invasion, being in the cella of the Athena Polias), where was heaped up the riches belonging to Athena, the gold and ivory of her chryselephantine statue—as much a monetary reserve for the city as a work of art—the golden crowns offered to the goddess as prizes for valiance in the battle of the giants, superb couches, and the throne of Xerxes.[3]

Certain themes of religious art throw light on this essentially human character of the gods. How often they are represented at their toilet, and without fear of compromising their dignity ! Aphrodite puts on a necklet (frieze of the Treasury of Cnidus; Pseliumene of Praxiteles); nude, she twists up her damp tresses; or Artemis fastens her mantle on her shoulder (the Artemis of Gabii). They all gladly accept gifts of homage in the shape of garments or ornaments to place on their statuary bodies, and, over the entrance of the Parthenon, at the place where the great Panathenaic procession converges, Athena receives from the hands of the chief priest the peplos that the Ergastikæ have woven and embroidered.

The animal, plant and aniconic forms of former days disappear; they persist only in certain cults as survivals of an outworn stage in so far as they have become the attributes of a god now human (the owl of Athena, the lizard of Apollo, the boar of Demeter), or in strange monstrous combinations in legends and metamorphoses. And these monstrosities, that unite in some form or another the body of a man with that of a beast, become more and more rare, eliminated by æsthetic feeling. They shock, not only because they are unreal and improbable but because they impair the dignity of the human body, the most beautiful gift that can be offered to the gods. The strange fauna of Ægean art, in which men with stag's heads, and human bees, abound, and then the fantastic

---

[1] **CLXXXV,** *s.v.* " Donarium."   [2] *Cf.* p. 45.   [3] **XXXIX.**

conceptions imported into Greece after the Dorian invasion by Oriental influence, such as the hare-headed man and the hippalectryon, gradually die out; a few alone survive: those to which the popular mind had become accustomed, a few mythical beings necessary because of the significance attached to them—Syrens, Centaurs, Sphinxes, Satyrs, Sileni, and Pan—but which the artist sought to render less bestial. The Sileni, Satyrs and Pan had their ugly faces ennobled and their animal origin was almost forgotten; the Gorgon's hideous mask was refined into the Rondanini Medusa (5th century). One very rarely sees, in Greece, supernatural beings represented with a multiplicity of limbs (arms and legs) with a view of emphasizing by such redundancy their infinite strength[1]—Argus with his hundred eyes, sometimes double-headed, and the two-headed Boreas are exceptions— or with an elongated head like the Chinese sage's disproportionate cranium. Any tampering with the human form, such as its union with that of a beast, was a blemish which was not lightly to be inflicted on its sovereign majesty.

All that concerned the gods was kept within due proportion. The Greek did not imagine, as was done in the Indian religions, fantastic and mountainous creations. Dimensions had to be kept within the scale of a superior humanity; the colossal statues and temples of Greece are actually small by comparison with those of Egypt, Mesopotamia or the Far East.[2]

Man, and not the gods alone, felt the influence of this anthropomorphic conception. This conception concentrated the Greek's attention on the human body, so that he offered this body in homage to, and organized for, the divinity, games in which athletes competed together, and set up in the sanctuaries the effigies of adorers and of victors who gave themselves to the god, at the same time ensuring for themselves that god's protection. It educated the eye of every man, whether artist or no, and it awakened pleasure in the sight of this body, nude or clothed, in its various attitudes whether in repose or in action. It inspired the artist in his plastic efforts and stimulated in him an æsthetic appreciation

---

[1] Deonna, " Essai sur la genèse des monstres dans l'art," REG, 1915, p. 288.

[2] *Cf.* p. 64.

that has never been equalled in other nations. The technical progress we have already examined in pose, rhythm, anatomy, drapery, action, and the rendering of volume, was accomplished thanks to this human body being taken for subject, and was all so much profit reaped by art that was directly due to anthropomorphism.

*   *   *   *   *

But what place does the Greek give to the other phases of the world of nature ? Animals[1] rarely interest the artist in themselves, for the pleasure of rendering their form and their movements. Archaic art left behind it some animal images of a sober naturalism (the Acropolis greyhound, 6th century), and the ancients praise Myron's talent for rendering animals, his cow, in particular, being so life-like that it deceived even bulls and shepherds. However, it was a long time—not till Hellenistic times—before animals were treated for themselves and became of as great artistic interest as man. Hitherto they had played but the secondary rôle of an attribute or servant of the god whose earliest form they often recalled, to whom their effigy was offered as an ex voto because it took the place of a live victim and kept the offering in continual memory; they figured as necessary accessories in the sacred combats of Heracles and Theseus. They also served man, drawing his chariot, accompanying him on funerary stelæ, and they glorified him. They exist only as a function of this divine or mortal man. In the 6th century the Attic horses (Acropolis statues, funerary reliefs) signify that the dedicator or the dead belonged to the Athenian hippeis class; in the 5th century, in the Olympian pediments, they draw the chariots of Œnomaus and Pelops, and in those of the Parthenon, the chariots of Helios and Selene, Zeus and Athena. The dog appears frequently on funerary stelæ with his master, and the hare is the favourite animal of the ephebi. Animals are also symbolical. The lion, that the Greeks had never seen but whose image had been inherited from the Ægeans and the Orientals, signified strength and courage; he guards the approach to temples (archaic lions at Delos, 6th century), and he protects the tomb.[2] The bull, emblem of valiance, is still set up on a tomb in the

[1] **VI**, vol. iii, p. 80.   [2] **LXIII**, p. 226.

Keramikos. But does this rôle not confirm the subjection of the animal to man and to the thought of man ?

*   *   *   *   *

Flowers and scenery very nearly vanished from art when the Dorian invasion took place;[1] the earliest Hellenic works, the vase-paintings of the Attic Dipylon, bear witness to this. Formerly, Cretans and Mycenæans covered their vases with flowers and foliage and seaweed. Now there were human scenes, funerals of the Eupatrids, or a network of geometrical lines. When a floral motif does appear on a vessel it is unrecognizable, its detached leaves are stylized and stiff. One feels that the artist saw in it nothing but a decorative element of sorts. If some vestige of a love for nature persists —but how attenuated !—in Ionian ceramics, which occasionally treats with truth buds and flowers and leaves, and which places divine and human action in a picturesque frame, it is because the Ionians have inherited something of the Ægean naturalism.[2] But in continental Greece the new ideal brought in by the Dorian invaders, characterized by its anthropomorphic spirit and its geometrical conceptions, eliminated nature. The artist, under the predominant Oriental influence of the 8th to 7th centuries, employed a number of floral— palmette and lotus—motifs, but they were transmitted to him already denatured and schematized by the art objects brought in by commerce and from which he copied them.

And, in painting, even these accessories were gradually driven from the field, which was left entirely to man. Mythological and human scenes took up all the space and there remained but a few palmettes, a traditional element in Greek design. In the Attic black-figure, and then in the red-figure vases, man stands out on a blank ground. At the most a tree, stark as a broomstick, indicates that the scene takes place in the open air. How characteristic is this charming painting, for instance, on a red-figure vase:[3] a bearded man, an ephebus and a small boy are watching a swallow's flight. " Look !" says one of them, " a swallow !" " Yes, by Zeus ! it is," says the other, and the third concludes: " It is the spring." Is not this a triumph in the way

[1] **VI**, vol. iii, Table, s.v. " Nature."   [2] See above, p. 135.
[3] *Monumenti dell' Instituto*, ii, Pl. xxiv; JOAI, 1913. Petrograd, The Hermitage.

of evoking the season of rebirth with no other means than human figures ? The three personages in the little scene stand out, as a fact, on a plain ground which is broken by nothing save the flying swallow; it could not be done without, because it was necessary to the understanding of the subject, but there is not a single flower or a blade of grass.

Nature, like animals, only comes in as a function of man. If we find in vase-paintings olive trees, vines, and water with fishes, it is only because a real or a mythical man is gathering in the olive or grape harvest, is fishing, or has an escort of dolphins. Does not Socrates claim that scenery can teach him nothing that he does not already know from the unique study of self ? This human conception lasts throughout Greek art. Hellenistic realism covers the background of paintings and reliefs with trees and views of nature. Scenery makes its appearance in art, but it is never more than a setting for human occupations. Nature alone and undisturbed by the presence or the toil of man is unknown in Greek art, and even modern art only arrived at this conception tardily. In fact, æsthetic feeling turns last of all to appreciate the beauties of nature; man begins by interesting himself in that which touches him nearest, that is to say in himself, and in nature in so far as it is useful to him, and he does not go back to virgin nature until he has tired of himself and of the civilization that weighs too heavily upon him.

And Nature herself becomes anthropomorphized. The poet beside the Hellenic sea, whose every clear-cut wave-crest sparkles in the sun, sings of their laughter. He dreams of the adventures of Dionysus and of the Tyrrhenian pirates, and he seems to see the flower-decked vessel of the god with its escorting dolphins. Mountain and plain and stream evoke the vision of mythic beings peopling them throughout the centuries. He hears the sound of Pan's hoofs, the wildly dancing feet of the Mænads, and in some hollow tree he spies Dryads and Hamadryads; a Nymph appears to him in the depths of a spring, and his rivers, dry for a part of the year, and impetuous, destroying torrents for the rest of it, are for him bulls and galloping horses whose forms are half animal and half human. Even the creations of man's handiwork, the houses and cities, have countenances: the city becomes an amply draped woman, seated, and wearing on her head a turreted crown (Tyche of Antioch,[1] by Eutychides, 3rd century).

Nothing can escape this obsession. Justice and Injustice, Peace, Victory, Tragedy, Comedy, all appear to the artist in human guise. Nor are these abstractions banal and cold as in modern art, in which they are no longer the direct transposition of an idea into a living body but an age-old worn-out tradition. In Greece, where they were realized for the first time, they had freshness and sincerity. The dominant thing about them was not so much their attributes, or the idea of them, as their corporeal beauty. Confronted by the numerous Nikes who commemorate so many Hellenic victories, we forget that they symbolize the abstract notion of victory. For us, as for the Greeks who contemplated them, they are supple feminine bodies with floating draperies and rustling wings who have fluttered to earth, as did the Nike of Pæonius of Mende at Olympia (after 425). That which charms us in the Cephisodotus group is the sentiment of mother-love bending the gentle head of Eirene, Peace, over Plutus, Wealth.[2] And it is only afterwards that we think of the real meaning of these themes: the abstraction vanishes in this plastic beauty.

This exaltation of the human body inspires a fervent love of life. The Greeks, like other men, knew the sorrows of terrestrial existence with its suffering and its injustice, and experienced the bitterness of death and the fear of the unknown beyond, and literature from the outset echoes these universal lamentations. But life for them was never a meditation on death. They did not, as the Egyptians did, trouble to prepare their eternal abode, nor, like the Chinese, to ensure for themselves a fine coffin; they did not, like the Christians, think of this life as a sad progress towards a better world. For the Greeks it seemed better to be the least among the living than the first among the dead.

*   *   *   *   *

Their art is the glorification of the healthy vigorous human body. They will have nothing to say to anything that impairs it or foreshadows its decline—such as physical or

_____

[1] **LXII,** vol. ii, p. 486.   [2] _Ibid.,_ vol. ii, p. 181.

mental infirmities, the decrepitude of age, ugliness or disease. Myth sometimes required such blemishes (the limping Hephæstus), and vase-painting, always closest to reality, reproduces them; but high art will have none of them until the time when it turned resolutely to realism, from the 4th century, and particularly in Hellenistic times.

The latter end of this corporeal decline, death,[1] has neither sadness nor æsthetic ugliness. Nevertheless it is everywhere present to the mind of the artist in the images of the necropoles and in the pediments and metopes of temples, where it lays warriors low. But the wounded and dying sink gently; their countenance is never anguished: it is even smiling in the archaic work of the 6th century, and it is calm in the idealism of the 5th. The pain of the Rome Niobid[2] is still full of restraint. On the funerary stelæ the dead is not rigid and corpse-like, but living. Erect, he still goes about his daily avocations, plays with his dog, looks at the jewels never again to be worn, or his relatives tenderly clasp him by the hand. There is no brutal separation between the dead and the living. There are no vain regrets. The dead do not appear to regret life, or at least betray it only by a few discreet gestures of sadness (statue of Penelope, Vatican, 5th century[3]); the pose is calm, the countenance serene. Relatives do not perpetuate about the tomb, through the agency of art, the lamentations with which they may have accompanied the corpse. The weepers who tear their hair on the Dipylon vases become rare, and their bemoaning rôle is given over to inferior beings who have more liberty in the expression of their feelings, to disconsolate servants at the feet of their master, on the stelæ, or to symbolic Syrens set up on the tomb.[4] With the humanizing of art which came about at the beginning of the 4th century a certain thoughtfulness and melancholy may pass like a gentle shadow across the countenance, and sorrowing gestures on stelæ become more frequent. On the Ilissus stele of the Athens Museum (4th century)[5] the hound seems still to scent his master, and the little crouching slave sleeps or weeps; but the dead, a fine and strong young man, is no way moved by this reminder of his former life: his arms folded in thought, his gaze

---

[1] **CXCVII.**   [2] REG, 1908, p. 350; REA, 1910, p. 325.
[3] **LXII,** vol. i, p. 407.   [4] **LXIII,** pp. 76, 198.   [5] *Ibid.,* p. 149.

bent on the far distance, he no longer even sees his father, who contemplates him with resigned grief.

This limit is never overstepped. The sad moment in which the soul quits the lifeless body is resolutely suppressed in Greek art; there are in funerary inconography only a very few exceptions to this rule (stelæ of young women who die in childbirth). The " recumbent " figure, stiff on its tomb, is not a Greek conception, and it was Egypt, Carthage, and Etruria that supplied its prototypes to the Christian medieval age. The dead is not even " sleeping," as in Etruria and in Romanesque art; if he reclines, it is on the couch of the funerary banquet whence he can see his wife seated near him and his servant who brings in the funeral meats.[1]

Thus even in funerary art it is still life that is exalted. The dead is depicted as he was upon earth, or such as he is in the Beyond, not such as he is when death has transformed him. Heroized, he lives among the blest, he is enthroned in dignity and receives homage from those near and dear to him (6th century Chrysapha relief, Harpy reliefs);[2] he has the features and the attributes of the chthonian deities, Hermes, Demeter, Cora, and Dionysus, to whom he is assimilated.[3] He is now a god, but pre-eminently he affords the artist an opportunity for modelling a handsome living body.

The damned are doomed to hard penances in Tartarus; Ixion must ceaselessly turn his flaming wheel, the Danaids must endeavour to fill their bottomless vessel, and Sisyphus pushes in vain his rock to the top of the mountain. But we do not find in Greek art the scenes of terror and cruelty that the Etruscans imagined—those hideous demons with the hooked beaks of birds of prey, greedy for the blood of their victims, which they transmitted to Christian imaginations.[4]

The personification of Death itself is not at all terrible, but keeps the aspect of life, resembling Sleep, and on the white Attic lecythi Thanatus helps his brother Hypnus to dispose the dead in the tomb. There is nothing formidable about him; he is a handsome ephebus on the chiselled column

---

[1] **LXIII,** pp. 347, 360, 372.
[2] **LXXXIV,** vol. viii, pp. 331, 439. [3] **LXIII,** pp. 267, 315.
[4] Weege, *Etruskische Malerei,* 1921; Poulsen, *Etruscan Tomb Paintings,* 1922.

of the temple at Ephesus (4th century);[1] at the very most, on the lecythi, he is somewhat sombre in aspect, with hair a little unkempt and muscles that are rather coarse. Charon scolds the souls who linger on the gloomy bank; he insists on his obolus for their passage, but although he is the surly ferryman he in no wise resembles the horrible monsters armed with instruments of torture who await the dead in the Etruscan hell.

The image of a skeleton finds no favour with the Greeks,[2] and its late appearance in Græco-Roman art denotes that the real Hellenic thought has suffered a change. And this skeleton is never that of the dead; the Greek never placed on the tomb this derisory image of the human body, nor did he ever show it, as it appears in Christian art, as a corpse half devoured by worms and oozing corruption. The skeleton-dead does not seek to freeze the blood of men with terror by unexpectedly appearing among them at their daily occupations or at feasts which it delights to disturb like some old ogress. In antique art the skeleton frisks joyously on the festooned vases, or on graven stones shows its stark head which is being contemplated gravely by some philosopher, or on which the butterfly of the soul alights. This is not a terrifying object, but a mere discreet reminder of the ephemeral nature of all existence, the expression of a natural antithesis between the joys of living and the sadness of death, but with nothing sinister or distressful about it.

*　　　*　　　*　　　*　　　*

Loving life and striving after truth the Greek artist saw things quite simply, just as they are, with no make-believe and without establishing hierarchic distinctions between them. Realism properly so-called, that is to say the keen, precise representation of the accidental and the momentary, whether it be feelings, age, or individual features, is doubtless late in coming in Greek art, but the themes of this art, even when treated with the idealism of the 5th century, are always borrowed from the real, often of the simplest and most humdrum variety. A young lad extracts a thorn that has run into his foot while he was running in the stadium—and we have the statue of the Capitol and its numberless replicas

[1] **LXII**, vol. ii, p. 398.　　　[2] **CLXXXV**, s.v. " Larvae."

up to quite late times. Another youngster, squatting, plays with his toes as he watches the preparations for the race between Œnomaus and Pelops—and is one of the figures on the east pediment at Olympia. Heracles, armed with a broom, vigorously sweeps away the manure in the Augean stables in the presence of a haughty Athena—this is one of the subjects in an Olympian metope. An ephebus slips on his chiton, and another is having his girdle fastened by a small serving lad; an impatient horse whisks away the flies—all these are motifs included in the Panathenaic frieze. Vase-painting, which has even greater liberty, does not shrink from trivial scenes: men vomit as they come from a banquet where they have feasted too well; ephebi embrace courtesans, and the most intimate subjects are displayed openly. The action may be banal and humble, even coarse—little the artist cares so long as it is human and true to life, and affords him a pretext for exalting, by the magic of his art, the body's beauty; nothing living is noble or ignoble when art transfigures it.

It is this sense of the real that permits the Greek artist to go further than his colleagues of other lands along the road of progress. Keenly observing life without prejudice, and directly his hand had got sufficient cunning—about 500—he realized that the conventions to which he had tamely submitted in the 6th century were arbitrary, and he triumphantly tore away the veil that divided him from truth.

*   *   *   *   *

The Greek artist, in consequence, is positive. His imagination does not wander away in reverie to the domain of chimæra and fantasy but is always held in check by reality; it does not create the visionary worlds of Indian imagining, nor people its mythology with strange phantoms, but makes it a counterpart of terrestrial life.

" In the beautiful as the Greek saw it there is neither dream nor fantasy nor mystery, not so much as a grain of opium, so intoxicating, so full of hallucination, and so curiously enigmatic for the beholder " (Goncourt). To refuse the slightest sense of mystery to the Greeks, as has so often been done, is somewhat excessive, but assuredly theirs was a spirit that loved daylight—that must have precision and clarity of idea in everything. All must be clear-cut, like the lines of a landscape in the bright Hellenic sunlight. Dim and hazy horizons, half-tones, all that is indefinite or holds a doubt, things vague, and indecision of soul, are unknown to that spirit, or at least have small attraction for it. The temple, precise and luminous, with its human decoration, does not stimulate the faithful to mystic reverie or introspection as do the half-lights and the architectural confusion of Gothic cathedrals and Oriental sanctuaries.

Everything is clear-cut, limited, finished. The temple is not a complex whole, like the Egyptian or Mesopotamian temple, or the Cretan palace, whose maze of courts and stairways and whose many halls, added one to another without upsetting the loose arrangement of the building, inspired in the Greeks the legend of the Labyrinth at Knossos. It had, in the Doric order which is the most frankly Hellenic, a rigorous plan which admitted neither of addition nor subtraction of any importance, and in which variation could only affect the details. The East loved compositions that can be unfolded without definite beginning or end, those long friezes in which the subject has no unity and the figures follow one another for as long as the field permits.[1] This narrative and continuous method is of eastern origin, and it is from the East that the Ionians borrowed it. The restricted and geometrical frame of the metope and pediment, on the other hand, is truly Greek: it does not allow the imagination to wander with no fixed aim, and it obliges the composition to be ordered.[2] On reliefs and in vase-paintings composition tends more and more to be strictly unified, to have a beginning, a centre, and an end, and to avoid looseness. In Greek decorative design there is no interlaced ornament that is unwound and prolonged indefinitely, as there is in early medieval Christian art and in Arab art.

*   *   *   *   *

It is likewise the rational character of Hellenic thought that explains the features we have seen revealed in art, this love of truth, of reality, and of precision. Reason and logic direct the Greek mind, inspiring in it from the 6th century onwards the exact and historical sciences which it progres-

[1] See above, p. 133.   [2] See above, p. 143.

sively freed from empiricism and mysticism, forcing everything to be brought within the bounds of probability. The evolution of the shapes of monstrous creatures gives another example of it.[1] Already reduced by the anthropomorphism which humanized them more and more, many of them disappeared in the course of time, incapable of surviving because their improbability was altogether too shocking to the Greek mind. The wings of the supernatural beings, imitated from the East, were reduced to a single pair, and Nike abandoned the useless second pair that Archermus still preserved for her. The Ionian Centaur, with human feet before and horses' hoofs behind, was an heterologous assemblage. How could such a creature move with regular gait, run as a man and gallop as a horse, with such disparate limbs ? So he was given an entire animal body surmounted merely by a human bust.

In architecture, each member testifies to the function it fulfils. The Doric column and architrave are only lightly painted and have no sculptural decoration because they are not themselves decorative fields but the supports of such. The flutings of the columns, which carry the eye upwards, still further accentuate their supporting rôle. The Ionic order, less purely Greek and contaminated by the East because it came into being in Asiatic territory, sometimes disregards these principles. More luxuriant and less sober than the Doric, it is likewise less rational; its plan is less logical and regular,[2] and ornament comes at last to dissimulate the architectural rôle of the various elements.

If the Greeks during a long time preferred the pure line and disregarded, in drawing, perspective and that modelling that gives roundness to bodies, it was, among other reasons, because it seemed to them illogical to transform a flat decorative surface into one that seemed to have depth.[3]

*   *   *   *   *

A rational spirit leads to the taste for symmetry. Instinctive in all ages and in every land, in Greece it became an æsthetic principle, doubtless developed by the Dorian invaders, since Ægean art pays little heed to it. The vase-

---

[1] See above, p. 278.   [2] See above, p. 129.
[3] See above, p. 264.

painters of the Attic Dipylon show evident care in balancing the elements of a decoration around a central motif; those of the 7th and 6th centuries hesitate between two tendencies, one Ionian and inspired from the East, which turns figures all in one direction, and the other, continental, which causes two equally balanced motifs to converge towards a centre.[1] Although the Corinthian and Attic potters employ the Ionian zone, they sometimes follow their own instinct and introduce into it this symmetrical equilibrium. All vase-painting from the earliest time to its close shows this seeking after equilibrium[2] (Figs. 63 and 64). How many motifs there are whose presence is necessitated only by this single desire not to

FIG. 63. SYMMETRICAL COMPOSITION ON A GREEK VASE, 5TH CENTURY.

break the symmetry, and how many stopgap figures! Symmetry at the outset may be very naïve, but with time it becomes more subtle, less apparent; instead of opposing identical figures, there are in Polygnotus' painting and in Phidias' sculpture[3] corresponding groups and masses; instead of counterparts on either side there are motifs which are only analogous.

The Greek temple shows the application of this principle. The front and back façades, the side faces, and the divisions of the cella all correspond; the entire building can be divided in two, as formerly could the organs of the human body

[1] **CXLV**, vol. ii, p. 449.   [2] **CXLV**, vol. iii, pp. 838-839, 956.
[3] *Ibid.*, p. 1050.

under the frontality rule, by a median line, to right and left
of which all is the same.   In the triangle of the pediment
each wing repeats the grouping of the other—with rigidity
at Ægina and Olympia, with suppleness in the Parthenon.[1]
Buildings are only apparently asymmetrical, because the
Propylæa (Fig. 64) and the Erechtheum (Figs. 13 and 14) are
undoubtedly unfinished.[2]

An innate desire for regularity and repetition inspires the
alternation of metope and triglyph, of the stones in the
regular courses known as " Hellenic "—known, it is true,

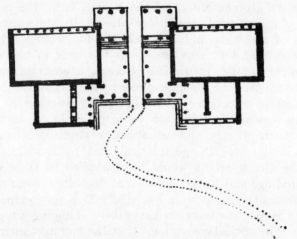

FIG. 64.   PRIMITIVE PLAN OF THE PROPYLÆA.

since Mycenæan times, but which became one of the characteristic elements of the beautiful Greek architecture—and of
the decorative motifs in vase-painting.

Symmetry, alternation and repetition, which introduce
order and logic into nature, awaken the æsthetic sense of the
Greeks, no matter what is the object to which they are applied
—pediment statue or kitchen cooking-pot: " It is beautiful "
said Isomachus,[3] " to see footgear ranged in a row according
to its kind, beautiful to see garments sorted according to
their usage, and coverlets; beautiful to see brass vases and
tableware so sorted, and beautiful, too, despite the jeers of
him who has no wits and is not a serious person, to see cooking-

[1] See above, p. 251 ff.   [2] See above, p. 142.
[3] Xenophon's *Œconomicus*.

pots arranged with intelligence and symmetry. Yea, all
things without exception, thanks to symmetry, will appear
more beautiful still when they are arranged orderly. All
these utensils will seem to form a choir; the centre which
these objects concur in forming creates a beauty which the
distance of the rest enhances."

＊　　　　＊　　　　＊　　　　＊　　　　＊

All this, together with rhythm, the canons of proportion
for the human body and for architectural building, denotes
a spirit that loves number and its reciprocal relations. The
instinctive geometrization of the human form, the predominance of geometrical over naturalistic motifs, the symmetrical
notion of grouping and a preference for settings that are
clearly delimitated, registers, from the time of the earliest
monuments of the continental Greeks, a contrary spirit to
the eastern tendency inspiring more particularly the Ionians.
One already perceives " a certain mathematical spirit " that
is " an essentially Hellenic element."[1] It is instinctive
rather than strictly and scientifically studied, because the
determination of the geometrical and mathematical laws
that the Greek artists would have applied to their statues
and buildings and to the shapes and decoration even of their
vases, remains confused and sterile.[2] This predominance of
number is not contrary to the subtly changing suppleness
of life. The optical corrections[3] that the architect introduced
in the Parthenon and other edifices had in view precisely the
avoidance of such coldness as would result from too mathematical lines, and the endowment of the temple with a soul.

＊　　　　＊　　　　＊　　　　＊　　　　＊

Greek art, which some people consider monotonous, is
full of infinite variety, but of a variety due to subtle rather
than sharp differentiation. The same fundamental principles are strictly observed in different Doric temples. Yet
the independence of the artist is manifested in a number of
details left to his individual choice, such as the number of
columns in the façade and along the sides, their height,
diameter and intercolumniation, the number and distribution
of the metopes and triglyphs which may either go right
round the building or be localized on the façade—sometimes

[1] **CXLV,** vol. ii, p. 450.　　　[2] **CXXX, CXXXV.**　　　[3] **LVI.**

with a return—and the subject of the decoration. Despite
the repetition of forms and themes, one never sees two painted
vases quite alike; even in the same palmette border there
are slight differences. Sometimes vases were made in pairs,
but the second is never an exact replica of the first; even
here there is some divergence. Even in a copy there was
the possibility of introducing variation.[1] And what ingenuity the potters employed in combining a very few
elements differently, so that with three models they could
compose pictures having ten figures![2] At Tanagra and
Myrina terra cotta statuettes differing in aspect and name
were none the less produced from the same mould, the variety
being obtained by the different methods of adjusting the
parts. " They only had to bend a head to one side, to raise
or lower an arm, to bring one leg forward, or to change a
fan from one hand to the other, to produce ten motifs instead
of one. And if we then imagine the combination of different
parts of moulds, it can be easily conceived that it was possible
to obtain an almost infinite multiplication of motifs."[3]

Sculptors repeated the same subjects tirelessly in sculpture
—the general themes of a nude man erect or in repose, and
the special themes of a boy plucking a thorn from his foot.
But there were subtle differences between each, in the pose,
the gestures of the arms, the attributes, the way the hair
was arranged, the features, and the style, and the rich series
of ephebi, from the old stiff 6th-century Kouros up to the
athletes of Lysippus, astonish us by their diversity as well
as by their continuity.[4]

The artist avoided monotony and coldness by these
subtle differences. He introduced into repetition an element
of change that is the life and personality of his work.
Centauromachy, Amazonomachy, Gigantomachy, exploits of
Theseus and Heracles—the subjects are ever the same, but
treated in different fashion every time. See how the artist
was able to vary the banal theme of the Centauromachy in
the Parthenon metopes![5] The snare and the risk lay in the
repetition of the same combinations, the same attitudes, the
same lines, in this perpetual dual between a Centaur and

---

[1] **CXLV**, vol. iii, p. 661; **CXLIV**, vol. x, pp. 328-329.
[2] **CXLV**, vol. iii, pp. 733, 840, 978, 986.
[3] **CX.** p. 254.   [4] See above, pp. 49, 181 ff.   [5] **XXXIX.**

a Lapith. Yet there are not two of these pieces that are identical. The centaur is at the right or the left, he is beaten or he is victorious, the battle is broken up into all its phases, the bodies are nude or lightly draped. The single rule is to get diversity while maintaining the unity of the whole. There is the same preoccupation in the distribution of the metopes on the building. In the primitive plan the continuity of the subject was doubtless intended to be respected —on the south the Centauromachy, on the north the Trojan legend and the Attic myths; but when the slabs of marble were put in place the order was upset. Had it not been so there would have been thirty-two metopes coming one after the other and each showing a Lapith and a Centaur, which would have been monotonous for so great a stretch. To obviate this, part of the metopes of the Centauromachy were transposed to the centre of the north face, and were replaced on the south by an equal number of scenes from the other series.[1] Here, the unity of the composition has been sacrificed in a small degree to the desire for variety.

Mechanical and routine repetition is essentially contrary to the Greek spirit. In industrial art, whose very principle is economic repetition, there was production of series of terra cotta figurines, and, coming after the painted vases, differing always by slight details, there were relief cups made in moulds, characteristic of the Hellenistic period.[2] But in the more carefully produced figurines the boasting-tool came into play, after the casting, to sharpen the blunted features and to give the work an individual character and the mark of the artisan, and this is why the best of the terra cotta figurines are as personal as the marble or bronze statues.

* * * * *

This sense of reality and this clear faculty of reason led to sincerity. One does not find subterfuge and still-life deception. There is no attempt to deceive as to the nature of materials. The Ægeans and the Egyptians already painted their walls and vases to look like marble, as did the Romans: this procedure is foreign to the real Greece. The Etruscans made imitations of bronze ware in clay, but

---

[1] **XXXIX**, pp. 133, 138.
[2] Courby, *Les vases grecs à reliefs*, 1922.

this technique, undoubtedly Ionian in origin, never came
into vogue in Greece to the extent it did in Italy, and the
Hellenistic ceramics of cups in relief betrayed a falling away
from Hellenic taste. The same scruple prevented the gilding
or silvering of statues in bronze and stone or of terra cotta
figurines until Hellenistic times.

*   *   *   *   *

The Greek had a sense of proportion, of fitness in environment, and of moderation, and the μεσότης became one of
the necessities of his æsthetic. It has been said that in
architecture and sculpture[1] the colossal, the exaggerated and
the disproportionate generally denote an Oriental influence.
In the Hellenistic period the sculptors of Pergamum and
Rhodes with their theatrical action, their emphatic muscles,
and their excessive pathos, belong to the Asiatic Greek
schools contaminated by the East. The Belvedere torso,[2]
however Lysippian it may be, is over-powerful, because it
dates from the 1st century B.C., from an epoch in which
Greek taste had suffered a change. Attica provides the
perfect example of this harmonious equilibrium. There, the
sculptor had it instinctively from the very beginning.[3] His
fellow-worker on Dorian soil gave to his statues a too vigorous
frame and a brutal physiognomy; there is an unnecessary
superabundance of strength in the Selinus Perseus and in
Polymedes' Kouros. In Ionia, on the contrary, grace and
refinement ran the risk of degenerating into affectation and
mannerism, and the human body was given no muscles.
In Attica, the earliest sculpture in soft stone on the Acropolis
is already preserved from such excesses in both directions;
the build of the body is strong but less brutal, and elegant
but with less affectation about it; the countenance is smiling,
but without exaggeration. This feature persists throughout
the evolution of Attic art, and " Atticism " is precisely that
exquisite sense of proportion in all things that finds its most
beautiful expression in the marbles of Phidias. In drapery,
musculature and composition the note is always true; one
feels that the motto of Attic art is μηδὲν ἄγαν. Ionian
work, on the other hand, continues to sin slightly in the

[1] See above, p. 65.   [2] **LXII**, vol. ii, p. 632.
                    [3] See above, p. 151.

direction of excess.[1] The friezes of the heröon at Trysa,[2] and of the Nereids' monument,[3] are too long, too prolix in their story, and their execution is too facile and flowing; in the Nereids' statues, beautiful as they are, there are weakness, ungraceful attitudes and careless workmanship. In the Peloponnese there still persists in Polyclitus a certain heaviness in the proportions and dryness in the anatomy of his figures. Athens was able to reconcile the qualities and to avoid the faults of both.

* * * * *

Sobriety and simplicity are other traits of Greek art. The archaic Peloponnesian work has an air of heaviness and awkwardness and that of the isles of elegance. But whereas the latter sacrifices something to luxuriance and redundancy of embroidery, to the minutiæ of the hair and drapery, the former is striking in its sobriety; the drapery has few folds, the hair is simple, sometimes merely shown in mass. When Ionian influence declined about 510, this Dorian ideal finally got the upper hand. And thenceforth the principle of Greek æsthetics was to obtain the greatest effect with the simplest of means.

* * * * *

The artist had a desire for perfection and for conscientious execution. Classic architecture clearly demonstrates this to us in the naked walls of the Parthenon and the Propylæa whose carefully trimmed stones fit with such precision that the joins are almost imperceptible. In plastic work the parts hidden from view are often not worked with the same care as the others; sometimes, however, they are. The feet of the Auriga at Delphi, hidden in the well of the chariot, are as carefully finished as the head or the arms which are visible.[4] And what care is evident, in bronzes, to hide the imperfections of casting by minute repairs, so finely done that they become imperceptible![5]—And in marble statues, to hide the joins of different portions![6] It was this feeling,

---

[1] See above, p. 137.   [2] LXII, vol. ii, p. 202.
[3] Ibid., p. 216; LXIII, p. 243.
[4] Bourguet, Les ruines de Delphes, p. 226.
[5] CLXXXV, s.v. "Statuaria ars."
[6] LXXIX, p. 227.

to some extent, that prompted the artist to leave on one side imperfect material such as wood, soft stone, or clay, for hard and homogeneous material which permitted careful and irreproachable workmanship.[1]

* * * * *

But the artist did not merely desire truth and perfection in his work, but beauty. He saw beauty everywhere, even in the humblest articles of daily use. The vase types had changed since the Mycenæan wreck; some of them, like the stirrup vase, disappeared because they no longer responded to the current needs and taste and had been supplanted by others. The Hellenic pottery forms entered on their long course of development. One sees them becoming modified by time, not only in a more practical but in a more beautiful sense that they may offer the most perfectly harmonious curves to the eye. Study, for example, the modifications in the amphora, or in the kylix; in this last the relation between the height of the foot and the bowl had to be established, and the outline of the bowl and its depth had to be determined; various experiments followed one another until the kylix arrived at its final and perfect form in the Attic productions of the first quarter of the 5th century.[2] The themes had to be chosen and adapted to the vessel, and the decoration had to be distributed over the field and its composition worked out. All these experimental efforts tended to the realization of the maximum of beauty even in industrial art. Indeed, " in no other country of the world has industrial art been at the level of art, properly so-called, as it was in Greece. . . . Whether in vase, terra cotta, hair ornament or coin, one is sure of finding some definite æsthetic quality " (Pottier).[3] The architect, by his preoccupation with the material he was to employ, and by his study of the proportions of his building and all the problems thereby raised; and the sculptor, by undertaking the various experimental efforts we have described in the foregoing pages, were always guided by their innate sense of beauty.[3] This beauty they all perceived in the human body, in its movements and in its attitudes of repose, both nude and draped. They were one and all sensitive

[1] See above, p. 173.   [2] **CXLIV**, vol. x, p. 213.
[3] See, however, p. 45.

to the contraction of a muscle, to the fall of a piece of drapery, to the translucid whiteness of Parian marble and the sombre hues of bronze, to the precision of a naked wall built in beautiful regular courses—in short, to the thousand and one details that stirred their æsthetic sensibility and set it vibrating, whereas these things leave so many people wholly indifferent.

CHAPTER II

EVOLUTION OF THE IDEAL

From the outset up to the end, from the time when works of art first appeared, after the Dorian invasion, to the day when the creative force had dried up and when art exhausted itself in vain repetitions, the æsthetic ideal was evolving, like everything else, and was never at a standstill. It is closely linked with technical progress which alone rendered its expression possible, and a knowledge of which is essential if we are to understand its various phases; it is likewise closely linked with the social vicissitudes that we studied further back. The various stages are as follow:

1. From the earliest days to the end of the 6th century. Elaboration of technique and ideal.
2. 5th century. Technical mastery. Idealism.
3. 4th century. Beginnings of Realism.
4. Hellenistic period. Apogee of Realism.
5. Decline. Exhaustion of Creative Power.

* * * * *

Each of these phases has new features proper to itself, differentiating it from the others. But at the same time each phase foreshadows, albeit in uncertain and timid fashion, the tendencies that are to dominate the succeeding period. It is this co-existence of separate traits that makes art so complex at any given moment and that prevents it from being completely reduced to an exclusive formula—to whose rule it would immediately supply modifying exceptions; it is this co-existence, too, that makes tradition, the regular seriation linking the art of each century to that which has gone before and that which is to follow.

No new creation ever quite disappears; it may fall out of fashion and usage, and be relegated to a lower stratum of art and of society, but it persists none the less. Greek art affords many characteristic examples of this. In vase-

painting the black-figure process was dethroned about the
close of the 6th century in favour of red-figure; but though
it may thenceforth lose its artistic value, and though its
rival may realize fresh progress, although it sinks socially
and is employed for vases of little value, and is merely a
ritual survival in the Panathenaic amphoræ, it yet lives very
nearly as long as red-figure, almost to the time of Alexander,
when both black-figure and red-figure are supplanted by
pottery in relief.[1]

In plastic art the archaic style of the 6th century is not
suppressed by the progress and the ideal of the 5th century.
About 413 one of the Erechtheum sculptors was still carving
the back of one of the Korai in the identical manner of one
of his predecessors of a hundred years earlier,[2] and archaistic
art,[3] in honour in Græco-Roman times, goes back in an
uninterrupted sequence to its inspiration in the 6th century.
A long line of sculptors carries on for hundreds of years
the creations and the style of Phidias, Polyclitus, Praxiteles,
Lysippus and Scopas, and these masters live on in the works
of their imitators.

As time goes on art becomes more and more complex
and varied, and at a given moment one may find all the
earlier tentatives existing side by side. In the centuries
just prior to and just after the beginning of the Christian
era, some will be inspired by the Hellenistic realism and by
the Pergamene and Rhodian schools, others will prefer the
gentleness of the Praxitelian tradition, and others will favour
athletic types in imitation of Polyclitus and Lysippus, whereas
still others will seek their models in a yet more distant past
in the classicism of the 5th century and the archaism of
the 6th.

Sometimes there are genuine renaissances. These are of
a technical order: pottery in relief, so quickly supplanted
by painted pottery, was known in the 7th and 6th centuries.
But when painted pottery declined at the end of the 4th
century, the old technique came into favour again, and
pottery in relief was characteristic of the Hellenistic period.[4]
Some were æsthetic: the Neo-Attic and archaistic renaissance
brought back into vogue an outworn ideal.

[1] **CXLV**, vol. iii, p. 647 ff.   [2] **LXXVIII**, p. 497.
[3] **XCII**.   [4] Courby, op. 1.

At a given moment, too, one may find an artistic formula adumbrated which was to flourish later. During the height of 5th-century idealism, realism claims its right to existence. It inspires certain details of the pediments at Olympia, and some masters yield more than others to it—for instance, Pythagoras, Myron, Lycius and Styppax. It was especially manifested in vase-painting, which had more liberty than sculpture, and in types of the lower social order.[1] All these essays prepared the way. If the 4th century was to see realism vindicate its sway over high art and introduce into it portraiture and passion, that is because these features were already dormant in the minor arts of the 5th century.

[1] See above, p. 81 ff.

FROM THE EARLIEST DAYS TO THE END OF THE 6TH CENTURY. ELABORATION OF TECHNIQUE AND IDEAL

DURING the few hundred years that elapsed between the beginnings of Greek civilization and the end of the 6th century, art was constituting its domain, elaborating types, and experimenting with technique. It was a slow preparation, as ever in the beginning, since development accelerates as time goes on, and the later stages are more rapid. Though the artist required several centuries in which to dominate his material and bend it to his archaic ideal, it only needed some hundred years for the idealism of the 5th century to be succeeded by the still timid realism of the 4th, and another century for this to develop into the keenly pursued Hellenistic naturalism. But we should not forget that this period of trial and groping enabled art, about 500, to become emancipated from its early fetters, and to arrive, a few decades later, at the perfection of Periclean Atticism.

And what a laborious task it was, indeed, that faced the artist on the morrow of the Dorian invasion ! The æsthetic of the Ægeans was no more, and a new spirit, characterized further back in this book, animated Greece. For its realization the Greeks possessed but a rudimentary technique, because the invasion had flung the old population back into barbarism. Art began to rise again out of the night of the " Hellenic medieval age," and in geometrical Greece the ivory idols of the Dipylon, the Bœotian terra cotta figurines resembling bells, and the triangular and rectangular figures painted on the vases show a primitive and infantine design.

The artist learned to choose his materials. In measure as his hand grew more skilled and his æsthetic sense was awakened, he gave up wood for soft stone, and soft stone for marble, both in sculpture and in architecture. From the first quarter of the 6th century marble was the material of

statuary *par excellence*, and although limestone still continued
to be used for a long time in architecture, marble, while it
had still to wait to be used alone in the beautiful temples
of the Periclean age, yet was already in demand, for certain
portions of the building, in the second half of the 6th century.
At the same time hollow bronze casting provided statuary
with resources hitherto unknown.

In architecture the Doric and Ionic orders were created,
the one in continental Greece, the other in Greece in Asia,
each of them asserting a special aspect of the Greek spirit,
and one of the opposite poles of Hellenic thought and Hellenic
æsthetics. Its elements, plans, forms of columns and capitals
and entablature, their disposal and reciprocal proportions,
and their polychromy were fixed. The temple, a living
organism, gradually lengthened its stunted column and
diminished the height of its entablature; the Doric capital
straightened its too depressed curve, and the Ionic volute
united horizontally its two scrolls. There was an effort to
discover what was the most suitable painted and plastic
ornamentation for this building, and the genre of the salient
of the pediments and metopes; the principles governing the
composition of this decoration were studied and these studies
resulted, from the end of the 6th century onwards, in the
symmetrical principle for the pediment and the binary for
the metope. At the end of the 6th century there was
no great progress left to realize, but there were subtleties
to introduce, and especially an increased harmony and
eurhythmy. These are all so many Hellenic innovations,
foreign to all other art whether anterior to or contemporaneous with Greek art.

In sculpture in the round the erstwhile human schema
of the geometrical period was evolving into something more
advanced. Types were fixed—for the erect male figure,
generally nude, the Kouros; and for the erect female figure,
nearly always draped, the Kore; as also for the enthroned
and dignified figure, and the horseman. These few themes,
very simple and always alike, which, being still indeterminate,
were equally suitable for gods and mortals, were erected on
tombs and in sacred precincts either as cult statues or as
ex votos of the dedicators.

Relief began to appear within the frame of Ionian friezes

and Dorian metopes, ex votos, and funerary sculptures in which the long narrow Ionian stele predominated, and was carved with a single erect figure in profile.

Painting on a large scale came into existence and experimented with manner and method, revealed to us, imperfectly, through the medium of industrial vase-painting. The potter worked out a rich repertory of forms for his vessels—the aryballus, alabaster, pyxis, œnoche, amphora and crater—some of which were to disappear as time went on while others persisted and were perfected, their contours being improved. The painter traced on them silhouettes in profile, in dark colour on a light ground, frequently obtained by the cast shadow method, and in which the interior details were shown by leaving blanks in Ionian, and by incisions in the Corinthian and Attic, ceramics. The beautiful Attic productions in black-figure (Plate XII) were soon to surpass earlier work and to supplant the products of other workshops, which gave up competing against Athens. It was in this city that, in the second half of the 6th century, the red-figure process was to come into existence by a reversal of the values of the ground and the figure, a process destined to a brilliant future in the 5th century.

Cast into these shapes and carried out in these materials, the subjects implicated technical problems that the artist had to solve—such as pose, gesture, anatomy, drapery, action, and composition, which we examined further back. It is here especially that we clearly perceive the technical limitations of this archaic art which imposed on it the convention of frontality in sculpture in the round, and of altogether ignoring foreshortening and perspective in drawing and relief. One may say that the part played by technique, up to the end of the 6th century, is tremendous; the artist's eye only gradually came to see reality in its actual aspect; his hand, at first maladroit, only grew firm very slowly. Convention and the preponderance of detail over ensemble obscured his view, and the material too often got the better of his hand.

Nevertheless an ideal emerged, the adumbration of the ideal that was to assert itself in the 5th century. It was a religious, social and patriotic ideal, exalting, in a closely interwoven union, the celestial and terrestrial world of the

Hellenes, by the building of their temples and tombs, by the erection of their cult and funerary statues, and by the varied ex votos they dedicated.

Man asserted a despotic sway. The sculptors carved and the painters painted in order to glorify him under his mortal or divine form. They commemorated the athlete and recounted the exploits of gods and heroes, because, haunted as it was by this human conception, mythology won a definite place in figured art. The ceramist, under Oriental influence, at first substituted floral and animal designs for the geometrical motifs of the early days, and then man came to take a more and more preponderant place in pottery decoration. Together with man, scenes borrowed from social and mythological reality made their appearance on vases, to such a point, indeed, as gradually to eliminate all other subjects, and the old motifs were relegated to second place according to the rules of the hierarchy of genres.[1]

The main æsthetic preoccupations of Greek art asserted themselves together with this anthropomorphic ideal—the anatomical features of the human body, drapery, pose, grouping—henceforth to be considered indispensable elements of beauty. This ideal called for a strong man presenting, in its nudity, his bodily beauty with its broad shoulders, slender waist and well-covered buttocks, such as it was fashioned by gymnastic exercises. And already a preference for masculine shapes asserts itself which was to influence the specific forms of woman and the child, giving to the former slender hips and a boyish chest, and turning the child into a small edition of the man. But woman's form also found favour: too masculine and austere in Dorian territory (Athena of the metope at Selinus, etc.), it was gentler, prettier and more finely decked among the Ionians. Woman's body provided the opportunity for qualities of grace and delicacy to reveal themselves, as man's body was the vehicle for the revelation of Dorian strength.

Countenances were not yet lit by mobility of feeling. At the beginning the artist did not seek to get any particular expression, because he was too busily occupied in giving to each part of the face its proper form and in linking these up more or less correctly, to think about the life of thought

[1] **CXLV,** vol. i, p. 250; VI, vol. ii, p. 495.

or of the soul. But, as time went on, two kinds of faces can be distinguished: one with stern features, rectilinear mouth and eyes, in Peloponnesian art; and the other, in Ionian art, with smiling lips and eyes with tip-tilted corners. This, however, was not due to a conscious seeking after real feeling. The smile bestowed indifferently on all—on the dying and on angry gods—which was perhaps born from some technical necessity, became stereotyped, a simple æsthetic convention (Plate XIII). Did it mean that man presented himself amiably to the gods and that they showed their goodwill towards him? It would seem more likely that it was already the social defence of man who disdained to show his feelings and who disguised them under an amiable expression, as we still do, and as the Japanese do. To be master of oneself in all circumstances, in anger, pain, and even agony, and not to allow human dignity to be upset by the accidents of life—this is the meaning of the archaic smile, as it is the meaning of Dorian austerity, and both foreshadow the serenity of the 5th century.

These technical and spiritual experiments and efforts were pursued in all the regional centres of Greek art. Ionia, enamoured of amiable delicacy and richness but sometimes lacking in real strength in its musculature, half Asiatic by its geographical situation and by its political relations, brings precious gifts to the common patrimony of the Greek æsthetic —the technical knowledge of bronze casting, the appreciation of the beauty of marble and the practical working of this material, the science of drapery, the spirit of grace and delicacy which was somewhat to temper that which was too rough in the Dorian ideal, movement and picturesque realism. Attic art especially, and the whole of the Peloponnese, felt this influence in the second half of the 6th century. It is Ionia who plays the leading part in the 6th century, who really initiated Greece artistically. When she lost her political independence and when her influence ceased to be dominant, about 510, the lessons learned from her were not lost, and Atticism owes to Ionia a share of its most beautiful qualities. It is from the Ionian spirit that a number of 5th-century works derive, works of rare delicacy in which light draperies allow the feminine form to be seen through them (pediments of the Parthenon, the Fréjus Aphrodite,

Nike of Pæonius) and, in the Hellenistic period, when Greece proper yielded the lead in artistic matters to Asia Minor and to the Hellenized East, a triumphant return to Ionianism inspires the realism, the love of scenery and of violent movement, qualities already in embryo in the 7th and 6th centuries, more particularly in Ionian vase-painting.

To this tendency is opposed the Dorian art of continental Greece, testifying to quite other qualities—austerity, sobriety, energy that is sometimes brutal. Just as the Ionian spirit persists throughout Greek art, so is the somewhat too massive strength of the Polyclitian ephebi in direct descent from the Selinus Perseus and the Kouroi of Delphi. Peloponnesian Greece ever preserves its instinctive preference for man, for musculature and bronze, over woman, drapery and marble.

Greek art had need to be stimulated by this tonic as a counterpoise to Ionian delicacy, which was in danger of degenerating into affectation and effeminacy. This Dorian spirit, hitherto confined to the Peloponnese and to the colonies of Magna Græcia and Sicily, was to become dominant about 500, and to replace the Ionian influence by its own; and Greek art, having learned from both, and uniting in a nice equilibrium Dorian strength and Ionian grace, was well on the way to achieve perfection.

This perfection was realized in the 5th century by the Attic artist who, from the earliest times, had known how to maintain a just balance between his two neighbours and to temper strength with grace; marvellously favoured by the circumstances of the Persian wars and the political prosperity of Athens, he was to become the æsthetic master of all Greece.

CHAPTER IV

THE 5TH CENTURY. TECHNICAL MASTERY, IDEALISM

THE Doric order in architecture, after the temples of Ægina and Olympia, achieved its most perfect expression in the Parthenon of Ictinus and brought the long efforts towards eurhythmy, proportion, and optical anticipations to completion. Henceforth Doric buildings could be multiplied; Mnesicles solved some difficult problems in the Propylæa—thought as much of by the Ancients as the Parthenon—and Ictinus also erected the temple at Phigalia. Nevertheless there was no further progress, rather even a decadence in the Doric order. The Ionic order, which came into being in Greece in Asia, had not yet been used in continental Greece except for isolated columns—supporting ex votos, and not architectural—and the Treasury of Siphnus was a purely Ionian work implanted in the soil of Delphi. The Ionic first made its way into continental Greece under the ægis of the Doric. Departures from the strict rules of the Doric order opened the door to the newcomer. The Parthenon, like the old Hekatompedon of the Pisistratidæ, maybe, had certain Ionic elements such as the frieze, and details of the mouldings, and the number of the columns of the façade. This was still but a small thing. Mnesicles went further: he placed two interior rows of three Ionic columns in the Propylæa. Other buildings of the second half of the 5th century show this same association of orders, the Ionic still playing a subordinate rôle (exterior frieze of the Theseum; columns and interior frieze of the temple of Phigalia, etc.). Finally, the Ionic became entirely emancipated from Doric tutelage. The temple of Athena Nike is conceived entirely in this order, of which the Erechtheum, larger and more sumptuous, was the ultimate consecration on Greek soil. Richer, more elegant and more supple in its ornament, it responded better to the new tendencies of luxury and wealth that appeared in the second half of the 5th century, and which developed progressively; it was to win general favour. But then comes the rise of the Corinthian capital in much the same way. A variant of the Ionic, inspired by the acanthus crowning funerary stelæ (Fig. 10), it was employed for the first time in the temple of Phigalia for the head of an isolated column, and this building demonstrates the hierarchical alliance of the three principles—the Doric constituting the mass of the building, the Ionic providing the columns and interior friezes, and the Corinthian limited to a single column in the cella. The tholos of Polyclitus the Younger at Epidaurus still preserved the subordination of Ionic to Doric. But the Choragic ex voto of Lysicrates at Athens (335-4), in the 4th century, is the first entirely Corinthian building. Still richer and more deeply sculped than the Ionic, the Corinthian capital—one can hardly speak of an order—corresponds with the third phase of an architecture that was evolving in the direction of a growing luxuriousness.

Thus the second half of the 5th century covers the apogee of the Doric, the final adoption of the Ionic, and the genesis of the Corinthian.[1]

In plastic art and in drawing, the conventions of the 6th century (Fig. 65, Plate VIII) had been useful in that they prevented the artist from prematurely grappling with problems still too difficult for him, and caused him to concentrate his attention on the details of anatomy, drapery and features, but they were in danger of arresting him on the path of progress, and of keeping him on the same level as his fellow-workers in other lands of antiquity.

The artist broke away from them from 500 onwards. Urged on by his feeling for the real, by his love of life and by his æsthetic feeling, he realized that frontality, oddities in drawing, incorrect outlining of muscles and drapery, were so many errors, and that the archaic smile and the advancing of the left leg and the left leg alone were not the sole possible aspects provided by reality. Henceforth observation was truthful, and, in consequence, to the monotonous schema there succeeded the variety of life afforded by the different attitudes of the body, alone or in groups, in repose or in action, and variety of subject. Some new technical problems

[1] See above, pp. 130 ff., 141 ff.

resulted, such as that of the more precise adaptation of the
details of drapery and musculature to this unceasing mobility,
giving rise to efforts to achieve rhythm, proportion and
composition.[1]

The horizon was broadened. Details no longer stood out
alone, but the artist's mind embraced the ensemble, and for
the old fragmentary analysis was substituted synthesis and
co-ordination, and a tendency towards simplicity and sobriety
was favoured by Peloponnesian influences.[2]

The emancipation of Greek art, begun about 500, was
almost complete by about the middle of the 5th century. By
then the last errors and awkwardnesses had disappeared, and
the artist knew his business to perfection and how to realize
his ideal without let or hindrance from technical difficulties.
The way for the great masters of the second half of the 5th
century, Phidias[3] and Polyclitus,[4] had been prepared by
their forerunners such as Critius and Nesiotes, Hegias and
Myron[5] in Attic art, Ageladas and his disciples in the Argive
school, the Æginetans,[6] Pythagoras of Rhegium,[7] and many
more besides. These artists likewise created masterpieces,
but they somewhat savoured, perhaps, of harshness; full
maturity was only reached just after their day (Plate XIV).

From now on artists impressed their personalities on art.
The names of Pythagoras, of Myron, Polygnotus, Micon, and
Panainus, to quote at random, could not be passed over in
silence. The 6th-century artist, no doubt, could be an
innovator, and Archermus of Chios invented, or rather transposed to Nike an Oriental type, but he was still incapable
of clearly asserting his originality; he modestly pursued his
work within the narrow limits imposed on him by convention,
the analytic study of details and the studio tradition. From
the beginning of the 5th century, being free to adopt the
pose and subject that best suited him, and having mastered
the technical rules of his art, he asserted himself, and the
rôle of the artistic individuality now began. The history
of Greek art which, hitherto, had been the history of local
and regional schools, now became that of individual great
masters who impressed on art their own æsthetic vision, thus

---

[1] See above, p. 179 ff. [2] See above, p. 237 ff.
[3] **XXXIX, CLVIII, CLXV-VI.** [4] **CLXVII, CLXX.**
[5] **CLXX.** [6] Furtwaengler, *Ægina*, 1906. [7] **CLXIV.**

giving rise to schools of disciples, and radiated their influence both spatially and in time. We can follow the fortunes of the styles of Phidias, Polyclitus, Praxiteles and Lysippus right up to the closing moments of Greek art.

The ideal sketched out by the 6th-century artists now acquired precision. The unceasing changes in man and in nature did not interest the artist any more than the savant or the philosopher, the poet or the historian. He desired to pass from the particular to the general, to create types which would not be of one time but of all time. Eliminating the accidental and the individual he retained only that which was eternal.

It was this desire for abstraction that imposed the Hellenic profile[1] on the 5th century. The earliest Peloponnesian heads of the 6th century already show this vertical nose and forehead in which one is but the prolongation of the other, whereas the Ionian foreheads are receding and the nose points out in front. From 500 we can see the profile straightening in Attic art at the same time that new principles were everywhere being introduced into the then flourishing Dorian schools (Ægina, Argos). The Hellenic profile, of which we get typical examples, often regularized to excess, in the painting of Attic lecythi in the middle of the 5th century, is not an imitation of nature but an æsthetic convention, no doubt resulting from a desire for abstraction to be seen at this period in all art. A just mean, a norm for all, was sought, such as would avoid the accidents of aquiline, or of pug noses, left to inferior mortals. A few sculptors, more realistic than the rest, already slightly accidented the athletic profile, and Myron, maybe, foreshadowed Praxiteles in this particular. But it was not till the 4th century gave proof of realism, by depressing the root of the nose and making the forehead swell, that this too uniform regularity was broken.

It was this desire for abstraction that eliminated all individual or fleeting expression from faces (Plate XV).[2] They reflect no definite feeling no matter what the action in which the body is engaged; they no longer smile as they did in the 6th century, nor pout as they did at the beginning of the 5th when the artist, having broken with the tradition

[1] See above, p. 85.   [2] **VI**, vol. iii, p. 231.

of the archaic smile, went rather to the opposite extreme
and gave a sulky-looking mouth to his statues.   Almost
impassive, they are equidistant from joy and sorrow, calm
with a superhuman serenity.   No trace of ugliness disturbs
the harmony of head and body.   There are no portraits; that
of Pericles by Cresilas, if we leave out of account the strategus'
helmet,[1] might as well be that of a god or a hero.   Nor is
there age that enfeebles the body and wrinkles the countenance, unless it be rejuvenated and ennobled and approxi-
mated, like that of the woman and the child, to the age type
that belongs to the adult in the plenitude of his youthful
and manly strength.   Nor yet historical scenes—unless under
the guise of legend and myth.   Nor scenery—merely an
indeterminate background.   On funerary stelæ, the dead,
whether they had been young or old, handsome or ugly,
have all the unalterable beauty, eternal youth and perfect
serenity of the Parthenon marbles.   This so noble art is
abstract, rational, idealist; it addresses itself more to the
intelligence than to the heart; and with this art we find
ourselves in the domain of the pure idea of Plato.   The
fugitive and changing side of things is displeasing to it, and
for it the only truth is eternal truth.

It is at this period of Greek development, and only then,
that we can speak of " serenity."   The dogma of " Greek
serenity,"[2] created by the pundits of the 18th century (Lessing,
Winckelmann), attributes to all Greek art a calm and absence
of passion, and, by the most ingenious subtleties, recognizes
this serenity even in the most tortured productions of
Hellenistic times—in the Laocoon, the *chef-d'œuvre* of pathos
at its most emotional.   This notion that still survives in
certain manuals and in the thought of certain ill-informed
writers is quite mistaken.   To admit it would be to believe
in the immobility of Greek art that was never to have
but one ideal before it which could never change by a
hair's-breadth.   The monuments themselves contradict this.
Serenity there is, but only in the 5th century.   Because,
from the 4th, art leans towards realism and makes a great
effort to achieve pathos—new tendencies developed to the
utmost by the Hellenists.

Perfect serenity conforms to the æsthetic thought of the

[1] **LXII,** vol. ii, p. 133.   [2] **VI,** vol. i, p. 97.

5th century in figured art as in literature—before it had been disturbed by Euripides. In the strong and healthy body the head cannot play a predominant part or attract attention by a too marked expressiveness. The harmony of the whole would thereby be upset. Thought and feeling do not yet reduce the body to slavery; the ideal is that of perfect balance between the life physical and the moral and intellectual life; gymnastics mould the body, in education, as reading, music, singing and poetry mould the mind. This impassiveness is suitable for such handsome creatures as nude ephebi and young women in the Dorian peplos, whose corporeal repose it seems to enhance. It is a little surprising in figures engaged in some violent form of exercise. Should not the countenance of the Diskobolos of Myron be contracted by the effort made at the moment when, his tense muscles strung like a catapult, he is about to hurl the discus far from him ? But he wears a mask of glacial calm; if we saw the head detached from the body we should think it belonged to a statue in the most complete repose. This is not incapacity on the part of the artist who knows quite well how to express the surprise caused by the discovery of the pipes in an inferior being like the Silenus Marsyas. It is the deliberate control of the athlete resembling the frigid reserve depicted on the countenance of Athena before Marsyas despite her haughty anger.

The Greek of the 5th century was proud of himself; he lived in that heroic epoch in which the small Hellenic nation, though weak, had gloriously beaten back the enemy and become conscious of its own valour. As already in the 6th century—if we admit the social significance of the smile— to yield to one's feelings or passions and to perpetuate them in art seemed unworthy of a member of a noble race who under all circumstances must show complete self-mastery. The ancients said that no one had ever seen Pericles laugh, and the death of his son, carried off by plague, in no way altered his calm or his energy; up to the end he was to encourage his fellow-citizens and to be the proud soul of the city.

This serenity is also a mark of human confidence in the divinity. The art of the 5th century, still entirely religious and civic, is an expression of gratitude to the gods for the

protection accorded to the Greeks in this decisive hour of
their national story, and it exalts the city in its victories.
Is not the Acropolis, that pedestal for Periclean monuments,
one vast act of homage in stone rendered to Athena and to
Athens, to the goddess and the city ?   Man was in the hand
of his gods: this is what gave him his strength of soul and
his calm; he was a member of a community to which he
owed his all—that is what constituted his impersonality.

Indications of expression are very discreet in plastic art,
and more precise in vase-painting (Fig. 66).[1]   And there are
slight subtle variations between one artist and another.
Myron and Polyclitus give to their ephebi countenances of

FIG. 66. WARRIOR, ON A 6TH-
CENTURY VASE.

perfect tranquillity untroubled
by thought; as artists who
were fascinated by the form of
the body, which they desired
before all else to make as
beautiful as possible, they did
not bother themselves at all
about the life of the mind.
But features are more expressive on the Parthenon.   The
ephebi and the young girls of
the Panathenæa, with heads
modestly bent, seem thought-
ful.   The others seem to be stiffened in an impassiveness
altogether physical, or strained by some effort (Olympia,
Polyclitus); these have really a peaceful serenity which
accepts life as it is without seeking to struggle against it.
Phidias seems already to foreshadow, by this attenuation
and softened aspect, the pensive and sensuous reverie of
Praxitelian countenances.

Expression, in the 5th century, consists only in slight
nuances.   The discreet smile praised by the ancients in the
mysterious Sosandra of Calamis, and the smile which gently
lightens the countenances of the Tralles Caryatid and the
Fréjus Aphrodite seems to be a reminiscence of the old archaic
smile.

The 5th century found its most beautiful artistic expression in Atticism.   The Ægina school had but a passing

[1] **VII.**

brilliance in the first half of the 5th century, disappearing amidst the political misfortunes of the island. The Peloponnese, it is true, was to see the school of Argos flourish, which was rendered illustrious by Ageladas and his immediate disciples, and then by Polyclitus and his successors, and which maintained from the beginning up to the very end the tradition inaugurated in the 6th century by Polymedes. But the artistic leadership that belonged to the Ionians up to the end of the 6th century was lost by them and now passed to Athens. From the 6th century onward, with the " century of Pisistratus," Athens was preparing for her commercial and political expansion which was to march side by side with her æsthetic domination. The 5th century brought the realization of both. In the short space of time separating the morrow of the great Persian battles (Delian league, 477) from the peace of 449, Athens became the unchallenged mistress of a great maritime empire, and jealous Sparta, occupied with her continental policy, did not contest her domination. At peace with Persia, the ruin caused by the invasion repaired, prosperous once more, having at her disposal the treasure transferred to her by her allies in 450, and her commercial fleet sailing the seas under the protection of her navy, Athens is also the intellectual and artistic capital of Greece. All the most illustrious men of the day throughout Greek lands flocked within her walls. Drawn by the great artistic projects of Pericles, artists from all over Greece mingled in Athens with the Attic artists, and Agoracritus of Paros, and many another, arriving from other cities of the Athenian empire, received there the teaching of Phidias. Athens now spread far and wide the fame of her art; she set up in the heart of the Peloponnese buildings inspired by the Parthenon, whose architect, Ictinus, subsequently to 420, built the temple of Phigalia; she influenced the Ionian artists who worked for the Lycian and Carian dynasts, and it was Athens that caused the style of Phidias and his pupils to find acceptance everywhere. Athens continued to play the part of the artistic metropolis of Greece up to the end; even after the centres of artistic production had been displaced in the Hellenistic period, she retained her glorious renown as the city in which Greek genius revealed itself in its most typical and lasting forms. The terrible Peloponnesian war (431-404)

did little to detract from this brilliant Attic efflorescence of
the second half of the 5th century, and work went on in
Athens in the calmer moments of the peace of Nicias, from
421 (Erechtheum about 420; the Erechtheum Korai, about
415) to the Sicilian expedition (415-413). The beautiful
Victories of the temple of Athena Nike were carved on the
morrow of the ephemeral successes of Alcibiades in the
Hellespont (408), and very little before the fall of Athens
(404). But the spiritual consequences of this war, which
ruined Greece, are sensible in the art of the 4th century.

CHAPTER V

THE 4TH CENTURY. BEGINNINGS OF REALISM[1]

THE 4th century, heir to a perfect technique and an exact knowledge of the problems that in the 5th century were still to solve, had the task of introducing subtleties rather than innovations. We have seen how in this century attitudes became more supple, the raising of one hip having been adopted,[2] and how a still too dry and schematic modelling had been softened by a more pictorial and picturesque vision of anatomy and drapery.[3]

But if themes and motifs were unchanged, the spirit animating them was quite different. The soul of the artist flew less high, and the pure and noble idealism of the Parthenon began to flag. The misfortunes of the Peloponnesian war transformed the Hellenic mentality. The relaxing of tradition, the growing incredulity and slackening of religious conviction, the invasion of more sensual and emotional foreign cults, the increasing luxury, and the individual freedom that is always clamant in troublous times to the detriment of any common bond, turned men's minds from the serene heights of other days to the agitations of humanity and the many fleeting happenings of ordinary daily life. The study of man, from every angle and in every possible manner, as private individual and not merely as mankind, not only in his heroism but in his weakness—this is the dominant note of the 4th century. Art now neglects the general and pursues the particular character. It was the same in society; this was the moment in which the individual sought to free himself from the trammels of a collectivity.[4]

The artist emancipated himself in the 4th century. He had no longer at heart the grandeur of the city and the glory of his gods; he no longer modestly joined his own efforts to those of all the other citizens for the attainment of a common

---

[1] **VI**, vol. iii, p. 261.
[3] See above, pp. 216, 237.
[2] See above, p. 198.
[4] See above, p. 110 ff.

ideal. He became independent and obedient unto himself alone, his preoccupation being now rather to produce personal work than to follow tradition. He no longer had the robust faith that animated his ancestors of the 5th century and he no longer believed himself called to a mission; he ceased to seek his aspirations uniquely in the national, patriotic and religious life. Man interested him more than the gods, and not only heroic man, the combatant who vanquishes barbarians and monsters, or the victorious athlete, but man *qua* man who has accomplished no brilliant act and whose only merit is that he lives, and the artist takes him even from the lowest classes of society, whereas for many a long day the vase-painters had had a monopoly of such familiar and often trivial scenes.

The art that becomes humanized in this way tends to quit the exclusive service of the gods to consecrate itself to that of men, and these men it secularizes. Phidias immortalized the glory of Athens before all else; Lysippus multiplies portraits of Alexander; he becomes, like Apelles and Pyrgoteles, a court artist.[1] Though the State no longer undertakes the construction of great groups of works in which the soul of an entire people is revealed, the luxuriousness of private persons increases. Funerary monuments, which become more and more sumptuous, and the official offerings which abound, testify more to pride than to gratitude towards the gods.

The differences between schools, still so marked in the preceding century, tend to become effaced. The masters travel about; Scopas works at Tegea and at the Mausoleum in Halicarnassus; Praxiteles works at Mantinea as well as in Athens, and they make disciples almost everywhere. The influence of individual studios is greater; Attic and Peloponnesian art borrow from one another, and from their union issues that eclectic style frequent in 4th-century work. There is a movement in the direction of that international character in art which was to be the distinctive mark of the Hellenistic period.

The gods come down from the ideal heights and become mere mortals. Aphrodite, a chaste and austere goddess in the 5th century, is now a real woman whose sensuous charm and

[1] See above, p. 111.

beauty are exalted, and her erstwhile virile contours are now languid. The Aphrodite of Cnidus[1] put off her divine majesty with her raiment, and now there is nothing left but a woman's exquisite body. Apollo is a youth who teazes a lizard,[2] and Artemis a young girl fastening her mantle.[3] Religious subjects now border upon genre, which begins to assert itself.

Arrogance now elevates mortals, on the contrary, to the level of the gods. Apelles is the first painter to represent men in the guise of gods, and Lysippus shows Alexander, leaning on his spear, regarding heaven with an air of defiance. " The bronze hero," says the epigram, " raises his eyes to Zeus as though to say: 'the earth is mine; thou, O Zeus, mayst reign on Olympus.' " Honorific statues are multiplied —another result of human vanity.

The dominant and genuinely original note of 4th-century art is the search for the accidental and the individual, briefly, the evolution of realism out of idealism. " Consequently " said Socrates, " combatants' eyes should express menace, and joy should be read in the countenances of victors? Undoubtedly. Then statuary should express in form all the impressions of the soul."[4] The art of the 5th century, however, had avoided this portrayal of the passions and emotions that the philosopher commends to the sculptor. But now the countenances of gods and mortals lose their superhuman serenity. This seeking after expression is one of the conquests of the 4th century: everything, attitude, gesture, drapery and countenance, unites in revealing that which moves the heart. Two quite distinct expressive tendencies appear—the sentimentalism of Praxiteles and the pathos of Scopas. Humble predecessors among the 5th-century ceramists, and the bronze-worker Pythagoras of Rhegium, a realist born before his time,[5] had already dimly seen the resources of pathos, but it was reserved for Scopas[6] to lead sculpture into the path of violent emotion, to render the physical or moral suffering that forces the head back (Plate XVIII), and raises the eyes to heaven, and half opens

---

[1] **LXII**, vol. ii, p. 276.   [2] *Ibid.*, p. 287.
[3] *Ibid.*, p. 283.
[4] Xenophon's *Recollections of Socrates.*
[5] **CLXIV**, p. 126.   [6] **CLIX, CLXX.**

the lips as though to groan (Tegea heads).[1] Praxiteles,[2] likewise, mingles with his marble the passion of the soul, to repeat the terms of the ancients, but in a different manner from Scopas. His ephebi and his gods are lost in a sensuous and gentle reverie, with a touch of romantic pensiveness about it, and sometimes a slight smile.

Not a countenance now remains indifferent. That of the Demeter of Cnidus,[3] that antique *Mater dolorosa*, with her gentle sadness, gazes into the distance, as do those of the figures on Attic funerary stelæ,[4] whose discreet resignation moves us more than any violent pain. Asclepius is a god full of compassion and kindliness. Zeus himself, whom Phidias had been the first to depict as human and compassionate, becomes yet more gentle, and thoughtful, too. Lysippus[5] endeavoured to react against the growing invasion of sentiment by means of the corporeal beauty of his robust athletes, without, however, depriving his Agias of a pensive and weary air (Plate XIX).

Suffering passion, gentle melancholy, sorrowful kindliness —these are some of the feelings revealed by the countenances sculptured by the great psychological artists of the 4th century. After the serenity of the 5th century, this is a new note, still timid, it is true, and subtly expressed—a long way from the Hellenistic exaggeration.

Grace and sensuousness also mark this period. Praxiteles renders the seductiveness of woman and the sometimes ambiguous languor of young people. The Tanagra Koroplastes,[6] his humble disciples, clothe all their fragile works in a delicious grace which avoids Hellenistic mannerism and affectation and is still lit by the glow of a dying idealism.

The artist interests himself in all the accidents that befall humanity. He observes the differences between ages, between the two sexes, individuals, and races, instead, as in the old days, of reducing them all to one common measure. Woman acquires her specific characters; children are no longer conceived as small adults. Portraiture seeks to reproduce exactly the individual features; Silanion excels in this, and effigies of orators, poets, and illustrious statesmen become frequent.

[1] **LXII**, vol. ii, p. 239. [2] **CLIX, CLXII-III, CLXXII**.
[3] **LXII**, vol. ii, p. 362. [4] **LXIII-IV.**
[5] **CLX, CLXVIII.** [6] **CVII, CX, CVI.**

Still, the realism of these countenances (Mausolus, Æschines, etc.) has not yet the cruel acuity of the Hellenistic period; it shuns excess, and it preserves a nobility which is too often absent from later portraits.

This change in ideal corresponds with the social transformation in art which we have already indicated.[1]

The 4th century is a period of transition from the idealism of the 5th century to the precise realism of the Hellenistic epoch. It is to this last that it belongs to develop these still timid tendencies and to carry them to their most extreme limit.

[1] See above, p. 110 ff.

CHAPTER VI

THE HELLENISTIC PERIOD. APOGEE OF REALISM[1]

THE monarchies of Alexander and the diadochi transformed social conditions, and art felt the inevitable repercussion whose effects we have already seen.[2]

The political centre of gravity having been displaced in an eastward direction in conjunction with the conquests of the Macedonian and the brilliant Egyptian, Syrian, and Asia Minor empires, art now finds its original forms at Pergamum, Tralles, Antioch, Alexandria and Rhodes, where schools come into existence. Art flows back again towards the East. And once more in contact with it, old qualities, that the classicism of continental Greece had curbed, are liberated, and link the Hellenists with their Ionian predecessors, and through them with the Ægeans,[3] qualities of realism, the feeling for life, love of nature, of the picturesque and of movement. Reacting since 500 against the preponderant influence of Ionianism and the Orient and accepting the teaching that came from the Peloponnese, especially from the school at Argos, art, in the 5th century, had been the expression of that part of Hellenic genius which was purely original and Dorian; now it is once more modified by coming back to Asia.[4]

Athens loses the artistic supremacy acquired in the course of the 5th century, and now plays but a secondary rôle, although maintaining her fame as an intellectual queen and the city of all the arts which foreign princes think themselves honoured in embellishing and protecting. Doubtless her studios still prospered under Demetrius of Phalerum (317-307):[5] it was then that Protogenes worked at the Bouleuterion, and the architect Philo at the great portico at Eleusis, and that the sons of Praxiteles, Cephisodotus and Timachus

---

[1] **VI**, vol. iii, p. 311; **LXI, LXV, LXIX, XCI.**
[2] See above, p. 111.   [3] **VI**, vol. iii, p. 59.
[4] See above, pp. 65, 135 ff.   [5] **LXII**, vol. ii, pp. 442, 613.

sustained with honour the reputation of the Attic school. It was the last flash of the brilliance of Athens—henceforth to live on her glorious past. From the 3rd to the 1st century she remained faithful to the traditions of the 5th and 4th centuries, especially keeping up the traditions of Phidias and Praxiteles, and sometimes of Scopas. But there was no more invention, and her artists limited themselves to combining with greater or lesser felicity the types created by the great masters, and to repeating and adapting them. Protected by the memory of the great names of Phidias and Praxiteles, Athens avoided the exuberant pathos and the *outré* realism of other Hellenistic centres, and preserved up to the very end that just sense of proportion and of harmonious balance of which she gave proof from the commencement of her æsthetic life. Up to the 1st century A.D. she engenders sculptors of greater skill than originality. It is these men who, having maintained the tradition, are the makers of the Neo-Attic and archaistic renaissance,[1] who bring back into honour the classic models, and propagate in Rome the most glorious themes of an older time, going back readily right past the 4th century to the archaism of the 5th and even of the 6th.

The artist has at his disposal for making his new aspirations concrete a highly skilled technique marked with that increasing subtlety whose principal traits we have already characterized.[2] He works his materials with a virtuosity that is more varied than of old. Sometimes it would seem as though, in art as in literature, the conquering of a difficulty is the artist's aim, and that he chooses, for the mere pleasure of solving them, difficult problems in pose, statics, grouping and musculature.

The characteristic note of the Hellenistic ideal is the triumph of the realism that was still timid in the 4th century. In every domain there is a passionate desire to see things in their most concrete reality. The sciences—geography, chronology, mathematics, anatomy, botany, astronomy, medicine—become experimental. Philosophy, following Aristotle, takes as its starting-point the particular fact. Historians give an individual idea of their heroes, showing the particu-

---

[1] **LXII,** p. 643; **XCII;** Hauser, *Die neu attischen Reliefs.*
[2] See above, pp. 174, 202, 217, 271.

larities of their private life. Theophrastus paints characters. Psychological analyses are the order of the day. The positive fact takes on a singular value in Greek eyes.

So, too, art is required to give the illusion of reality and of life. In one of Herondas' mimes, two women admire the works of art in the temple of Asclepius. One of them exclaims: "Look at this child how he strangles the goose! If the marble were not before your eyes you would take your oath he was about to speak. Sure enough, the day will come when men will end by making the stone itself come to life." "I was within an ace of taking that bunch of grapes," says an epigram in the Anthology, "deceived by its colouring." This is the same sort of illusion as that which the author of another epigram, on Andromeda, would suggest when he says of the monster that one could not tell whether it was painted on the rock or whether he was really about to come up out of the sea. Myron's heifer and his Ladas seemed to be alive. There is here, at all events for the 5th-century work, an obvious literary exaggeration, but Hellenistic works bear witness to this constant effort to make art the faithful counterpart of life, and no longer to look upon it as an idealized transposition of life.

The artist scrutinizes the human body in the manner of a scientist,[1] profits by the new medical studies which are making anatomy known with precision, and is interested in physiological blemishes. Whereas in the 5th century he avoided anything that subtracted from the integrity of the ideal human being, he now regards with a curious and an instructed eye a body whose development is abnormal, or warped by disease, and vacant faces, of which the terra cotta statuettes, particularly those from Smyrna, provide numerous examples.[2]

Pathos, which first appeared in the 4th century with Scopas and Praxiteles, remained a little conventional and without revealing any clearly defined feelings or running over the whole gamut of possibilities. These two masters opened up the way, but the Hellenistic artists got the maximum effect out of these formulas. Every kind of passion now moves the body and is expressed in the face. Whereas in the 5th century the head did not attract more attention than

[1] See above, p. 218; **VI**, vol. iii, p. 415.　　　　[2] **CXI**, p. 95.

the rest of the figure, it now begins to be the most important part of it.

Physical pain causes the giants of the Pergamum frieze,[1] the Galatian and Persian combatants,[2] and Laocoon and his sons,[3] strangled by the serpents, to cry out. It would be impossible to push further this pathos that is already theatrical and that seeks effect rather than sincerity (Plates XXII and XXIII). Mental anguish exasperates to the point of equalling physical suffering, and the old Centaur, writhing under the dart of Eros, has a face as tormented as that of Laocoon.[4] Anger contracts the masks, and the sculptor must himself have felt the rage of Ajax, said an author, to be able to render it with such intensity. Art and literature are penetrated by a dolorous sentimentality of which few traces were to be found earlier. Everywhere there is effusiveness and tragic passion. Along with love that is tender or sensual there is also the love that is terrible, exasperated by disdain, of which Daphnis and Polyphemus die. There are sickly pallor, languishing eyes, inexhaustible tears, sighs, and bad and troubled dreams. A veil of sadness spreads over the face of Hellenistic sculpture. It is the sadness of the Pourtalès Apollo,[5] grown thin with melancholy in the Castellani Apollo,[6] and in the Attis type, sullen and restless in the Vienna Zeus, and dejected in the Smyrna terra cottas of the Heracles type. Sculpture chooses unhappy and sentimental countenances. The very gods have lost their Olympian serenity. In the 4th century Athena transpierces Enceladus with a conventional smile on her lips, and in the 5th she remains calm; but now, in the Scopasian statue at Florence[7] and in the terra cottas of Asia Minor, she turns heavenwards a face full of woe. Serapis is occasionally a sombre and romantic god. The Olympians all seem to be somewhat discouraged. Are they conscious, perhaps, of their decrepitude ? Do they feel that they are no longer the ardent expression of the popular faith, and does this sadden them ? One asks oneself if the art of Greece in her decline, with its sceptical and disturbed soul, wanted to represent its gods grown old, wearied of the long business of divinity and,

[1] **LXII**, vol. ii, p. 513.   [2] *Ibid.*, p. 500.   [3] *Ibid.*, p. 550.
[4] **LXXXVIII**, Pl. 229.   [5] **LXII**, vol. ii, p. 456.
[6] *Ibid.*, p. 457.   [7] **LXX**, p. 306, Fig. 130.

having lost their strength, mourning sadly their departed powers.[1]

The pathos of Scopas led to the exasperation of painful passion, both physical and moral; the sentimental tendencies of Praxiteles are accentuated in the romantic art of the Praxitelidæ who, in the Hellenistic period, kept up the Attic tradition. In the heads, gentle reverie mingles with sensuousness, the regard is veiled in languor, and all the contours are softened as though dissolved in mist. This morbidezza and sentimentalism are generally characteristic of the Hellenistic spirit whose literary equivalent is supplied by Alexandrian poetry (Plate XXIV). Passion is not stilled even in sleep. Formerly, painting had represented sleeping persons, but this theme did not find its way into plastic art till the Hellenistic period, when man allowed his body to yield to fatigue and no longer sought, as in the classic period, to resist and to retain his mastery of himself. Eros, Nymphs, Satyrs, fishers and shepherds lie sleeping. Often it is a troubled sleep. The Satyr of Naples is sodden with drink; one almost seems to hear the more bestial Barberini Faun snoring. Hermaphrodite dreams sensual dreams (Plate XXIV), and the goddess appears to Endymion; on Ariadne's face the artist paints the sorrow caused by her lover's defection.[2]

All kinds of feelings now appear. Laughter lighting up the faces of children, Satyrs and young girls does not appear in plastic art until this period. Maternal tenderness causes mothers to yearn over their little children.

Physiognomies are asked to express more than they can possibly say. In Euphranor's Paris, according to Pliny, one could recognize at one and the same time the judge of the three goddesses, the lover of Helen, and the murderer of Achilles. What we see in Niobe's image is the precise moment in which the mother has not quite given up hope but, cruelly tried, thinks she may still be able to save the last of her children. The Medea theme fascinates the imagination. " When the hand of Timomachus painted the cruel Medea, torn between her jealousy and her maternal love, he took infinite pains to characterize these two feelings, one of which drives to anger and the other to pity. He knew how to render both—look at his work ! In the midst of her

[1] **VI**, vol. iii, p. 354. [2] *Ibid.*, p. 356.

threats she weeps; even while she feels pity she is carried away by her passion." Iphigenia is furious, but the sight of Orestes evokes in her the sweet memory of her brother. Then we have the Cyclopian lover: " The painter has preserved his savage and terrible aspect; he shakes his locks, thick and straight as pine stems; he tries to assume a tender expression in conformity with his love, but this love has something savage and terrible about it, like the desire of a wild beast yielding to nature's call." The commentators on these works may have attributed to the authors intentions that were never theirs, but which are quite in accordance with Hellenistic taste, going so far as to reconcile in the same countenance feelings that are contradictory.[1]

Realism lends precision to portraiture, and multiplies images of a truth that is often cruel (example: the so-called Seneca portrait).[2] Not content with noting the physiognomy of their contemporaries, they gave to people who were dead and gone expressions that seemed caught from the life; they no longer idealized but they conferred on Æsop his traditional hump,[3] and their Homer has open and sightless eyes in a worn and lined face.[4] Everyone wants to possess an image of himself and of the members of his household. These portraits lack speech only, repeat the old authors *ad nauseam.* " See, Cunno," says Coccale, " that statue of Battale, the daughter of Mutes, how life-like she stands ! He who does not know Battale has but to look upon this image and needs not to see her in person." A portrait is said to be so lifelike that " the little housedog barked, thinking it saw its mistress." Physical resemblance was not all they sought; it was desired to read in the face the complex feelings of the living model. If a woman be honest one should see in her the nobility of her soul, her wisdom, and her virtue, as well as her charming beauty. " It is Sappho herself; one sees in her eyes, sparkling with light, the vivacity of her imagination. Her firm slim contours bespeak her candour and her simplicity, and from her face, in which joyousness and thought are depicted, one sees that she combines her service of the muses with Cytherean pleasures." As for Aristotle, " the

---

[1] **VI**, vol. iii, p. 358. [2] **LXII**, vol. ii, p. 600.
[3] Helbig-Toutain, *Guide dans les musées d'archéologie classique de Rome*, vol. ii, p. 29, No. 756. Villa Albani.
[4] **LXII**, vol. ii, p. 599.

bronze even bespeaks the activity of his thought, and he looks like a man who is deep in meditation. The slight fullness of the cheek reveals the doubt in his mind, whilst his eyes show the crowding thoughts that haunt him." Realism in sculptured funerary portraits did not appear before the Hellenistic period.[1] But then there was an effort to preserve a more personal image of the dead. " Thy mother has placed on thy marble tomb a young girl," says an epigram in the Anthology, " who has thy stature and thy beauty, O Thersis, and, dead, thou art such that one may still speak to thee." There is complaint of this too speaking likeness which revives the sorrow of those left behind. In order to make sure of it, casts taken from the dead were resorted to according to a method brought into vogue by Lysistratus, the brother of Lysippus, as is testified by many funerary effigies (example : terra cotta bust at Brussels.).[2]

The 4th-century artist understood better and rendered better than his predecessors the charm of children's bodies, but he did not yet care for the child for its own sake and for the pleasure of seeing its plump and rounded form, and its clumsy and naïve gesture; he would bring a child into a composition whose interest was centred elsewhere. But now the child invades art as he invades literature, and artists achieve a correct knowledge of what he is like.[3] Boethus, in the 2nd century B.C., and his imitators, set babies to quarrelling with a goose;[4] others play at knuckle-bones, run, fish, ride on dolphins, and play a hundred pranks. They may be immobile, erect in their little shirts, or, tired, they may be slumbering. They steal his arms from Heracles. Or they run about, carrying their shoes in their hands so as not to wear them out. Childhood is now so tenderly appreciated that the gods take on the shapes of children. Eros is no longer the youth he was in the 5th century, but a plump and chubby infant, a Love, who finds his way in everywhere, laughing and crying, alone, or escorting other gods and mortals. The child has become the favourite motif of artists, and everyone knows with what facility of invention the koroplastes of Asia Minor, and the painter, treated this

---

[1] **VI**, vol. iii, pp. 297, 376.   [2] *Ibid.*, pp. 378-379.
[3] See above, p. 101.   [4] **LXII**, vol. ii, p. 603.

theme in graceful genre scenes. The infant Heracles is more interesting than the labours of Heracles the athlete, and artists love to show him from his cradle up wrestling with the serpents of Hera. Pan becomes a child, and baby Satyrs gambol, and infantine laughter brightens their joyous countenances. What charm there is in these plump little forms with their big heads, round bellies and dimpled limbs, and in the naïve clumsiness of their poses !

The Hellenistic artists realized that there was monotony in rendering the human body in its robust youth alone and that even wrinkled age might have an interest of its own.[1] The gaunt face of the so-called Seneca is full of intense intellectual life. A pedagogue is shown walking with bent back, holding in his hand his little pupil's bag of knuckle-bones (Myrina statuette);[2] or a peasant woman with skinny bosom and withered breasts, her knees bent with years, painfully carries a lamb.[3] They do not shrink from trivialities: Myron of Thebes (3rd century) sculps an old woman, whose features are hideous in their mock gaiety, lovingly clasping in her arms the flagon of wine whose contents have made her drunk.[4]

Thus the cycle of human existence, from infancy to age, from the cradle to the grave, is followed in its full circle. It would seem, too, that the idea of death moved men more at this period. Tragic adventures abound in literature; in art, funeral scenes take on a mournful character that had hitherto been absent, and awaken a sentimental feeling of pity. The Ludovisi Galatian, having killed his wife who sinks in his arms, stabs himself with his sword, and the two of them, united in life, are together in the Beyond.[5] The Galatian child, in the Epigonus[6] ex voto, fondles its dead mother, and this picture of maternal love is calculated to bring tears to the eyes of many sensitive folk. On funerary stelæ, the young woman, seated, or stretched on her couch, sinks in the arms of her parents and servants. The Pagasæ stele may be considered the *chef-d'œuvre* in this genre. The dying woman lies on her couch, her head supported by many pillows; the nurse approaches, holding the swaddled infant in her arms; at the foot of the couch a man watches with

[1] See above, p. 103; **VI**, vol. iii, p. 396.   [2] **CXII.**
[3] **LXII**, vol. ii, p. 566.   [4] *Ibid.*, p. 594.
[5] *Ibid.*, p. 505.   [6] *Ibid.*, p. 508.

profound sadness this young mother dying in childbed. And it is here that we see appear the skeleton and the death's head.[1]

Though industrial art represents at an early date people of other races such as Semites (vase in the Phalerum style)[2] and Negroes (6th century vase, among others the Busiris hydria),[3] the classical sculpture of the 5th century knows nothing of Negroes, and only depicts barbarians such as Amazons and Persians in order to illustrate Hellenic victories. One would search in vain, too, for the realism with which the vase-painters occasionally treat them; their features are idealized like those of the Greeks; they are characterized alone by their costume and their attributes. The Negro, who was never an enemy for the Greeks and who was known to them mainly through their commercial relations with Africa, is relegated to industrial art in which he decorates vessels of perfume; but his ethnic type, easy to seize, is conventionalized and occasionally caricatured. The Hellenistic period aims at ethnographic verity even in so far as to render the differences between individuals of the same foreign race. The beautiful head of the Cyrene Lybian[4] is that of an individual substituted for the type. Negro youngsters abound, and in them the ethnic quality is united with the charm of childhood. As wandering musicians they play some instrument in the squatting attitude of their race; or, as pedlars, they doze, sitting on their heels beside their wares; or else, their monkey playmate on their shoulder, they are dancing, or as little slaves they gravely hold some dish (The Negro Boy of Tarragona).[5] The faces of the Persians (Dying Persian's Head, Terme Museum, Rome; mosaic of the Battle of Issus, Naples) have also assumed a perfect realism. But the original creation of the Hellenists is the Gaul, the Galatian who struck terror into the Greek world and who plays in Hellenistic times the rôle of the Persian in the 5th century. By celebrating the valour of those whom they have conquered, the Attalids who immortalize them in their ex voto at Pergamum and Athens glorify their own courage and call men to witness that they, too, have delivered Greece from

---

[1] **VI**, vol. iii, p. 380; see above, p. 284.   [2] **CXLIV**, vol. x, p. 667.
[3] *Ibid.*, vol. ix, p. 521.   [4] **LXII**, vol. ii, p. 567.
[5] **VI**, vol. iii, p. 398.

the barbarian. The ethnic features of the Gaul, his shaggy hair and long moustache, his rude muscles contrasting with the supple musculature of the Greek trained in physical exercises, are rendered with nuances shading from the sharpest naturalism to the most attenuated idealism.[1]

From the 4th century onward the artist had given more attention than hitherto to animals, and he had begun to endow them with an individual life (example, Lysippus). In the Hellenistic period,[2] circumstances are still more favourable. The progress made in natural science had made the shapes and habits of animals better known; the decoration of palaces and private houses, parks and gardens, open up to this genre new opportunities. What intense life that group must have had which was admired by the two gossiping women of Herondas' mime: "Look at that bull, and the man leading him, and the woman walking behind, and him with the button of a nose, and him with the snub. Aren't they all alive—made of real flesh and blood! If it weren't for my womanly reserve I should scream—that bull really scares me: look at his eye, Kunno! He is positively glaring at me!" One thinks of the Florentine boar and the Palermo ram, extraordinarily accurate works.

On a lower plane there was still life.[3] Epigrams describe fruit and various other objects. At Pergamum, Sosus executes the *asarotos œkos* mosaic: there were to be seen reliefs of a feast which seemed to have been left lying by mistake on the ground. This genre was to develop in Rome: Possis modelled fruits which could not be distinguished from real fruit, and the Pompeii paintings are full of still life subjects.

The merit of the Hellenists was to have brought back into honour that feeling for nature[4] that the exclusive cult of man had stifled since the Dorian invasion. Scepticism had driven out the personifications of nature, and Pan, the Nymphs and the Satyrs are become no more than graceful allegories. The sciences—geography, astronomy, botany, and zoology—made soaring flights. The addition of Asia to the Greek patrimony opened up new researches in a vast unexplored domain, the sight of which awakened the sentiment of the beauties of nature. The refined and complicated

[1] **VI**, vol. iii, p. 397 ff.   [2] *Ibid.*, p. 81.
[3] *Ibid.*, p. 407.   [4] *Ibid.*, p. 72.

civilization of the great Hellenistic cities provoked a reaction in favour of the country; people went there to rest and recuperate, and parks were laid out in cities, and gardens were made for private houses; they took passionately to the sport of hunting, which enabled them to find again in the calm of the woods the simplicity they had lost. The entire literature bears witness to this new love of nature. In art the picturesque element, hitherto sporadic and timid, takes a larger place; it inspires those groups of metamorphoses into tree or plant (Apollo and Daphne, Dionysus and Ampelus), and those marine or woodland creatures whose bodies, faces and beard are covered with seaweed, with leaves and berries (Oceanus, Scylla, etc.). Foliage unites the human and animal elements in giants and monsters, and the artist intermingles with their scales little acanthus leaves. Combinations of animate beings with ornamental foliage are common— winged children whose bodies end in leafy branches, busts or heads emerging from a collarette. In architecture a naturalistic decoration covers the capitals of Asia Minor. Picturesque groups are placed in frames of verdure, and in " picturesque "[1] reliefs, funerary reliefs, and painting, blank backgrounds are abandoned and are invaded by scenery.

Hellenistic art has not the simplicity of the classic periods. It understands the complexity of life and interests itself in everything, taking pains to render the subtle shades and differences in physical life that shape the infinite variations in the bodies of women and children, the appearances of disease and of blemishes, and which make the contrast between one race and another. It is no longer limited by the old restrictions or the long-lasting predilection for the ephebic body. It is interested in intellectual and moral life, and the indifferent countenances of older days with their conventional serenity reflect henceforth all the human feelings from the simplest to the most delicate. It is interested in social life, and it takes note of the ranks of society and of occupational deformations. How much more varied is this conception ! One seems to hear a great modern symphony played by a huge orchestra instead of the sober and straightforward music of the past, which was somewhat thin and uniform in tone.

[1] XCI.

This variety, however, is not accomplished without mistakes being made. Taste is less sure than it once was. Thanks to the search for the new, to the desire to be original, to be sensitive to all the facets of life, the instinct for proportion and equilibrium of the classic period is somewhat hesitant. There is bad taste in the complicated, skilfully built up hair of the Myrina terra cottas; there is theatrical emphasis in Laocoon, even already in the Pergamum frieze; there is mannerism in the gestures, in the exaggeration of a bulbous and declamatory anatomy; all so many forms of excess that had been unknown hitherto.

CHAPTER VII

THE DECLINE. EXHAUSTION OF CREATIVE POWERS

THERE is one theme repeated century after century which clearly shows the modification of ideal which we have indicated. The Boy Plucking a Thorn from his Foot has inspired a number of replicas[1] until quite late times. In the 5th century, when the theme was invented, it was not a genre subject but a type of the athletic and religious statue, the image of a young victor whose wounded foot did not cause him to slacken in the race. The early form was slim and dry, somewhat schematized; and gaucheries had not completely disappeared because the carefully combed locks did not fall, as they should, by their own weight, and the junction of thorax and pelvis is still a little reminiscent of the old frontal ankylosis. The Rothschild bronze shows a robust fellow with expressive physiognomy, knit brows, picturesque hair and powerful muscles: here we have the dawning realism of the 4th century. Still later, the Priene image-maker[2] transforms the graceful lad of archaic times into a common little street urchin who, barely clothed in a small cloak and wearing a cap, makes a pleasing grimace of pain: here we get the keen and somewhat trivial realism of the Hellenists with its predilection for the lower orders of society and its transformation of the grave and religious subjects of olden times into genre.

The funerary group of San Ildefonso,[3] the work of an eclectic artist of the 1st century A.D., united the formulas of three centuries of art. The little idol recalls the 6th century: she holds up her drapery with its regular and schematic folds in the manner of the Korai. The ephebus on the right is an adaptation of the Doryphoros of Polyclitus, and that on the left has a thoroughly Praxitelian rhythm; one evokes the 5th and the other the 4th century. Finally, the altar placed between them is Roman in its taste. If

[1] **LXII**, vol. i, p. 416.   [2] Wiegand, *Priene*.   [3] **LXIII**, p. 339.

there had but been a Hellenistic motif as well we should have had all the schemas of Greek art represented from archaic times up to its fusion with the art of Rome.

The evolution of Greek art may be considered to have ceased about the 1st century B.C. To its spiritual and technical formative period (6th century) had succeeded the time in which the artist, liberated from his last maladroitnesses, realized the ideal dimly perceived hitherto, and of which the Parthenon marbles supply the most finished expression (5th century). But realism crept in (4th century) to triumph in the Hellenistic period. And it could go no further. Was inspiration now to renew itself, and still to find fresh formulas ? It would not seem so; it would seem that this evolution is complete and that art now could only oscillate between the two extreme phases of idealism and realism which it had passed through successively, now preferring one and now the other, and now welcoming both simultaneously.[1]

Creative imagination already showed symptoms of exhaustion with the Hellenists. There was a great deal of copying, and of combining together earlier conceptions in order to achieve types that were original in appearance; the action and pose of one celebrated statue was transposed into another subject, and motifs were rejuvenated by treating them according to the taste of the day, and invention was apparent only in the arrangement of disparate parts. These expedients often denote real ingenuity which yet does not dissimulate the too frequent reminiscence.[2] In literature, erudition takes the place of imagination; we see the birth of the history of art and of art criticism, which likewise bear witness to an analogous impoverishment. And thus theory is substituted for action, and science for emotion, the memory of the past for thoughts of the future and of progress.

Arrived at this impasse, Greek art turned readily back to its past. The Neo-Attics and archaists[3] take up again the themes and styles of the 6th, 5th, and 4th centuries, and we now see all the ideals which succeeded one another from the 6th century co-existing. In the Rome of the 1st century A.D., crowded with Greek works, we can study the development of plastic art from the statues of Bupalus and Athenis

---

[1] **VI,** vol. i, p. 318.   [2] **VI,** vol. iii, p. 450.
[3] **LXII,** vol. ii, pp. 631, 643; **XCII.**

(6th century) in the temple of the Palatine Apollo built by Augustus, up to the most realistic forms of the Hellenistic age. And the artists of that day take their inspiration indifferently from the one or the other. Art exhausts itself in vain repetitions, but it is already Græco-Roman art.

This evolution is not particular to Greece, since the same thing happens in the Christian world whose art follows the same course from its beginnings in the medieval age to the 16th century, and with an analogous rhythm. In both there is a formative period, submitting to the same technical conventions—comprising the 6th century B.C. and the 12th century A.D.; idealism dominates both in the 5th and 13th centuries; then comes the dawn of realism in the 4th and 14th centuries whose full harvest is reaped in the Hellenistic age and in the Christian 15th and 16th centuries.[1]

However original it may have been, and however profound its influence, Greek art had in common with the art of other periods and lands certain features which are due, not to borrowing or filiation, but to spiritual and technical necessities. Filiation and borrowing on one hand, coincidences on the other, art by contact and spontaneous art—these are the two formulas which explain analogies in different lands and times.[2] So-called influence exerted by Greece is really only a spontaneous similitude. To quote but a few instances: in pre-Columbian America the presence of the " Greek " fret—though it is a universal ornament—on Peruvian vases, certain Maya art motifs, and a creature resembling the classic Gorgon on certain objects of the Cuenca treasure, has given rise to a suppositional and imaginary communication between the old and the new world. One could show by hundreds of examples that a large number of material and spiritual appearances in Greek art are to be found everywhere, not only in its beginnings when it had to obey primitive conventions that are general, but even later in its most developed phases. Greek art loses nothing by such an admission. Shorn of anything absolutely unique, the Hellenic artist is no longer an exceptional being but a man who, having to submit to the same psychological and material necessities as other men, nevertheless was capable of realizing more perfectly than they the common ideal because he was more sensitive to beauty and more highly gifted in his ability to express it.

[1] **VI**, vol. iii.　　　　　　　　[2] **VI**, vol. ii.

CONCLUSION

THE PLACE OF GREEK ART IN THE HISTORY OF CIVILIZATION

IN order to realize how original Greek art was we must note how it has reacted to the numerous influences exerted on it in the course of its history, and how it exerted its own influence. To receive, adapt to its own temperament with lesser or greater individuality, and then to give out to others, is the law of all art.

I

WHAT GREECE OWES TO FOREIGN ART

Greece owes the foreign elements of its art to what it inherited at its inception, and to what it borrowed as a result of historic contacts, both commercial and political. Outside influence was most active in the first stages, at the beginning of the 6th century; art was then docile to such influence, not yet having become clearly conscious of its ideal, and being in course of elaborating its themes and acquiring a technique. It was likewise active after the great national period of the classic 5th century, when Greece had once more come into regular contact with the East, especially in the Hellenistic age, and also towards the end, when creative imagination sought to renew itself and when Greek art fused with the art of Rome.

Though a new world may have come into being after the Dorian invasion, there was yet no absolute break between Ægean civilization and the Hellenic civilization which followed it. Subject to the conqueror, the old population of the Peloponnese preserved its technical procedures despite the regression brought about by the cataclysm and continued to produce for the newcomers, who left the manual work they themselves despised to this population, and who, as a minority caste in a hostile country, retained in their own hands military

337

strength and civil power.[1] Certain regions, protected by their geographical situation, remained untouched, such as mountainous Arcadia, and Attica, separated from the Peloponnese by the isthmus and saved by the heroism of the legendary Codrus. Fleeing before the invasion, the Ionians, who were the descendants of the Ægeans, crossed the Ægean Sea and established themselves on the Asiatic coast. The Ægean tradition was actively maintained by these technical survivals in districts which had not felt the invasion, such as Attica and Ionia, and was adapted to the Dorian spirit in the Peloponnese. Is not Ionian naturalism, contrasting as it does with continental schematism, due to this difference in origin ?[2]

All forms of spiritual, material and artistic activity in Greece betoken Ægean survivals. How many Hellenic deities have pre-Hellenic ancestors ! Such was the Delphic Apollo himself, whose sanctuary, the omphalos of the Greek world, was raised on the site of the ancient establishments. Certain divinities sink from favour and become monsters and demons; such were the sacred bull of Crete, who was now only the Minotaur; and Theseus, his vanquisher in the labyrinth which recalls the palace of Knossos, symbolized Hellenic Greece which overthrew the Minoan empire; the cuttle-fish, whose image, no doubt prophylactic, ornamented so many vases and other objects, now became the redoubtable Hydra against which Heracles fought. How many were the reminiscences in rites and cult objects, even as far afield as Italy where the fiddle-shaped shield which decorated the Ægean gems and frescoes (Tiryns fresco) persists in the sacred ancilia of the Salian priests ! Many elements of Greek costume, especially the Ionic, and the citharist's dress, originated in the Ægean. The seven-stringed lyre was not invented by Terpander because it had already appeared on the Haghia Triada sarcophagus. The Hellenic language preserved a number of vocables, endings and roots, and toponymy in many places was reminiscent of pre-Greek settlements. In literature, Homer, who was an Ionian, could still trace, at a distance of centuries, a dim picture of this vanished world.

In architecture the so-called " Doric " temple was a

[1] **CCXI.**   [2] See above, pp. 121, 161.

descendant of the Mycenæan megaron. How many ornamental motifs persisted in the geometric pottery of orientalistic, Ionian, or Corinthian complexion !¹ And what is more, the old Ægean æsthetic had not entirely disappeared. Elongated proportions, which lasted for centuries after the geometric Greek period, were still inspired by the slim and slender figures beloved of the Cretan and Mycenæan artists.² These already had a taste for human musculature, which was to become almost exclusive in Greece;³ they affected those great ritual games in which athletes took part in pugilistic and acrobatic exercises and in racing. The direct heir of the Ægeans, Ionian art especially preserved an attenuated naturalism and a love for plants and animals, movement and life, and of the picturesque, features that were very different from the continental tendencies brought in by the Dorians; this art inspired the rare picturesque velleities that are occasionally evident in the full classical period, and it was to triumph once more when Greek art flowed back towards Asia with the Hellenistic monarchies. Many links thus unite the two civilizations; Ægean survivals explain certain accents in Greek art.

To this legacy from the past Greece added the influences she received from countries with which she had relations. Oriental influence was exerted indirectly in all that the Ægeans themselves had already borrowed from Egypt, Mesopotamia, and the Hittites, and which was transmitted to the Hellenes. But it was also exerted directly, during the formative period, from the Greek geometric phase to the end of the 6th century, and especially in the 7th, so much so that the Greek art of that time may be called " Orientalistic."⁴ A science that has become more subtly discriminating no longer believes in the " Oriental mirage " and no longer makes out the Hellenes to be the servile imitators of that East from which they were supposed to have got everything. Truth lies midway between, and the scholar has to discern which elements were inherited and borrowed, and which were spontaneously Greek. We no longer think of evoking the influence of India, once a dogma when that country was

---

[1] **CXLV**, vol. ii, pp. 487, 558.
[2] See above, p. 245. [3] See above, p. 206.
[4] **CCXII**; Karo, AM, xlv, 1920, p. 106.

dimly recognized as the cradle of all civilization. We smile when we recall that Burnouf explained the enigmatic characters of the Trojan spindle whorls by the old Chinese ideographs. One is inclined to think that contemporary " pan-Babylonianism " is only a belated form of the old Oriental mirage and the expression of a mentality among scientific men which refuses to admit similitudes and puts everything down to influence.

Nevertheless one cannot fail to recognize Eastern influence. The Greek artist for long sought his technical processes, his themes, and his decorative motifs in the East. Geometric pottery already betokened such influence, which became stronger in the vases of orientalistic style, in the productions of Ionian, Rhodian and Corinthian workshops. The decoration, which covered the vessel like a variegated carpet, was imitated from Eastern stuffs; we see the monsters created by the fertile imagination of Asia and Egypt fighting upon them, and cuneiform characters there become ornament (Rhodian vases).

The scholar determines the share of each of the Oriental civilizations in the make-up of Greek art.

Mesopotamia gave mythological themes, whose form the Greek spirit changes, Ixion on his flaming wheel being the solar god of Assyria; ornamental motifs, such as the tress which appeared as early as in Elam and which was perpetuated up to the time of the barbaric art of the early Middle Ages, despite Alexander's cutting of it in the Gordian knot;[1] and the cosmic tree, and the Potnia Theron. The thickset proportions of the Ionian figures are in imitation of Assyrian statuary. The Ionic order borrows the idea of the frieze, and the torus of column bases.

The Hittites supplied their contribution. The Greeks took from their religion the legend of the Amazons, which they denatured, and the motif of the Chimæra, may be, as well as many other features.

Lydia,[2] semi-Hellenized and mistress of the Ionian cities, exerted on them fruitful influence in that she was the agent of transmission between coast and interior.

Ionian art, as a whole, thanks to the privileged topographical situation of the Ionian settlements which received

[1] " Le nœud gordien," REG, 1918, pp. 39, 141.   [2] **CCXIII.**

the products of Anatolia, Cappadocia and the basin of the
Tigris and Euphrates, by sea and by island caravan routes,
was penetrated through and through by Asiatic influences,
and served as the intermediary between Asia and continental
Greece.[1]

Egypt's share is no less. Her priests justifiably said to
the Hellenes: " You Greeks are mere children."   At the time
when Greece was first coming into existence, Egypt, indeed,
had behind her a long past of glorious art which attracted
the attention and called forth the admiration of the Greeks.
But the Greeks had also a more practical interest in the Nile
valley; their trade was established there, and they founded
cities at Naucratis and Daphnæ. Friendly relations were
established with the phil-Hellene pharaohs, Amasis and
Psammeticus, and there was continual coming and going of
men, things and ideas from one shore of the Mediterranean
to the other. Perhaps the cult of Dionysus and of Demeter
at Eleusis may have borrowed its elements from that of Isis
and Osiris. Were Heracles, and Atlas who supports the
world, the heirs, perhaps, of Shu holding up the heavens ?
In architecture the taste for colonnades, characteristic of
Greek temples, and the use of stone instead of wood—may
these have been suggested by the sight of the great sanctuaries
of Egypt ? It was there that Rhœcus and Theodorus of
Samos studied the technique of hollow bronze casting which
was destined to such a great future in statuary. Was the
Kouros, with closed fists and the left leg uniformly put
forward, imitated from the Egyptian pose, or was this only
an instinctive and universal schema ?[2] Because, among the
borrowings that have been so often pointed out and in
such great numbers, some are certain and some are doubtful,
the analogy being capable of explanation by spontaneous
similitudes.

Among this company of protectors surrounding the cradle
of Greek art place should be found for the Phœnicians.
Doubtless the Phœnician like the other Oriental mirages has
been dissipated; we no longer believe that those hardy
mariners brought everything to Greece, as was credited prior

[1] **CCIX, CCXII.**
[2] Deonna, " L'influence égyptienne sur l'attitude du type statuaire
debout dans l'archaïsme grec," *Festgabe für O. Blümner*, 1914, p. 102.

to the pre-Hellenic discoveries. The Ægean thalassocracy flourished long before the Phœnician, and it was the Minoans who transmitted to the Greeks those elements which once were attributed to the Phœnicians, as, for example, writing and the alphabet. But after the Ægean shipwreck these traffickers were dominant in Mediterranean waters from the 9th to the 7th centuries at a period when Greece, barely emerged from the disturbance following the invasion, was constituting her art, and in which they themselves, flung back by the Assyrians at the end of the 8th century, turned once more towards their western trading bases and wherever they had maintained commercial relations in being. They served as intermediaries between the East and Greece, bringing in with their cargoes a number of ornamental motifs.[1]

Oriental influence declined in measure as Greece made progress and asserted her own technique and ideal. Towards the end of the 6th century, that useful intermediary, Ionia, lost her independence and her artistic preponderance. From 500 onwards the Greek artist turned his eyes towards the Peloponnese and sought his artistic guidance in that direction. The tyranny against which Sparta had always struggled was finally beaten down in 510—that tyranny which was Asiatic in origin and conceived after the pattern of the Lydian, Gyges, and which knit close the relations of the peninsula with the Oriental monarchs; the Persian war was to break these bonds. And then there came a reawakening of national sentiment, not only in political matters but in art, which, having assimilated the contributions from without, was thenceforth to reject all foreign interference.

Very little in the way of foreign elements penetrated into art during the classic period covered by the 5th and 4th centuries. From the 5th century onwards, nevertheless, Asia and Thrace introduced the gods of the senses and the passions and of the mysteries—Dionysus, Cybele, Atys, Bendis, and Sabazius—whose acceptance was brought about by the misfortunes of the Peloponnesian war, since they promised that comfort for the troubled spirit which the official gods could no longer provide. The wild and stirring music of the Phrygians effected a change in the calm Grecian music. The pathos of 4th-century art may be in some measure

[1] **CCXII.**

due to this contribution.   Artists of exotic origin, especially ceramists, introduced dissonances into 5th-century art such as a repugnance to nudity and a predilection for drapery and fringes.

Whenever Greek art set foot on Asiatic soil it became modified by the contact.   Hellenistic art was the fusion of the purely Hellenic spirit with the spirit of Ionia, of the Ægean, of Asia, and from that moment the old link with the East and with Egypt was again renewed.

Greek art subjected Rome to its own domination; but when the ancient world was sinking into decadence the old Oriental spirit triumphed; the Græco-Roman world was invaded by the cults and the arts of Persia, Babylonia, Syria and Egypt.

Christian art is a mixture of those two tendencies, Græco-Roman and Oriental, and we find in every period of this art this twofold current, now mingling, now running distinct, for example in Byzantium where the Hellenistic tradition exists side by side with the Oriental.

Our modern civilization itself presents this dual aspect, Oriental in its religion, Greek and Roman in its science and its art.   In this art the image of the Crucified is an Oriental conception which would have been abhorrent to Greek genius; however much pathos it occasionally exhibited, it never knew gods who died to save humanity and never conceived for them this despised rôle of slave, this voluntary abasement in suffering.   But the Greek spirit slowly but surely won empire over the Christians, who, at first antagonistic to anthropomorphic images and to the translation of this human body into plastic form, gradually disrobed it that its musculature might be seen, as, of old, the Hellenic gods had had theirs displayed.

In the earliest days of Greek art, as at its close, the East stands revealed; it directed the first steps of the artist, and inspired him when his creative strength was exhausted and when troubled souls, weary of the clear light of Hellenic reason, sought a new ideal.

II

WHAT GREECE HAS GIVEN TO THE OLD WORLD AND THE NEW

If Greece received much from others, she did not slavishly copy from them. There are countries of the ancient world whose art docilely followed foreign impulses and whose native qualities were not adequate to transform what they borrowed into fresh creations of beauty stamped with their own individual genius. Such was the art of Cyprus, a reflection of the political vicissitudes of the island, incapable of doing aught but copy carelessly and clumsily, and without a vestige of·original imagination, by turns Egyptian, Assyrian, and Hellenic.

With Greece it was quite otherwise. Her native originality was such that she transformed all that the foreigner gave her so thoroughly as to make of it a new creation. "All that we Greeks borrow from the Barbarians we transform and make into something more beautiful" (Plato). Egypt might supply Greece with the technique of hollow bronze casting, but Greece immediately extracted from the process effects never dreamed of by the Egyptian artist, who had never tried to make large statues by this method and who had never realized what freedom of pose could be achieved in bronze, or appreciated its artistic possibilities so different from those of stone. The sphinx and the bird-soul had their meaning and their form modified by their passage into Greek art; the human-headed bird became the symbolic Syren lamenting over the tomb, and the Ægina sphinx with its beautiful Phidian head bears not the remotest resemblance to the androcephalous monster of Egypt and Mesopotamia, nor even to the Ægean sphinx. When adaptation is impossible and is shocking to good sense and æsthetic feeling, the borrowed notion is gradually eliminated. Thus disappeared in the course of time certain archaic motifs such as the hippalectryon, the hare-headed man, and the duplex beast with a single head.

Although there was a link with the Ægean world, yet it was a new world that arose and revealed such fruitful promise in its earliest and still naïve productions. Greek art alone got beyond the point reached by its rivals in antique lands. The rupture of the frontal convention, the knowledge of foreshortening and perspective, the understanding of human beauty and of musculature and drapery, of attitudes, rhythm and composition—all these innovations were essentially Hellenic, and the artist had to rely on his own genius alone in order to realize them. They opened up for Greece the way of progress; they enabled her art rapidly to dominate the art of all those other lands which had gone before or were contemporaneous, and to become a master of beauty, unchallenged, even among the ancient peoples themselves, as for us to-day.

This ascendancy was not a question of time, for predominance was not assured to Greece on account of the long ages her art had been in existence. How formless were her earliest artistic manifestations ! The Dipylon idols, the funeral scenes traced by the Attic artist of about the 9th century on the flanks of the great clay vases—all this betokens an art in its infancy and governed by all the conventions to which beginners must submit. There is no comparison possible with the often beautiful images that the Egyptian had been carving for thousands of years, or with those of the Chaldæan of Tello, or those of the Ægeans who were the immediate predecessors of the Greeks on their own soil, or with those that the Assyrian was then creating.

And yet, starting from these naïve attempts, the Greek artist was able to surpass in a very short time those whom he might consider his masters. Towards the middle of the 5th century B.C. he had nothing left to learn. His term of artistic education had been completed and he was in possession of his technique and of his ideal. How rapid this progress had been ! How rapid, too, the entire evolution of Greece, since it took place within some eight hundred years, that is to say from about the 9th to the 1st century B.C.— from the primitive barbarism of the " geometric " period to the time of her exhaustion. If maturity had come quickly, decadence was equally rapid.

Egypt and the Mesopotamian East, on the contrary, measure their artistic life in thousands of years. The works of the first pharaonic dynasties, and those of Elam and Chaldæa, are as far advanced as those of many centuries

o

later. These countries did evolve, and we can no longer admit the immobility of Egyptian art. But their evolution was of a different order from that of Greece: there is change, doubtless, subtle shades of style which alter with the periods, but not progress in the ordinary sense of the word, that is to say a gradual modification towards something better achieved by essays which subsequently succeed.

Greek art, if it received, had above all given much to the world.[1]

How is it that, wherever Greek products have gone, Greek art has modified age-old native traditions, leading all, from one side of the world to the other—Indians and Gallo-Romans alike—to the understanding of an ideal so different from their own ? Was this the result of historical hazard, of circumstances external to Greek art ? No, it was due to its innate qualities, to its amazing æsthetic and technical superiority.

Its influence was substituted for that of the Ægeans, which had extended all over the Mediterranean basin, to Egypt, Palestine, Italy and even Spain, and which had penetrated, perhaps, even to the Far East. Greek art began the accomplishment of its civilizing mission when the maritime trade of the Ionians, Corinthians and Attics took the products of their cities everywhere, initiating barbarian peoples into Greek culture, and carrying afar the radiance of Hellenic intelligence and the limpid Hellenic idea of beauty. To the north the shores of the Black Sea and even of the Sea of Azov bear witness to Greek colonization by the fragments of Ionian vases found there;[2] to the south, Egypt opened her gates to Greek commerce in the times of Amasis and Psammeticus, and Saïte art already bore witness to qualities which were not altogether Egyptian but partly Hellenic. In Asia Minor, Lycia and Caria called for Greek artists from the 6th century, and continued so to do in subsequent centuries. It was they who in the 5th and 4th centuries carved the magnificent sarcophagi destined for the princes of Sidon, the earliest of which, by their anthropoid form, resemble the Egyptian mummy cases, and by the faces resemble the Greek statues of the first half of the 5th century.[3] It was they,

[1] **CCXIV-CCXXIII.**   [2] **CCXX-I.**
[3] Hamdy-Bey and Th. Reinach, *Une nécropole royale à Sidon*, 1892.

doubtless Ionians, who, at the end of the 5th and beginning
of the 4th centuries, carved the sculptures of the heröon at
Trysa and of the Nereids' monument at Xanthus, for the
benefit of the Lycian dynasts. In Persia the grandiose
buildings of Darius and Xerxes borrowed Hellenic[1] elements.
It was Greek art that was revealed in the Carthage sarcophagi. The East, that had given so much to Greece, now
received from her in turn and ever more abundantly.

Etruria was a province of Ionian art; Rome was hellenized
indirectly by her and directly by the Greek settlements of
Magna Græcia and Sicily, before being pacifically conquered
by her conquest.[2]

In Gaul, Greek commerce, starting from Marseilles, passed
up the Rhone Valley, leaving here and there numerous
fragments of vases and figurines, and took into the heart
of Switzerland, as far as Graechwyl, the beautiful 7th-century
Ionian bronze vase of the type of the goddess taming the
deer. Gaulish coins were crude imitations of Massiliot and
Macedonian coins; the alphabet was introduced by the Greeks
of Marseilles; fibulæ, swords and torques betoken importation
and imitation. When the Roman conquest took place the
ground was already prepared, and it was still Greece, under
the name of Rome, that was dominant, imposing on the
native artist an anthropomorphic conception of divinity to
which he had hitherto felt repugnance, no doubt on religious
grounds, and giving Hellenic forms to the old local gods.

Greek art penetrated everywhere, long before the conquests of Alexander hellenized the whole world—Egypt,
Syria and Asia[3]—and long before Rome, already prepared
by its antecedents, finally learned its lesson.

But this influence was exerted still further afield. Greece
was early linked in close relations with India; it is possible
that the nude Jain saints, who resemble the old 6th-century
Kouroi, were imitated from some Greek statue imported
from Asia Minor. Do not the ivories of the old Artemisium
of Ephesus recall Buddhist types? The seated Buddha
himself derives from an Ionian type of which examples are
to be found in Cyprus, in the terra cottas of Asia Minor, and
in the Marseilles statues. But this influence which was

---

[1] Dieulafoy, *L'Art antique de la Perse*, 1884-1889.
[2] **CCXV, CCXIX.** [3] **CCXVI-VII.**

uncertain hitherto became so decisive in India from Hellenistic times as to give rise to that mixed art known as " Græco-Buddhist " which flourished especially at Gandhara. The Buddha took on the appearance of a Greek Apollo; Praxiteles contributed the characteristic raised hip of his statues which was there exaggerated; Leochares' Ganymede became Garuda carrying off a Nagi; Mara, dæmon and god of Passion, now took the pug features and unkempt beard of a Satyr or a Silenus, and now those of Eros.

The contagion crept gradually to the Far East. In 4th-century China we have a winged figure with Hermes' cap carrying a trident and a thyrsus. We get mirrors of Han times (A.D. 202) whose vine-leaf ornament is inspired by Hellenic prototypes and coincides with the introduction of the vine into China at the period when there were relations between Alexandria and Canton, and between Persia and China. Invented in Greece and mentioned for the first time by Aristophanes, the optical lens was transmitted to the Hellenistic East and then passed into China at the beginning of the 7th century.

It would not be possible to enumerate here all the effects of the influence of Greek art. Less profound than that of science and technics, artistic influence only touches visual forms without modifying their thought content. If it gives to the divine and mythological beings of India Hellenic raiment it does not transform the essence of religion. If, in Gaul, the one-time aniconic deities now have the appearance of a Mercury, a Mars or a Jupiter they preserve their early character and their ancient functions. Christianity itself was to maintain the Oriental character of its religion under the anthropomorphic forms which were to triumph over its hostility to the image.

Modern art is the direct heir to the art of the Greeks and it bears the indelible stamp of it. Breaking with the Græco-Roman paganism it abhorred, Christianity, triumphant, wanted to annihilate that which seemed to it the work of the devil, but its efforts were in vain, and from the days of the Catacombs it was ever the themes and the craftsmanship imposed on Rome by Greece that appeared on the earliest sarcophagi, as, for instance, Orpheus amidst animals, or the Dionysiac vine. The Christian's divinity was to be incarnated in that human body so extolled by the Greeks, and to accept the antique beauty.   Contrary to the teachings of Scripture, new wine was poured into old skins—new thoughts, in order to win comprehension, were materialized in pagan semblance, and, after some twenty centuries have elapsed, the spirit of Greece once again regulates our æsthetic.

Again and again attempts have been made to tighten the bonds that attach us to that spirit, to imitate more closely the antique beauty in its Roman and Greek forms.   Hence those returns to the past in the Middle Ages, in the time of Charlemagne and of Frederick II., and hence the inspiration of certain statues at Rheims cathedral dating from the 13th century.   Hence, finally, after these abortive efforts, the great Renaissance that erected into a dogma the supremacy of the antique art obscured and impaired by Christian work, and the necessity to imitate it.   The Renaissance brought back into honour the cult of the human form, of the long proscribed nudity, of æsthetic anatomy, and it recommenced the study of foreshortening and perspective that the ancients had pursued.   Later still, there was a return to the antique at the close of the 18th century, and in the first half of the 19th, with David and Ingres in painting, and Canova, Thorwaldsen and Pradier in sculpture.

Contemporary art, desirous of originality at all costs, is restless and rudderless.   It tries all manners of tentative experiments.   Some seek renewal in abstract and mathematical conceptions, and elaborate the already abandoned theories of cubism and futurism.   Some, the Bolshevists of art, reject all and every principle, and realize the absolutely arbitrary by " dadaism," which is even more ephemeral. Others, hoping to recover a lost naïveté and the freshness of vision and imagination withered by a too lengthy classical education, take their models from among the African primitives, the strange civilizations of Oceania or the refined ones of the Far East, or, nearer home, in the rudimentary art of the naïve Breton Calvaries or in the drawings of children.   Diverse as these experiments may seem to be, they all proceed from the same desire—to escape from the domination of Greece and Rome, to forget age-old teachings, to abandon deliberately all the principles that took so long in the acquiring that they might be transmitted in turn to posterity. One sees artists of the present day giving up correct perspective, establishing foreshortenings that are deliberately false, neglecting all harmony of proportion, even finding anew the frontality of the early days and of the decadence. But there are other artists, too, who still keep their eyes on Greece the everlasting, who docilely learn in her school, and, while retaining their own originality, do not fear to treat the same old themes, such, for example, as Bourdelle, whose Heracles slaying the birds of Lake Stymphalus has the rude savour of the Æginetans, or Landowski, who goes so far as to take his inspiration from the Homeric and Hesiodic shields.

How many forms are there in our daily life which we inherit from Greece—architecture with Ionic and Doric columns and triangular pediments; masks of Phidian style, even on street lamps ! Greek art, which educated antiquity and the modern world, lives yet.

III

THE GREEK MIRACLE AND GREEK PERFECTION

In the evolution of æsthetics Greek art appeared to be a phenomenon so peculiar in its beauty that it has readily been set down as something in the nature of a prodigy, and the " Greek miracle " has become for many people an article of faith.[1] The word *miracle* always seems to connote something theological, to signify an event outside the laws of nature and of humanity, whereas science, on the contrary— and the history of art should be conceived scientifically— seeks to eliminate the supernatural, and, says Livy, *rem miraculo eximere*. Let us then use this term judiciously. Let us remember that there is no such thing as a miracle on this earth where all can be explained by causes, and is more or less easy to discern. Greek art, the product of human activity, cannot escape the laws governing human affairs. Doubtless its genius was more than any other instinct with the sentiment of beauty and the desire to achieve perfection. But these masterpieces did not come into being suddenly in some incomprehensible manner like a bolt from the blue;

[1] **VI**, vol. i, p. 81 ff.

their development was the culmination of long and often clumsy attempts, and they appeared in the fulness of time like ripened fruit. It is essential to have a knowledge of this slow elaboration and of the favourable circumstances which permitted the artists to attain to the culminating point. "To admire is to understand " it has often been said. We shall admire this great art all the more in that we understand it the better not only through the æsthetic emotion it still arouses in us, but through its psychological, social, technical, and—in a word—anæsthetic factors; we shall admire it all the more that we see in it a human necessity of the most logical order. Miracle, then, let us call it, if we mean by that something worthy of admiration, but not some phenomenon confronted with which our reason ceases to function and we merely contemplate; not some phenomenon unique in history, because there have been other " miracles," that is to say, other moments in which art, freed from too particular contingencies, has imposed itself on the emotion of all human beings by its characters of lasting and universal beauty. Yes, indeed, the Greeks achieved a miracle—the miracle of imposing on the world their own spiritual and emotive pre-eminence. They triumphed in that struggle for existence which is history, despite the smallness of their country, despite their own paucity of numbers. The past of vast empires is buried for centuries, and is only revived very slowly, thanks to the efforts of archæological science. But Greece taught Rome, and through Rome the entire modern world, which still admires her and recognizes her as the mistress of thought and beauty.

Greek art, it has frequently been said, is perfect, and the dogma of " Greek perfection " is a corollary of the precedent article of faith.[1] This perfection has been vaunted ever since the Renaissance. Models that are insurpassable are sought in Greece, and in Greece is found " a place where perfection exists " (Renan) and " perfection is not to be achieved except—and always provided the ancients can be surpassed—by imitating them " (La Bruyère). The golden age of art, the paradise lost for ever by modern decadence !— it is still a current belief. The " Quarrel of the Ancients

[1] **VI,** vol. i, p. 81 ff.

and Moderns " goes on for ever, because it sets in opposition
two spirits, two temperaments to be found in every age
both in individuals and in society—the one exclusively
enamoured of the past, the other accepting the present and
interesting itself in it with face set towards the future. We
have been moulded by the classic education that almost
unconsciously imposes on us admiration for the Greeks and
Romans, and tradition inculcates in us belief in the magic
virtue of the humanities in a thoroughly modern society
which has quite other tendencies and aspirations. We are
often the playthings of an instinctive psychological illusion:
the past always seems to be more beautiful than the reality,
and we deck it in the iridescent veil of memory. Let us
beware of terminology that is too absolute. Æsthetic judgment is subjective, varying according to time, social environment, individuals and races. This Greek perfection has not
been recognized as such by all peoples, and Far Eastern
artists, whose æsthetic principles are very different, are quite
unable to admit it. And do not we, modern folk, continually
modify our judgment of Greek art ? That which was
admired from the Renaissance to the beginning of the 19th
century, and that which was decreed to be perfect, was the
work of that last artistic period in Greece when her art had
grown old and was more concerned with virtuosity than
sincerity: it was the declamatory emphasis of the Laocoon,
the coldness of the Apollo Belvedere that were considered
perfection. Then, when a number of classical monuments
were unearthed during the discoveries of the 19th century,
these at first astonished rather than charmed. The Ægina
marbles, people said, were " hyperantique, and that was
their only merit," and those of the Parthenon left them
indifferent. Greek art, in fact, by no means always resembled
itself from the earliest days to the end, and, as we have seen
further back, it had various stages emotionally and techni-
cally. Each of these stages has its own admirable beauties,
whether the charm of the 6th century, naïve and precious at
the same time, the ideal abstraction of the 5th, the sweetness
and sensuousness of the 4th, or the penetrating realism of the
Hellenists. It was beauty that varied according to the
different tendencies of those who conceived it, just as those
who now admire it differ in their tendencies. Was every

phase of this beauty perfect, or did one particular phase realize " Greek perfection " ?

Let us understand this term " perfection " relatively to the efforts of those who sought it—as a correlation of the artist's ideal with his realization of it—rather than relatively to our own modern mentality in its judgment of the past, which itself is subject to change. Then we can admit that there was a time in Greece when art arrived simultaneously at its maximum æsthetic, social, spiritual and technical development. Perfection in the sense of a perfect adaptation of art to the needs, thought, and highest aspirations of the Greek people. Perfection in the sense of a technique arrived at its maturity, and having broken with the faults of earlier days, but which had not yet come to seek a sterile virtuosity. Perfection, when art reflected a pure, harmonious, sober and sincere taste as far removed from the gaucherie and naïveté of its infancy as from the bad taste which sometimes appeared among the Hellenists. Perfection, if we mean by that the beauty of an art which, being in full possession of its material means of expression, still preserves the freshness, the spontaneousness and enthusiasm of youth. All these conditions were realized in the 5th century. This 5th-century art seems to some a trifle abstract, even cold, lacking in emotion and sweetness, deliberately ignoring the variety of human sentiment. But in the evolution of Greece it realized this perfect harmony. The centuries that followed were more skilled from the technical standpoint, more varied and more subtly discriminating, but they no longer possessed that marvellous balance of all the conditions called for in a work of art. Towards the middle of the 5th century Greek art arrived at the plenitude of its development, achieved the glorious possession of strength and beauty. It had reached that stage of development that the artists depicted in their ephebic statues—the age of youth of some twenty summers, strong and calm, conscious of its own worth yet modest withal.

To retain this anthropomorphic comparison of art with an individual, we may say that up to the 6th century Greek art is in its childhood, growing and learning how to live. In the first half of the 5th century it is adolescent, and still a little gauche. But from 450 onwards it has just arrived at maturity, having ahead of it great projects for the future and full faith that they will be realized. In the 4th century the ideal is already somewhat less lofty, more conscious of mundane realities, just as a man, towards his fortieth year, has greater experience and is more given to reflect but is also more disillusioned. The Hellenistic age heralds life's decline, when a man understands the complexity of existence but has less energy and verve. Old age approaches, creative power grows feebler, thought readily turns back to the contemplation of a glorious past as a man's thoughts towards memories of his youth, until the time comes when Greek art, exhausted, disappears altogether as an independent entity. Yet, like the human procreator who dies, the task accomplished has been fruitful, and there is a long posterity left in token of it.

BIBLIOGRAPHY

GREEK ART IN GENERAL

BRUNN, *Griechische Kunstgeschichte*, 2 vols., 1893-97 ....   **I**

BÜLLE, *Handbuch der Archæologie*, I, 1913 ....   **II**

BURKHARDT, *Griechische Kulturgeschichte*, 3rd ed., 1909,
4 vols. ....   **III**

CAROTTI, *Storia dell'arte*, I, 1907; ID., *History of Art*, I,
Ancient Art, 1908 ....   **IV**

COLLIGNON, *L'Archéologie grecque*, 2nd ed., 1907 ....   **V**

DEONNA, *L'Archéologie, sa valeur, ses méthodes*, 3 vols.,
1912 ....   **VI**

— *L'Expression des sentiments dans l'art grec*, 1914 ......   **VII**

— *Les lois et les rhythmes de l'art*, 1914 ....   **VIII**

— *L'Archéologie, son but, son domaine*, 1922 ....   **IX**

DUCATI, *L'arte classica*, 1920 ....   **X**

FOUGÈRES, " Grèce," *Guide Joanne*, 1911 ....   **XI**

— *Athènes*, 1912 ....   **XII**

GARDNER (P.), *The Principles of Greek Art*, 1914 ....   **XIII**

— *A Grammar of Greek Art*, 1905 ....   **XIV**

GERCKE and NORDEN, *Einleitung in die Altertumswissen-
schaft*, 1910 ....   **XV**

KOEPP, *Archæologie*, 2nd ed., 1919-21 ....   **XVI**

LÜBKE, *Grundriss der Kunstgeschichte*, 15th ed., I, *Die
Kunst des Altertums* ....   **XVII**

RIZZO, *Storia dell'arte greca*, 1913-14 ....   **XVIII**

ROBERT (C.), *Archæologische Hermeneutik. Anleitung zur
Deutung klassischer Bildwerke*, 1919 ....   **XIX**

VON SALIS, *Die Kunst der Griechen*, 1919; 2nd ed., 1922   **XX**

SPRINGER-MICHAELIS, *Handbuch der Kunstgeschichte*, I,
Das Altertum, 11th ed., 1920 ....   **XXI**

WOERMANN, *Geschichte der Kunst*, I, 2nd ed., 1915 ......   **XXII**

ARCHITECTURE

GENERAL.

ANDERSON-SPIERS, *Die Architektur von Griechenland und
Rom*, 1905; ID., *The Architecture of Greece and Rome*,
1907 ....   **XXIII**

BELL, *Hellenic Architecture : Its Genesis and Growth*, 1920   **XXIV**

BENOIT, *L'architecture*, I, *Antiquité*, 1912 ....   **XXV**

BROWN, *Greek Architecture*, 1909 ....   **XXVI**

CHOISY, *Histoire de l'architecture*, 2 vols. (s. d.) ....   **XXVII**

— *Histoire critique de l'origine et de la formation des ordres
grecs*, 1876 ....   **XXVIII**

DURM, *Handbuch der Architektur*, I, *Die Baukunst der Griechen*, 3rd ed., 1910 XXIX

HARTMANN, *Die Baukunst in ihrer Entwicklung von der Urzeit bis zur Gegenwart*, I, *Die Baukunst des Altertums und des Islams*, 1910 XXX

KOHTE, *Die Baukunst des klassischen Altertums und ihre Entwicklung in der mittleren und neueren Zeit*, 1915 XXXI

MARQUAND, *Greek Architecture*, 1909 (good bibliography) XXXII

NOACK, *Die Baukunst des Altertums*, 1910 XXXIII

STURGIS and FOTHRINGHAM, *A History of Architecture*, 4 vols., 1906-15 XXXIV

UHDE, *Die Architekturformen des klassischen Altertums*, 2nd ed., 1909 XXXV

THE TEMPLE.

LECHAT, *Le temple grec*, 1902 XXXVI

LEROUX, *Les origines de l'édifice hypostyle*, 1913 XXXVII

PERROT-CHIPIEZ, *Histoire de l'art dans l'antiquité*, Vol. VII, 1898 XXXVIII

DORIC.

COLLIGNON, *Le Parthénon*, ed. in folio, 1911, and in 4to 1912 XXXIX

FOUGÈRES, *Les origines du Parthénon et l'influence de l'ionisme sur l'architecture dorique à Athènes*, 1911 XL

KATTERFELD, *Die griechischen Metopenbilder*, 1911 XLII

LAUM, "Die Entwicklung der griechischen Metopen-bilder," *Neue Jahrbücher f. d. klass. Altertum*, 1912, 29, pp. 612, 671................................... XLIII

LEICESTER B. HOLLAND, *Amer. Journal of Archæology*, 1917, XXI, p. 117 ("Origin of the Doric Entablature") XLI

MICHAELIS, *Der Parthenon*, 1871 XLIV

WASHBURN, "The Origin of the Triglyph Frieze," *Amer. Journal of Arch.*, 1919, 23, p. 33; 1918, 22, p. 434 XLV

WILBERG, JOAI, XIX-XX, 1919, p. 167 ("Evolution of the Doric Capital").

IONIC.

BRAUN-VOGELSTEIN, "Die ionische Saüle," *Jahrbuch d. d. arch. Instituts*, 1920, XXXV, p. 1 XLVI

HOMOLLE, "L'origine des Caryatides," *Rev. arch.*, 1917, I, p. 1 XLVII

LEHMANN-HAUPT, "Zur Herkunft d. ionischen Säule," *Klio*, 13, 1913, p. 468 XLVIII

VON LICHTENBERG, *Die ionische Säule als klassisches Bauglied rein hellenischen Geistes entwachsen*, 1907 XLIX

VON LUSCHAN, *Entstehung und Herkunft d. ionischen Säule*, 1912 L

PUCHSTEIN, *Die ionische Säule als klassisches Bauglied oriental. Herkunft*, 1907 LI

THIERSCH, "Zur Herkunft d. ionischen Frieses," *Jahreshefte d. Oest. arch. Instituts*, 1908, p. 47 LII

CORINTHIAN.

GUTSCHOW, *Untersuchungen zum Korinthischen Kapitell,*
JDAI, 1921, 36, p. 44 .... **LV** *bis*

HOMOLLE, "L'origine du chapiteau corinthien," *Rev.
arch.,* 1916, II, p. 17 .... **LIV**

LETTUM, *Die Erfindung d. korinthischen Säule,* 1909 .... **LIII**

WEIGAND, *Vorgeschichte d. korinthischen Kapitells,* 1920 **LV**

VARIOUS.

BERTHA CARR RIDER, *The Greek House: Its History and
Development from the Neolithic Period to the Hellenistic Age,* 1916 .... **LVII**

Exploration archéologique de Délos, VIII, CHAMONARD,
Le quartier du théâtre. Étude sur l'habitation délienne
à l'époque hellénistique, 1923.

GOODYEAR, *Greek Refinements ; Studies in Temperamental
Architecture,* 1913 .... **LVI**

SCULPTURE

ARNDT-AMELUNG, *Photographische Einzelaufnahmen* .... **LVIII**

BRUNN-BRUCKMANN, *Denkmäler griech. und römischer
Skulptur* (1897 ff.; in 1920, 137th printing) .... **LIX**

BULLE, *Der schöne Mensch,* I, *Altertum,* 2nd ed., 1910 .. **LX**

CESSI, *Vita ed arte ellenistica,* 1910 .... **LXI**

COLLIGNON, *Histoire de la sculpture grecque,* 2 vols., 1892-
97 .... **LXII**

— *Les statues funéraires dans l'art grec,* 1911 .... **LXIII**

CONZE, *Attische Grabreliefs* .... **LXIV**

CULTRERA, *Saggi sull'arte ellenistica e greco-romana,* I,
1907 .... **LXV**

DEONNA, *Les statues de terre cuite en Grèce,* 1906 .... **LXVI**

— *Les statues de terre cuite dans l'antiquité,* 1908 .... **LXVII**

— *Les Apollons archaïques,* 1908 .... **LXVIII**

DICKINS, *Hellenistic Sculpture,* 1920 .... **LXIX**

FURTWAENGLER, *Meisterwerke der griechischen Plastik;
Masterpieces of Greek Sculpture,* 1895 .... **LXX**

GARDNER, *Handbook of Greek Sculpture,* 2 vols., 1905,
1909 .... **LXXI**

HEBERDEY, *Altattische Porosskulptur. Ein Beitrag zur
Geschichte der archaïschen griech. Kunst,* 1909 .... **LXXII**

JOUBIN, *La sculpture grecque entre les guerres médiques et
l'époque de Périclès* 1901 .... **LXXIII**

KEKULÉ VON STRADONITZ, *Die griechische Skulptur,* 3rd
ed., 1922 .... **LXXIV**

KLEIN, *Geschichte der griechischen Kunst,* 3 vols., 1904-05 **LXXV**

KOESTER, *The Masterpieces of Greek Sculpture,* 1910 .... **LXXVI**

LECHAT, *La sculpture grecque. Histoire sommaire de son
progrès, de son esprit, de ses créations,* 1922 .... **LXXVII**

— *La sculpture attique avant Phidias,* 1904 .... **LXXVIII**

LECHAT, *Au Musée de l'Acropole d'Athènes, études sur la sculpture en Attique avant la ruine de l'Acropole par l'invasion de Xerxès*, 1903 LXXIX

LERMANN, *Altgriechische Plastik*, 1907 LXXX

LOEWY, *Die griechische Plastik*, 2 vols., 2nd ed., 1918 LXXXI

VON MACH, *A Handbook of Greek and Roman Sculpture*, 1905 LXXXII

OVERBECK, *Geschichte der griech. Plastik*, 2 vols., 1893-94 LXXXIII

PERROT-CHIPIEZ, *Histoire de l'art dans l'antiquité*, Vols. VII and VIII, 1898, 1903 LXXXIV

PICARD (CH.), *La sculpture antique*. I, *Des origines à Phidias*, 1922. II, *De Phidias à l'ère byzantine* LXXXV

REINACH (S.), *Répertoire de la statuaire grecque et romaine*, 4 vols., 1897-1910 LXXXVI

— *Répertoire des reliefs grecs et romains*, 3 vols., 1909-1912 LXXXVII

— *Recueil de têtes antiques idéales ou idéalisées*, 1903 LXXXVIII

SCHMIDT, *Archaistische Kunst in Griechenland und Rom*, 1921 XCII

SCHRADER, *Archaïsche Marmorskulptur im Akropolis Museum zu Athen*, 1909 LXXXIX

— *Auswahl archaïscher Marmorskulpturen im Akropolis Museum*, 1913 XC

SCHREIBER, *Hellenistische Reliefsbilder* XCI

WASER, *Meisterwerke der griechischen Plastik*, 1914 XCIII

WIEGAND, *Die archaïsche Porosskulptur der Akropolis zu Athen*, 1904 XCIV

UXHULL-EYLLENBAND, *Archaïsche Plastik der Griechen*, 1920 XCV

COINS

BABELON, *Les monnaies grecques, aperçu historique*, 1921 XCVI

— *Traité des monnaies grecques et romaines*, 1901 XCVII

BARCLAY HEAD, *Historia Nummorum. A Manual of Greek Numismatics*, 2nd ed., 1911 XCVIII

GARDNER (P.), *A History of Ancient Coinage*, 1918 XCIX

PERROT-CHIPIEZ, *Histoire de l'art dans l'antiquité*, Vol. IX, 1911 C

REGLING, *Die Münze als Kunstwerk*, 1921 CI

REINACH (TH.), *L'Histoire par les monnaies*, 1902 CII

GEMS

FURTWAENGLER, *Antike Gemmen*, 3 vols., 1900 CIII

LIPPOLD, *Gemmen und Kameen des Altertums und der Neuzeit*, 1922 CIV

TERRA COTTA FIGURINES

KAUFMANN, *Aegyptische Terrakotten d. griech., römischer und koptischen Epoche*, 1913 CV

LAUMONIER, *Catalogue des terres cuites du Musée archéologique de Madrid*, 1921 CVI

LECHAT, *Tanagra* (s. d.) CVII

MENDEL, *Musées impériaux ottomans, Catalogue des figurines grecques de terre cuite*, 1908 CVIII

PERDRIZET, *Les terres cuites grecques d'Égypte de la collection Fouquet*, 1921 CIX

POTTIER, *Les statuettes de terre cuite dans l'antiquité*, 1890 CX

— *Diphilos et les modeleurs de terres cuites grecques*, 1909 CXI

POTTIER-REINACH, *La Nécropole de Myrina*, 1888 CXII

WEBER, *Die aegypt. griech. Terrakotten d. aeg. Sammlung kgl. Museen zu Berlin*, 1914 CXIII

WINTER, *Die Typen der figurlichen Terrakotten*, 2 vols., 1903 CXIV

PAINTING

BERGER, *Die Wachsmalerei des Apelles und seiner Zeit, Neue Untersuchungen und Versuche über die antike Malertechnik*, 1917 CXV

BLÜMNER, "Die Maltechnik des Altertums," *Neue Jahrbücher*, 1905 CXVI

BULARD, "Peintures murales et mosaïques de Délos," *Monuments Piot*, XIV CXVII

GIRARD, *La peinture antique*, 1892 CXVIII

HERMANN, *Denkmäler der Malerei des Altertums*, 1906-15 CXIX

LAURIE, *Greek and Roman Methods of Painting*, 1910 CXX

PFÜHL, "Die griechische Malerei," *Neue Jahrbücher*, 1911 CXXI

— *Malerei und Zeichnung der Griechen*, Munich, 1923, 3 vols. CXXII

RAEHLMANN, *Ueber die Maltechnik der Alten*, 1910 CXXIII

REINACH (A.), *Recueil Milliet, Textes grecs et latins relatifs à l'histoire de la peinture ancienne*, I, 1921 CXXIV

REINACH (S.), *Répertoire de peintures grecques et romaines*, 1922 CXXV

WEIR, *The Greek Painter's Art*, 1905 CXXVI

WEISBACH, *Impressionismus. Ein Problem der Malerei in der Antiken und Neuzeit*, 1910 CXXVII

WÖRMANN, "Die Malerei des Altertums," in *Geschichte der Malerei* of Woltmann, I, 1879 CXXVIII

VASE PAINTING

BUSCHOR, *Griechische Vasenmalerei*, 1912; *Greek Vase Painting*, trans. Richards, 1921 CXXIX

CASKEY, *Geometry of Greek Vases*, 1922 CXXX

Corpus vasorum antiquorum, I, 1922, Recueil général des vases du Louvre .... **CXXXI**

DUCATI, " Saggio di studio sulla ceramica attica figurata del secolo IV a C.," *Memorie Acad. Lincei*, 1916, XV, p. 211.. **CXXXII**

— *Storia della ceramica greca*, I, 1922, Florence .... **CXXXIII**

FURTWAENGLER-REICHHOLD, *Griechische Vasenmalerei*, 1904-09 .... **CXXXIV**

HAMBIDGE, *Dynamic Symmetry. The Greek Vase*, 1920 .. **CXXXV**

HARTWIG, *Die griechischen Meisterschalen der Blüthezeit des strengen rothfiguren Stiles*, 1893 .... **CXXXVI**

HERFORD, *A Handbook of Greek Vase Painting*, 1919 .... **CXXXVII**

HOPPIN, *A Handbook of Attic Red-figured Vases signed or attributed to the various Masters of the sixth and fifth centuries B.C.*, I, 1919; II, 1920 .... **CXXXVIII**

LANGLOTZ, *Zur Zeitbestimmung der Strengrotfiguren Vasenmalerei und der gleichzeitigen Plastik*, 1920 .... **CXXXIX**

— *Griechische Vasenbilder*, 1922 .... **CXL**

LEROUX, *Lagynos, Recherches sur la céramique et l'art ornemental hellénistique*, 1913 .... **CXLI**

VON LUECKEN, *Greek Vase Painting*, 1922 .... **CXLII**

NICOLE, " Corpus des céramistes grecs," *Rev. arch.*, 1916, II, p. 373, and *Rev. des études grecques*, 1917, p. 237; cf. HOPPIN, *Amer. Journal of Arch.*, 1917, p. 308 .... **CXLIII**

PERROT-CHIPIEZ, *Histoire de l'art dans l'antiquité*, Vols. VII, IX, X, 1898, 1911, 1914 .... **CXLIV**

POTTIER, *Musée national du Louvre, Catalogue des vases antiques de terre cuite*, 3 vols., 1896-1906; ID., *Vases antiques du Louvre*, 3 vols., 1897-1922 .... **CXLV**

— *Douris et les peintres de vases grecs* (s. d.) .... **CXLVI**

REICHHOLD, *Skizzenbuch griechischer Meister. Ein Einblick in das griechische Kunststudium auf Grund der Vasenbilder*, 1919 .... **CXLVII**

REINACH (S.), *Répertoire des vases peints grecs et étrusques*, 2 vols., 1899-1900; 2nd ed., I, 1923 .... **CXLVIII**

RICHTER (GISELA), *The Craft of Athenian Pottery*, 1922 **CXLIX**

WALTERS, *History of Ancient Pottery*, 2 vols., 1905 ...... **CL**

DECORATIVE ART

BERCHMANS, " L'esprit décoratif dans la céramique grecque à figures rouges," *Annales de la Société d'archéologie de Bruxelles*, XXIII, 1909 .... **CLI**

POULSEN, *Die Dekorative Kunst des Altertums*, 1914 .... **CLII**

ARTISTS

GENERAL.

BÉNÉZIT, *Dictionnaire critique et documentaire des peintres, sculpteurs . . . de tous les temps et de tous les pays*, 1911-13 .... **CLIII**

BRUNN, *Geschichte der griechischen Künstler*, 2 vols., 2nd ed., 1889 CLIV

ERRERA, *Dictionnaire-répertoire des peintres depuis l'antiquité jusqu'à nos jours*, 1913 CLV

OVERBECK, *Die antiken Schriftquellen zur Geschichte der bildenden Kunst bei den Griechen*, 1868 CLVI

THIEMÉ-BECKER, *Allgemeines Lexikon der bildenden Künstler von der Antike bis zur Gegenwart* CLVII

PRINCIPAL MONOGRAPHS.

COLLIGNON, *Phidias*, 1886 CLVIII

— *Scopas et Praxitèle*, 1907 CLIX

— *Lysippe* (s. d.) CLX

GARDNER (E. A.), *Six Greek Sculptors*, 1910 CLXI

KLEIN, *Praxiteles* CLXII

— *Praxitelische Studien* CLXIII

LECHAT, *Pythagoras de Rhegion*, 1905 CLXIV

— *Phidias* (s. d.) CLXV

— *Phidias. L'Acropole d'Athènes* (s. d.) CLXVI

MAHLER, *Polyklet und seine Schule*, 1902 CLXVII

MAVIGLIA, *L'attivita artistica di Lisippo ricostruita su nuova base*, 1914 CLXVIII

MIRONE, *Mirone d'Eleutera*, 1921 CLXIX

NEUGEBAUER, *Studien über Skopas*, 1913 CLXX

PARIS, *Polyclète*, 1895 CLXXI

PERROT, *Praxitèle* (s. d.) CLXXII

ÆSTHETIC AND TECHNICAL PROBLEMS

BLÜMNER, *Technologie und Terminologie der Gewerbe und Künste bei den Griechen und Romern*, 2nd ed., 1912 CLXXIII

RHYS CARPENTER, *The Esthetic Basis of Greek Art*, 1921 CLXXIV

DIELS, *Antike Technik*, 1914 CLXXV

LANGE, *Darstellung des Menschen in der älteren griechischen Kunst*, trans. Mann, 1899 CLXXVI

LOEWY, *Die Naturwiedergabe in der älteren griechischen Kunst*, 1900; ID., *The Rendering of Nature in Early Greek Art*, 1907 CLXXVII

NEUBERGER, *Die Technik des Altertums*, 1922 CLXXVIII

PETERSEN, " Rhythmus," *Abhandl. d. kgl. Gesell. d. Wiss. zu Göttingen*, Phil.-hist. Klasse, XVI, 5, 1917 CLXXIX

DELLA SETA, " La genesi dello scorcio nell'arte greca," *Reale Accad. dei Lincei*, 1907 CLXXX

MANNERS AND INSTITUTIONS

STANLEY CASSON, *Ancient Greece*, 1922 CLXXXI

CROISET (M.), *La civilisation hellénique, aperçu historique*, 2 vols., 1922 CLXXXII

362 BIBLIOGRAPHY

JARDÉ, *La Grèce antique et la vie grecque*, 1915 .... **CLXXXIII**

PAULY-WISSOWA, *Realencyclopaedie*, 2nd ed., 1893-1901 (in course of publication) .... **CLXXXIV**

SAGLIO-POTTIER, *Dictionnaire des antiquités grecques et romaines*, 1877-1919 .... **CLXXXV**

UTILITARIAN ART

GLOTZ, *Le travail dans la Grèce antique*, 1920 .... **CLXXXVI**

GUIRAUD, *La main-d'œuvre industrielle dans l'ancienne Grèce*, 1900 .... **CLXXXVI**

POTTIER, "Les origines populaires de l'art," *Gaz. des Beaux-Arts*, 1907; *Comptes rendus Acad. Inscr.*, 1907 **CLXXXVIII**

THE CITY

CROISET (A.), *Les démocraties antiques*, 1909 .... **CLXXXIX**

GLOTZ, *La cité grecque. Développement des institutions* (*L'Évolution de l'Humanité*, No. 14) .... **CXC**

RELIGION

FARNELL, *The Cults of Greek States* .... **CXCI**

— *Greek Religion and Mythology*, 1914 .... **CXCII**

GRUPPE, *Griechische Mythologie und Religionsgeschichte* **CXCIII**

HARRISON, *Themis : A Study of the Social Origins of the Greek Religion*, 1912 .... **CXCIV**

MOORE, *The Religious Thought of the Greeks from Homer to the Triumph of Christianity*, 1916 .... **CXCV**

PETTAZONI, *La religione nella Grecia antica sino ad Alessandro*, 1921 .... **CXCVI**

DE RIDDER, *L'idée de la mort en Grèce à l'époque classique*, 1886 .... **CXCVII**

ROSCHER, *Lexikon der griechischen und romischen Mythologie* (in course of publication, begun in 1884) .... **CXCVIII**

DELLA SETA, *Religione e arte figurata*, 1912 .... **CXCIX**

SOURDILLE, *Le génie grec dans la religion* (*L'Évolution de l'Humanité*, No. 11) .... **CC**

ATHLETICS, NUDITY, COSTUME

ABRAHAMS, *Greek Dress*, 1908 .... **CCI**

DEONNA, *Les toilettes modernes de la Crète minoenne*, 1911 **CCII**

GARDINER, *Greek Athletic Sports and Festivals*, 1910 .... **CCIII**

HEUZEY, *Histoire du costume antique d'après des études sur le modèle vivant*, 1922 .... **CCIV**

WOOBURN HYDE, *Olympic Victor Monuments and Greek Athletic Art*, 1921 .... **CCV**

KLEE, *Zur Geschichte der gymnischen Agonen an griechischen Festen*, 1918............................. **CCVI**

MÜLLER, *Nacktheit und Entblössung in der altorientalischen und älteren griechischen Kunst*, 1906 .... **CCVII**

SCHROEDER, *Der Sport des Altertums*, 1921 .... **CCVIII**

REGIONAL ART: INFLUENCES

HOGARTH, *Ionia and the East*, 1909 .... **CCIX**

PICARD, *Éphèse et Claros, recherches sur les sanctuaires et les cultes de l'Ionie du nord*, 1922 .... **CCX**

POTTIER, *Le Problème de l'art dorien*, 1908 .... **CCXI**

POULSEN, *Der Orient und die frühgriechische Kunst*, 1912 **CCXII**

RADET, *La Lydie et le monde grec au temps des Mermnades*, 1893 .... **CCXIII**

EXPANSION OF GREEK ART

VON BISSING, *Das Griechentum und seine Weltmission*, 1921. — ID., *Der Anteil der ägyptischen Kunst am Kunstleben der Volker*, 1912 .... **CCXIV**

COLIN, *Rome et la Grèce, de 200 à 146 av. J.-C.*, 1905 .... **CCXV**

GRENIER, *La civilisation romaine* (*L'Évolution de l'Humanité*, No. 17) .... **CCXIX**

L'hellénisation du monde antique (by different scholars), 1914 .... **CCXVI**

IMMISCH, *Das Nachleben der Antike*, 1919 .... **CCXXIV**

JAMES, *Our Hellenic Heritage*, 1921 .... **CCXXII**

JOUGUET, *L'Impérialisme macédonien et l'hellénisation de l'Orient* (*L'Évolution de l'Humanité*, No. 15) ...... **CCXVII**

LIVINGSTONE, *The Legacy of Greece*, 1922 .... **CCXVIII**

ROSTOWTZEFF, *Iranians and Greeks in South Russia*, 1923 **CCXX**

THOMPSON, *Greeks and Barbarians*, 1920 .... **CCXXI**

ZIELINSKI, *Die Antike und wir*, 2nd ed., 1921 .... **CCXXIII**

JOURNALS

Bulletin de correspondance hellénique .... **BCH**

Revue archéologique .... **RA**

Revue des études grecques .... **REG**

Journal of Hellenic Studies .... **JHS**

Revue des études anciennes .... **REA**

American Journal of Archæology .... **AJA**

Athenische Mittheilungen .... **AM**

Jahrbuch d. deutsch. Arch. Instituts, Berlin .... **JDAI**

Id., Anzeiger .... **AA**

Jahreshefte d. arch. Instituts in Wien .... **JOAI**

Monuments et mémoires Piol .... **MP**

Monumenti antichi .... **MA**

Gazette des Beaux-Arts .... **GBA**

INDEX

I.
GORGON (*Athens, Acropolis Museum*)
6th Century

II.
DELPHI.
TREASURY OF THE ATHENIANS
First quarter of the 5th Century

III.

DRAPED FEMALE FIGURE FROM A
FUNERARY STELE
(*Athens, National Museum*) 5th Century

FRÉJUS APHRODITE (*Louvre*)
Second half of the 5th Century

IV.
MEDICI APHRODITE
(*Uffizi, Florence*)

V.
ANDROMEDA AND PERSEUS
(*Capitol Museum, Rome*)

VI.
TEMPLE RUINS AT OLYMPIA

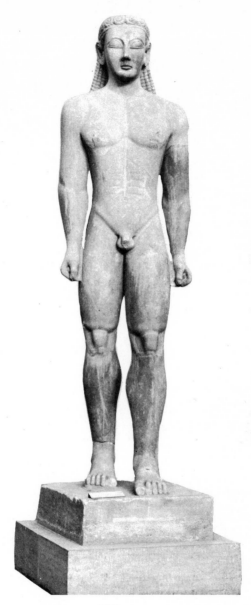

VII.
SUNIUM KOUROS
(*Athens, National Museum*)
6th Century

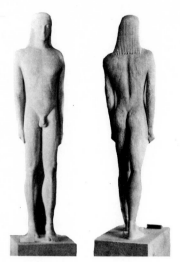

Fig. 37. MELOS KOUROS
(*Athens, National Museum*)
6th Century

Fig. 38. VOLOMANDRA KOUROS
(*Athens, National Museum*)
6th Century

Fig. 39. KEA KOUROS
(*Athens, National Museum*)
6th Century

Fig. 65. ANAVYSSOS KOUROS
(*Athens, National Museum*)
6th Century

IX.
HESTIA GIUSTINIANI
(*Torlonia Museum, Rome*)
About 460

X.
HEAD OF THE OLYMPIA HERMES
BY PRAXITELES

XI.
HERMES OF ANDROS
(*Athens, National Museum*)
School of Praxiteles

XII.
BLACK-FIGURED ATTIC AMPHORA.
BANQUET SCENES (*Louvre*)

XIII.
THE 6TH CENTURY SMILE

XIV.
THE HELLENIC PROFILE.
FEMALE HEAD FROM
WEST PEDIMENT AT OLYMPIA
About 460

XV.
LACK OF FACIAL EXPRESSION.
THE BRIDE OF PEIRITHOOS
ATTACKED BY A CENTAUR,
FROM TEMPLE OF ZEUS AT
OLYMPIA

RED-FIGURED CUP
5th Century

XVI.

HEAD OF HYGEIA
(*Athens, National Museum*)
5th Century

XVII.
EAD OF APHRODITE
(Athens, National Museum)
4th Century

XVIII.
HEAD OF A MAN BY SCOPAS
(*Athens, National Museum*)
4th Century

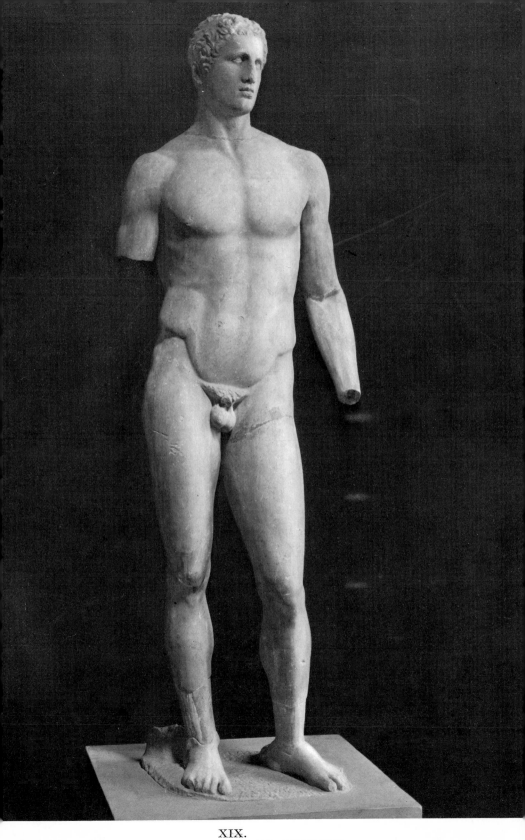

XIX.
THE DELPHI AGIAS BY LYSIPPUS
4th Century

XX.
THE EPHEBE OF ANTICYTHERA
(*Athens, National Museum*)
4th Century

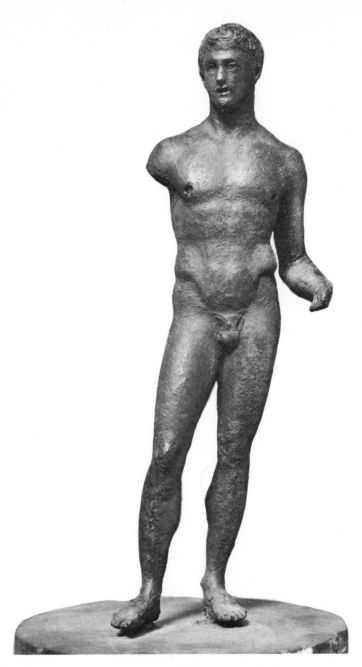

XXI.
ATHLETE (*Athens, National Museum*)
4th Century

XXII.
HELLENISTIC PATHOS.
HEAD OF THE LAOCOON
(*Vatican Museum*)

XXIV. SLEEPING HERMAPHRODITE (*Uffizi, Florence*)

HELLENISTIC PATHOS.
THE SO-CALLED DYING
ALEXANDER (*Florence*)

XXIII.

HEAD OF THE PERGAMUM
APHRODITE